Other
Sisterhoods

EDITED BY

SANDRA KUMAMOTO STANLEY

Other
Sisterhoods

◇ Literary Theory and
◇ U.S. Women of Color

UNIVERSITY OF

ILLINOIS PRESS

Urbana and Chicago

Library of Congress Cataloging-in-Publication Data

Other sisterhoods : literary theory and U.S. women
  of color / edited by Sandra Kumamoto Stanley.
      p.   cm.
  Includes bibliographical references and index.
  ISBN 0-252-02361-7 (alk. paper).—
  ISBN 0-252-06666-9 (pbk. : alk. paper)
    I. American literature—Minority authors—
History and criticism—Theory, etc.   2. American
literature—Women authors—History and criticism—Theory, etc.   3. American literature—
20th century—History and criticism—Theory, etc.
4. Women and literature—United States—History—
20th century.   5. Literature and society—United
States—History—20th century.   6. Minorities
in literature.   7. Ethnic groups in literature.
I. Stanley, Sandra Kumamoto.
PS153.M56O85   1998
810.9'9287'08996073—dc21   97-4689   CIP

◇ Contents

◇ Acknowledgments

We gratefully acknowledge permission to use the following material in this book:

Chapter 1: Excerpts from "that dark shining thing," by Gloria Anzaldúa, in *Borderlands/La Frontera: The New Mestiza* (San Francisco: Aunt Lute, 1987). Reprinted by permission of Gloria Anzaldúa.

Chapter 3: Excerpts from "There It Is," "They Came Again in 1970 and 1980," "If the Drum Is a Woman," and "Rape," by Jayne Cortez, in *Coagulations: New and Selected Poems* (New York: Thunder's Mouth Press, 1984). © 1984 by Jayne Cortez. Used by permission of the publisher.

Chapter 6: Excerpts from "If I Am Too Brown or Too White for You," "Notes on a Conspiracy," "The Well-Intentioned Question," "Margaret Neumann," "Excavation at Santa Barbara Mission," "Muskogee," "For the Campus Committee on the Quality of Life," "For the Complacent College Students Who Don't Think People Should 'Live in the Past,'" and "To Make History," by Wendy Rose, in *Going to War with All My Relations* (Flagstaff, Ariz.: Northland-Entrada, 1993). Used by permission of Wendy Rose.

Excerpts from "Vanishing Point: Urban Indian," "Builder Kachina: Home-going," "The Endangered Roots of a Person," "The Day I Was Conceived," "Walking on the Prayerstick," "Anthropology Convention," "Matriculation," "Handprints," "Academic Squaw," and "Indian Anthropologist: Overhanging Sand Dune Story," by Wendy Rose, in *Lost Copper* (Banning, Calif.: Malki Museum Press, 1980). Used by permission of the publisher.

Excerpts from "Ya Don Wanna Eat Pussy," "I Walk in the History of My People," "I Am Not Your Princess," "Ceremony for Completing a Poetry Reading," and the preface, by Chrystos, in *Not Vanishing* (Vancouver,

B.C.: Press Gang, 1988); from "Going Through," "I Like to Think," "Just Like You," "The Women Who Love Me," "Lesbian Air," and "Urban Indian," by Chrystos, in *Dream On* (Vancouver, B.C.: Press Gang, 1991); and "Askenet, Meaning 'Raw' in My Language," by Chrystos, in *Inversions: Writing by Dykes, Queers, and Lesbians,* ed. Betsy Warland (Vancouver, B.C.: Press Gang, 1991). Used by permission of the publisher.

Chapter 8: Excerpts from "The Underground Parking" and "After Tonight," by Gary Soto, in *The Elements of San Joaquin* (Pittsburgh: University of Pittsburgh Press, 1977). Used by permission of Gary Soto.

Excerpts from "Shooting a Wren," "Night Stand," and "On Touring Her Hometown," by Lorna Dee Cervantes, in *From the Cables of Genocide: Poems on Love and Hunger* (Houston: Arte Publico Press, 1991). Used by permission of the publisher.

Excerpts from "Uncle's First Rabbit," "Cannery Town in August," "Emplumada," "Caribou Girl," "Poem for the Young White Man Who Asked Me How I, an Intelligent Well-Read Person Could Believe in the War between the Races," "Four Portraits of Fire," and "Starfish," by Lorna Dee Cervantes, in *Emplumada* (Pittsburgh: University of Pittsburgh Press, 1981). © 1981. Used by permission of the publisher.

I would like to thank the wonderful contributors to this volume for their hard work and faithful commitment to women of color scholarship. Thanks also to my friends and colleagues for their help and advice, including Mark Rocha, Kathleen Lundeen, Marilyn Moss, and Wendy Furman, and especially Donald Hall, for his unfailing support and for providing me with the benefits of his good sense and sense of humor. I appreciate the encouragement I received from my department chair, William Walsh, and my dean, Jorge Garcia, to work on projects committed to issues of diversity. The University of Illinois Press provided me with the expert advice of many people, including Margie Towery, Cope Cumpston, Veronica Scrol, and Theresa Sears.

The contributors to this volume acknowledge, with deep appreciation, the many women of color who have provided us with the inspiration to write and compile this work. We dedicate *Other Sisterhoods* to them.

◇ *Introduction*

Resistance . . . Difference . . . Multiplicity . . . These words have characterized the intervention of U.S. women of color into the narrative history of American feminism. In the sixties and seventies, the "first wave"
of U.S. women of color challenged and critiqued the "second wave" of
the white women's movement. Regarding themselves as outsiders,
women of color have often taken on the subversive roles of women warriors, tricksters, wild women, and guerrilla tacticians—critiquing multiple systems of domination. In academia, many women of color often
felt excluded or even invisible: Where were the literatures written by
women of color? Where were their theoretical voices? In the succeeding decades, however, women of color—actively engaging in *haciendo
caras*—began to help reshape the face of academia—or so it seemed.
Works by women writers of color were being incorporated into or, as
many have argued, appropriated by the academic system. As such,
women academics of color inevitably found themselves asking the question: Have we, too, been incorporated, even appropriated by the system?
Many women critics of color have asserted that their works have continued in the interventionist mode of the "first wave" of women of color—
marked by a desire to resist and resignify dominant modes of theorizing.
In fact, because of this resistance, some women scholars of color have
garnered the reputation for being "antitheory." *Other Sisterhoods* seeks
to explore this complicated relationship between women of color and
literary theory, a relationship often characterized by resistance, difference, and multiplicity. The very name "women of color" is embedded by
these complex markers, raising corollary complex theoretical questions.
Hence, we start the collection by asking an ostensibly simple question:
Who are women of color?

Scholars writing on women of color must inevitably face a central irony: the very term "women of color" resists definition. Is this classification based on biological, social, political, and/or discursive contexts? How do such issues as race, ethnicity, class, gender, and sexuality impact this category? From the outset, we must acknowledge that the category "women of color" is a complex, multiple, and problematic site of representation. In two recent collections, Maxine Baca Zinn and Bonnie Thornton Dill's *Women of Color in U.S. Society* (1994) and D. Soyini Madison's *The Woman that I Am: The Literature and Culture of Contemporary Women of Color* (1994), however, the editors are less interested in interrogating the category of women of color than they are in recognizing its coalition-building and counterhegemonic possibilities—color penetrating/diversifying a hegemonic whiteness. As such, both collections—defining through elaboration—list four racial/ethnic groups that constitute women of color: African Americans, Asian Americans, Native Americans, and Latina Americans. Obviously, their list includes categories defined by historically discriminatory U.S. racial laws, in which the racial universe is demarcated by five "color" categories: black, yellow, red, brown, and white.[1] Although recognizing that women of color are a group "governed by a dynamic of difference" (Madison 2), these editors stress the issues that unite this diverse group: a history of oppression and exclusion and a shared desire to combat racist and sexist domination. *Other Sisterhoods* also recognizes both the diversity of women of color and the shared assumptions that define the groups associated with the name of U.S. women of color, acknowledging it as both a term of imposition, constructed from historical, social, and discursive matrices of power, and a term of resignification, reconceived by women of color as a means of challenging and displacing oppressive dominant ideologies.

Nevertheless, the act of defining, naming, classifying—especially in the production of a "constituted otherness"—can be fraught with difficulties. We might ask—why do Zinn, Dill, and Madison limit U.S. women of color to only four identified racial/ethnic groups? Is this very limitation essentialist and exclusionary? In *Third World Women and the Politics of Feminism,* for instance, Chandra Talpade Mohanty not only includes such "new immigrant" groups as Arabs in her "women of color" classification but also asserts that the term "designates a political constituency, not a biological or even sociological one": women of all colors (including white women) constitute an "imagined community" based upon a "*common context of struggle* rather than color or racial identifications" (7). Others might argue that this category threatens to be not too exclusive but rather too inclusive. Both bell hooks and Gayatri Chakravorty Spivak warn that the very designation of women of color may posit an illusory homogeneous subject, working "to erase class and other differences" (hooks and Childers 78) and to ignore the shifting significations of "color" in different societal contexts (Spivak 294).

Chela Sandoval, however, argues that U.S. women of color—which she primarily refers to as "U.S. third world feminists"—are defined by discourses of difference, eluding any essentialist, totalizing criteria. Escaping a monolithic unity, these "constantly speaking differences" coalesce into a mutating dynamic unity: "This connection is a mobile unity, constantly weaving and reweaving an interaction of differences into coalition" (18). As a self-identified collective, U.S. women of color become a trope for a heterogeneity that can be mobilized for political opposition. Highlighting terms such as oppositional and differential consciousness, Sandoval perceives this collective not as a monolithic subject but as a tactical position of resistance.

Nevertheless, we could point out that the name women of color itself was first produced and then legislated by discriminatory racialist practice; hence, we could contend that the very name validates racial/ethnic/color categories that many agree belong to a discredited racial universe.[2] Moreover, if "woman of color" is perceived as a "marked" category of difference defined against whiteness as an "unmarked" category representing a normative center, then the very term could, ironically, reinscribe a marginal positionality for those attempting to subvert hierarchies of domination.[3] In answer to these objections, some critics argue that self-identified women of color have reconceived the name as a site not of subjection but of political agency. Perceiving the potential for both subjugation and resistance in the act of naming, Trinh T. Minh-ha points to "the pain and frustration of having to live a difference that has no name and too many names already" (*Moon* 14). Yet she also acknowledges "the necessity of re-naming so as to un-name" (*Moon* 14). For Trinh, the act of naming can become an act of resistance—to undo "established models and codes" in which "plurality adds up to no total" (*Moon* 15). Moreover, Carole Boyce Davies argues that any act of naming originates in an act of misnaming. Whether one identifies with such representational constructs as black, Hispanic, woman of color, or third world, each term carries a "string of echoes and inscriptions": "Each represents an original misnaming and the simultaneous constant striving of the dispossessed for full representation" (Davies 5). Both Trinh and Davies discern that they live in a discursive world of "the already said," a world filled with misnamings, with slippery signifiers subverting any transcendent signified. At the same time, the "dispossessed" striving for "full representation" must engage in the insurgent act of "re-naming so as to un-name." Women of color as a representational construct has a

complex history of "misnaming" that, within the purview of this introduction, we can only briefly investigate.

Women of color—the term itself has been in use at least since the
nineteenth century and, in all probability, since the seventeenth or
eighteenth centuries.[4] Winthrop Jordan notes that the symbolic use of
color (whiteness identified with purity, darkness with sin) permeated
the early European mind and was transported to the English colonies
(7). With the rise of racial slavery in the United States, the "initially common term *Christian*"—with its more universal assumption of the common ancestry of the human "race"—was transformed to "the terms
English and *free*": "After about 1680, taking the colonies as a whole, a
new term appeared—*white*" (Jordan 95). Furthermore, Michael Omi and
Howard Winant argue, for most of its existence, the United States, first as
a European colony and then as an independent nation, was a racial dictatorship—defining " 'American' identity as white, as the negation of
racialized 'otherness'—at first largely African and indigenous, later
Latin American and Asian as well." The "color line" became the "fundamental division of U.S. Society" (66).

Early in this century, Alain Locke perceived "color prejudice" as "a
strange sort of aberration . . . peculiar to the modern mind" (64), and
certainly contemporary sociologists such as David Goldberg and Howard
Winant have aligned racialist thought and practice with the rise of
modernity—that is, the rise of the West with its imperial form of domination. In fact, Winant asserts that "to imagine the end of race is thus to
contemplate the liquidation of Western civilization" (xiii); color became a means of justifying colonization and the domination of indigenous people. Early in the nineteenth century, Pequod William Apes,
noting the linking of color with race prejudice, asked with an exas-
perated irony, "If black or red skins, or any other skin of color is disgrace-
ful to God, it appears that he has disgraced himself a great deal—for he
has made fifteen colored people to one white, and placed them here
upon this earth" (qtd. in Krupat 174). Although predicting that "the
problem of the twentieth-century" would be "the problem of the color-
line," W. E. B. Du Bois also recognized the possibilities for coalition
building among people of color. Indeed, the black movement—with
such diverse pioneering leaders as Du Bois, Booker T. Washington, and
Marcus Garvey—would build the foundations for the modern civil
rights movement that would impact all people of color. Although a
number of groups arising from the modern civil rights movement—like
the Black Power Movement, La Raza, the American Indian Movement
(AIM), and the Asian American Political Alliance—would emphasize

cultural nationalism, others would see the issues of "difference" as, paradoxically, their very point of unity. Women of color would constitute one such group.

A product shaped by the civil rights and women's movements, women of color—as a self-identified collective—participated in, as well as critiqued, the "second wave" of feminism in the late sixties and early seventies. Since that time, women of color groups—such as the Combahee River Collective and Women of Color Association—have challenged race and class blindness in the white women's movement and sexist practice in male-centered antiracist groups. Even as white feminists earlier sought to decenter a hegemonic male subject, feminists of color seek to dislodge any mythos of a homogeneous female subject identified with white middle-class norms. Recognizing women of color "as speaking subjects of a new discursive formation," Norma Alarcón asserts that these women became increasingly aware of "the displacement of their subjectivity across a multiplicity of discourses: feminist/lesbian, nationalist, racial, socioeconomic, historical, etc." (356).

Women activists of color, often working in both women's and nationalist liberation movements, acknowledged the complexities of multiple positionings—in terms of both the construction of identity and the systems of domination. In the context of their syncretic experiences, women of color—such as Audre Lorde, Gloria Anzaldúa, and Cherríe Moraga—reconfigured Du Bois's classic paradigm of double consciousness into the paradigm of the multiple, borderland, and "mestiza" consciousness. For Du Bois, double consciousness entails an understanding that black subjectivity is constructed against the social fact of whiteness—"this sense of always looking at oneself through the eyes of others" (5). Hence, the Du Boisean subject always feels a sense of doubleness: "One ever feels his two-ness,—an American, a Negro; two souls, two thoughts, two unreconciled strivings; two warring ideals in one dark body" (5).

For many U.S. women of color, multiple consciousness involves a recognition of their hybrid existence—of the ways they are multiply inflected—and a challenge of paradigms based on binary oppositions. Written in the eighties, Gloria Anzaldúa's *Borderlands/La Frontera* offers a key reading of this multiple consciousness in her figuration of the new mestiza. This new mestiza, aware of her "in-between" borderland state, "copes by developing a tolerance for contradictions, a tolerance for ambiguity" (79). Constructing a mestiza or borderland consciousness, she challenges the "unitary aspect of each new paradigm" and straddles two or more cultures: "The work of mestiza consciousness is to break down the subject-object duality that keeps her a prisoner and to show in the flesh and through the images in her work how duality is transcended" (80). At the same time that Anzaldúa acknowledges the plurality of the subject, she also recognizes the importance of the historical and geographical determinants in which that subject is situated, comprehending the importance of the "politics of location" and the "simultaneity of oppression."[5] For Anzaldúa, the borderlands/la frontera is not only a space accommodating multiple discourses of race/ethnicity, class, gender, and sexuality but also a political and social site of resistance: "The border is the locus of resistance, of rupture, implosion and explosion, and of putting together the fragments and creating a new assemblage" ("Border *Arte*" 107). For many women of color, acknowledging their hybridity and constructing theories of multiplicity have allowed them to challenge hegemonic Western metanarratives. Although they challenge oppressive foundationalist thought, they can still embrace a politics of location and experience—borderland sites of resistance and hybridity. Transforming theory into practice, women of color attempt to become instruments for social change, claiming the right to articulate—to name/misname/rename/unname—their own experiences.

Other Sisterhoods seeks to examine the growing women of color scholarship of the last several decades. Although we recognize a discernible body of women of color scholarship—work that crosses the boundaries among groups—we also acknowledge that many women of color still primarily identify themselves by their race/ethnicity, and, working from this position, they have made significant contributions to women of color scholarship.[6] In fact, the tendency in theorizing by and about women writers of color has been to compartmentalize these women according to race or ethnicity. Thus, we have come to expect to see works such as Cheryl Wall's *Changing Our Own Words: Essays on Criticism, Theory, and Writing by Black Women,* Barbara Smith's *Home Girls: A Black Feminist Anthology,* Debra Castillo's *Talking Back: Toward a Latin American Feminist Literary Criticism,* Tey Diana Rebolledo and Eliana Rivero's *Infinite Divisions: An Anthology of Chicana Literature,* the Asian Women United of California's *Making Waves: An Anthology of Writings by and about Asian American Women,* Shirley Geok-lin Lim's *The Forbidden Stitch: An Asian American Women's Anthology,* and Paula Gunn Allen's *The Sacred Hoop: Recovering the Feminine in American Indian Traditions* and *Spider Woman's Granddaughters: Traditional Tales and Contemporary Writing by Native American Women.*

Although these books, as well as many other works, have had a significant impact on women of color scholarship, there have also been several key works that emphasize concerns shared among women of color who identify themselves as a collective. Certainly, many regard Gloria Anzaldúa and Cherríe Moraga's *This Bridge Called My Back: Writings by Radical Women of Color* as *the* groundbreaking women of color anthology, a work signaling a "shift in feminist consciousness"[7] and highlighting a "theory in the flesh" that attempts "to bridge the contradictions in our experience": "We are the colored in a white feminist movement. / We are the feminists among the people of our culture. / We are often the lesbians among the straight. / We do this bridging by naming our selves and by telling our stories in our words" (23).

During the early 1980s, other groups were also demonstrating their commitment to coalitional women of color projects. For example, a group of predominantly black women organized the Kitchen Table/ Women of Color Press in 1980 to create a press for all women of color. As Barbara Smith recalls, "We were saying that as women, feminists, and lesbians of color we had experiences and work to do in common, although we also had our differences" (11). Despite the developing interest in coalitional women of color projects, however, Anzaldúa, by the late eighties, felt frustrated with the lack of women of color anthologies and thus compiled *Making Face, Making Soul/Haciendo Caras: Creative and Critical Perspectives by Feminists of Color,* perceiving her anthology as an extension of the earlier *Bridge* anthology. In the nineties, several other key women of color texts were published, including Chandra Mohanty, Ann Russo, and Lourdes Torres's *Third World Women and the Politics of Feminism,* Madison's *The Woman that I Am: The Literature and Culture of Contemporary Women of Color,* and Zinn and Dill's *Women of Color in U.S. Society.* Moreover, this burgeoning academic interest in women of color has been reflected in the increase in women of color conferences and in publications by and about women of color—which have been aided by the active work of women of color presses such as Kitchen Table and Third Woman Press.

Interestingly, this increasing attention to women of color has led to the concern that women of color texts, now that they have garnered academic credibility, are being transformed into an academic commodity and appropriated by men and white women.[8] Nevertheless, the increase of interest in women of color has also affected the academic community, forcing the community to respond to issues raised by women of color—a reaction that, admittedly, may take the form of evasion, ghettoization, and "racial lumping," as well as serious confrontation. In the end, a number of theoretical texts—such as Barbara Christian's "The Race for Theory," Sandoval's "U.S. Third World Feminism: The Theory and Method of Oppositional Consciousness in a Postmodern World," and Trinh's *Woman, Native, Other*—have attracted some attention from the general academic community (although typically from groups most interested in gender studies and "minority discourse"), impacting not only theoretical issues specifically concerning women of color but also the broader purview of "literary theory" itself.

Articulating some of the central theoretical and academic issues that have affected women of color scholarship, the present collection also seeks to examine the relationship of women of color texts to corollary issues in literary theory. Of course, the term "literary theory(ies)"—like women of color—is a complex and problematic category. From the outset, we regard both terms as heterogeneous and, in the case of theory, recognize that "doing theory" can include a variety of methodologies derived not only from philosophical or sociohistorical paradigms but also, as Christian argues, from narrative constructs. Although acknowledging that "the 'question of theory' is unavoidable," Christine Di Stefano has noted that some women critics of color—such as Christian—have voiced a suspicion of theory, especially if it is aligned with "the hypertheoreticism of postmodernism": "Some critics attuned to issues of race and racism suggest that 'theory' may be getting in the way of our ability to engage the lived experiences and social and cultural contributions of people who have traditionally been excluded from academic attention" (87). But this, of course, depends upon how "theory" is defined. As hooks suggests, "theorizing" in its most fundamental form is simply making sense of what is happening (*Teaching* 61). Trinh warns that "theory no longer is theoretical when it loses sight of its own conditional nature, takes no risk in speculation, and circulates as a form of administrative inquisition. Theory oppresses, when it wills or perpetuates existing power relations, when it presents itself as a means to exert authority—the Voice of Knowledge" (*Woman* 42). But, as Trinh also notes, theory can be a "tool of survival" (*Woman* 43), and as hooks observes, theory can also "be a healing place" (*Teaching* 61).

Exploring theory's potential for both oppression and healing, *Other Sisterhoods* seeks to interrogate various modes of theory making—as a multivoiced project. Recognizing that there is no homogeneous woman of color voice, this book aims to present diverse voices in this field. Women of color constitute complex and multiple sites of representation, and thus, I attempt to locate the issues concerning women writers of color and literary theory within "sites of contestation and negotiation,"[9] reflecting some of the diversity and complexity of these issues. I use the term "sites" self-consciously; for, in women of color scholarship, subject formation is often described in the context of spacial metaphors—for example, "borderlands" (Anzaldúa), "house of difference"

(Lorde), "migrations of the subject" (Davies), "constraining walls of social location" (Zinn and Dill), "cartographies of struggle" (Mohanty), and so on. These descriptions reflect not only general theoretical shifts in the thinking about identity—in which Bonnie Zimmerman has noted the subject has been deconstructed as a unified being and reconstructed as a subject position (3)[10]—but also the importance of "the politics of location" in the works of women of color. For my purposes, imagining the discussion of issues within the context of "sites of contestation and negotiation," rather than of oppositional "debates," also allows for the inclusion of various writers' points of view and acknowledges that these views are ever transforming as we all continue to dialogue with one another. Organized into three sections, this collection foregrounds intersecting theoretical issues that recur in the writings concerning women of color: part 1 focuses upon the ways that key issues in the "race for theory"—the politics of identity, subject formation, and the "question of theory"—impact the works of women writers of color; part 2 examines the ways that women writers of color deal with specific social issues relating to gender, class, race, ethnicity, and sexuality; and part 3 explores the ways that women writers of color create their own ethnopoetics within the arena of literary and cultural theory, helping to redefine the nature of theory itself.

Women of Color and Literary Theory

One of the central theoretical issues facing women of color is the question of identity. What is the role of agency, experience, ideology, and identity politics in the formation of the subject? The first four essays in this collection are dialogically arranged. In the first two essays, the authors explore diverging views of two key theoretical issues closely associated with women of color: theories of multiplicity and the politics of identity. In the next two essays, the authors interrogate the abuses and uses of current mainstream criticism (specifically poststructuralism and postmodernism) in relation to political commitments and social struggle. In the final two essays of part 1, the authors raise questions concerning the limits of ideological assumptions: What happens when critics themselves perpetuate the very ideology they wish to challenge? What happens when writers find themselves caught between various ideological commitments?

In "(De)Centering the Margins? Identity Politics and Tactical (Re)-Naming," AnaLouise Keating voices her concerns about any rigid definition of identity politics in which identity politics is played out as a scenario of binary oppositions: us versus them, self versus other, center versus margin. She notes that the rhetoric of marginality can ultimately undermine the very goals of empowerment that many women of color seek, for implicit in the structure of such binary oppositions, the center/self/us is conceived of as a "privileged site" that defines the margin/other/them. Through a comparative analysis of the ways Paula Gunn Allen, Gloria Anzaldúa, and Audre Lorde appropriate and alter the rhetoric of marginality, Keating argues that these writers subvert not only traditional humanist concepts of an autonomous, unified self but also the various forms it assumes in conventional identity politics.

In "Women of Color and Identity Politics: Translating Theory, *Haciendo Teoría*," Dionne Espinoza argues that current multiplicity theories associated with women of color can work hand in hand with identity politics, empowering women of color to confront oppression through multiple sites of resistance. Distinguishing between an enabling multiplicity (that allows for an affirmative claiming of multiple subject positions) and a disabling multiplicity (that would fragment and tear the individual apart), Espinoza traces the implications of the *teorías* proposed by the Chicana critics Gloria Anzaldúa, Norma Alarcón, Chela Sandoval, and Cherríe Moraga and finds that, for women of color, the formation of identity—haciendo caras—is a complex process in which women of color not only acknowledge the societal interpellations that shape them but also investigate ways to resist and rewrite those interpellations.

Kimberly N. Brown, in her essay "Of Poststructuralist Fallout, Scarification, and Blood Poems: The Revolutionary Ideology behind the Poetry of Jayne Cortez," revisits the questions posed by such critics as Barbara Christian and Joyce A. Joyce: Do certain academic theories—such as poststructuralism—constitute an alienating discourse that excludes some critics/writers of color? Although Brown is uninterested in dismantling poststructuralism, she is concerned with what she assesses to be the dictatorial role of poststructuralist criticism in African American literary theory—specifically as articulated by Henry Louis Gates Jr. and Houston A. Baker Jr. She is especially concerned when poststructuralist theorists dismiss literature shaped by revolutionary ideologies—such as those inspired by the Black Arts and Power Movements—that helped to transform the U.S. social and political landscape. Juxtaposing her theory of scarification against Gates's theory of signification, Brown asserts that Cortez's poems are revolutionary writings that work from the scars of experience and revolution, demonstrating that works inspired by the Black Arts and Power Movements can create the opportunity to "theorize from the scars."

Although Brown questions the hegemonic role of poststructuralism in African American literature, Marilyn Edelstein argues that postmodern theories (which she is careful to distinguish from the related but distinct concepts of poststructuralism and postmodernity) can be used in the service of revolutionary efforts, as well as a tool for social transformation. In "Resisting Postmodernism; or, 'A Postmodernism of Resistance': bell hooks and the Theory Debates," Edelstein notes that many women of color dedicated to radical social and political change have been distressed by some of the fundamental concepts associated with postmodernism, including the deconstruction of an autonomous self and foundationalist notions of truth. Edelstein argues, however, that reconceiving subjectivity is not the same as rejecting the power of human agency and questioning the centrality of truth does not mean undermining political agendas that work to challenge racist and sexist oppression. Edelstein first reviews various feminist concerns about postmodern theories and then specifically explores the ways women of color have engaged in debates over postmodern theories. Examining hooks's recent work in the contexts of the "theory debates" among feminists of color, Edelstein argues that hooks is one woman theorist of color who enacts a "postmodernism of resistance."

In "Psycholinguistic Orientalism in Criticism of *The Woman Warrior* and *Obasan*," Tomo Hattori voices a concern about the ways that critics may appropriate certain theoretical strategies without interrogating the ideological assumptions embedded in the production of those theories. Although several critics have raised the issue of "orientalism"—that is the "West's" stereotypical projections upon the "East" as the silent, alien, often female other—in the reception of such works as Maxine Hong Kingston's *The Woman Warrior*, Hattori focuses on the ways that this very orientalist discourse may be embedded in the sympathetic readings of critics—especially those influenced by feminist psychoanalytic theories. Critiquing several readings of *The Woman Warrior* and *Obasan* that have been informed by American and French psychoanalytic and feminist perspectives, Hattori is disturbed to find that these critics have chosen to relegate the Asian mother to the maternal, preverbal, pre-oedipal realm of the "semiotic" or the "imaginary." Hattori warns that critics should carefully examine the cultural basis of a theory so that they do not replicate ideological assumptions (in this case, orientalism) that they would, in fact, desire to challenge.

In "Who Speaks, Who Listens? Questions of Community, Audience, and Language in Poems by Chrystos and Wendy Rose," Robin Riley Fast examines the limits of identity politics in the works of two Native

American poets who have commitments to diverse communities. Fast explores the ambivalent and fluid relationship to community and audience that Chrystos (Menominee/Euramerican) and Wendy Rose (Hopi/ Miwok/Euramerican) evoke and address in their poetry. Both writers (Chrystos challenging the boundaries of the Native and lesbian communities and Rose acknowledging the importance of Euramerican influence upon her work and her complex relationship to the academy) raise explicit and implicit questions according to how they position themselves in terms of their various audiences: Who is "us" and who is "them"? Who reads their poetry? How do they voice their anger? How can they engage their audience in creative response? As these two poets negotiate complex relationships with their diverse communities and audiences, they also seek ways, through their work, to empower themselves to effect social and political change.

In part 2, the authors focus upon some of the ways that women of color have been instrumental in rethinking issues concerning gender, class, race, ethnicity, and sexuality—the theoretical mantra of the 1980s and 1990s. Although this section may appear to compartmentalize these markers of identity, I do not wish to imply that these categories are isolated from each other. In fact, women of color groups—such as the Combahee River Collective—were among the first to propose theoretical frameworks for understanding how women are multiply marked by these categories. The authors in this section demonstrate how women of color continue to investigate these key markers, often noting the ways they are imbricated in one another.

In "Of Men and Men: Reconstructing Chinese American Masculinity," King-Kok Cheung explores key issues concerning gender politics in Asian American literature. Cheung argues that the dominant U.S. perception of Asian men as "emasculated" reflects the inextricability of gender and race. In response to this perception, some Asian American male writers and critics have attempted to reconstruct images of Asian manhood by privileging so-called Asian heroic traditions, a strategy that has troubled many Asian American women. These contrasting responses have led to a conflict between Asian American feminists intent on dismantling Asian patriarchy and Asian American nationalists who complain that feminist writers reinforce and perpetuate negative stereotypes about Asian American men. Interested in reconfiguring the American feminist project, Cheung explores the possible reconciliation between these conflicting feminist and nationalist agendas.

In "Rethinking Class from a Chicana Perspective: Identity and Otherness in Chicana Literature and Theory," Timothy Libretti notes the importance of class issues—explicit and implicit—in both the criticism and literature of Chicana writers. Focusing specifically upon the poetry of Lorna Dee Cervantes, Libretti notes that criticism of Cervantes's work has tended to privilege either the ethnic or the feminist aspect of Chicana identity, despite the urgings of such Chicana feminist scholars as Yvonne Yarbro-Bejarano to demonstrate how "elements of gender, race, culture, and class coalesce" in Chicana works. Concerned that the category of "class" has not been sufficiently explored in Cervantes's work, Libretti argues that her poetry offers a version of Chicana Marxism. In opposition to poststructuralist and post-Marxist critical methods that question the "totality of social relations," Libretti consciously reinserts the category of totality in examining how Cervantes's poetry accomplishes a radical retheorizing of identity and identity politics through a poetic reconceptualization of the relations between identity and otherness in terms of race, class, and gender, experience and totality, and nationalism and internationalism.

Renae Moore Bredin, in "Theory in the Mirror," formulates a theory of guerrilla ethnography in the works of Leslie Marmon Silko and Paula Gunn Allen, examining the social construction of race implicit in their works. Bredin observes that the current balance of power in the dialectics of identity politics tends to perpetuate a binary formulation of race—white empowerment and nonwhite disempowerment; in fact, such a formulation has the potential to reinscribe the subject/object status of races mirrored in past ethnographic practices in which white anthropologists regarded Native Americans as "objects of ethnographic investigation." Bredin argues that writers such as Silko and Allen enact a guerrilla ethnography in which they become the ethnographers writing about constructions of "whiteness." In their interrogation of the social construction of whiteness, these two writers destabilize Euramerican historical and sociological versions of culture and society.

In "Mothering the Self: Writing through the Lesbian Sublime in Audre Lorde's *Zami* and Gloria Anzaldúa's *Borderlands/La Frontera*," Jennifer Browdy de Hernandez locates both works in the context of queer theory. Browdy de Hernandez argues that these texts, which engage in a written performance of "acting up," anticipate some of the key engagements of queer theorists, specifically the postmodern critique of essentialist identities. Lorde and Anzaldúa rewrite the genre of autobiography, rejecting the conventional, autonomous, individual autobiographical subject in favor of nonessential, nonhierarchical, shifting and multiple identities (exemplified in Lorde's notion of the "house of difference" and Anzaldúa's "new mestiza"), thus representing the hybrid identities of the women of color who inhabit the U.S. borderlands. Likewise, Lorde and Anzaldúa rewrite the sublime, a traditionally masculine mode, in a lesbian key: reconfiguring the dynamics of the sublime, they produce an embodied, visceral textual performance that celebrates the power of lesbian sexuality as a source of creative energy.

The essays in part 3 suggest ways that women of color are reconfiguring the site of literary theory and raising questions about how writers go about "doing theory." This section takes seriously Barbara Christian's contention that narrative is also a form of theorizing; in fact, these writers argue that some of the most powerful theorizing is enacted in the production of literature itself. Moreover, each of these writers experiments with form and/or voice, attempting to transform the genre of conventional academic discourse.

In this section's opening essay, "Like 'Reeds through the Ribs of a Basket': Native Women Weaving Stories," Kimberly M. Blaeser asks a key question: How effective are the tools of a U.S. or continental literary theory for reading the hieroglyphs of a Native American system? Instead of attempting to impose the codes of another system upon Native literature, Blaeser argues that critics would do well to investigate the ways that theory is already embedded in a work, the ways that literature itself provides a site for literary theory. Native storytelling itself teaches critics new ways of seeing how the literary and academic are intertwined with—not separated from—the sacred and the daily.

Working on the borders between "black" and "queer" theory, Kathryn Bond Stockton, in "Heaven's Bottom: Anal Economics and the Critical Debasement of Freud in Toni Morrison's *Sula*," explores how Morrison turns theoretical views concerning penetration and debasement upside down and, in so doing, shapes a new poetics of value and exchange. Rather than assert that Freud impacts Morrison's work and thinking, Stockton argues that Morrison, in fact, "outruns" Freud. Noting that critics such as Christian have challenged the alienating effects of academic discourse (specifically continental/French feminist views), Stockton also extends this idea of "debasement" to the enterprise of critical theory, using Morrison's poetics as a means of questioning any notion of "high/low," "privileged/debased" criticism.

In "Reading the Figure of Dictation in Theresa Hak Kyung Cha's *Dictée*," Eun Kyung Min reflects upon the performance artist Cha's *Dictée*— a genre-defying work that includes photographs, Chinese calligraphy, letters, historical documents, and language exercises. Min argues that *Dictée* is a theoretical work, testing the formal boundaries of literature, as well as the record of a specific Asian American immigrant experience of crossing linguistic and national boundaries. In exploring the figure of dictation—as both genre and trope—in Cha's work, Min uses the form of meditation to articulate the often contradictory nature of dictation (suggesting issues of obedient reproduction and subversive appropriation, boundaries between the oral and written, and questions of authenticity and compulsion). Min's meditation raises questions about the nature of boundaries—not only in the context of immigrant experiences but also in the context of language, art, and critical theory itself.

In our final essay, "A Journey toward Voice; or, Constructing One Latina's Poetics," Cecilia Rodríguez Milanés explores the boundaries between critical theory and narrative discourse and argues for a writing praxis that challenges the conventions of traditional "academic discourse." Asserting that the boundaries between narrative writing and literary theory, between subjective and academic voices are fluid, Rodríguez Milanés presents her own autobiographic cultural criticism, a form she calls the *testimonio*. In this form of cross-genre, hybrid writing—which allows her to cross borders—she preserves her own voice, with all its tonality, inflections, and accents.

Other Sisterhoods represents a diversity of voices, demonstrating the various ways that women of color are articulating—naming/misnaming/renaming/unnaming—their own experiences as theory and praxis. Although this book was inspired by the idea of women of color working as a collective, we do not deny the importance of the historical location or specificity of any group. As many of the essays show, different groups are currently emphasizing specific theoretical issues: for example, it is not by accident that Asian American critics are especially interested in the issues of orientalism and the conflict between feminist and nationalist agendas; that Chicana critics are committed to investigating class issues and the ways that the multiple markers of race, class, gender, and sexuality are imbricated in a mestiza borderland consciousness; that Native American critics are concerned about the West's continuing appropriation of their land and cultural identity; that African American critics continue to investigate ways of resignifying power and challenging issues of oppression and cultural debasement. But, as is evident in this collection, many of their key concerns are shared concerns about identity and community that cross racial and cultural boundaries. Moreover, women of color can find strength in working as a collective, a community sharing their "otherhood" status, an alliance of outsiderhood/outsisterhood. The challenge for women of color is to maintain their interventionist identity—even as they work in the inner circles of academia, even as they become key spokeswomen of theoretical discourse. Resistance . . . Difference . . . Multiplicity . . . As women of color find ways to create coalitions, to build bridges, to construct empowered communities, they must be wary of disappearing into, of being co-opted by, the larger academic system. Works such as *This Bridge Called My Back* and *Making Face, Making Soul* urge women of color to embrace difference and multiplicity, to resist the desire of predominant systems to resolve and neutralize those differences. As such, *Other Sisterhoods* remains an open-ended collection: we realize that there are many more voices to be heard, for this work records only part of an ongoing conversation that is multiple, hybrid, and ever evolving.

NOTES

1. These racially defined minorities have faced a history of oppression: Native Americans were invaded and many were systematically exterminated, African Americans were enslaved, Mexican Americans were colonized, and Asian Americans were systematically excluded. Nevertheless, as a number of scholars have noted, these racial and "color" categories are ambiguous and problematic. What about individuals who are multiracial? What about those who identify themselves with people of color but either "pass" for or are white? What about those nationalities—such as Arabs and South Asians—who do not "fit" neatly into any of these categories? Moreover, since the concept of race in the twentieth century has been transformed from a biological and essentialist category to a historically and socially constructed one, race and color must be understood within a dynamic sociopolitical system of "racial formation" (Omi and Winant).

2. The sociologists Omi, Winant, and Goldberg point out that the concept of "race" as a "natural, biological category" has been successfully challenged in the twentieth century. Winant observes that "a clear racial identity does not, and cannot, exist" (3). Nevertheless, even though these race and color categories might be judged as "absurd," all three sociologists agree that race is one of the most powerful social constructions of modernity operating in the national and global body politic.

3. For a fuller discussion of this topic, see Frankenberg, *White Women, Race Matters*, Trinh, "Not You/Like You," and Keating, "(De)Centering the Margins?" (in this collection).

4. The *Oxford English Dictionary* records the use of "women of color" in Sir Charles Lyell, *Second Visit to the U.S.* (1849). This term—especially in relation to the more inclusive category "people of color"—is actually much older; it was used at least since the eighteenth century and, initially, to refer to women of African descent. Of course, such names continue to undergo transformation—demonstrating their often positional and transitional status. For instance, in England the term "blacks" broadly designates people of Latin, Caribbean, Asian, as well as African descent. And while South Africa was under the system of apartheid, its "coloured category" reflected ambiguous hierarchies in which, for instance, the Chinese were regarded as Asians while the Japanese were considered "honorary whites."

5. Both "simultaneity of oppression" and "politics of location" are terms that have accrued their own historical significance. First highlighted by the Combahee River Collective and in the works of Barbara Smith, the term "simultaneity of oppression" foregrounds the desire of black feminists to challenge multiple sources of oppression, including racial, sexual, heterosexual, and class oppressions. Other writers, such as Mohanty and Henderson, continue to explore the

implications of this term in a postcolonial and postmodern context. In "The Politics of Location as Transnational Feminist Practice," Kaplan presents an insightful reading of the term "politics of location," a phrase coined by Adrienne Rich and later deployed as a "particularly North American feminist articulation of difference, and even more specifically as a method of interrogating and deconstructing the position, identity, and privilege of whiteness" (139). For women scholars of color, these terms are especially important in that they highlight the significance of not only such issues as multiplicity and difference but also such issues as positionalities, material history and existence, and the local (in contrast to the "universal") in the shaping of identity/subjectivity.

6. Especially important in this group has been the work of black feminist scholars. For a list of some of these key scholars, see duCille, "The Occult of True Black Womanhood."

7. These are Teresa de Lauretis's words quoted in Alarcón, "The Theoretical Subject(s) of *This Bridge Called My Back* and Anglo-American Feminism," a key essay assessing the importance of the *Bridge* anthology.

8. Critics such as Valerie Smith, Ann duCille, and Margaret Homans have astutely explored different aspects of the question of appropriation: Who has the right to speak for whom? What is the role of cultural experience in writing about texts on women of color? How are women of color texts used—do they act as an objectified trope for material experience (Smith), for sacred texts (duCille), for heterogeneity (Homans)?

9. I borrow this phrase from Gates (302)—although it has become common, spacializing discourse and undermining binary oppositions.

10. Here I generalize from Zimmerman's specific review of the theories on lesbian identity. She notes that this shift in emphasis in the theories of subject formation is reflected in the current theoretical tropes: "They refer less to the act of seeing than to the place from which one sees. Metaphors of position and space now dominate in the way those of sight did a decade ago. . . . Another way of putting this is that we are less focused on essential, 'deep' *knowledge* than on historically situated *knowing*" (3).

WORKS CITED

Alarcón, Norma. "The Theoretical Subject(s) of *This Bridge Called My Back* and Anglo-American Feminism." *Making Face.* Ed. Anzaldúa. 356–69.

Allen, Paula Gunn. *The Sacred Hoop: Recovering the Feminine in American Indian Traditions.* Boston: Beacon Press, 1986.

———, ed. *Spider Woman's Granddaughters: Traditional Tales and Contemporary Writing by Native American Women.* Boston: Beacon Press, 1989.

Anzaldúa, Gloria. "Border *Arte: Nepantla, El Lugar De La Frontera.*" *La Frontera/The Border: Art about the Mexico/United States Border Experience.* San Diego: Centro Cultural De La Raza, Museum of Contemporary Art, 1994.

———. *Borderlands/La Frontera: The New Mestiza.* San Francisco: Aunt Lute, 1987.

———. *Making Face, Making Soul/Haciendo Caras: Creative and Critical Perspectives by Women of Color.* San Francisco: Spinsters/Aunt Lute, 1990.

Asian Women United of California, ed. *Making Waves: An Anthology of Writings by and about Asian American Women.* Boston: Beacon Press, 1989.

Castillo, Debra A. *Talking Back: Toward a Latin American Feminist Criticism*. Ithaca, N.Y.: Cornell University Press, 1992.

Christian, Barbara. "The Race for Theory." *Making Face*. Ed. Anzaldúa. 335–45.

Combahee River Collective. "A Black Feminist Statement." 1977. *This Bridge Called My Back*. Ed. Moraga and Anzaldúa. 210–18.

Davies, Carole Boyce. *Black Women, Writing and Identity: Migrations of the Subject*. New York: Routledge, 1994.

Di Stefano, Christine. "Who the Heck Are We? Theoretical Turns against Gender." *Frontiers* 12.2 (1991): 86–108.

Du Bois, W. E. B. *The Souls of Black Folk*. 1903. New York: Penguin, 1989.

duCille, Ann. "The Occult of True Black Womanhood: Critical Demeanor and Black Feminist Studies." *Signs* 19 (1994): 591–629.

Frankenberg, Ruth. *White Women, Race Matters: The Social Construction of Whiteness*. Minneapolis: University of Minnesota Press, 1993.

Gates, Henry Louis, Jr. "'Ethnic and Minority' Studies." *Introduction to Scholarship in Modern Languages and Literatures*. Ed. Joseph Gibaldi. New York: Modern Language Association, 1992. 289–302.

Goldberg, David Theo. *Racist Culture*. Cambridge, Mass.: Blackwell, 1993.

Henderson, Mae Gwendolyn. "Speaking in Tongues: Dialogics, Dialectics, and the Black Woman Writer's Literary Tradition." *Changing Our Own Words*. Ed. Wall. 16–37.

Homans, Margaret. "'Women of Color' Writers and Feminist Theory." *New Literary History* 25 (1994): 73–94.

hooks, bell. *Teaching to Transgress: Education as the Practice of Freedom*. New York: Routledge, 1994.

hooks, bell, and Mary Childers. "A Conversation about Race and Class." *Conflicts in Feminism*. Ed. Marianne Hirsch and Evelyn Fox Keller. New York: Routledge, 1990. 60–81.

Jordan, Winthrop. *White over Black: American Attitudes toward the Negro, 1550–1812*. 1968. New York: Norton, 1977.

Kaplan, Caren. "The Politics of Location as Transnational Feminist Practice." *Scattered Hegemonies: Postmodernity and Transnational Feminist Practices*. Ed. Inderpal Grewal and Caren Kaplan. Minneapolis: University of Minnesota Press, 1994. 137–52.

Krupat, Arnold. *The Voice in the Margin: Native American Literature and the Canon*. Berkeley: University of California Press, 1989.

Lim, Shirley Geok-lin, Mayumi Tsutakawa, and Margarita Donnelly, eds. *The Forbidden Stitch: An Asian American Women's Anthology*. Corvallis, Ore.: Calyx, 1989.

Locke, Alain LeRoy. *Race Contacts and Interracial Relations: Lectures on the Theory and Practice of Race*. Ed. Jeffrey C. Stewart. Washington, D.C.: Howard University Press, 1992.

Madison, D. Soyini. *The Woman that I Am: The Literature and Culture of Contemporary Women of Color*. New York: St. Martin's Press, 1994.

Mohanty, Chandra Talpade, Ann Russo, and Lourdes Torres, eds. *Third World Women and the Politics of Feminism*. Bloomington: Indiana University Press, 1991.

Moraga, Cherríe, and Gloria Anzaldúa, eds. *This Bridge Called My Back: Writings by Radical Women of Color*. New York: Kitchen Table/Women of Color Press, 1983.

Omi, Michael, and Howard Winant, eds. *Racial Formation in the United States: From the 1960s to the 1990s.* 2d ed. New York: Routledge, 1994.

Rebolledo, Tey Diana, and Eliana S. Rivero, eds. *Infinite Divisions: An Anthology of Chicana Literature.* Tucson: University of Arizona Press, 1993.

Sandoval, Chela. "U.S. Third World Feminism: The Theory and Method of Oppositional Consciousness in a Postmodern World." *Genders* 10 (Spring 1991): 1–24.

Smith, Barbara, ed. *Home Girls: A Black Feminist Anthology.* New York: Kitchen Table/Women of Color Press, 1983.

———. "A Press of Our Own Kitchen Table: Women of Color Press." *Frontiers* 10.3 (1989): 11–13.

Smith, Valerie. "Black Feminist Theory and the Representation of the 'Other.'" *Changing Our Own Words: Essays on Criticism, Theory, and Writing by Black Women.* Ed. Cheryl A. Wall. New Brunswick, N.J.: Rutgers University Press, 1989. 38–57.

Spivak, Gayatri Chakravorty. "Can the Subaltern Speak?" *Marxism and the Interpretation of Culture.* Ed. Cary Nelson and Lawrence Grossberg. Urbana: University of Illinois Press, 1988. 271–313.

Trinh T. Minh-ha. "Not You/Like You: Post-Colonial Women and the Interlocking Questions of Identity and Difference." *Making Face.* Ed. Anzaldúa. 371–75.

———. *When the Moon Waxes Red: Representation, Gender and Cultural Politics.* New York: Routledge, 1991.

———. *Woman, Native, Other: Writing Postcoloniality and Feminism.* Bloomington: Indiana University Press, 1989.

Wall, Cheryl A., ed. *Changing Our Own Words: Essays on Criticism, Theory, and Writing by Black Women.* New Brunswick, N.J.: Rutgers University Press, 1989.

Winant, Howard. *Racial Conditions: Politics, Theory, Comparisons.* Minneapolis: University of Minnesota Press, 1994.

Zimmerman, Bonnie. "Lesbians Like This and That: Some Notes on Lesbian Criticism for the Nineties." *New Lesbian Criticism: Literary and Cultural Readings.* Ed. Sally Munt. New York: Columbia University Press, 1992. 1–15.

Zinn, Maxine Baca, and Bonnie Thornton Dill, eds. *Women of Color in U.S. Society.* Philadelphia: Temple University Press, 1994.

PART I

Theory and the Politics of Identity

1 ❖ (De)Centering the Margins?

Identity Politics and Tactical (Re)Naming

> We have been organizing on the basis of identity,
> around immutable attributes of gender, race and class
> for a long time, and it doesn't seem to have worked.
> —June Jordan, *Technical Difficulties*

> Not quite the Same, not quite the Other, she stands in
> that undetermined threshold place where she
> constantly drifts in and out.
> —Trinh T. Minh-ha, *When the Moon Waxes Red*

In their attempts to create a discourse that empowers oppressed peoples, theorists in contemporary U.S. literary and ethnic studies have relied on oppositional terms such as margin and center—where the margin represents historically disempowered social groups and the center represents those in power. Yet their very language reinforces a problematic binary structure, thus undermining the goals they seek to achieve. As Henry Louis Gates Jr. asserts, theorists utilizing the rhetoric of marginality overlook the ways their references to "marginalized" and "central" writers and texts reify existing categories of meaning. Because the center defines the margin, the margin's "privileged site of cultural critique" is itself authorized by the dominant hegemonic cultural system. Consequently, the other's oppositional worldview remains locked in a dyadic relationship that inadvertently reinforces existing power structures. Gates maintains that attempts to transcend this self/other binary construction are equally ineffective and result only in a proliferation of margins, "breeding new margins within margins . . . an ever renewed process of differentiation, even fragmentation" (298).

Sara Suleri makes a related point in her discussion of "postcolonial" U.S. feminist theory when she challenges contemporary feminists to explore "the excesses and the limitations" in marginal locations, claiming that, "until the participants in marginal discourses learn how best to critique the intellectual errors that inevitably accompany the provisional discursivity of the margin, the monolithic and untheorized identity of the center will always be on them" (757–58). Like Gates, she emphasizes the constrictive, relational nature of all margin/center rhetoric, yet she takes her critique even further by questioning the epistemic privilege recently associated with feminists marginalized by both their gender and their ethnicity. As Suleri points out, mainstream feminism's automatic acceptance of the doubly marginalized feminist voice has led to a highly ironic situation: "Even though the marriage of two margins should not necessarily lead to the construction of that contradiction in terms, a 'feminist center,' the embarrassed privilege granted to racially encoded feminism does indeed suggest a rectitude that could be its own theoretical undoing" (758). In other words, the unquestioned authority granted to self-identified[1] women of color makes it impossible to develop sophisticated analyses of the complex systems of differences inscribing contemporary social actors. Cultural critique is reduced to "unthinking celebrations of oppression, elevating the racially female voice into a metaphor for 'the good'" (759).[2]

These objections to marginal positionality raise significant questions concerning the political (in)effectiveness of identity politics and other oppositional forms of resistance, especially when applied to writings by contemporary U.S. feminists who locate themselves on the margins and speak in the voice of the other(s). If, as Gates suggests, "keeping inside and outside distinct is a means of keeping the other elsewhere" (298), then marginal theories do not provide social actors with a "location of radical openness and power" (hooks) that effectively intervenes in hegemonic discourse. Instead, the margin becomes a reified oppositional enunciative position, defined (and thus controlled) by the invisible center. And if, as Suleri argues, the automatic acceptance of the doubly marginalized voice leads to the construction of a new center, marginal discourse inadvertently reinforces binary structures, creating overly simplistic dualisms between "oppressor" and "oppressed." But what happens when the self-identified other neither dissolves nor maintains all inside/outside oppositions? When, for example, s/he identifies as both oppressor and oppressed, does s/he remain "elsewhere"? Or does s/he open up intermediary space(s)—neither inside nor outside the dominant cultural inscriptions?

In this chapter, I argue that an analysis of recent writings by Paula Gunn Allen, Gloria Anzaldúa, and Audre Lorde indicates the possibility of developing configurations of identity that destabilize self/other, margin/center dichotomies by challenging traditional humanist notions of a unitary self and its various forms in conventional identity politics.[3] As self-identified lesbians of color, these three writers could be considered *triply* marginalized; however, they do not reify their multiply marginal positions into the paradoxical feminist center Suleri describes. Instead, they use their epistemic privilege performatively to negotiate diverse sets of socially constructed spaces: Allen, who calls herself a "multi-cultural event . . . raised in a Chicano village in New Mexico by a half-breed mother and a Lebanese-American father" (Review 127), is a Native American scholar and professor of English at UCLA; Anzaldúa, a self-described "Chicana *tejana* feminist-dyke-*patlache* poet, fiction writer, and cultural theorist"[4] from the Rio Grande Valley of south Texas, is the daughter of sixth-generation Mexicanos; and Lorde, the daughter of working-class West Indian immigrants and a self-identified "Black woman warrior poet," was born and raised in New York City yet "returned" to the Caribbean during the last years of her life. To borrow Victor Turner's phrase, they are "threshold people" who "elude or slip through the network of classifications that normally locate states and positions in cultural spaces" (95).[5]

Although the socially constructed spaces each writer "slips through" and the liminal identities she invents reflect the specificity of her regional, ethnic, and economic background—as well as other differences such as native languages, religion, education, and skin color—Allen, Anzaldúa, and Lorde enact their liminality in similar ways. As they translate their "threshold" identities into their writings, they engage in what I call tactical (re)naming, or the construction of differentially situated subjectivities that, deployed contextually, deconstruct oppositional categories from within. Although the identities they deploy occasionally resemble what Gayatri Chakravorty Spivak terms "strategic essentialism," I describe their (re)naming processes as tactical, rather than strategic, to underscore the temporary, plural, transformational nature of their maneuvers.[6] Allen, Anzaldúa, and Lorde engage in multiple conflicts simultaneously, thus enacting a series of displacements that confound preestablished divisions between margins and centers. To borrow Trinh T. Minh-ha's words, because their struggles are "multiple and transversal—specific but not confined to one side of any border war" (*Moon* 18), they oscillate between margin/center, oppressor/oppressed, and self/other. In short, they "use marginality as a starting point rather than an ending point . . . cross[ing] beyond it towards other affirmations and negations" (*Moon* 19).

Allen, Anzaldúa, and Lorde invent differential subjectivities and nondualistic modes of thought that they use to establish points of similarity among readers of diverse backgrounds. Instead of limiting herself to a single-voiced discourse on topics such as sexism or racism, each writer draws from her experiences and assumes complex speaking positions enabling her to explore issues crossing ethnic, sexual, national, and economic lines. This flexibility provides an important challenge to readers' generally more stable notions of subjectivity and selfhood. As Trinh asserts, "Essential difference allows those who rely on it to rest reassuringly on its gamut of fixed notions. Any mutation in identity, in essence, in regularity, and even in physical place poses a problem, if not a threat, in terms of classification and control. If you can't locate the other, how can you locate your-self?" (*Moon* 73). In various ways, and to varying degrees, Allen, Anzaldúa, and Lorde destabilize preestablished concepts of ethnic, cultural, and gender identity; in so doing, they demonstrate the limitations of any fixed sociocultural inscription. By disrupting the restrictive networks of classification that inscribe us as racialized, engendered subjects, they provide nonbinary models of subject formation, thus opening up psychic spaces where alterations in consciousness can occur.

> You say my name is ambivalence? Think of me as Shiva, a
> many-armed and legged body with one foot on brown soil,
> one on white, one in straight society, one in the gay world,
> the man's world, the women's, one limb in the literary world,
> another in the working class, the socialist, and the occult
> worlds. A sort of spider woman hanging by one thin strand
> of web.
> —Gloria Anzaldúa, "La Prieta"

Lorde's shifting positionality throughout *Sister Outsider* illustrates one possible form this (re)naming process can take. More specifically, she uses potentially essentializing self-definitions tactically. As Gloria Hull points out,

> Lorde's seemingly essentialist definitions of herself as a black/lesbian/
> mother/woman are not simple, fixed terms. Rather, they represent her
> ceaseless negotiations of a positionality from which she can speak. Almost as soon as she achieves a place of connection, she becomes uneasy
> at the comfortableness (which is, to her, a signal that something critical
> is being glossed over) and proceeds to rub athwart the smooth grain to
> find the roughness and the slant she needs to maintain her difference-
> defined, complexly constructed self. (155–56)

Although I agree with Hull's assertion that Lorde defines herself through her differences from others, I think it's also important to note that an equally necessary part of her "difference-defined, complexly constructed self" is the way she utilizes these differences to generate commonalities among differently situated readers. Consider, for example, her use of shifting subject positions in "Age, Race, Class, and Sex: Women Redefining Difference" to deconstruct binary oppositions between oppressor and oppressed. In the opening paragraphs she describes herself as a "forty-nine-year-old Black lesbian feminist socialist mother of two, including one boy, and a member of an inter-racial couple" and asserts that this diverse set of labels ensures her membership in a number of subjugated groups (*Sister Outsider* 120). Although she draws on her own experiences of oppression to discuss racism, heterosexism, and other forms of discrimination, she does not reify these margins into a new center. Instead, she blurs the boundary between oppressors and oppressed by locating herself, as well as her audience, in both groups. Rather than speak from a position of epistemic privilege based on her marginalization in U.S. culture, Lorde extends her experience outward to include all—regardless of color, sexuality, gender, age, or class—who do not fit this country's "mythical norm": "Institutionalized rejection of difference is an absolute necessity in a profit economy which needs outsiders as surplus people. As members of such an economy, we have *all* been programmed to respond to the human differences between us with fear and loathing and to handle that difference in one of three ways: ignoring it, and if that is not possible, copy it if we think it is dominant, or destroy it if we think it is subordinate" (*Sister Outsider* 115).

Lorde's shifts in this essay and elsewhere are tactical and illustrate Trinh's contention that, in order to resist self-reification and closure, "the challenge has to be taken up every time a positioning occurs: for just as one must situate oneself (in terms of ethnicity, class, gender, difference), one also refuses to be confined to that location" (*Moon* 229–30). Throughout her work, Lorde positions herself in response to the specific audience she addresses and to the particular social issues she confronts. By rejecting simplistic labels, she demonstrates that the recognition of differences can, paradoxically, create commonalities that serve to unite, rather than divide, apparently disparate groups.

Although Allen's tactical (re)naming takes different forms, she too utilizes her diverse personal experiences to explore complex sets of ethnic-, sexual-, and gender-related concerns. In essays such as "Where I Come from Is Like This" and "Something Sacred Going on Out There: Myth and Vision in American Indian Literature," she uses her formal training as a literary scholar, as well as her personal knowledge of Native traditions, to examine issues affecting all Native Americans, American Indian women, lesbians, mixed bloods, and contemporary U.S. feminists. There is, however, a significant difference between Allen's and Lorde's politics of enunciation. Whereas Lorde draws on different elements of her experiences and positions herself in a variety of ways, Allen generally draws on her Native ancestry and writes from the perspective of a half-breed American Indian woman. As Elizabeth Hanson puts it, "Allen remains for herself and for us (*at least as she wishes us to know her*) the quintessential 'breed'" (15, emphasis added). Yet Allen's "breed" identity is no more static than Lorde's shifting positionality for, as Hanson's comment indicates, Allen's (re)naming process is performative, not descriptive. In other words, Allen is not reconstructing a monolithic gender/ethnic-specific standpoint; instead, she redefines herself and other mixed-blood peoples in ways that challenge readers to rethink existing identity categories. For example, by describing herself as the "confluence" of numerous, sometimes conflicting identities, Allen destabilizes conventional notions of a unitary self. As she explained in an interview,

> I am Lebanese-American, I am Indian, I am a breed, and I am New Mexican and they have a lot to do with how I act and what I think and how I interpret things. I was raised in a family and in a world that was multicultural, multiethnic, multireligious, and multilinguistic, with a number of social classes involved. . . . And then I have a kind of overlaying or underlaying American or Anglo culture that I mostly picked up in school. It is all me. It sometimes comes into conflict with itself, but it is all me. (qtd. in Eysturoy 103)

Given this complex background, it is perhaps not surprising that Allen claims that her Laguna/Sioux/Lebanese/Scotch/German ancestry makes her "split, not in two but in twenty, and never . . . able to reconcile all the *places* that I am" (qtd. in Bruchac 18, emphasis added). However, by portraying herself as the convergence of apparently irreconcilable places, Allen gives her marginal status a central role in U.S. culture. More specifically, she maintains that "half-breeds" function as catalysts for cultural change: "We have a mediational capacity that is not possessed by either of the sides. What we are able to do is bridge variant realities because everybody is pissed off at us and we are pissed off at ourselves. What we are able to do is move from flower to flower, so to speak, and get the pollen moved around among each of our traditions. Then we can plant back into them" (qtd. in Bruchac 19). Significantly, Allen does not use this epistemic privilege to reify already existing categories of meaning. Instead, she employs her marginality to engage in a to-and-fro movement that takes up yet disrupts conventional interpretations of Native American identities. She stages a fluid, indianized self/worldview that she invites her readers—whatever their biological/cultural backgrounds—to adopt.

The title character in Allen's novel, *The Woman Who Owned the Shadows,* illustrates one form these negotiations can assume. A mixed blood cut off from tribal traditions and educated at Catholic schools, Ephanie Atencio must painfully discover the ways her identity has been (mis)-shaped by Native American, Mexican, and Anglo cultures. Like shadows, which as Allen notes are neither light nor dark but rather the interplay of both (*Sacred Hoop* 244), Ephanie represents the mingling of apparent opposites. Although her mixed heritage prevents her from aligning herself with a single group, it enables her to establish new connections between and among diverse peoples. As Allen points out, at the novel's conclusion Ephanie "goes back to teach white people. So her resolution is that this is not about race; this is about vision. *The people who live on this continent are Indians,* that is to say, they live on the Indian continent, and what we must do is teach them how to live here. We tried and they kept killing us. That was then; but now maybe there are people here, lots of them, who are ready" (qtd. in Eysturoy 105, emphasis added).

I have quoted this passage at length because I believe it provides an important key to understanding the performative dimensions of Allen's tactical (re)naming. Allen, like Ephanie, teaches "white people" how to live like Indians. Yet Allen takes this educational process even further, for her lessons are designed to teach North American "white people" that they *are* "Indians." Throughout her scholarly writing, Allen draws on her mixed-blood heritage to authorize her position as "spokesperson within the scholarly community" (Hanson 14). Consequently, readers generally assume that she functions as a native informer who simply reveals previously hidden aspects of American Indian life. Indeed, Allen herself often reinforces this interpretation by presenting her literary and cultural criticism under the guise of *explaining* Native American traditions to "outsiders." Yet she is at least equally concerned with developing new woman-centered "Native American" traditions capable of transforming her readers as well as herself. In other words, Allen does not simply attempt to explicate the intersection of gender and ethnicity in Native American texts. Instead, she uses her gendered/ethnic identity performatively in order to alter her readers' self-perceptions, as well as their views of tribal cultures. Thus, in the essays collected in *The Sacred Hoop: Recovering the Feminine in American Indian Traditions,* Allen reinterprets the historic and mythic beliefs of indigenous North American peoples from a twentieth-century feminist perspective and develops a highly distinctive woman-focused tradition. Similarly, in *Grandmothers of the Light: A Medicine Woman's Sourcebook,* Allen combines theory, myth, and story to construct a twentieth-century feminist pan-Indian worldview that she invites her readers to adopt. She implies that—read

from the proper mythic perspective—the Aztec, Cherokee, Navajo, and
other Native American stories she retells function as a guidebook for any
woman interested in learning to develop her own shamanic powers and
"walk the medicine path" (3). By fully participating in the "sacred myths"
collected in her anthology, contemporary English-speaking women of
any ethnicity or cultural background can develop a spiritual mode of perception that empowers them to bring about psychic and material change.

As coeditor of *This Bridge Called My Back: Writings by Radical Women
of Color* and editor of *Making Face, Making Soul/Haciendo Caras: Creative
and Critical Perspectives by Women of Color,* Anzaldúa is equally concerned
with creating transformative dialogues among people of diverse backgrounds. Like Lorde, she converts simplistic binarisms between oppressor and oppressed into complex interconnecting fields. Within the
space of a single passage in *Borderlands/La Frontera,* for example, Anzaldúa identifies herself with both the "oppressed" and the "oppressors"—
with the "Chicano, *indio,* American Indian, *mojado, mexicano,* immigrant
Latino, Anglo in power, working class Anglo, Black, [and] Asian"—as she
describes the psychic struggles facing all twentieth-century peoples and
insists that "we need to meet on a broader communal ground" (87). And
like Allen, Anzaldúa uses her marginal status to redefine existing categories of identity. Consider, for example, her discussion of "new *mestiza*
queers" in "To(o) Queer the Writer," where she explains that "the new
mestiza queers have the ability, the flexibility, the amorphous quality of
being able to stretch this way and that way. We can add new labels,
names and identities as we mix with others" (249). As the term suggests,
Anzaldúa's new mestiza represents a hybrid, a complex mixed breed
who can neither be reduced to a single category nor rigidly classified according to a specific set of traits (*Borderlands* esp. chap. 7). The product of
two or more cultures—each with its own value system—the mestiza is in
a "state of perpetual transition" as she attempts to reconcile, rather than
reject, the many voices in her head.

Anzaldúa's theory of *mestizaje* represents at least two significant de-
partures from its earlier usage. First, by feminizing "mestizo," her mestiza
provides an important in(ter)vention into twentieth-century Chicano
literary and theoretical movements that, as Ramón Saldívar observes,
have been dominated by "male-centered themes and values" (39). Second, by extending conventional definitions of the mestizo as a member
of a biologically based cultural group, Anzaldúa de-essentializes and
pluralizes culturally specific notions of identity. As Marcos Sanchez-
Tranquilino asserts, Anzaldúa's theory represents an innovative shift from
earlier views: "Her interpretation goes beyond the traditional concept of
mestizaje. For Anzaldúa, that concept cannot ever again be thought of as

a simple mixing of blood or cultures but rather that what has always been in effect a mixing of identities many times over—beyond the old dualities be they gender, historical, economic, or cultural, etc." (568).

Like Allen and Lorde, Anzaldúa transforms essentialized conceptions of identity into transcultural, transgendered models of subjectivity. By positing the nonduality of self and other, they construct multilayered discourses recognizing both the diversities *and* commonalities between and among apparently dissimilar peoples. They invent nonunitary plural subjectivities illustrated, for example, in "Between Ourselves," where Lorde writes, "We are all children of Eshu . . . / and we each wear many changes / inside of our skin." Yet she stipulates that until we recognize these many faces as our own and "stop killing / the other / in ourselves / the self that we hate in others," we remain blinded by our own self-denial and unable to create alliances among people of diverse backgrounds (*Black Unicorn* 114).

But what can it mean to discover the "other" within one's "self"? Or to have "many changes" within "our skin"? By blurring the boundaries between self and other, Lorde destabilizes Western culture's dominant/subordinate worldview and the subsequent dichotomy between subject and object. In psychoanalytic terms, her invitation to recognize the other in ourselves entails a reversal and subsequent reincorporation of the displaced projections that occur during ego splitting. I describe this nonbinary subject formation as re(con)ceiving the other in order to emphasize its twofold nature: We redefine the other as a part of ourselves by acknowledging our own otherness. Alicia Ostriker finds a similar process in writings by a number of twentieth-century U.S. women poets. As she explains in her discussion of their attempts to reconcile "internal antinomies," "for many women writers, the quest to reintegrate a split self is simultaneously a drive to topple the hierarchy of the sacred and the profane, redeeming and including what the culture has exiled and excluded. To deny the other is to deny the self. Conversely, it is dread of what seems loathsome within the self that produces a projection of it onto another" (194–96).

There are, however, two important differences between the reintegration Ostriker describes and the processes Lorde enacts in her work. First, on a collective level, Lorde extends the need for reintegration outward to encompass the bifurcation experienced by people of the African diaspora. Second, on an individual level, her writings illustrate the particular resonance this quest for reintegration has for people who, because of their ethnicity, gender, and/or sexuality, have been portrayed as the profane, especially when they have internalized this negative self-image. The myth of feminine evil, for example, often has further implications for dark-skinned women: Because the dominant ideology privileges male over female and light over dark, both their gender and their ethnicity seem to confirm their inferior status. As Virginia R. Harris and Trinity A. Ordoña explain, when dark-skinned women accept this dualistic world-view and believe that "dark is inferior and evil; woman is inferior, evil, and must be controlled sexually," they suppress themselves and distrust their ability to speak (306).

Anzaldúa addresses this issue in "Speaking in Tongues: A Letter to Third World Women Writers" where she describes her own desire to write as a

> quest for the self . . . which we women of color have come to think as "other"—the dark, the feminine. Didn't we start writing to reconcile this other within us? We knew we were different, set apart, exiled from what is considered "normal," white-right. And as we internalized this exile, we came to see the alien within us and, too often, as a result, we split apart from ourselves and each other. Forever after we have been in search of that self, that "other" and each other. (169)

As these complex interconnections between inner and outer forms of self/other-alienation suggest, Anzaldúa's quest for the self-become-other(ed) indicates more than a desire to reconcile internal divisions. To my mind, her search represents an attempt to develop new modes of perception and alternate subjectivities capable of reconciling both internal and *external* antimonies. Like Lorde, she implies that this re(con)-ceived otherness, or recognition of the other in ourselves, indicates the possibility of inventing nonbinary models of subject formation that open up new interconnections among people. Yet she stipulates that this self-othering process entails a painful rebirth, a self-confrontation that requires simultaneously accepting and transforming the dominant society's label.

Anzaldúa's "that dark shining thing" graphically illustrates the highly emotional, terrifying nature of this encounter with the self-become-other(ed). In this poem, she recalls her own experience as she simultaneously observes and assists as another mestiza—"colored, poor white, latent queer / passing for white / seething with hatred, anger"— learns to recognize the other as a part of herself. Significantly, her shifts between first- and second-person pronouns enable her to extend this transformational experience outward and invite readers to undergo a similar alteration in consciousness. Consider, for example, the following stanza. By depicting herself as the repository of other people's projected self-hatred, Anzaldúa redefines herself as the other, thus blurring the boundaries between writer and reader:

I am the only round face,
Indian-beaked, off-colored
in the faculty lineup, the workshop, the panel
and reckless enough to take you on.
I am the flesh you dig your fingernails into
mine the hand you chop off while still clinging to it
the face spewed with your vomit
I risk your sanity
and mine.
(*Borderlands* 171)

Despite her desire to "turn [her] back" on this other mestiza, she does not, for she recognizes the similarities between their experiences:

my feet know each rock you tread on
as you stumble I falter too
and I remember
he/me/they who shouted
push Gloria breathe Gloria
feel their hands holding me up, prompting me
until I'm facing that pulsing bloodied blackness
trying to scream
from between your legs.
(*Borderlands* 171–72)

In this poem and others, such as "Letting Go" and "I Had to Go Down," Anzaldúa associates this self-othering process with an exploration of internalized oppression, a period of psychic and emotional pain so intense that it forces her to confront her self-loathing. When she does so, she faces her own dread of the other and discovers that this other is also a part of herself. Thus in the conclusion Anzaldúa enacts a complex series of negotiations between herself and her mestiza-reader:

I know that I am that Beast that circles your house
peers in the window
and that you see yourself my prey

But I know you are the Beast
its prey is you
you the midwife
you that dark shining thing.
(*Borderlands* 172)

By identifying both herself and her reader with this "Beast," Anzaldúa illustrates an alternate model of subject formation analogous to the transformational process Chela Sandoval refers to in "U.S. Third World

Feminism." According to Sandoval, self-splintering—or what she describes as a "violent shattering of the unitary sense of self" (23)—leads to the development of an alternate mode of perception she calls differential consciousness. Sandoval uses this term to represent the nonbinary oppositional tactics effectively deployed by self-identified U.S. third world feminists in their efforts to confront simultaneously racism, sexism, and other forms of oppression. She outlines a "four-phase hegemonic typology" of traditional oppositional ideologies and describes differential consciousness as a fifth form that enables social actors to use already existing binary oppositional strategies in new ways (3). Differential consciousness represents "a new subjectivity, a political revision that denies any one ideology as the final answer, while instead positing a tactical subjectivity with the capacity to recenter depending upon the kinds of oppression to be confronted. This is what the shift from hegemonic oppositional theory and practice to a U.S. third world theory and method of oppositional consciousness require" (14).[7] In other words, differential consciousness utilizes conventional oppositional readings of culture, but it does so selectively. When social actors employ differential consciousness, they convert binary forms of opposition into "ideological and *tactical* weaponry" capable of transforming oppressive sociolinguistic and political systems (14). By enabling movement " 'between and among' " traditional binary oppositional strategies, differential consciousness "permits functioning within yet beyond the demands of the dominant ideology" (3).

Although Sandoval associates differential consciousness with U.S. third world feminists, she maintains that the mobile subjectivity it requires is "accessible to all people."[8] Indeed, she believes that Anzaldúa, Lorde, and other twentieth-century self-identified U.S. third world feminists have demonstrated that differential consciousness provides the most effective form of resistance for *all* contemporary social actors. Whereas conventional "hegemonic" oppositional theories "rigidly circumscribe what is possible" by establishing binary categories between dominant and subordinate groups and by demanding an internal consistency that eventually fractures resistance movements from within, differential consciousness remains flexible and acknowledges its partial containment in hegemonic power structures (10).

But how do social actors—of whatever gender, ethnicity, sexuality, or class—begin to utilize this shifting, nonbinary oppositional practice? Sandoval herself offers few clues. Although she briefly mentions the "violent shattering of the unitary sense of self" (23) necessary for the development of differential consciousness, she does not explain how, more precisely, this self-splintering occurs. I would argue that re(con)-ceived otherness indicates one way this mobile identity develops. Consider, for example, Anzaldúa's confrontation with the other in "that dark shining thing." By deconstructing self/other binaries and redefining herself as the other, she constructs a flexible self/worldview enabling her to shift subject positions contextually. Anzaldúa associates this alteration in consciousness with performative language. She can use words in new ways, for she rejects the binary thinking that separates good from evil, light from dark, up from down, and subject from object, by dissolving the boundaries between them.

Allen depicts a similar deconstructive process in *The Woman Who Owned the Shadows*. Only at the point of death—when she has surrendered entirely to the dark and attempted to hang herself—does Ephanie recognize her intense desire to live. The conflicting worldviews she has internalized lead to fragmentation, alienation, and guilt, and throughout almost the entire novel Ephanie undergoes an intense inner struggle as she attempts to escape or transcend the "lifelong duality, dichotomy, twinning of her own self with a monstrous other" (133). But it is not until she accepts this "monstrous other" as a part of herself and becomes immersed in the isolation she fears that she can transform this "lifelong duality" into a nondualistic self/worldview.

Both the transmutation of self/other dichotomies and the corresponding insight that extremes meet and turn into their opposites are central to the tactical (re)naming processes developed by Allen, Anzaldúa, and Lorde. By positing the nonduality of self and other, they destabilize fixed notions of selfhood, thus opening up the transformational possibilities contained within any apparently self-enclosed subject. As I will explain in the following section, these nonbinary models of subject formation have important implications for developing what I call transformational identity politics—a complex interactive process that displaces conventional boundaries between apparently disparate social groups.

> Otherness becomes empowering critical difference when it is not given, but re-created. Defined with the Other's newly formed criteria.
> —Trinh T. Minh-ha, *When the Moon Waxes Red*

> I am who I am, doing what I came to do, acting upon you like a drug or a chisel, to remind you of your me-ness, as I discover you in myself.
> —Audre Lorde, *Sister Outsider*

Identity politics—or the development of political theories and strategies based on social actors' personal ethnic, gender, and/or sexual identities—has played a pivotal role in contemporary feminist and ethnic movements. By enabling oppressed people to unite across differences, identity politics makes it possible to develop coalitions for social change. Too often, however, this radical potential is greatly diminished. When personal identities become reified and defined as monolithic, social actors focus almost entirely on the differences *among* what they perceive to be discrete gender, ethnic, or sexual categories. By so doing, they inadvertently reinscribe inflexible boundaries between apparently separate groups. This emphasis on mutually exclusive identities makes it impossible to recognize commonalities among differently situated social actors, thus preventing the establishment of effective alliances.

Pratibha Parmar makes a similar point in her assessment of self-identified black British women's attempts to develop a cohesive feminist movement. Parmar acknowledges the importance of identity politics yet emphasizes its limitations, explaining that "while the articulation of self-identities has been a necessary and essential process for collective organizing by black and migrant women, it also resulted in political practices which became insular and often retrograde" (102). She too attributes these limitations to rigid, exclusionary definitions of identity based on static conceptions of sexuality, ethnicity, and class. She asserts that when feminists relied on "a language of 'authentic subjective experience'" derived from restrictive self-definitions they developed hierarchies of oppression that prevented the establishment of alliances across differences. Moreover, the appeal to authentic experience led to claims of epistemic privilege and guilt-tripping, or the "self-righteous assertion that if one inhabits a certain identity this gives one the legitimate and moral right to guilt-trip others into particular ways of behaving" (107).

In short, it seems that conventional identity politics often bases political strategies on humanist notions of stable, unitary identities that fragment groups from within. Yet the solution is not to abandon all references to personal experiences but rather to take experientially based knowledge claims even further by redefining identity. As Andrea Stuart states in her discussion of British feminists' identity politics,

> The problem was not, in a strange way, that we took the implications of organizing around identity too far, but that we didn't take it far enough. Had we really pushed this debate far enough, we would have come to appreciate that we are all oppressor *and* oppressed. . . . Instead of appreciating the interconnectedness of our oppressions we saw all our interests as mutually antagonistic, instead of making alliances we were in competition with one another. (39)

Stuart's critique applies to U.S. identity politics as well.[9] As Barbara Smith, Gloria Yamato, and other contemporary feminists point out, racism and racist behavior are so deeply embedded in twentieth-century U.S. culture that people of all colors have been (mis)shaped by this "patriarchal legacy" (Smith 25). Similar statements could be made about heterosexism, sexism, and (perhaps) classism.[10] They too are the widespread manifestations of a rigidly dualistic hierarchical mode of thought that, to greater or lesser degree, has affected us all. But until we begin "actually *feel[ing]* what we have been forced to suppress each time we were a victim of, witness to, or perpetrator of racism" or other forms of discrimination, we remain unaware of our own complicity in oppressive social structures (Yamato 23). However, this exploration of previously unacknowledged emotions involves suffering, as social actors of all colors, genders, sexualities, and classes realize the various ways we function as both oppressor and oppressed. Because the deconstruction of self/ other binaries serves as the potential trigger for such insights, it is less painful to deny internal differences by creating unitary models of identity. Yet these monolithic identity concepts reinforce dominant/ subordinate dualistic thinking, and, as Lorde points out, this denial of difference keeps us divided. To establish effective alliances, we must leave the safety of unitary, insular conceptions of identity by recognizing, expressing, and accepting both the differences *and* the similarities among ourselves and others (*Sister Outsider* 114–23).

In psychoanalytic terms, the recognition of difference(s) cannot occur without the existence of a prior, though often erased, point of contact. As Homi Bhabha explains in his discussion of the ambivalent identification and slippage between colonizer and colonized, "the disavowal of the Other always exacerbates the 'edge' of identification, reveals that dangerous place where identity and aggressivity are twinned. For denial is always a retroactive process; a *half*-acknowledgement of that Otherness that has left its traumatic mark" ("Remembering Fanon" 144). But what if this disavowal of the other is only partially enacted? Or what if the other is first disavowed and then re(con)ceived, as it is in writings by Anzaldúa, Allen, and Lorde? I believe this emotionally charged recognition of the other effects a shift in consciousness where transformational identity politics can occur.

If, as I argued in the preceding section, re(con)ceiving the other triggers the emotional commitment and the violent shattering of a unitary sense of self Sandoval associates with differential consciousness, then this nonbinary model of subject formation makes it possible for social actors of whatever gender, sexuality, or ethnicity to develop politics based on differential identifications with diverse groups of people.

Although this deconstruction of self/other binaries necessitates a period of intense psychic/emotional pain, the acknowledgment of previously suppressed emotions should not be equated with guilt. The point is not to encourage feelings of personal responsibility for the slavery, decimation of indigenous peoples, land theft, and so on that occurred in the past. It is, rather, to enable social actors to comprehend more fully how these oppressive systems that began in the historical past continue to (mis)shape contemporary conditions. Only then can we work to bring about a more equitable distribution of resources in the present. Guilt-tripping plays no role in this process. Indeed, I would argue that guilt functions as a useless, debilitating state of consciousness that reifies the boundaries between apparently separate groups. As Nancie Caraway suggests, "guilt depoliticizes us by instilling a sense of fatalism" (16). When people feel guilty, they become paralyzed, deny any sense of agency, and assume that their privileged positions in the contemporary sociosymbolic system automatically compel them to act as "the oppressor." However, as I have emphasized throughout this essay, there are no permanent, unitary identities. Even the notorious "white male" is far less monolithic than we often assume. As Patrick McGee notes, "every subject is an other; that is, it is destabilized by the social system that constitutes it" (14). In order to recognize the heterogeneity of every subject, we must deconstruct simplistic conceptions of self-identity. In the words of Anzaldúa, we must "leave the permanent boundaries of a fixed self . . . and see . . . through the eyes of the other" ("En rapport" 145).

The work of Anzaldúa, Allen, and Lorde demonstrates that this "fixed self" only becomes fixed when we perceive it as such. When we define "difference" as "deviation," and "other" as "not-me," we rely on binary oppositions and create inflexible speaking subjects, pseudo-universal concepts of wo/manhood, that erect permanent barriers between mutually exclusive sexual/ethnic identities. However, by redefining differences as ever changing fields of interplay occurring within, between, and among speaking/reading subject(s), subjectivity becomes pluralized; we reject humanist models of self-identity and create multilayered discourses that replace the unified subject with fluid, shifting speakers.

Each writer exhibits what Trinh describes as a "critical difference from myself"—the ability to perceive difference within, between, and among speaking subject(s), which "means that I am not i, am within and without i. I/i can be I or i, you and me both involved. We (with capital W) sometimes include(s), other times exclude(s) me. You and I are close, we intertwine" (*Woman* 90). As this proliferation of I's, we's, and you's suggests, Trinh deconstructs the notion of a fixed, stable identity and claims that, because speaking subjects are always defined contextually in relation to others, each individual is herself composed of *"infinite layers."* Consequently, each discourse we enter requires a tactical (re)naming, another variation of nonunitary plural subjects (or I/i's). It is this fluid speaker we hear when Lorde writes, "I am blessed within my selves / who are come to make our shattered faces / whole" (*Black Unicorn* 61–62), or when Allen claims that her "life is the pause. The space between. The not this, not that, not the other" ("Autobiography" 151), or when Anzaldúa insists, "I remain who I am, multiple / and one of the herd, yet not of it" (*Borderlands* 173). They enact their nonunitary identities differentially, based on the particular contexts in which they speak.

Indeed, Anzaldúa, Lorde, and Allen take Trinh's deconstruction of "the line dividing *I* and *Not-I, us* and *them*" (*Woman* 94) even further. In Lorde's words, they *become* "the sharpened edge / where day and night shall meet / and not be / one" (*Black Unicorn* 7). Not one, but not two either. Each writer locates herself on Trinh's ever-shifting marker separating I from Not-I, us from them, and invents new spaces for convers(at)ions—transformational dialogues—between and among nonunitary plural subjects. As they position themselves within the intermediary space between I/i, I/Not-I, subject/object, self/other, and other binary pairs, they subvert dualistic forms of thinking by destabilizing the categories from within. This subversion is transformative. As Françoise Lionnet points out in her discussion of Friedrich Nietzsche's writing practice,

> It is by rejecting the whole Western tradition of binary thinking which contributes to the naturalization of such distinctions as male/female, master/slave, autonomous/dependent, writer/reader that Nietzsche succeeds in reaffirming a principle of interconnectedness in which subjects and objects, self and other, are conditioned by their interactions in the world and thus become open to transformations of all sorts. To privilege autonomous subjectivity or original writing as the locus of the authentic self is a way of ignoring that subjectivity (and writing) is always already filled with the voices of others. (68)

In their texts, Anzaldúa, Allen, and Lorde speak with the voices of re(con)ceived others, thus opening up spaces where this "interconnectedness" can occur. Whereas social actors who rely on conventional identity politics base their actions on static notions of an authentic (engendered, racialized, and/or sexualized) self, Allen, Anzaldúa, and Lorde do not. Instead, they create nonessentialized, constantly shifting locations where transformational identity politics can arise. Naming the other(s) in herself, and herself in the other(s), each writer constructs flexible models of identity that deconstruct monolithic notions of difference and similarity.

By translating their liminality into their works, Allen, Anzaldúa, and Lorde transform the margins into convers(at)ions among writers, readers, and texts. As they destabilize the binary oppositions between margin and center and locate the other(s) within both themselves and their readers, they open up new intersubjective spaces, or what Bhabha describes as "a space of 'translation': a place of hybridity . . . where the construction of a political object that is new, neither the one nor the Other," can occur ("Commitment" 117). These convers(at)ions (can) play a significant role in the transformational identity politics I advocate here. As we—whatever color, class, ethnicity, or sex "we" are—see (ourselves) through the eyes of the other, we recognize the other(s) in ourselves, and ourselves in the other(s). We too enter new spaces where transcultural/sexual/gender/class identifications—mestizaje connections—can occur.

NOTES

1. I use the term "self-identified" to indicate the volitional dimension of contemporary feminist identity politics. Throughout this essay I will use the term "U.S.," rather than "American," when referring to the United States. As I see it, the word "American" is too general, for it incorporates Canada, Mexico, and all of Central and South America. I borrow the phrase "U.S. third world feminists" from Chela Sandoval. In my work, as in Sandoval's, it denotes a constructed category: "the political alliance made during the 1960s and 1970s between a generation of U.S. feminists of color who were separated by race, class, or gender identifications but united through similar responses to the experience of race oppression" ("U.S. Third World Feminism" 17).

2. Suleri's essay, "Woman Skin Deep," contains a biting critique of bell hooks's and other recent "postcolonial" feminists' (mis)use of the rhetoric of the margin/center discourse. Finke makes a related point, asserting, "There are no oppressed groups pure and simple, only shifting relations between oppressors and oppressed. Yet, the relational nature of marginality frequently remains unacknowledged, even by feminists" (253). For an additional analysis of the epistemic privilege claimed by some self-identified women of color, see Bar On, "Marginality and Epistemic Privilege."

3. For an analysis of this humanist self, see P. Smith, *Discerning the Subject,* and the first chapter of S. Smith, *Subjectivity, Identity, and the Body.*

4. This self-description appears in Anzaldúa's 1992 vita.

5. I discuss threshold identities in greater detail in *Women Reading Women Writing.*

6. Spivak discusses strategic essentialism in *In Other Worlds* (197–221) and *Outside in the Teaching Machine* (3–8). For a useful explanation of the differences between strategies and tactics, see de Certeau, *The Practice of Everyday Life.*

7. Sandoval's "four-phase hegemonic typology" of oppositional ideologies

consists of "equal rights," "revolutionary," "supremacism," and "separatism" ("U.S. Third World Feminism" 10–14).

8. Sandoval explains that differential consciousness represents a "learned intellectual and emotional skill" rather than an inborn biological trait ("U.S. Third World Feminism" 23).

9. Giroux provides a useful analysis of the correlations between U.S. and British identity politics in *Living Dangerously* (esp. chaps. 3 and 4). For additional critiques of the limitations in U.S. feminists' identity politics, see Butler, *Gender Trouble;* Ferguson, *The Man Question;* Jordan, *On Call* and *Technical Difficulties;* and Suleri, "Woman Skin Deep."

10. For a discussion of how class issues are generally overlooked in feminist theory, see Ferguson, *The Man Question.*

WORKS CITED

Allen, Paula Gunn. "The Autobiography of a Confluence." *I Tell You Now: Autobiographical Essays by Native American Writers.* Ed. Brian Swann and Arnold Krupat. Lincoln: University of Nebraska Press, 1987. 143–54.

———. *Grandmothers of the Light: A Medicine Woman's Sourcebook.* Boston: Beacon, 1991.

———. Review of *This Bridge Called My Back. Conditions* 5 (1982): 121–27.

———. *The Sacred Hoop: Recovering the Feminine in American Indian Traditions.* Boston: Beacon, 1986.

———. *The Woman Who Owned the Shadows.* San Francisco: Spinsters/Aunt Lute, 1983.

Anzaldúa, Gloria. *Borderlands/La Frontera: The New Mestiza.* San Francisco: Aunt Lute, 1987.

———, ed. *Making Face, Making Soul/Haciendo Caras: Creative and Critical Perspectives by Women of Color.* San Francisco: Aunt Lute Foundation, 1990.

———. "La Prieta." *This Bridge Called My Back.* Ed. Moraga and Anzaldúa. 198–209.

———. "En rapport, In Opposition: Cobrando cuentas a las nuestras." *Making Face.* Ed. Anzaldúa. 142–48.

———. "Speaking in Tongues: A Letter to Third World Women Writers." *This Bridge Called My Back.* Ed. Moraga and Anzaldúa. 165–74.

———. "To(o) Queer the Writer—Loca, escritora y chicana." *Inversions: Writing by Dykes, Queers, and Lesbians.* Ed. Betsy Warland. Vancouver: Press Gang, 1991. 249–64.

Bar On, Bat-Ami. "Marginality and Epistemic Privilege." *Feminist Epistemologies.* Ed. Linda Alcoff and Elizabeth Potter. New York: Routledge, 1993. 83–100.

Bhabha, Homi K. "The Commitment to Theory." *Questions of Third World Cinema.* Ed. Jim Pines and Paul Willeman. London: British Film Institute, 1989. 111–32.

———. "Remembering Fanon: Self, Psyche, and the Colonial Condition." *Remaking History.* Ed. Barbara Kruger and Phil Mariani. Seattle: Bay Press, 1989. 131–50.

Bruchac, Joseph. *Survival This Way: Interviews with American Indian Poets.* Tucson: University of Arizona Press, 1987.

Butler, Judith. *Gender Trouble: Feminism and the Subversion of Identity.* New York: Routledge, 1990.

Caraway, Nancie. *Segregated Sisterhood: Racism and the Politics of American Feminism.* Knoxville: University of Tennessee Press, 1991.

de Certeau, Michel. *The Practice of Everyday Life.* Trans. Steven Rendall. Berkeley: University of California Press, 1984.

Eysturoy, Annie O. "Paula Gunn Allen." Ed. John F. Crawford, William Balassi, and Annie O. Eysturoy. *This Is about Vision: Interviews with Southwestern Writers.* Albuquerque: University of New Mexico Press, 1990. 95–107.

Ferguson, Kathy E. *The Man Question: Visions of Subjectivity in Feminist Theory.* Berkeley: University of California Press, 1993.

Finke, Laurie A. "Rhetoric of Marginality: Why I Do Feminist Theory." *Tulsa Studies in Women's Literature* 5 (1986): 251–72.

Fuss, Diana. *Essentially Speaking: Feminism, Nature, and Difference.* New York: Routledge, 1989.

Gates, Henry Louis, Jr. " 'Ethnic and Minority' Studies." *Introduction to Scholarship in Modern Languages and Literatures.* Ed. Joseph Gibaldi. New York: Modern Language Association, 1992. 289–302.

Giroux, Henry. *Living Dangerously: Multiculturalism and the Politics of Difference.* New York: Peter Lang, 1993.

Hanson, Elizabeth I. *Paula Gunn Allen.* Boise State University Western Writer Series. Boise, Idaho: Boise State University Press, 1990.

Harris, Virginia R., and Trinity A. Ordoña. "Developing Unity among Women of Color: Crossing the Barriers of Internalized Racism and Cross-Racial Hostility." *Making Face.* Ed. Anzaldúa. 304–16.

hooks, bell. *Yearning: Race, Gender, and Cultural Politics.* Boston: South End Press, 1990.

Hull, Gloria. "Living on the Line: Audre Lorde and *Our Dead Behind Us.*" *Changing Our Own Words: Essays on Criticism, Theory, and Writing by Black Women.* Ed. Cheryl A. Wall. New Brunswick, N.J.: Rutgers University Press, 1989. 150–72.

Jordan, June. *On Call: Political Essays.* Boston: South End Press, 1987.

———. *Technical Difficulties: African-American Notions and the State of the Union.* New York: Pantheon, 1993.

Keating, AnaLouise. *Women Reading Women Writing: Self-Invention in Paula Gunn Allen, Gloria Anzaldúa, and Audre Lorde.* Philadelphia: Temple University Press, 1996.

Lionnet, Françoise. *Autobiographical Voices: Race, Gender, Self-Portraiture.* Ithaca, N.Y.: Cornell University Press, 1989.

Lorde, Audre. *The Black Unicorn.* New York: Norton, 1978.

———. *Sister Outsider: Essays and Speeches.* Freedom, Calif.: Crossing Press, 1984.

McGee, Patrick. *Telling the Other: The Question of Value in Modern and Postcolonial Writing.* Ithaca, N.Y.: Cornell University Press, 1992.

Moraga, Cherríe, and Gloria Anzaldúa, eds. *This Bridge Called My Back: Writings by Radical Women of Color.* New York: Kitchen Table/Women of Color Press, 1983.

Ostriker, Alicia. *Stealing the Language: The Emergence of Women's Poetry in America.* Boston: Beacon, 1986.

Parmar, Pratibha. "Black Feminism: the Politics of Articulation." *Identity.* Ed. Rutherford. 101–27.

Rutherford, Jonathan. *Identity: Community, Culture, Difference*. London: Lawrence and Wishart, 1990.

Saldívar, Ramón. *Chicano Narrative: The Dialectics of Difference*. Madison: University of Wisconsin Press, 1990.

Sanchez-Tranquilino, Marcos, and John Tagg. "The Pachuco's Flayed Hide: Mobility, Identity, and Buenas Garras." *Cultural Studies*. Ed. Lawrence Grossberg, Cary Nelson, and Paula Treichler. New York: Routledge, 1992.

Sandoval, Chela. "Feminism and Racism: A Report on the 1981 National Women's Studies Association Conference." *Making Face*. Ed. Anzaldúa. 55–71.

———. "U.S. Third World Feminism: The Theory and Method of Oppositional Consciousness in the Postmodern World." *Genders* 10 (Spring 1991): 1–24.

Smith, Barbara. "Racism and Women's Studies." *Making Face*. Ed. Anzaldúa. 25–28.

Smith, Paul. *Discerning the Subject*. Minneapolis: University of Minnesota Press, 1988.

Smith, Sidonie. *Subjectivity, Identity, and the Body: Women's Autobiographical Practices in the Twentieth Century*. Bloomington: Indiana University Press, 1993.

Spivak, Gayatri Chakravorty. *In Other Worlds: Essays in Cultural Politics*. New York: Metheun, 1987.

———. *Outside in the Teaching Machine*. New York: Routledge, 1993.

Stuart, Andrea. "Feminism: Dead or Alive?" *Identity*. Ed. Rutherford. 28–42.

Suleri, Sara. "Woman Skin Deep: Feminism and the Postcolonial Condition." *Critical Inquiry* 18 (1992): 756–69.

Trinh T. Minh-ha. *When the Moon Waxes Red: Representation, Gender and Cultural Politics*. New York: Routledge, 1991.

———. *Woman Native Other: Writing Postcoloniality and Feminism*. Bloomington: Indiana University Press, 1989.

Turner, Victor. *The Ritual Process: Structure and Anti-Structure*. Chicago: Aldine, 1969.

Yamato, Gloria. "Something about the Subject Makes It Hard to Name." *Making Face*. Ed. Anzaldúa. 20–24.

2 ◇ Women of Color and Identity Politics

Translating Theory, *Haciendo Teoría*

In her introduction to the anthology *Making Face, Making Soul/Haciendo Caras* (1990), the editor, Gloria Anzaldúa, explains how the book continues the work that she and Cherríe Moraga started in their groundbreaking collection *This Bridge Called My Back: Writings by Radical Women of Color* (1983):

> For years I waited for someone to compile a book that would continue where *This Bridge Called My Back* left off. A book that would confront the Racism in the white women's movement in a more thorough, personal, direct, empirical, and theoretical way. A book that would deepen the dialogue between all women and that would take on the various issues—hindrances and possibilities—in alliance-building. A book that would explode the neat boundaries of the half dozen categories of marginality that define us and one that would unflinchingly bring us *cara a cara* with our own *historias*. (*Making Face* xvi)

Anzaldúa perceives her anthology as part of a larger project of decolonizing the "white women's movement" and of strengthening coalitions among women of color as they dialogue with Anglo feminism. Yet Anzaldúa points out that the project of encountering "our own" histories still awaits elaboration. What does it mean to come face to face with "our own" histories? Are these histories of the individual or of the collective? Who is included in the collective that proclaims ownership and how is she (are they) included? It would seem that we would know the answers to these questions if we only had the right *teorías,* not the theories given to women of color by Anglo American liberal feminists to interpret their experience, but those that women of color are making, often in reaction to and in dialogue with, a number of "dominant academic" communities. Anzaldúa enjoins:

> What is considered theory in the dominant academic community is not necessarily what counts as theory for women-of-color. Theory produces effects that change people and the way they perceive the world. Thus we need *teorías* that will enable us to interpret what happens in the world, that will explain how and why we relate to certain people in specific ways, that will reflect what goes on between inner, outer and peripheral "I" 's within a person and between the personal "I" 's and the collective "we" of our ethnic communities. *Necesitamos teorías* that will rewrite history using race, class, gender and ethnicity as categories of analysis, theories that cross borders, that blur boundaries—new kinds of theories with new theorizing methods. (*Making Face* xxv)

Anzaldúa's call for the engagement of women of color in debates about "what counts as theory" comes at a time when women of color are rethinking key issues concerning knowledge, identity, politics, and experience within the context of identity based social movements. As a result, *Making Face, Making Soul/Haciendo Caras* includes works by academic and activist women of color who are interested in "doing theory in other modes of consciousness" and in translating theory into a language relevant to the lives of women of color.

Skeptical of "dominant academic" theories that are potentially oppressive, Anzaldúa continues to be wary of an institutionalized mode of theory making she perceives as potentially monolithic, totalizing, and appropriative. She fears that women of color speaking the "dominant" language will be "blanked out" (xxi) and that they will find themselves rearticulating the power plays that make women of color invisible when they inhabit "theorizing space" without transforming it (xxv). Expressing a similar concern, Barbara Christian, in her well-known polemic "The Race for Theory" (reprinted in *Making Face*), criticizes the way theory monolithicizes: "Inevitably, monolithism becomes a metasystem in which there is a controlling ideal, especially in relation to pleasure" (341). Ironically, Christian's critique of the monolithic tendencies of most theoretical operations allies her with a variation of an academic poststructuralist skepticism, where claiming to disavow grand narratives and overarching explanations in the service of a theoretical project is virtually commonplace. But the suspicion of theory voiced by many feminist theorists of color originates not only from their concern with finding themselves mimicking postures of domination or with being duped by the "master's tools"; the suspicion also comes from a grounded and (dare I say) *visceral* response to exclusion. For example, Valerie Smith closes "Black Feminist Theory and the Representation of the 'Other'" as follows:

> I have approached the subject from three perspectives in part because of my own evident suspicion of totalizing formulations. But my approach reflects as well the *black feminist skepticism* about the reification of boundaries that historically have excluded the writing of black women from serious consideration within the academic and literary establishments. Since, to my mind, some of the most compelling and representative black feminist writing treads the boundary between anthology and criticism, or between cultural theory and literary theory, it seems appropriate that a consideration of this critical perspective would approach it from a variety of points of view. (57, emphasis added)

Smith's "black feminist skepticism" leads her to argue for a mode of theory generated from multiple sites, from a "variety of points of view," including writing that transgresses generic boundaries.

In this essay, I explore the ways that women of color—even from a point of skepticism—are rethinking key theoretical issues, especially those related to the politics of identity and theories of multiplicities. Here, I am most interested in the way in which teorías, when juxtaposed against contemporary Anglo feminist theory with which they also powerfully resonate, can provide an interpretive framework for understanding the self-formation processes of "women of color." Briefly commenting on the debate on identity politics, I investigate how the Anglo feminist theorist Diana Fuss interrogates identity politics as potentially problematic for women of color. Then I turn to the work of the Chicana *teoristas* Gloria Anzaldúa, Norma Alarcón, and Chela Sandoval and examine their theories of multiplicity and subject formation—woven against particular Anglo feminist critiques of identity politics. At this point, I admit that my own mode of "doing theory" takes a circuitous route—dramatizing the dynamics of negotiation, engagement, resistance, and qualification. In this way, I demonstrate how Anzaldúa, Alarcón, and Sandoval activate a dynamic and complex form of identity politics that allows for theories of multiplicity and the politics of unity, social determination and individual agency, and negotiation and resistance to negotiation. Finally, I turn to "La Güera," a piece by the Chicana feminist lesbian writer Cherríe Moraga, that was initially published in *This Bridge Called My Back*. Drawing from the framework suggested in the works of Anzaldúa and Alarcón, I offer a reading of how Moraga comes *cara a cara* with her own history and how, in doing so, she becomes a woman of color. Proposing a theory of self-formation that takes place through what I call "retrospective ontologizing," I argue that Moraga's piece enables us to consider the foundational claims involved in self-formation and naming, claims that are usually simultaneous with undermining previous foundational self-understandings.[1] This move is fundamental to the process of "coming to consciousness" and illustrates the complex dynamics and dialectics involved in deploying an identity politics.

"Women of Color"

First, it is important to consider that women writers, activists, and critics of color have "bodies that matter," as evidenced in the battles over interpretations of race, class, gender, and sexuality that are taking place in a context of multiple social interests.[2] In the academy, the field of literary study in particular has rendered women of color hypervisible, a fact that has been commented upon by feminist critics of color such as Valerie Smith and Anglo feminists such as Margaret Homans. Smith has been concerned about the ways that both African American male critics and Anglo American female critics have used African American women critics and writers to represent the material body; hence, they appropriate the black woman's body to lend materialist credibility to their arguments, to reembody and "to rematerialize the subject of their theoretical positions" (44). Highlighting another side of this argument, Homans takes on other Anglo feminists, such as Donna Haraway, who in their critical procedures also make women of color do the work of embodying theory—but this time, they use "women of color" as a term to represent hybrid identities, to "negate the possibility of an essential identity of 'woman'" (76). In developing her argument, Homans puts women of color in quotation marks to counteract the appropriative moves of Anglo feminists who have used that figure to deconstruct identity categories. She herself admits that such a move is inadequate, for it quickly becomes evident that writing "women of color" doubly underscores and symptomatizes the visibility/invisibility dilemma of women writers and critics of color who often become unwilling magician's assistants: Now you see her. Now you don't.

Nevertheless, for most women of color invisibility may be—to quote Mitsuye Yamada—"an unnatural disaster" (35). Thus, the aim of anthologies by/for/about women of color has been to make visible a self-named collectivity. Within this collectivity, the referent that "women of color" is presumed to name—as Michael Omi and Howard Winant claim for the category "race"—is "a matter of both social structure and

cultural representation" (56). Women of color are shaped by what Maxine Baca Zinn and Bonnie Thornton Dill call "the constraining wall of
social location" (that is, their specific positioning at the intersection of
categories that describe their location(s) based on class, race, gender, and
sexuality) and of cultural representations that reflect, repress, or distort
these social locations, offering yet another possible placement (4-5).

In either case, women of color can also resist constraining locations
and representations through various forms of agency. Activism makes
visible the organization of race, class, gender, and sexuality in the
United States and renders women of color visible as a result. However,
while social and political activism may be the most evident exercise of
agency, it is the narratives women of color produce—cultural forms of
self-inscription—that consolidate the oppositional self-naming initiated by activist organizing and coalition politics. Of these inscriptions,
the testimonial style most effectively narrates individual and collective
histories as layered expressions of individual embodiment in a society
that is hierarchically organized around powerfully established ways of
legislating the diverse meanings of race, class, gender, and sexuality.[3]

How we read these expressions of embodiment, oppression, and self-
naming (i.e., questions of politicization, cultural self-awareness, anger
turned to knowledge) is central to the politics of interpretation and to
the politics of identity. Here, I am most interested in the ways that women
of color think through issues of multiplicity, identity, and subjectivity
to develop a social theory grounded in the lives of women of color.

The Subject of Multiplicity

The subject, "woman of color," has moved from a positioning as an object of oppression to one as a subject who responds to oppression
through multiple modes of resistant self-understanding (Alarcón, "Theoretical Subject[s]"). For many women theorists of color, this move has
led them to talk about subject formation as heterogeneous; the "theoretical subject" is comprised of "a multiplicity of identity" or "plural selves."
This description, however, can be both enabling and disabling. On the
one hand, embracing plural identities can be a liberatory practice for
women of color who often find themselves committed to multiple subject positions. On the other hand, as Alarcón has noted ("Theoretical
Subject[s]" 356), it tears women of color in many directions when it derives from the hegemonic legislation of reality leading to the fear, as
voiced by Anzaldúa, that "they would chop me up into little fragments"
(*This Bridge* 205). It is this external pull, enacted from a position of dominance, that leads to the overwhelming sense that to resist as the subject

of oppression one would have "to fight the whole world" (Michele Wallace, qtd. in Combahee River Collective 215). Ultimately, however, the language of multiplicity has taken hold of the theoretical field of identity politics and become dominant in the most revealing theories of how selves are made and are able to resist oppressive externalities.

Nonetheless, while proclaiming the liberatory possibilities of multiplicity, many women theorists, critics, and activists of color also affirm the importance of identity politics, asserting that a commitment to identity politics is not at odds with multiplicity. For example, statements such as that by the Combahee River Collective—a group of black lesbian activists—present an early theory of identity politics based on multiple oppressions. In "A Black Feminist Statement" (1977), the collective, "concerned with any situation that impinges upon the lives of women, Third World and working people," early on indicted racism in the white feminist movement and affirmed their own "vision of a revolutionary society" (217–18). Recognizing the multiplicity of identity and oppression, they asserted that racial, sexual, heterosexual, and class oppressions were often enacted simultaneously.

However, the Anglo feminist theorist Diana Fuss has cited the Combahee River Collective as a problematic example of lesbian identity politics deployed in the context of social struggle. Referring to the particular identity politics that she sees lesbians of color, such as the African American women of the Combahee River Collective and Chicana Cherríe Moraga promoting (1983), Fuss is concerned that they advance a definition of identity politics that lacks "a full awareness of the complicated processes of identity formation, both psychical and social" (100). Fuss argues that these, as well as other gay and lesbian, activists establish a causal relationship between identity and politics, invoking confused binary choices in which the subject is expected to "claim" and "discover" a ready-made identity or to "make" and "construct" such an identity out of scratch. Without exploring the tension between these two modes as simultaneously occurring and/or more complexly coded in the textual production of the marginalized (99), Fuss also invokes "causality" and "determination" as interchangeable terms when, in fact, these terms are not precisely synonymous but carry important nuances of difference.

According to Fuss, "practitioners of identity politics," such as the black lesbian feminist Barbara Smith, formulate the relationship between identity and politics as follows: "The link between identity and politics is causally and teleologically defined; for practitioners of identity politics, identity *necessarily* determines a particular kind of politics" (99). Fuss's representation of identity politics, derived largely from the statement of the Combahee River Collective, misses the complexity of the

relationship being outlined and claimed. To say that there is a "causal"
relationship is to say that, because one has an identity, one must have a
politics, as in one of Smith's statements cited by Fuss: "We have an identity and *therefore* a politics." However, while Smith *is* insisting upon the
implication of identity in politics, she is not *necessarily* making a claim
for the kind of politics one would have to espouse, at least not at this
point. Fuss reads Smith as stating that "identity *causes* politics," a reading that fortifies Fuss's argument that the "personal is political" slogan
has circulated in such a way that it diffuses "real" politics.[4]

Identity certainly does not "cause" politics in any simple way, nor
does it *necessarily* "determine" the particularities of those politics. Politics and identity can be relationally linked, though, and such a claim
can be made, depending on the social theory that is advocated. In this
respect, the Combahee River Collective identifies a social theory within
which they view their identity as determined through the simultaneous
register of oppressions based on the "lived experiences" of black women.
Such an experience is, *theoretically,* the experience of multiplicity, or the
"piling up" of significant identity categories—black, female, working
class, for example—that are felt in the midst of one's oppression: "We
believe that sexual politics under patriarchy is as pervasive in Black
women's lives as are the politics of class and race. We also often find it
difficult to separate race from class from sex oppression because in our
lives they are most often experienced simultaneously" (213). These
things can only be separated with difficulty, which is why a conception
of the "all at once" becomes an important site of theoretical elaboration.
Nevertheless, the difficulty of identifying the sources of oppression does
not keep the Combahee River Collective from articulating the resource-
fulness of a black feminist identity politics whereby black women
"might use our position at the bottom . . . to make a clear leap into revolutionary action" (215).[5] Using that position calls for a formulation of
selfhood that involves a reading of one's position. One can then see how
that position calls for an invocation of categories that adequately describe one's perspective and positioning.

Attempting to describe the "all at once" positioning of women of
color in terms of multiplicity theories can be paradoxical and confusing,
giving way to a set of vagaries and ambiguities that present as many
questions as answers. The way this paradox functions can be seen in the
title of the anthology *Making Face, Making Soul/Haciendo Caras,* in which
Anzaldúa announces the ambiguous relationship between the construction of a unified "front" and a strategy of multiplicity. The English part
of the title, *Making Face, Making Soul,* evokes the process of constructing

face and soul "all at once" while the Spanish subtitle, *Haciendo Caras* ("making faces"), calls upon either the multiplicity of the many in the one or perhaps the one as many. Moreover, Anzaldúa is also interested in the role of agency—as the subject finds herself wearing masks of a predetermined cultural identity, she must also find a means "to make face/caras."

Contributing to the proliferation of possibilities, Anzaldúa spends a great deal of time in the introduction, "Haciendo caras, una entrada," explaining the multiple interpretations offered by the culturally inflected turn of phrase "haciendo caras." For example, "face" is the surface on which "each aspect of identity" is "inscribed by a subculture" (xv). Women of color are "written all over" by these subcultural attempts to put women of color in particular social-cultural positions. So the face is inscribed with externally imposed constructions. On top of this are layered *máscaras*—which in Spanish means both "masks" and "more faces"—that "we are forced to wear" (xv). In other words, women of color are imposed upon both through the very construction of the self as derived from the inscriptions of an external source and through the masking of the self by these same external sources. In any case, it is not clear whether the masks are chosen by women of color or are imposed by an outside force. At this point, the difficulty of putting these layers together is evident. First, the self is constructed, as women of color are written upon as blank slates. Second, the self either consciously takes on masks or is forced to wear them. In either case, the possibility for agency appears to be utterly thwarted or immensely compromised.

Anzaldúa then says that "making faces" is her metaphor for constructing an identity, as "you create your face and your soul" (xvi). This suggests that the external masks (*las más/caras*) are eliminated and that the inscribed face is the one with which we work in an attempt to establish a "face and a soul" or "a body and a soul." Agency derives from refiguring the faces we have already been given—when we change faces—but before that we have nothing to call our own.[6]

Can we say more about how one rewrites the onslaught of outside interpellations? Or, as many theorists would have it, are we merely constituted by these outside interpellations? Anzaldúa's "ambiguities" are productive but we must do the work of pulling pieces together. This means, of course, that the issue of how useful and critical meanings emerge out of the máscaras available needs further exploration. For, if we "make face," there must be some way in which the face we make gains a meaning that would be recognizably different from its oppressive inscriptions. In what follows, I will explore how this process of resistance occurs on the terrain of theory as the signal way in which theories generated by women of color resist subsumption into already available paradigms.

"The Half Dozen Categories of Marginality That Define Us"

In the opening of her essay, "The Theoretical Subject(s) of *This Bridge Called My Back* and Anglo-American Feminism," Norma Alarcón describes the beleaguered subject struggling to make sense of her multiple experiences and identities:

> As speaking subjects of a new discursive formation, many of *Bridge*'s writers were aware of the displacement of their subjectivity across a multiplicity of discourses: feminist/lesbian, nationalist, racial, socioeconomic, historical, etc. The peculiarity of their displacement implies a multiplicity of positions from which they are driven to grasp or understand themselves and their relations with the real, in the Althusserian sense of the word. (356)

Of course, Louis Althusser's theories—with their exploration of ideology and social formation—have informed not only Alarcón's readings of the *Bridge* anthology but also my own reading of Anzaldúa (Althusser 121–73). Alarcón's "speaking subjects" find themselves in a world in which they are caught by "ideological state apparatuses," finding that even when they act in resistance they "endure ideological subjection," "sustaining and reinforcing the dominant social order" (Sandoval 2). But, as Chela Sandoval has argued, Althusser also suggests that "individuals and groups in opposition are able to effectively challenge and transform the current hierarchical nature of the social order" (2).

In her seminal essay, "U.S. Third World Feminism: The Theory and Method of Oppositional Consciousness in a Postmodern World," Sandoval critiques and further develops this Althusserian account of ideology. Building on Althusser's theories, Sandoval formulates a theory of an "oppositional consciousness" that becomes possible when the "citizen-subject can learn to identify, develop, and control the means of ideology, that is, marshal the knowledge necessary to 'break with ideology' while also speaking in and from within ideology" (2). Thus, when women of color can identify the ideological implications of their "half dozen categories of marginality," they can also begin to create a space for an oppositional consciousness.

Alarcón, Anzaldúa, and Sandoval outline the genealogy of consciousness not as a definitive break with the impositions of ideology but as an ongoing process, allowing for an empowered reconstruction of the multiple self.[7] However, their theory of consciousness and subjectivity rejects an ideal of consciousness as "synthetic unificatory power" (Alarcón, "Theoretical Subject[s]" 357) that allows the subject easily to pull together an identity and freely to map the world according to her experience of it. Alarcón relentlessly critiques this theory of consciousness in "The Theoretical Subject(s)" and in her more recent essay, "Conjugating Subjects: The Heteroglossia of Essence and Resistance" (1994). But in critiquing a particular kind of subject—the "autonomous self making subject important to the kind of struggle made necessary by current hegemonic views of juridical equality" ("Conjugating Subjects" 133)—Alarcón finds it necessary to pose an alternative theory, in spite of the way in which theory "monolithicizes." Teoría, in this terrain, becomes the name for the defensive posture of wholeness or "all at once"-ness that works in conjunction with an enabling multiplicity and subverts the outward pull toward fragmentation and compartmentalization.[8] Thus, although Alarcón rejects a vision of the self as an illusory "synthetic unificatory power," she nonetheless affirms the need to situate an enabling multiplicity within a site of resistance and agency. Furthermore, teoría desires a dialogue that would produce a deeper account of, to recall Anzaldúa's mandate, "what goes on between inner, outer, and peripheral 'I's' within a person and between the personal 'I's' and the collective 'we' of our ethnic communities" (xxv). Such an account entails not only acknowledging the undeniable resonances between "theory" and "teoría" that are apparent on the face of things but also translating the differences and disengaging apparently compatible meanings.

In Translation: Haciendo Caras in Theory

How does this process take place? I will explore the workings of this process through my own construction of a dialogic encounter among Norma Alarcón, Diana Fuss, and Judith Butler on the issue of situatedness and multiplicity. Then I will suggest how the theoretical differences translate into real differences in the realm of the social.

In "Conjugating Subjects," Alarcón critiques Fuss's argument that multiplicity theory fails "to challenge effectively the traditional metaphysical understanding of identity as unity" (Fuss 103). Although Fuss, like Alarcón, desires to avoid an essentialist definition of identity, she is troubled by a perception of identity either as a "subject composed of multiple identities" or as a primarily sociopolitical construct (103). Fuss argues that "the deconstruction of identity, then, is not necessarily a *disavowal* of identity." Thus, she argues for acknowledging "fictions of identity" that focus upon psychic life ("the spaces *within* identity") rather than "the production of political subjects" ("the spaces *between* identities") (103–4).

Alarcón, in turn, is suspicious of Fuss's desire to reinstate a "fictional unity," which Alarcón perceives as the undercover preservation of the "autonomous self-making liberal subject," which occurs despite Fuss's own relentless rejection of the "humanist fantasy of wholeness." Moreover, Alarcón questions Fuss's call for a reexamination of the spaces *"within* identity," since the shift in emphasis appears to pull subjects back into a preoccupation with their own subjectivities and avoids an analysis of "the spaces *between* identities," which allow for cross-cultural analysis ("Conjugating Subjects" 133).

Interestingly, Alarcón and Fuss share a desire to disrupt the very categories they assert. Fuss's argument for looking at "spaces within identity" is also a call to examine the fragmentation of the "discourses themselves" (e.g., as Alarcón names them, "feminist/lesbian, nationalist, racial, socioeconomic, historical, etc.") so that even the multiplicitous "discursive themes" can be called into question as already internally riven. That Alarcón takes for granted the self-evidence of these "whole" categories can be read as an argument for the thematic unities of these discourses of identity as salient interpretive registers of self-understanding.[9] In challenging Fuss's argument, Alarcón implies a social theory that she nevertheless also desires to undermine, as the resistance of her text to what she calls a desire for "tidiness" (134). Therefore, when Alarcón states that "categories such as nation, class, race, gender, sexualities, and ethnicities were intermittently questioned and disrupted" (135), she is underlining the "in-process" aspect of the identity construction of women of color, on the one hand concurring with Fuss's call to look at "spaces *within* identity" but on the other hand challenging any "fictional unity," given that she affirms the salience of these "whole" categories as sites of self-evident displacement.

Cataloging sites of self-evident displacement has become commonplace in discussions of the multiplicity of the subject. Judith Butler has pointed out the way in which cataloging sites of (dis)placement has become a familiar move in contemporary feminist theory, leading to an exhaustive outward proliferation: "The theories of feminist identity that elaborate predicates of color, sexuality, ethnicity, class, and ablebodiedness invariably close with an embarrassed 'etc.' at the end of the list. Through this horizontal trajectory of adjectives, these positions strive to encompass a situated subject, but invariably fail to be complete" (143). Butler also suggests that the "embarrassed 'etc.'" is a "sign of exhaustion" and of the "illimitable process of signification itself."

Nevertheless, her conclusion ("This illimitable *et cetera,* however, offers itself as a new departure for feminist political theorizing" [143]) resonates with Alarcón's "etc." because proliferation as multiplicity is *the* point of departure for the social and cultural theories of consciousness—oppositional, differential, or what have you—of many women theorists of color. At this point, the theoretical affinities between women of color who are advocates of multiplicity, such as Alarcón, Anzaldúa, and Sandoval, and Anglo American feminists who are rethinking identity politics, such as Butler and Fuss, are often undeniable. Yet there is a significant difference, for these women theorists of color insist upon positioning women of color as an oppositional identity and thus demonstrate what Sandoval has called "the refusal of U.S. third world feminism to buckle under, to submit to sublimation or assimilation within hegemonic feminist praxis" (3). Despite its often uncanny resonance with Anglo American feminist theory, teoría demands, on the part of women of color, the consistent exploration of the nuances of difference, as well as the development of an oppositional consciousness.

Finally, while Butler argues that there is no way to "encompass a situated subject" since signification is "illimitable," Sandoval and Alarcón always refer to specific locations and placements. Sandoval specifies these locations as "cultural regions" that call for a "charting of realities" (11) within a "dominant social order," and Alarcón speaks of the "subject-insertion" into a "geographical economy and politics" (135). For both theorists, the referent of the contemporary "real" is graspable and structures the social positioning of women of color—"constraining walls of location" that are also potential sites of resistance. Indeed, it is precisely that particular social positioning that women of color seek to contest, even as it marks them in specific ways, including for many a position conceptualized in spatial terms as "at the bottom."

"*Cara a Cara* with Our Own *Historias*"

This understanding of the self/subject and her social placement provides the basis for a reading of Cherríe Moraga's "coming out" as a lesbian of color in *This Bridge Called My Back.* "La Güera," Moraga's testimonial narrative as editor of *Bridge,* illustrates how she comes to understand a positionality that she consequently refigures. She grasps this knowledge that she is a "woman of color" while simultaneously expressing anxiety about both her "claim to color" (33) and her authority to "work on an anthology which is to be written 'exclusively by Third World Women'" (33).

After the invocation of the two "labels" that head the essay ("La Güera" and Cherríe Moraga),[10] Moraga begins her narrative by writing about her "illiterate" mother's memories of her own life, memories that slowly fade into Moraga's memories of her mother (28). These memories—both Moraga's and her mother's—foreground a representation of her mother as an illiterate laborer, the paradigmatic positioning of women of color in the political economy (Zinn and Dill). So that her mother might have a voice, Moraga, acting as a writing instrument, helps her mother with filling out job applications and writing checks at the market. Interestingly, in helping her mother, Moraga does not appropriate and usurp her mother's voice, for the two of them negotiate from positions of mutual authority gained through dialogue. As Moraga explains, "We would have the scenario all worked out ahead of time" (29).

Moraga moves between identification as appropriation/self-authorization and identification as empathetic understanding, a kind of "world traveling" to use a term coined by Maria Lugones.[11] In contrast to Lugones's account of her own initial "arrogant perception" of her mother, Moraga opts right away for an account of identification as empathetic understanding and as a disavowal of "power differentials."[12] Therefore, the activity of "world traveling" enables Moraga's "claim to color," through a process of discovery that requires her to examine the mutual implication of herself and her mother in "making" the difference. At the same time, however, she says, "I was la güera. . . . I had it made" (28), suggesting an already constructed identity that is marked as ontological through the intransitive verb. Furthermore, with the help of her mother—both her mother's memories and how they "color" Moraga's own—and with the tacit encouragement of distance and difference, Moraga comes to think of "Chicana" as poor and illiterate, while la güera can pass (28).

Thinking of la güera in this way, Moraga ontologizes it as a perception of the difference between what she was "born into" and what she grew up "to become" (28). Despite these perceptions and inscriptions of her cara as la güera, her mother's stories "crept under [her] güera skin" (28). She says, "I had no choice but to enter into the life of my mother. *I had no choice.*" Although her skin is coded a certain way, making it possible for her to pass by enjoying the privilege of a certain kind of interpellation as la güera, Moraga claims that underneath that skin crept another possibility in an alternative history—the narrative of her mother's life as a Chicana. Under the skin, then, the other life—stories of her mother—lurks as a kind of "body knowledge." Not necessarily "a true self" or "true identity" waits there but rather a set of stories that are viewed as the substance, "the flesh," of a knowledge that she disallows into her self-understanding as a "happy, upwardly mobile heterosexual" (28).

It is the flesh that Moraga comprehends as the site of her knowledge of her lesbianism (28), so that she locates sexuality as the body's knowledge of itself and its desire as the repressed secret of her self. But might we find disturbing the binarization of the skin as surface onto which interpellations are etched and the flesh as the substantial body, the one that, given a voice, would speak of the alternative histories and the repressed desire? These moves appear to give credit to Fuss's reading of "gay and lesbian literature," in which "a familiar tension emerges between a view of identity as that which is always there (but has been buried under layers of cultural repression) and that which has never been socially permitted (but remains to be formed, created, or achieved)" (100). Fuss also notes that "some writers shift from one position to the other with relative ease" and do not seem to notice "contradictions generated by the juxtaposition of two radically different assumptions" (100).

This is the contradiction Moraga initially outlines and then undermines. She argues that she felt her "lesbianism in the flesh," suggesting an essentialism of the flesh (under the skin), and then says that the flesh is just as constructed or narrated, that is, just as "made up" of stories and memories that imbue it with meaning, as her skin. With this maneuvering, Moraga provides a powerful instance of the workings of Anzaldúa's suggestion that resistance and self-formation take place through the manipulation of external constructions and interpellations. In Moraga's account, both flesh and skin are coded by external sources. These sources include her mother, whose views about race and class Moraga internalizes and puts alongside her observation of her mother's life as a laboring Chicana.

Through conversations, letters, and listening to others, then, Moraga rereads her self as la güera so that "La Güera," as a written testimony, becomes a second reading of these events and "clicks." In this second reading, Moraga "puts it all together" and forges a new epistemology based in retrospective readings of the positions she occupied in the past. Therefore, she becomes an agent and a woman of color not just through the act of writing her experience of embodiment and her narrative of discovery but also through writing her rereadings and rewritings of those experiences, events, and conversations; hence, she not only recognizes and claims a subject position but does so through a retrospective process.[13]

Moraga asserts the necessity of making the connection between oppressions but also realizes that starting with your own oppression—"the 'ism' that is sitting on top of my head"—is the only way of moving toward coalition politics. In externalizing our "ism(s)," she reminds us that, for those grappling with the effects of living in a racist society, the "real" battle "begins under the skin" (30). In other words, it is not just about what others do to me—those external forces that manipulate the process of haciendo caras—but also about what I do to myself. Not just a restatement of the "personal is political," Moraga's call to accountability of the self to the self also engages the implication—and constitution—of the self in the social, which is where the skin and flesh take on meaning.

Once again, Moraga leans toward essentialism when she claims, "What prompted me in the first place to work on an anthology by radical women of color was a deep sense that I had an insight to contribute by virtue of my birthright and background." As if that were not enough to set bells ringing—What does she mean by birthright?—the next sentence takes us in an entirely different direction: "And yet, I don't really understand first-hand what it feels like being shitted on for being brown" (30). So Moraga both claims and disclaims her authority to speak as a "woman of color" in the same way that she can both choose to "enter into the life of my mother" and choose not to enter into the life of herself as a woman of color. It is this claiming/disclaiming that is engaged when she later reflects upon the experience of listening to Ntozake Shange's poetry and says, "The reading had forced me to remember that I knew things from my roots. But to remember puts me up against what I don't know" (31).

Finally, Moraga, while not having been able to make a choice about "entering into the life of" her mother, says that she is able to make a choice about claiming color, since, after all, the surface of her skin still signifies güera in a racist society. Making that choice becomes, in her account, the launchpad for agency, when she insists, "What is my responsibility to my roots—both white and brown, Spanish-speaking and English? I am a woman with a foot in both worlds; and I refuse the split" (34). Moraga thus acknowledges the binaries that have constructed her (Chicana/la güera), shows that both reside within and without, and then refuses the binary altogether.

Through what I call "retrospective ontologizing," Moraga offers testimonial revisions of her subject "constitutions" understood as the externally imposed limits or discourses through which a subject might be made: "I was la güera. . . . I had it made." These "retrospective ontologizations" shift other "constitutions"—which she interprets as ontologizations, "What I was born into"—in order to highlight the fact that constitutions (or external constructions) may initially set the limits of resistance *without* making it impossible to supersede those limits and the parameters of interpretation they allow. In that sense, Moraga sees herself as having been "born" la güera and as having "become" a woman of color. Here, Moraga constructs whiteness as that which was supposed to be "natural" to her and effects a reversal. Through this reversal, whiteness is first rendered momentarily hypervisible, along with the privilege and power it encapsulates in a racist society, but then it is relegated, in an English dominant society, to a silent Spanish-language encoding of a past self that Moraga supersedes, even as she claims to have "a foot in both worlds." Consequently, it is color that comes to the surface.

In Moraga's work, the process of self-formation and "coming to consciousness" functions as both a poetic and a rhetoric. As a poetic, self-formation operates in the manner described by Alarcón (and other theorists), in which "a critical subject in process who reorganizes 'contents' upon the demands of the contingent moment and context may discover that it is in the inaugural transitional moment from being traversed to reconfiguration that the political intention as well as the combinatory transculturating takes place" ("Conjugating Subjects" 132). As a rhetoric, it is an acknowledgment of the limits of language to describe the movement of the self and an insistence on the need to engage the "illimitability" of possibilities, even as the social real within which multiplicitous selves/subjects live provides enclosures of its own. Thus, Moraga recognizes the multiplicity of her identity at the same time that she locates herself within a particular subject position; she recognizes that she is enclosed by the constraining wall of social location while she also situates herself in a specific social/cultural location—making face, making soul.

The voicings of women of color have yet to be fully examined in terms of the layers of interpretation that women of color work through while they attempt to theorize (as) women of color. I look forward to further elaborations of the ways in which women activists, theorists, and critics of color live their oppositional multiplicity, as they engage in the critical project of what Anzaldúa has called "haciendo teoría."[14]

NOTES

I would like to thank Sandra K. Stanley for her comments and assistance in preparing this essay. The idea for the piece originated from my participation in a graduate reading group at Cornell University, "Women of Color Doing Theory," spring 1992. Thank you to those who were there with me.

1. My use of retrospective ontologizing may resonate with "strategic essentialism," defined by Gayatri Spivak as "the strategic use of a positivist essentialism in a scrupulously visible interest" (3), but it is very different. However, because it is a "retrospective ontologizing," it entails an "after the fact" effect that is an interpretive call based on the construction of a narrative of identity and that, furthermore, is based in a theoretical reading of the social. It is the "theoretical" part that undermines the charge of "positivist essentialism" insofar as it involves

gauging multiple external mappings of identity and selfhood through a process of information gathering, as I show in my reading of Moraga.

2. On this, see duCille's essay on black feminist studies, in which she outlines the problematic in the case of African American women.

3. Should it seem that the division between grassroots social movements and elite literary movements is being reproduced here, remember that many women of color who took up writing in the 1970s and 1980s physically moved from one space to another or had contact with activist communities.

4. The status of *necessarily* used so often in theories of causality, determination, and various coimplications of levels of the realms of the political, identity, the social, and the economic operates to affirm a relationship of causality between identity and politics. To say that one thing "determines" another is to say that it sets up the parameters of possibility. That would be very different from a simple statement of a causal relationship between A (identity) and B (politics).

5. Aragon de Valdez asks of the Chicana: "Does her position within the dominant society afford her any resources which can be used to overcome these constraints? It may seem ironic, but the flagrant inequities and the subordinate and oppressed condition of the Chicana within the dominant society may provide her with one of the major resources for organizing—motivation. The Chicana's position in this society almost demands that she become an agent of change—a revolutionary" (9).

6. This schema is further complicated by the persona, which in Spanish means "person" but also carries the connotation in English of a pretense.

7. Elsewhere, Alarcón states, "The traces of a process of elimination may construct the subject as much as efforts to incorporate," and therefore points to the implication of the subject in ideology and the way in which ideology structures the kinds of oppositional responses that are available to the subject ("Conjugating Subjects" 136).

8. Here I think of Moschkovich's opening statement in "—But I Know You, American Woman": "I am Latina, Jewish and an immigrant (all at once)" (Moraga and Anzaldúa 79).

9. See Frankenberg, *White Women, Race Matters,* for a useful account of the way these categories take on meaning, an account largely derived initially from women of color theory and brought into dialogue with white women whom Frankenberg interviewed. See especially chap. 6, "Thinking through Race."

10. Moraga's choice to claim the name of her mother and to title the piece "La Güera"—the only Spanish in the essay—already sets up the subject. "La güera" means blond and white but also carries the connotation of "vain" and "empty." In addition, it is a term that, in the Mexican context, refers to light-skinned people and also carries with it the signification of class privilege. In Mexican and Mexican American communities, it can be a compliment to be called güera— even brown-skinned women of a perceived upper class might be called güera as a form of flattery. In some cases, it is used as a descriptive term, but it always carries a trace of the valuation of "white" skin or the possibility of a betrayal related to one's evidencing "whiteness."

11. In "Playfulness, 'World'-Travelling, and Loving Perception," Lugones examines her "coming to consciousness as a daughter" and "as a woman of color," providing an interesting parallel to Moraga's confessional.

12. Lugones writes about her own "arrogant perception" of her mother: "I was disturbed by my not wanting to be what she was. I had a sense of not being quite

integrated, my self was missing because I could not identify with her, I could not see myself in her, I could not welcome her world. I saw myself as separate from her, a different sort of being, not quite of the same species" (393). Here, Lugones shows how "absolute difference" can be used in the service of "arrogant perception." Her solution, to enter into a relation of love through "world traveling," may not be altogether without its own problems, many of which are predictable. The question remains: How can we resist the ways in which power relations saturate our contexts, pulling us into them in various ways, rendering our desires and intentions suspect?

13. Here I concur with Scott's assertion that Samuel Delany's description of the salience of gay identity is not a "discovery of truth, but the substitution of one interpretation for another" (Scott 34).

14. See Yarbro-Bejarano, "Gloria Anzaldúa's *Borderlands/La Frontera*," for an engaging reading of the workings of the nonunitary subject.

WORKS CITED

Alarcón, Norma. "Conjugating Subjects: The Heteroglossia of Essence and Resistance." *An Other Tongue.* Ed. Alfred Arteaga. Durham, N.C.: Duke University Press, 1994. 125–38.

———. "The Theoretical Subject(s) of *This Bridge Called My Back* and Anglo-American Feminism." *Making Face.* Ed. Anzaldúa. 356–69.

Althusser, Louis. *Lenin and Philosophy and Other Essays.* Trans. Ben Brewster. New York: Monthly Review Press, 1971.

Anzaldúa, Gloria, ed. *Making Face, Making Soul/Haciendo Caras: Creative and Critical Perspectives by Women of Color.* San Francisco: Aunt Lute, 1990.

Aragon de Valdez, Theresa. "Organizing as a Political Tool for the Chicana." *Frontiers* 5.2 (1980): 7–13.

Butler, Judith. *Gender Trouble: Feminism and the Subversion of Identity.* New York: Routledge. 1990.

Christian, Barbara. "The Race for Theory." *Making Face.* Ed. Anzaldúa. 335–45.

Combahee River Collective. "A Black Feminist Statement." 1977. *This Bridge Called My Back.* Ed. Moraga and Anzaldúa. 210–18.

duCille, Ann. "The Occult of True Black Womanhood: Critical Demeanor and Black Feminist Studies." *Signs* 19 (1994): 591–629.

Frankenberg, Ruth. *White Women, Race Matters: The Social Construction of Whiteness.* Minneapolis: University of Minnesota Press, 1993.

Frankenberg, Ruth, and Lata Mani. "Crosscurrents, Crosstalk: Race, 'Postcoloniality' and the Politics of Location." *Cultural Studies* 7.2 (1993): 292–310.

Fuss, Diana. *Essentially Speaking: Feminism, Nature, and Difference.* New York: Routledge, 1989.

Homans, Margaret. "'Women of Color' Writers and Feminist Theory." *New Literary History* 25 (1994): 73–94.

Lugones, Maria. "Playfulness, 'World'-Travelling, and Loving Perception." *Making Face.* Ed. Anzaldúa. 390–402.

Mohanty, Chandra Talpade, Ann Russo, and Lourdes Torres, eds. *Third World Women and the Politics of Feminism.* Bloomington: Indiana University Press, 1991.

Moraga, Cherríe, and Gloria Anzaldúa, eds. *This Bridge Called My Back: Writings by Radical Women of Color.* New York: Kitchen Table/Women of Color Press, 1983.

Moschkovich, Judith. "—But I Know You, American Woman." *This Bridge Called My Back*. Ed. Moraga and Anzaldúa. 79–84.

Omi, Michael, and Howard Winant, eds. *Racial Formation in the United States: From the 1960s to the 1990s*. 2d ed. New York: Routledge, 1994.

Sandoval, Chela. "U.S. Third World Feminism: The Theory and Method of Oppositional Consciousness in a Postmodern World." *Genders* 10 (Spring 1991): 1–24.

Scott, Joan W. "Experience." *Feminists Theorize the Political*. Ed. Judith Butler and Joan W. Scott. New York: Routledge, 1992. 22–40.

Smith, Barbara. "The Truth that Never Hurts: Black Lesbians in Fiction in the 1980s." *Third World Women*. Ed. Mohanty, Russo, and Torres. 101–31.

Smith, Valerie. "Black Feminist Theory and the Representation of the 'Other.'" *Changing Our Own Words: Essays on Criticism, Theory, and Writing by Black Women*. Ed. Cheryl A. Wall. New Brunswick, N.J.: Rutgers University Press, 1989. 38–57.

Spivak, Gayatri Chakravorty. *Outside the Teaching Machine*. New York: Routledge, 1993.

Yamada, Mitsuye. "Invisibility Is an Unnatural Disaster: Reflections of an Asian American Woman." *This Bridge Called My Back*. Ed. Moraga and Anzaldúa. 35–40.

Yarbro-Bejarano, Yvonne. "Gloria Anzaldúa's *Borderlands/La Frontera*: Cultural Studies, 'Difference,' and the Non-Unitary Subject." *Cultural Critique* 28 (Fall 1994): 5–28.

Young, Robert. *White Mythologies: Writing History and the West*. London: Routledge, 1990.

Zinn, Maxine Baca, and Bonnie Thornton Dill, eds. *Women of Color in U.S. Society*. Philadelphia: Temple University Press, 1994.

3 ◇ Of Poststructuralist Fallout, Scarification, and Blood Poems

The Revolutionary Ideology
behind the Poetry of Jayne Cortez

> For those of us who read and write books and plays
> and poetry, the Black Aesthetic has to do with both
> love and killing, and learning to live, and *survive,* in
> a nation of killers so that our children may breathe
> a purer and freer air.
>
> —Julian Mayfield, "You Touch My Black Aesthetic"

We live in an age where multiculturalism and canon formation rarely mean more than the minimal inclusion of people seldom heard (or thought) of outside of the realm of popular culture by the dominant, white, middle-class culture; in an age of videotape and virtual reality, where seeing is no longer believing; in the age of Barney the purple dinosaur—"I love you, you love me"—juxtaposed with images of Rodney King being beaten and a teary-eyed Susan Smith inventing imaginary black assailants to camouflage her own crimes; in an age where everyone wants to be black, or at least "ethnic," without the annoying, nagging baggage that color brings. We live in an age of poststructuralist "fallout."

In such an age, it is not surprising that a former male colleague once stated that we talk about the Black Arts (or Black Aesthetic) and Power Movements of the sixties in simplistic terms because they were just that—simplistic. However, these same "simplistic" movements challenged people to be confrontational (either nonviolently or in acts of violent self-defense) to the point where they would shut down entire institutions and were prepared to die in order to effect social change. From an academic standpoint, many such confrontations paved the way for scholarships and fellowships (from which both my former colleague and I have benefited directly), the establishment of black studies departments, the hiring of more black faculty, and the academy's inclusion of

African American literature and its criticisms in the curriculum. These things were not just gifts from the established power, nor did they reflect an inevitable response to the changing times—people *fought for* these things. Graduate school introductory theory courses had taught my colleague that black literary theory in the 1980s and 1990s meant a suppression and denial of the revolutionary language of the past and an immersion in poststructuralist theory.

Because poststructuralism is a theoretical device that works simultaneously with deconstruction to resist the notion of *a* center or concepts of totalization, many scholars have found various forms of poststructuralism(s) helpful in reading texts by people of color—thus giving voice to the marginal and expanding notions of what society and/or the academy deems "literary." What is paradoxical about poststructuralist theory is that on the surface it announces its project as antitotalization; in the *teaching of theory,* however, poststructuralism has become the dominant ideology while all other theories have become marginal. The issue of poststructuralist theory, then, becomes problematic when it dominates—as it has from the mid-1980s to the late 1990s—how people theorize about texts by people of color so that the student of theory thinks that poststructuralism is the only vehicle for examining those texts.

The inauguration of the current poststructuralist school of thought has unfortunately also included the trivializing of past theories, which leads students (like my colleague) to believe that the scars of the past have healed and not merely become keloids. Moreover, those who actively critique or challenge the use of poststructuralism to analyze texts by people of color have been openly attacked and criticized for not being smart enough to participate in the "theoretical" arena.

When Joyce A. Joyce's essay appeared in the infamous series of articles in the 1987 winter issue of *New Literary History* with the poststructuralists Henry Louis Gates Jr. and Houston A. Baker Jr., she argued: "Black poststructuralist critics have adopted a linguistic system and an accompanying world view that communicates to a small, isolated audience. Their pseudoscientific language is distant and sterile" (339). Joyce also questioned the motives behind adopting a "pseudoscientific language" in respect to the type of audience (the academic elite) that Gates and Baker attempt to attract.

Joyce lumps Baker and Gates into the same poststructuralist category for good reason. Although it has been noted previously by other theorists that Baker is a product of the black aesthetic school of theory while Gates is clearly influenced by continental theorists, the polemics of both writers have moved closer through the years. Gates gives a greater emphasis to the vernacular while Baker has developed a heavier reliance on poststructuralist theory and the act of signification. R. Baxter Miller argues that the "alleged differences" between Baker and Gates are minimal, considering that both rely on language laced with "jargon" to create a "fraternal space" for debate among themselves.

Theodore O. Mason Jr., in "Between the Populist and the Scientist: Ideology and Power in Recent Afro-American Literary Criticism or, 'The Dozens' as Scholarship," summarizes Baker and Gate's objections to Joyce's article: "Professor Joyce's objections to Afro-American poststructuralism stem from a faulty understanding of culture, a general intellectual 'laziness and complacency' ('Battle' 369 and 'Love' 357), the persistent ethos of 'minstrelsy' ('Battle' 368), and a fundamental ignorance of recent modes of criticism. . . . Her desire to rededicate criticism to the service of black people and black culture then is nothing more than a naive and fuzzy-headed populism" (Mason 607). Here Baker and Gates develop tag team wrestling tactics for dealing with defectors from their theoretical camp. The joining of these two critics is interesting when we consider that, to many teachers of "theory" and to editors of mainstream anthologies, Henry Louis Gates and Houston Baker—above all other present-day African American theorists—both literally and figuratively define the "black literary tradition." Gates's theory of signifyin(g) and Baker's blues matrix and theory of generational shifts have collectively become road maps through which many trace black literary and critical thought. When two supposed theoretical giants like Baker and Gates reinforce the idea that those who do not agree with their theoretical project are not able to "do theory" or are naive, idealistic, essentialist, and "fuzzy-headed," when they reinforce the idea that political struggle is no longer needed—implying that we need not, as academics, be concerned about the masses, they misuse the pedagogical power of poststructuralism.

Moreover, this rigid type of poststructuralism—emphasizing the process of signification—allows for the illusion that we can free ourselves through language, shifting an understanding of oppression to the symbolic. In this instance, the very thing that constitutes poststructuralism's strength—its desire to critique master narratives and prevalent ideologies—can also be viewed as its weakness. When practitioners of poststructuralism undermine foundations, they also run the risk of trivializing the foundations of people's beliefs—the very core of political struggle. As Terry Eagleton eloquently states: "One advantage of the dogma that we are the prisoners of our own discourse, unable to advance reasonably certain truth-claims because such claims are merely relative to our language, is that it allows you to drive a coach and horses through everybody else's beliefs while not saddling you with the inconvenience of having to adopt any yourself" (144).

Gates and Baker develop an antiessentialist polemic that enables them to disrespect and disregard other people's attempts to theorize about African American culture. Under their totalizing pedagogical poststructuralist doctrine—where students are taught to believe that "theory" is synonymous with "poststructuralism"—the Black Aesthetic and Power Movements, and consequently the theories therein, have been defined as essentialist, monolithic, sexist, homophobic, and ahistorical. In fact, Mason, in the *Johns Hopkins Guide to Literary Criticism* (1994), uses all those adjectives to define the literary criticism, fiction, poetry, and prose of the Black Arts Movement. Critics such as Elliot Butler-Evans and Gates follow suit by labeling the Black Arts Movement as "nationalist essentialism" (Butler-Evans 123) and as a movement that didn't "think deeply enough" and was bounded by a naive idealization of an imaginary black essence (Gates, *Black* 7).

The purpose of my essay, however, is not to argue that certain writings of the Black Aesthetic Movement were not essentialist, often sexist, or even homophobic—of course, they were—but by lumping all of the writers into this essentialist category, Baker, Gates, and Mason—in his overview of the Black Arts Movement—in effect essentialize that movement. Nor am I suggesting that we discard poststructuralist theory and its applications to texts by African American authors. As Baker states, "It is not theory, I think, that Afro-American detractors mean when they attack *the Afro-American literary project,* but rather *the politics of theory* as they have manifested themselves in recent years" ("There Is No More Beautiful Way" 141, emphasis added). In the late 1990s, the "politics of 'theory'" is the elitist and essentialist notion that Baker's statement demonstrates when he implies that poststructuralist theory is *the* "Afro-American literary theoretical project." In advancing their own programs, Gates and Baker are so focused on their efforts to deconstruct the essentialism of the Black Aesthetic Movement that they ignore their own essentialist tendencies.

In "Baptized Infidel: Play and the Critical Legacy," R. Baxter Miller states: "Perhaps nothing distinguishes the sacred bibliography of the post-structuralist from that of the literary historian, or indeed from that of the Black Aesthetician, more than does tone" (404). Indeed, language is the overarching concept with which many of Gates and Baker's critics (e.g., Richard K. Barksdale, Barbara Christian, Norman Harris, Dolan Hubbard, Joyce A. Joyce, and R. Baxter Miller), though coming from various angles, find fault. It is therefore problematic to suggest that one type of theory is any more essentialist than any other.

In *Blues, Ideology, and Afro-American Literature* (1984), Baker explains: "I know that I have appropriated the vastness of the vernacular in the United States into a single matrix. But I trust that my necessary selectivity will be interpreted, not as a sign of myopic exclusiveness, but as an invitation to inventive play" (14). Why should Baker be let off the hook by this disclaimer when the Black Arts Movement in its entirety is not? Likewise, is Gates's insistence on a distinctive African American theory any less essentialist than black aesthetic theories of "blackness"? It could be argued that all that has happened is a shift in "essences," from skin color to the vernacular.

African American critics who use poststructuralism in the 1990s are no more removed from the essentialist label than black aesthetic critics were when they attempted to define African American culture. As bell hooks reminds us in her essay "Essentialism and Experience," when we speak of essentialism and its dangers, we are often referring to its usage by people of color and other marginal groups in their attempts to speak from a position of authority, ignoring the fact that those who enjoy the greatest amounts of privilege in our society can also be implicated (*Teaching*). Whenever there is an attempt made by a person of color or other marginalized person to define a theoretical practice that is "unique" to her or his culture, there is always the risk of being labeled essentialist by fellow (sister) poststructuralists, black or white. Ignoring this fact and suggesting, as Butler-Evans does, that we should move beyond criticism coming out of the black aesthetic create yet another binary opposition—either the school of black aesthetics or poststructuralism.

As a new century nears and as we witness many of the gains of the black liberation and civil rights movements on the verge of regressing (the infamous *New Literary History* debate is now a decade old), a reassessment of black aesthetics might prove useful as at least one attempt greatly needed to deal with the poststructuralist fallout age. An approach that acknowledges that it might not be possible to articulate a cohesive collective culture or tradition without essentializing and that recognizes and respects the oppressed subject's need to create her or his own identity and to articulate her or his own experience, could serve as a much needed middle ground. I am speaking of theorizing from the wound, working through the scars—a theory of scarification.

When Gates defines his theory of signifyin(g), he states: "Signification is a theory of reading that arises from Afro-American culture; learning how 'to signify' is often part of our adolescent education. I had to step outside of my culture, had to defamiliarize the concept by translating it into a new mode of discourse, before I could see its potential in critical theory" (" 'Blackness' " 685–86). Scarification is a theory that also "arises from Afro-American culture"; learning how to use "scars" is often a part of our early childhood education—when parents teach their children ways to cope and react to oppression (e.g., what to do the first time she or he is called "nigger"). Unlike Gates, I had to step deeper *within* my culture. I had to look back and remember how I defined for myself what it meant to be a "marked" person in the United States. I had to step inside my anger, my humiliation, my pain, and ultimately, my pride and determination in order to see the greater potential for using scars to theorize critically.

I borrow the term "scarification" from the title and revolutionary message behind Jayne Cortez's second book of poetry, a product of the Black Aesthetic Movement. Scarification can be interpreted in two ways: (1) in terms of the scars left by oppression, mental as well as physical scars, and (2) as ritualistic tribal markings that define not only the people to whom you belong but also the place. The referential grounding of oppression can have theoretical implications if we consider Valerie Smith's comments: "The conditions of oppression provide the subtext of all Afro-Americanist literary criticism and theory. Whether a critic/theorist explores representations of the experience of oppression or strategies by which that experience is transformed, he/she assumes the existence of an 'other' against whom/which blacks struggle" (57).

I realize that my metaphoric use of scarification could be perceived as yet another "essentialist" attempt to define "the black experience" and therefore be easily dismissed. However, although there is no one "black experience," black people (as well as other exploited ethnic groups) worldwide are united by the shared experience of oppression—be it imperialism, colonialism, or capitalism. Racial oppression crosses class barriers; you cannot buy your way out of racism. And oppression goes deeper than skin color because when a fairer-skinned African American is "unmasked," she or he is left exposed to the effects of racism, not to mention the damage that hiding one's supposed identity can do to one's psyche.

Scarification does not mean that we should ultimately define ourselves through oppression; instead, it attempts to validate the real-life pain that oppression can cause for the African American subject. Scarification theory serves as a ritualistic invitation to marginalized critics/theorists to assert actively their simultaneous presence as both individuals and as part of a collective within the theoretic arena. Scarification theory is born out of the Black Aesthetic Movement's desire to acknowledge the materiality of African American existence and the poststructuralist notion that each person is a social construction—a blending of time, circumstance, environment, religion, ethnicity, gender, and sexual preference. In this respect, testimonies of oppression or personal experiences in general become historicized. Scarification, then, recognizes that both the nature of oppression and the marks that oppression leaves behind vary.

Jayne Cortez's poetry serves as an excellent example of how one can theorize through scars. Her poetry also illustrates how "theory" can be found in many forms. In *Scarification,* as well as in her other books of poetry, Cortez creates an ethnopoetics that blurs the lines between lived experience and theory. By ethnopoetics, I mean a theoretical ideology—in this instance, of revolution informed by her position as a third world subject—that can be located within and extracted from Cortez's poetry. Her project mirrors both the goals of black female anthologies, such as *Sturdy Black Bridges* (edited by Bell, Parker, and Guy-Sheftall) and *The Black Woman* (edited by Bambara) (both of which were published in the early seventies, where we see revolutionary black female writers as the precursors to "women of color" projects),[1] and the goals of the Black Arts Movement, which saw art as "functional, collective, and committed" (Karenga 391).

To say that the types of analyses performed in the academic arena are "theoretical" and working from lived/learned experience is not to create a hierarchical binary in which lived experience is forever on the bottom. As Cortez states: "The intellect and the intuition—that's all one thing. Can't be one without the other" (qtd. in Melhem 206). The pedagogical poststructuralist model that bell hooks provides is an excellent example of how the "intellect and the intuition" can come together, for she shows how notions of "experience" and "commitment" can have a place in poststructuralist teaching. In her "Essentialism and Experience," hooks finds useful ways to include and validate "experience"—both her own and her students—without letting either academic theory or the theory derived from lived experience stand as the only legitimate authority (*Teaching*). Instead of inverting the hierarchical positions, and therefore placing lived/learned experience on the top, she gives both "experiential" theory and "hypothetical" theory equal time in conjunction with each other.

By dividing these two types of theory, as it normally does, the academy contains and suppresses revolutionary ideologies. Moreover, the academy reductively treats the various revolutionary ideologies within the black aesthetic as monolithic. Students are taught to think that revolution is Marxist jargon and political slogans; "What we need is a revolution"; "No Justice, No Peace"; "Power to the People, Off the Pigs." Driven by the whip of wayward poststructuralists, the academy disavows the more complicated legacy of the black aesthetic and ignores writing such as Cortez's work—a poetry that, in fact, thwarts such monolithic definitions. Despite all of its faults, the black aesthetic was a movement that not only constructed "white" as the objectified other by deconstructing the notion of "whiteness" as a "universal" state of being but also simultaneously empowered blacks to define themselves and their art instead of both being defined by whites—that is, the movement empowered blacks to theorize from the scars.

Cortez theorizes from her scars by speaking on behalf of third world people from the simultaneous vantage points of both spokesperson and sister worker. Her poetry focuses on the abuses third world people face collectively: the exploitation of their labor, their bodies, and their land. Cortez also undercuts the notion of an academic theoretical hierarchy—as seen in her poem "There It Is," which serves as a perfect example of how she uses poetry as a space through which to filter notions of upheaval.

Cortez writes:

> My friend
> they don't care
> if you're an individualist
> a leftist a rightist
> a shithead or a snake
> They will try to exploit you
> absorb you confine you
> disconnect you isolate you
> or kill you.
>   (*Coagulations* 68)

The bottom line, then, is that no matter what type of political agenda you adopt, no matter what your ideological stance, on the level of lived experience, your politics won't save you from being victimized and manipulated by the power structure: exploitation, like death, knows no ideologies. Revolution through organization and unification, Cortez concludes, is the only means of combating the ruling class and saving ourselves from the perils of victimization:

> And if we don't fight
> if we don't resist
> if we don't organize and unify and
> get the power to control our own lives
> Then we will wear
> the exaggerated look of captivity

the stylized look of submission
the bizarre look of suicide
the dehumanized look of fear
and the decomposed look of repression
forever, and ever and ever
And there it is.
(Coagulations 69–70)

Cortez is able to give us the "bottom line" because she too has been at the bottom, been the last in line. As a product of the Watts School in Los Angeles—one of the several Black Arts schools set up during the sixties—she and her fellow (sister) poets were able to "take [their] poetry to the taverns and parks, to city squares and parking lots. Instead of taking the poems to the academic level, they took them back to the people" (Troupe and Schulte xxxix). During her years with the Watts School, Cortez also did factory and office work. Performing poetry and having once worked at blue-collar jobs are experiences that Cortez draws upon in the creation of her work. Both types of jobs are equally important to her poetry because they brought her into contact with "ordinary people,"[2] that is, people with whom she identifies, whose lives and struggles she has shared.

The overlapping connection between manual labor and poetry (performance poetry can also be seen as manual work) is best exhibited in Cortez's poem "I'm a Worker" (*Festivals* 14–15), which she dedicates "to all my sisters in the garment industry." In one sense, this poem is autobiographical, for she draws directly from her own experience as a factory worker. In "I'm a Worker," the blue-collar speaker believes that all of her problems would be solved by getting some "survival money"—money that will be just enough to get by: "If I had some honey / If I had some gunnie / I think I'd have that thing called survival money." The speaker believes her life would improve if she had either a man who could supply her with money or a gun so she could get money on her own. Here she exhibits the fact that existence in itself is material. Cortez suggests that possession of material goods serves as access to power—making the contrary also true.

In her poetry, Cortez often emphasizes her identification with blue-collar workers. She realizes that living from paycheck to paycheck with dirt wages can create a heavy sense of desperation and justifiable anger. At the end of this poem, the speaker states:

I got the landlord   gas   lights
the union   telephone   department store
subways buses & 4 human beings

to feed
so tell me   tell me   tell me
do you think a revolution is what I need
                    (*Festivals* 15)

It is interesting to note that the last sentence does not have a question mark, or any punctuation at all for that matter, suggesting that the question is rhetorical—the answer is obvious. What Cortez means by "revolution," however, is less clear. She could mean both overturning the system and destroying its oppression of working-class citizens or a personal revolution—the speaker needs to undergo a self-revolution so that her life is not preoccupied by the come and go of the dollar. However, in order for the latter to happen, the first must occur, because when bills must be paid it's very hard to devalue the importance of money. Indeed, I suspect Cortez would say that devaluing the importance of material goods is a luxury afforded only to the rich. In this respect, Cortez becomes both spokesperson for and sympathetic product of the working class.

In "They Came Again in 1970 and 1980" (*Coagulations* 82), a poem about the effect of missionaries and scientists on "developing" countries in Africa, Cortez extends the metaphor of the worker as exploited to the exploitation of all third world people:

And in the name of god and progress and
stuffed pockets
after so much torture
and so many invasions in the blood
your veins are
air strips for
multi-national corporations
Your native sweat is
aviation fuel for
drilling rigs

This poem links the abuse of third world people with the exploitation of third world countries. The bodies of third world people are depicted as sites for exploitation—"after so much torture / and so many invasions in the blood / your veins are / air strips for / multi-national corporations." Land is personified in the black body. Thus, the abuse of the human body equals the abuse of the land.

To place this in an African American context, we must join these two definitions so that "scarification" means that as African Americans we all belong to the same tribe and bear the markings of oppression to prove it. The place that defines us (notice I did not say the place that accepts us or that we can always call home) is also the place where we received our markings—the United States. In "To Our Oppressed Countrymen" (1847), Frederick Douglass expressed the *North Star*'s commitment to African Americans who remained in bondage:

> Remember that we are one, that our cause is one, and that we must help each other, if we would succeed. We have drunk to the dregs the bitter cup of slavery; we have worn the heavy yoke, we have sighed beneath our bonds, and writhed beneath the blood lash;—cruel mementoes of our oneness are indelibly marked in our living flesh. We are one with you under the ban of prejudice and oppression—one with you under the slander of inferiority—one with you in social and political disfranchisement. What you suffer, we suffer; what you endure, we endure. We are indissolubly united, and must fall or flourish together. (*Life* 283)

Cortez's poem "To the Artist Who Just Happens to Be Black" (*Festivals* 8) serves as an appeal to the artist who denies her or his markings, as an entreaty to the artist who believes in "art for art's sake," who views "blackness" as an accident of birth and would rather look past the color of her or his skin toward a contemplation of seemingly more productive issues. Here Cortez echoes Langston Hughes in his landmark essay, "The Negro Artist and the Racial Mountain," in which he writes: "One of the most promising of the young Negro poets said to me once, 'I want to be a poet—not a Negro poet,' meaning, I believe, 'I want to write like a white poet'; meaning subconsciously, 'I would like to be a white poet'; meaning behind that, 'I would like to be white.' And I was sorry the young man said that, for no great poet has ever been afraid of being himself" (88). This essay shows that even during the Harlem Renaissance, Hughes was deconstructing the notion of "whiteness."

Hughes's reminiscence also shows that although the circumstances of revolution might change, we need to revisit revolutionary ideologies to determine what possibilities might be unleashed when confronted with current political situations. While Cortez piggybacks on Hughes's notion of the role of the black artist by critiquing the same type of art-for-art's-sake philosophy that negates lived-through oppression, it is important to note the differences between Cortez's subject positioning and Hughes's. Hughes appropriates a folk culture that is not his own, fancying himself as a vanguard of the people, unlike Cortez who is decidedly "one of the people."

Cortez also uses graphically offensive, violent language to describe the legacy of oppression the African American poet might choose to disown. Cortez asks:

> Listen
> why is your grandaddy's chopped up penis the

magic mallets of truth you hide from
your grandmamma's vagina torn by mangy dogs
her hemorrhaging womb the blood mouth of
the blues you deny
Listen to us our own.
(*Festivals* 8)

Cortez transforms the notion of oppression into a concrete, physically brutal manifestation: an experience that moves the poet from writing a poetry that is mere contemplation (art for art's sake) to a poetry that is actively engaged with the African American heritage. The overall message, then, is that black writers who would rather write without acknowledging their race/culture are not only indirectly denying oppression but also denying the emasculation of their grandfathers, the rape of their grandmothers, and the whole ideology behind the blues. To deny oppression, then, is to devalue the experience of millions of African Americans who lived, loved, and died under the lash. To deny oppression is to efface the scars lashed into the very matrix of U.S. society. To deny oppression is to deafen your ears to a song that sings not only of pain but also of the victory found in surviving and fighting back.

Instead of attacking the wayward poet, Cortez attempts to enlist the artist into this fight. While she questions the poet's choice of audience, she refuses to call the artist a traitor or an "Uncle Tom" but rather labels the poet "our own." In the last stanza she asks, "Why are you forsaking us?" This question follows a plea—an invitation—for the artist to join the struggle and to rise up and "kill" the oppressor.

Cortez also uses the appeal as a thematic and rhetorical tool in order to critique sexist abuse and simultaneously affirm racial solidarity. The issue of scarification gets further complicated when the body as a site for exploitation is occupied by a black female and when the person doing the scarring wears her brother's face. In "If the Drum Is a Woman" (*Coagulations* 57), Cortez discusses violence against the black female body, violence initiated by her black male counterpart.

Using the drum as the representation of the black female body is not a metaphor that Cortez initiated; however, Cortez, being familiar with the negritude movement, could be expanding the metaphor for her own purposes. "If the Drum Is a Woman" could be read as a response to Leopold Sedar Senghor's poem "Black Woman." Senghor exclaims:

From the crest of a charred hilltop I discover you, Promised Land
. . .
Naked woman, dark woman
. . .

Savanna of clear horizons, savanna quivering to the fervent caress
Of the East Wind, sculpted tom-tom, stretched drumskin
Moaning under the hands of the conqueror. (8)

"If the Drum Is a Woman" begins:

> If the drum is a woman
> why are you pounding your drum into an insane
> babble
> why are you pistol whipping your drum at dawn
> why are you shooting through the head of your drum
> and making a drum tragedy of drums
> if the drum is a woman
> don't abuse your drum don't abuse your drum
> don't abuse your drum.
>   (*Coagulations* 57)

Cortez creates a dialogue between herself and Senghor, intertwining the notion of the drum as a beaten object with the notion of the woman as an abused object. While Senghor proclaims the black male speaker as "conqueror" of the female "Promised Land," Cortez thwarts and subverts his language of domination by *personifying the drum* instead of *objectifying the woman* by giving her drum-like qualities.

In personifying the drum as female, Cortez emphasizes the need to create a dialogue between black women and men. Here Cortez moves out of the us/them binary language of the black aesthetic toward a space in which the white "other" is marginalized—faded into the background. Asking black men to take responsibility for their own actions, Cortez appeals to black men to stop abusing black women. Recognizing the scars they share, Cortez appeals to rather than accuses black men in order to include them in the dialogue. Indeed, Cortez's example shows poststructuralists who dismiss the Black Arts Movement how a woman with a revolutionary mission successfully negotiates through layers of sexism and still holds a strong commitment to feminism/womanism. The black feminism/womanism Cortez uses, unlike much Anglo-feminist writing, and unlike Senghor and other black male writers, defines a space for the black woman beside and in connection with—not in opposition or subordination to—her black male counterpart.

Amiri Baraka, who seems to be an ardent supporter of Cortez's work, presents us with an interesting contrast to Cortez. He includes Cortez's work in his 1983 anthology of African American woman's writings, *Confirmation*. In his introduction to this anthology, Baraka asks the following questions:

What is it like here in the United States to be a black woman under the hammer of national oppression? What does this poison do to the woman herself, her life, her lovers, family? What does it take to survive? Can one "survive" and not survive at the same time? What does it take not only to survive but to triumph? How does one live under the rule and sway of national oppression, racism, and white supremacy? How does one keep one's sanity and balance in such a world, and how is this further complicated by being not just black, but a woman? (20)

The problem I have with the above questions is that Baraka implies that being a black male is synonymous with being black—"How is this further complicated by being not just black, but a woman?" No one is "just black." Nevertheless, that he could envision that someone could be "just black" is an excellent example of Baraka's attempt to work on his sexism. The attempt falls short, however, because, although there are differences between types of oppression black women and men face, Baraka's questions leave little room for an intersection between the two experiences. Are we to assume that he doesn't know the answers to any of his questions?

Unlike Baraka, Cortez, in "If the Drum Is a Woman," demonstrates an understanding of the plight of black men that Baraka—at least the Baraka of the 1960s to 1983—lacks. Cortez empathizes with the oppressed, implied black male worker:

I know the night is full of displaced persons
. . .
I know the ugly disposition of underpaid clerks
they constantly menstruate through the eyes
I know bitterness embedded in flesh
the itching alone can drive you crazy.
        (*Coagulations* 57)

She then traces how these men, in their pain and "bitterness" at the system, translate their frustration into acts of violence against the black female. Thus, Cortez recognizes the scars oppression has left on her brothers in a way that Baraka does not.

Although Cortez acknowledges how the exploited male worker, frustrated and scarred by racist oppression, can turn and then abuse his wife/ mate/sister/daughter, she does not condone it. She seems to agree with Audre Lorde when Lorde states: "As Black people, we cannot begin our dialogue by denying the oppressive nature of *male privilege*. And if Black males choose to assume that privilege, for whatever reason, raping, brutalizing, and killing women, then we cannot ignore Black male oppression. One oppression does not justify another" ("Feminism" 19). Here the victimized male assumes the role of the oppressor and is in the position to produce further potential scar victims. In "If the Drum Is a Woman," we remember the speaker's plea, "don't be forced into the position as an oppressor of drums and make a drum tragedy of drums," urging the oppressed male not to fall further prey to the evils of capitalism. What Lorde's insertion makes clear is that when theorizing from the scars, we must not for the sake of unity believe that everyone scars in the same manner, or that we are incapable of inflicting scars on each other.

Although Cortez, like Lorde, challenges sexism, she herself has been accused of homophobia, particularly in her earlier works. Some critics have questioned the inclusiveness of Cortez's revolutionary agenda and her notion of collective black scarring. The first line from her poem "Race" reads: "Men do not lay with men to claim god-hood." Cortez also demonstrates in this poem her belief that homosexuals cannot be revolutionaries and in fact are a detriment to the revolution (and should be eliminated).

> Bleeding as we must slaughter these our sons to bring a revolution on For what good will there be when time is here a non functioning product used openly against We as he pleads his creative ability Ability to create what? A Race called Faggot Oh black man quick please the laxative so our sons can shit the White Shit of Fear out and Live. (*Pissstained Stairs* 13)

In *Home Girls,* Cheryl Clarke, a black lesbian critic, discusses a printed flyer left on every seat at a conference on self-determination that she attended in 1981. The contents of this flyer explain the ideology working behind Cortez's poem:

> Revolutionary nationalists and genuine communists cannot uphold homosexuality in the leadership of the Black Liberation Movement nor uphold it as a correct practice. Homosexuality is a genocidal practice. . . . Homosexuality does not produce children. . . . Homosexuality does not birth new warriors for liberation. . . . Homosexuality cannot be upheld as correct or revolutionary practice. . . . The practice of homosexuality is an accelerating threat to our survival as a people and as a nation. (197–98)

In a 1990 interview with D. H. Melhem, Cortez attempted to explain her poem "Race," stating: " 'Race' was written for a friend of mine. I don't think it indicts homosexuals. I think it talks about the contradictions of a particular person. The poem is about contradictions and inconsistencies. . . . I wrote the poem in 1968 at the request of a friend. He never rejected the tone of the piece" (207). This statement, however, scarcely absolves Cortez from the charge of homophobia. Nonetheless, I submit that homophobia during the black liberation movement was not a notion that Jayne Cortez created. Indeed, what makes the poem "Race" even more interesting as a study of homophobia during this time period is that Cortez labels homosexuality as a product of oppression. Homosexuality, then, is coded as white: if you are a black homosexual then not only are you antirevolutionary, but you are also emulating your oppressors.

In 1970, Huey P. Newton published a response to this type of thinking in the *Black Panther*. He suggested that maybe the opposite is true, that "maybe a homosexual could be the most revolutionary" because of the various levels of oppression she or he had to fight against (15). Of course, Audre Lorde agrees with Newton. Lorde's project specifically attempts to examine the implications behind America's homophobic notions of lesbianism. Alexis DeVeaux, a black lesbian writer, has often stated that attacks on lesbianism exhibit society's ultimate fear of women's total independence of men. Lesbianism also threatens the established order because it subverts conventional notions of the feminine.

In actuality, both Lorde and Cortez are committed to reshaping society's perception of the independent woman and what it means to be feminine. Both writers challenge women to assert rather than replace their anger, to use anger as a revolutionary tool. Lorde explains: "My response to racism is anger. I have lived with that anger, ignoring it, feeding up it, learning to use it before it laid my visions to waste, for most of my life" ("Feminism" 38). In an interview with DeVeaux, Cortez elaborates: "There is something within me, an intense feeling of outrage. I've always felt it. I don't know where it comes from. I just know it's there and I use it. It's the thing, the energy that makes you you, how you put it down, how you use it, how it comes out" (106). By conceding that anger can be useful, both make a distinction between nihilistic rage and revolutionary rage. Nihilistic rage is anger for its own sake; revolutionary rage defines anger as an act of self-defense/self-preservation or as an act of protection.

Cortez's agenda goes beyond mere anger by advocating murder as a "strategy of resistance." As hooks states: "Naming the pain or uncovering the pain in a context where it is not linked to strategies for resistance and transformation created for many women the conditions for even greater estrangement, alienation, isolation, and at times despair" (*Talking Back* 32). Cortez also realizes that naming the pain is not enough when pain can be recurring and voices can be silenced. By advocating violence as a necessary self-defense—retaliatory violence—Cortez moves away from the language of victimization not only by valorizing the right to be angry over America's scarring of the body of the person of color (in this case female) with its systematic oppression but by advocating violence as a means of preserving the self.

Cortez's stance on retaliatory violence as a means of self-defense not only threatens mainstream America but also influences what anthologies, such as *Giant Talk* (edited by Troupe and Schulte) and *Confirmation* (edited by Baraka), as well as the *Norton Anthology of African-American Literature* (edited by Gates and McKay), will even expose to their readership. Coming from very different angles and working under very different motives in their representative Black Arts Movement selections, these anthologies privilege works focusing upon blues and jazz rather than revolution. Therefore, these anthologies select poems by Cortez that praise jazz "greats"[3] of the past rather than her more violent and graphic poems.

It seems that while she is readily accepted into the Black Aesthetic Movement, even that movement—as well as the established powers—are not radical enough to accept revolutionary/retaliatory violence, and the language it brings, from a black woman. In her book *Justifiable Homicide,* Cynthia Gillespie states:

> Our culture's expectation is, always, that a woman is not supposed to defend herself; she is supposed to rely on a man to defend her—her husband, her boyfriend, her father or brothers, or the police. . . . There is something that strikes us as obscene, against nature, or unholy about a woman who kills, that goes way beyond the illegality or even the immorality of her act. It shakes some of our most deeply held cultural stereotypes to their roots. . . . Society is outraged when a woman challenges all of these assumptions, refuses to take the blame, refuses to be a helpless victim but instead picks up a weapon and defends herself. It is doubly outraged when she then brazenly claims that she was reasonable and justified in doing so and should pay no penalty. (12)

Likewise, when Cortez applauds women who refuse to become victims or to rely on a man's assistance and who instead turn into ice-pick-wielding, gun-toting warriors, editors and academics become nervous. Perhaps this type of anger, along with its justification, makes many poststructuralists shy away from creative works coming out of the Black Arts Movement.

The *Norton Anthology* includes only one poem by Cortez: "How Long Has Trane Been Gone," a relatively tame work, considering the fact that it does not utilize graphic or violent imagery.[4] We could conclude that the Norton anthologies, as a series of books that reflect the unwritten lists of the canonical texts of the academy—the "must read" texts for students—is necessarily conservative. However, the fact that a subsection entitled "The Primeval Mitosis," from Eldridge Cleaver's *Soul on Ice*,[5] is included suggests that black women's poetry that is graphically violent and profane is not soon to be accepted by the predominantly male canon, black or white. Until she learns to talk like a lady, the move seems to be to include only works where we catch Cortez whispering rather than shouting for vengeance.

In "Rape" (*Coagulations* 63), Cortez uses aggressive obscenities to redefine radically what constitutes a woman's language, insisting that it includes a vocabulary of rage and retribution—a language that has also been claimed by many contemporary female poets such as June Jordan, Audre Lorde, and Adrienne Rich. On the surface, "Rape" deals with issues of violence as it occurs interracially and outside of personal relationships. Yet a deeper reading shows that Cortez uses the language of colonization to address the subject of rape. The poem is based on the highly publicized trials of Inez Garcia and Joan (pronounced and often cited as Joanne) Little. In 1974, Inez Garcia killed a man who held her down while another man raped her.

This poem not only shows Cortez's commitment to the Black Aesthetic Movement but also to feminist/womanist ideology as it relates to the unification of third world women. The two women mentioned, Inez and Joanne, one Hispanic, the other black, unify the dual heritage Cortez possesses as an African American woman with a Latin name— the implications of her skin color and the implications of her name (the name comes from her grandmother who was born in the Philippines) (Melhem 181).

Cortez asks, "What was Inez supposed to do for the man who declared war on her body / the man who carved a combat zone between her breasts" (again, a rhetorical question without a question mark). The woman's body is no longer a beaten drum, but a war zone. Man—specifically coded as the white male, according to Cortez's project—is then depicted as the oppositional country, colonizing into submission through brutal penetration of the female body/nation. The woman in turn retaliates in war/rape time like a defending country bearing arms against an unwanted invasion. The woman's act of violence is redefined as self-defense, and her victory has her dancing over her dead rapist, celebrating his defeat by proclaiming it a holiday:

> She pumped lead into his three hundred pound of shaking flesh
> Sent it flying to the Virgin of Guadalupe
> then celebrated day of the dead rapist punk
> and just what the fuck else was she supposed to do.
>
> (*Coagulations* 63)

Using poetic license in the rendition of Inez Garcia's story, Cortez envisions Garcia's retaliation as more immediate than it actually was. Immediate action is necessary for Cortez's program in order to emphasize the need for immediate revolution.

In the next section, Cortez defines Joanne—a black woman—as another female "country," this time besieged under a vicious police state. In this section, the country in question is the United States. Cortez questions the godlike power of U.S. police and their racist brutality. The fact that the rapist is a white policeman and the victim is his black woman prisoner serves to show how violence, rape, and racism are institutionalized. The fact that Joanne—written as a country—kills the policeman can be read as an attempt to dismantle and overthrow such institutions on a level that surpasses individual revolution:

> This being wartime for Joanne
> she did what a defense department will do in times of war
> and when the piss drinking   shit sniffing guard said I'm
>   gonna make you wish
> you were dead black bitch
> come here
> Joanne came down with an ice pick in
> the swat freak motherfucker's chest . . .
> Joanne did the dance of the ice picks and once again from
>   coast to coast
> house to house
> we celebrated day of the dead rapist punk
> and just what the fuck else were we supposed to do.

The excessive use of curses and "filthy" language throughout the poem is necessary to emphasize the filthiness and ugliness of rape itself. Since rape is, most of the time, a uniquely female experience, perhaps we can see this language as also being feminine—a specific female anger, speaking as a therapeutic tool to be used by all women against rape. Barbara Christian elaborates: "Her [Cortez's] precise naming of rape as a declaration of war on a woman's body reminds us why we talk of countries being raped; that rape of a woman is as evil an act as an attack on one's country. . . . It is clarity about what *is* really happening, the ability to name the truth beyond the muddle of propaganda, that characterizes Cortez's poetry" ("There It Is" 238).

I discovered the "truth" behind Cortez's poetry when I glanced at a library copy of her *Coagulations*. A person, whom I assume to be female, had changed the poem "Rape" into a first-person narration: "she" crossed out the names of Inez and Joanne and replaced them with "I" and "me." I can envision this woman's balled fist, tight around a scribbling ink pen, marking the margins with the memory of pain not forgotten—leaving her scars on paper. Here is where theory and experience meet, in the margins—a poststructuralist stomping ground informed by the pain of lived experience. This poem obviously served as an outlet for the anonymous woman's rage, because when she arrived at the section where Joanne kills the policeman, she wrote, "I am at that step." Cortez, then, has inspired at least one person to revolt.

The poetry of Jayne Cortez is about blood and revolution. Informed by the language of the Black Arts Movement, Cortez stands as proof that all has not yet been said about theories of the black aesthetic. Speaking as both "one of the people" and spokesperson "for the people," Cortez proudly asserts her commitment to speak always through her scars to reach others who have also participated in the ritual. Academics and teachers of "theory" and black literatures should not regard a commitment such as this as antithetical to the goals of the academy. If multiculturalism is true to its definition, theories that validate the various experiences of marginalized people should be readily accepted. If we are truly to heal the wounds of the past and not fall prey to the romantic language that poststructuralism often espouses, we must lessen the gap between the academy and those who exist outside of the ivory tower.

As Cortez's fifth book of poetry, *Coagulations,* reminds us, scarification is about blood, revolution, and, most of all, healing. Coagulation is the clotting of blood—the start of a healing process—and we can envision Cortez's poetry as a "clotting of blood poems." Blood poems could then be taken racially to mean poems that were concerned with the blood connection of blacks and their subsequent uplifting—an attempt to soothe and yet remember the scars left by oppression. Blood poems could also indicate that the commitment to the uplift of blacks is part of our heritage, passed down from "blood" to "blood" (meaning sister to sister, brother to brother, sister to brother) through the bloodstream, through the blood that was shed by our ancestors, from generation to generation. Seen in this respect, the theorist/critic who theorizes through scars is not being naive but rather is fulfilling a legacy. And if we don't accept this responsibility as African American theorists, what will we do if "they" come cracking the whip again? The past repeats itself if we do not learn from history. The message behind Cortez's blood poems is that if we adhere to the heritage in our blood the artist within all of us will openly acknowledge what it means to be black in America—to learn to endure and overcome oppression; brother will not beat sister and sister will not be afraid to draw blood to save her own.

Blood poems are the core of the black aesthetic, our "racial memory." Incorporating our racial memory into the mission of poststructuralism—reassessing the black aesthetic in relation to poststructuralism—can create a wider angle from which to analyze texts by people of color. Julian Mayfield states, "[The] Black Aesthetic . . . is our racial memory, and the unshakable knowledge of who we are, where we have been, and, springing from this, where are we going. Where have we been? Up a hell of a long, hard road" (26). The revolutionary blood poems of Jayne Cortez epitomize the amalgamation of both theories, a coming together of the "intellect" and "intuition." Not only is Cortez committed to our racial memory by recalling our tribal markings—our scarification—but she is also developing ways to use that memory, to use the scars, to fight oppression. Cortez writes to dismantle all oppressive institutions, to unpave all "hard roads" by all possible means. In the words of Jayne Cortez, "and just what the fuck else was she supposed to do?"

NOTES

1. Both texts exhibit this "blur" by serving as examples of the kind of reconstituted practice that more or less, for good or bad, has begun to be associated with "women of color" theoretical projects—the combining of poetry, fiction, and "theoretical" essays in one text to imply the equal importance of all forms.

2. It is precisely this simultaneous insider/outsider position, the ability to live "it" (whatever "it" may be) and to come back and share with authority what you learn that bothers Diana Fuss in classroom situations. Fuss is concerned that when marginalized students take center stage and speak from experience, they may silence others. There has to be a middle ground where we accept a difference between sympathy and empathy. When the white professor, John Howard Griffin, dyed his skin and went down South disguised as a "Negro," as chronicled in *Black Like Me* (1961), he also knew that in certain instances there is no substitute for experience.

3. Cortez is well known for her jazz poems, but since there has already been considerable work done on these types of poems, I chose not to focus on them in this essay.

4. Cortez appears in the *Norton Anthology* under the section entitled "The Black Arts Movement," edited by Houston Baker. Coincidentally (?), the *Norton Anthology* also leaves out Nikki Giovanni's infamous "The True Import of Present Dialogue Black vs. Negro," in which she asks, "Nigger can you kill?" And although *Giant Talk* (edited by Troupe and Schulte) includes a section entitled "Violence: Blood in the Thermometer Rises in Arms," Cortez is found in the section entitled "Music, Language, and Rhythm: Divine Wailing Alone in the Dark Cone."

5. In this section, Cleaver makes many offensive statements, such as "If a lesbian is anything she is a frigid woman, a frozen cunt, a warp and a crack in the wall of her ice" (184).

WORKS CITED

Baker, Houston A., Jr. *Blues, Ideology, and Afro-American Literature: A Vernacular Theory*. Chicago: University of Chicago Press, 1984.
———. "In Dubious Battle." *New Literary History* 18 (1987): 363–69.
———. "There Is No More Beautiful Way: Theory and the Poetics of Afro-American Women's Writing." *Afro-American Literary Study in the 1990s*. Ed. Houston A. Baker Jr. and Patricia Redmon. Chicago: University of Chicago Press, 1989. 135–63.
Bambara, Toni Cade, ed. *The Black Woman: An Anthology*. New York: Signet, 1970.
Baraka, Amiri. "Introduction." *Confirmation: An Anthology of African American Women*. Ed. Amina Baraka and Amiri Baraka. New York: William Morrow, 1983.
Bell, Roseann P., Bettye J. Parker, and Beverly Guy-Sheftall, eds. *Sturdy Black Bridges: Visions of Black Women in Literature*. New York: Anchor, 1979.
Butler-Evans, Elliot. "Beyond Essentialism: Rethinking Afro-American Cultural Theory." *Inscriptions* 5 (1989): 120–34.
Christian, Barbara. "There It Is: The Poetry of Jayne Cortez." *Callaloo* 9 (Winter 1986): 235–38.
Clarke, Cheryl. "The Failure to Transform: Homophobia in the Black Community." *Home Girls: A Black Feminist Anthology*. Ed. Barbara Smith. New York: Kitchen Table/Women of Color Press, 1983. 197–208.
Cleaver, Eldridge. *Soul on Ice*. New York: Dell, 1968.
Cortez, Jayne. *Coagulations: New and Selected Poems*. New York: Thunder's Mouth Press, 1984.
———. *Festivals and Funerals*. New York: Phrase Text, 1971.
———. *Pissstained Stairs and the Monkey Man's Wares*. New York: Phrase Text, 1969.
———. *Scarification*. New York: Bola Press, 1978.
DeVeaux, Alexis. "A Poet's World: Jayne Cortez Discusses Her Life and Her Work." *Essence*, Mar. 1978, pp. 77–79, 106, 109.
Douglass, Frederick. *The Life and Writings of Frederick Douglass: Early Years, 1817–1849*. Ed. Philip Foner. New York: International Publishers, 1950.
duCille, Ann. *The Coupling Convention: Sex, Text, and Tradition in Black Women's Fiction*. New York: Oxford University Press, 1993.
Eagleton, Terry. *Literary Theory: An Introduction*. Minneapolis: University of Minnesota Press, 1983.
Gates, Henry Louis, Jr., ed. *Black Literature and Literary Theory*. New York: Methuen, 1984.
———. "The 'Blackness of Blackness': A Critique of the Sign and the Signifying Monkey." *Critical Inquiry* 9 (1983): 685–723.
Gillespie, Cynthia. *Justifiable Homicide: Battered Women, Self-Defense and the Law*. Columbus: Ohio State University Press, 1989.
hooks, bell. *Talking Back: Thinking Feminist, Thinking Black*. Boston: South End Press, 1989.
———. *Teaching to Transgress: Education as the Practice of Freedom*. New York: Routledge, 1994.
Hughes, Langston. "The Negro Artist and the Racial Mountain." *Speech and Power: The African American Essay and Its Cultural Content, From Polemics to Pulpit*. Vol. 2. Ed. Gerald Early. Hopewell, N.J.: Ecco Press, 1993. 88–91.
Joyce, Joyce A. "The Black Canon: Reconstructing Black American Literary Criticism." *New Literary History* 18 (1987): 335–44.

Lorde, Audre. "Feminism and Black Liberation: The Great American Disease." *Black Scholar* 10.8–9 (1979): 17–20.

Mason, Theodore O., Jr. "Between the Populist and the Scientist: Ideology and Power in Recent Afro-American Literary Criticism or, 'The Dozens' as Scholarship." *Callaloo* 11 (Summer 1988): 606–15.

Mayfield, Julian. "You Touch My Black Aesthetic and I'll Touch Yours." *The Black Aesthetic*. Ed. Addison Gayle. Garden City, N.Y.: Doubleday, 1987. 23–30.

Melhem, D. H. *Heroism in the New Black Poetry: Introductions and Interviews*. Lexington: University Press of Kentucky, 1990. 180–212.

Miller, R. Baxter. "Baptized Infidel: Play and the Critical Legacy." *Black American Literature Forum* 21.4 (1987): 393–414.

Newton, Huey P. "A Letter from Huey to the Revolutionary Brothers and Sisters about the Women's Liberation and Gay Liberation Movements." *Black Panther*, Aug. 15, 1970, p. 15.

Senghor, Leopold Sedar. *The Collected Poetry of Leopold Sedar Senghor*. Trans. Melvin Dixon. Charlottesville: University Press of Virginia, 1991.

Smith, Valerie. "Black Feminist Theory and the Representation of the 'Other.'" *Changing Our Own Words: Essays on Criticism, Theory, and Writing by Black Women*. Ed. Cheryl A. Wall. New Brunswick, N.J.: Rutgers University Press, 1989. 38–57.

———. "Gender and Afro-Americanist Literary Theory and Criticism." *Speaking of Gender*. Ed. Elaine Showalter. New York: Routledge, 1989. 56–70.

Troupe, Quincy, and Rainer Schulte, eds. *Giant Talk: An Anthology of Third World Writings*. New York: Random House, 1975.

4 ◇ Resisting Postmodernism; or,
"A Postmodernism of Resistance"

bell hooks and the Theory Debates

Can postmodernism and feminism be good allies? Can either contribute effectively to the struggle against racism? It depends on *which* postmodernism and *which* feminism. If postmodernism and postmodernists have not always foregrounded or even acknowledged gender issues, race has been even less visible. Yet those concerned with gender, race, and their intersections have recently begun contributing to and thus reshaping postmodernism. Since the publication of her first book, *Ain't I a Woman: Black Women and Feminism* (1981), bell hooks has been an influential feminist writer and theorist. Just as that book helped to transform feminism—to make it more inclusive and liberatory—hooks's more recent work may help to transform postmodernism.[1] Her contributions to current debates about identity, experience, agency, culture, ethics, politics, and theory open a space both for a revitalized and repoliticized postmodernism and for more productive alliances among those of us committed to social change and social justice.

Currently Distinguished Professor of English at City College of CUNY, hooks is a scholar, an activist against racism and sexism, and a "public intellectual." She seems equally adept at feminist theorizing, movie and music reviews, cultural critique, and political commentary.[2] She has become an increasingly popular interviewee and speaker at college campuses, local schools, community events, and recently on PBS programs such as *To the Contrary*. She is committed to reaching a large, diverse audience so that she can promote the development of liberatory theories and practices and assist in the long struggle toward a hoped-for human emancipation from all forms of oppression.

As a black feminist, hooks has been especially concerned with pointing out and remedying the marginalization of black women—in U.S. society as a whole, within African American communities, and within feminism. In *Ain't I a Woman* and *Feminist Theory: From Margin to Center* (1984), hooks argues that white feminists have claimed to speak for all women but have actually taken their own white, middle-class experiences as normative, ignoring or marginalizing the concerns and contributions of black women. Indeed, hooks has helped to move these concerns and contributions "from margin to center"[3]—and in doing so she has illuminated the shifting relations between margin and center, normative and "other." Along with other feminists of color, hooks has helped to make feminist practices and theories more inclusive and more self-reflexive and thus more likely to achieve their liberatory goals.

In spite of her critiques of it, hooks has long insisted on her commitment to feminism. In fact, at a 1994 lecture at Santa Clara University, hooks stated that she preferred the term "feminism" to Alice Walker's term "womanism," since feminism, unlike womanism, is connected to an organized political movement. hooks has tried to convey to women, especially young black women, the importance of feminism to their survival and sustenance. She has also frequently stated her commitment to *theory* as a crucial corollary and complement to practice and as a necessary part of black liberation, decolonization, and feminist activism.

What has been less obvious is hooks's increasing engagement with postmodernism—an engagement that is, like hers to feminism, both critical and dialogic. Among contemporary thinkers, hooks is distinctive in her intersecting commitments to feminist and antiracist struggles, critical pedagogy, theory, and postmodernism. Through an analysis of her relations to feminists (white and black) who reject theory and/or postmodernism,[4] to feminists and theorists of race who engage postmodernism, and to some contemporary species of postmodernism itself, I wish to show how bell hooks's work enables us to imagine a different, more inclusive, and more politically effective postmodernism.

Postmodernism and the Theory Debates

Like other terms used for periodization and categorization, postmodernism has, as Ihab Hassan notes, a "certain *semantic* instability" (*Dismemberment* 263). There are probably as many definitions of postmodernism as there are definers. But unlike other terms used for intellectual, social, or literary historical periods (e.g., Renaissance or Romanticism), postmodernism and postmodernity include the name of that which preceded them: "modernism" and "modernity." Since these latter terms have been variously defined and widely debated, and since postmodernism/ity's *relation* to modernism/ity—whether one of continuity, exaggeration, or rupture—is *also* widely debated, postmodernism may be an inevitably contested and polysemic term. Nonetheless, since it is central to my analysis, I will provide a working, provisional definition of it.

"Postmodernism" is a term that began to be applied to some innovative literary texts in the late 1950s and early 1960s; its use then expanded to architecture, photography, dance, and other arts.[5] By the early 1970s, many critics were using "postmodernism" to designate recent artistic and cultural avant-gardes (including new forms such as performance art); theorists also began to define and evaluate postmodernism. Some of the most frequently cited characteristics of postmodernist literature and art were fragmentation, experimentation, heterogeneity, intertextuality, irony, parody, pastiche, self-reflexiveness, genre blurring, and playfulness. Definitions of postmodernism were often derived inductively, through examination of a group of works that had been selected in advance as somehow representative of this not-yet-defined phenomenon.[6] No agreement has yet been reached on whether objects or practices are postmodern by virtue of their intrinsic features and/or by virtue of their place in (post-1950) history. For example, I, like many other literary scholars, do not think that all contemporary novelists are postmodernists (even though we might agree that all postmodernists are contemporary—with exceptions being made, perhaps, for Cervantes, Sterne, or Stein as proto-postmodernists). So is postmodernism a style, a movement, a perspective on the world, and/or a historical period?

The conceptualization of postmodern*ity* as a historical marker seems to have followed—and been influenced by—that of postmodernism in literature, art, and architecture. Some scholars cite Jean-François Lyotard's *Postmodern Condition* (published in France in 1979) as the first work to theorize about postmodernity as a historical "event" and a philosophical concept.[7] I follow Lyotard's understanding of postmodernity as the social, historical, and cultural condition in which we now live: the post-Enlightenment, post-atomic, multimedia, high-tech, globalized world of late postindustrial capitalism.[8] Yet postmodernity's precise temporal boundaries, like those of modernity, are difficult to fix. Does modernity begin with the Renaissance or with the Enlightenment? Does it only come into being after Nietzsche and Freud, or do Nietzsche and Freud signal the beginning of *post*modernity? Should we trace postmodernity's origins to the Holocaust and World War II? Or is its emergence coincident with the student and cultural revolutions of the 1960s, with the invention of the personal computer, or with the rise of multinational corporations?

What, then, is the relation of postmodern*ity* to postmodern*ism*? As Andreas Huyssen notes, "By the early 1980s the modernism/postmodernism constellation in the arts and the modernity/postmodernity constellation in social theory had become one of the most contested terrains in the intellectual life of Western societies" (184). And these constellations had begun to overlap, as they still do for those of us who see postmodernism as both reflecting and shaping postmodernity.

Since at least the mid-1980s, the adjective "postmodern" has been applied not only to avant-garde literary and artistic works but also to culture and society as a whole and to specific post-1960 philosophies and theories, especially poststructuralism. I use "poststructuralism" to designate a group of theories developed largely in France, including, but not limited to, deconstruction (Jacques Derrida being the "founder" of deconstruction), with Jacques Lacan, Michel Foucault, and Julia Kristeva as some of the major nondeconstructive poststructuralists. French poststructuralism emerged concurrently with American postmodernist fiction, art, and architecture, and both may be responses to the same historical and social conditions of postmodernity.[9] I distinguish between postmodern *theories,* which are themselves shaped by and reflective of "the postmodern condition," and theories *about* postmodernism— what it is, whether it's a good thing, and so on.[10]

Postmodernity, postmodernism, and poststructuralism all involve a decentering of the world (or a recognition of its decenteredness); a critique of Enlightenment/modernity's belief in the universal, rational, unified subject and in history as progress; an awareness of heterogeneity and indeterminacy; and a foregrounding of issues of language and representation. In the rest of this essay, I use the terms "postmodernism" and "postmodern" to designate both specific contemporary artistic and theoretical avant-gardes and the wider social, cultural, historical, discursive, economic, technological, and ideological conditions in which they are embedded.

It might seem that postmodernism and feminism would be natural allies—in critiquing traditions, rejecting the universal (read: male) subject, embracing differences, rethinking margin/center dichotomies, and deconstructing existing power relations. Yet it took until the mid-1980s—two decades after the emergence of postmodern practices, postmodern theories, and theories *about* postmodernism—for serious feminist interrogation of postmodernism to occur.[11] Then, some of us began to notice that postmodernism had so far been discussed, defined, and exemplified primarily by (white) men who had largely ignored feminist theory, the work of women artists and writers, and issues of gender. Yet two of the most important figures in the U.S. importation of deconstruction are women who are also feminists: Barbara Johnson and Gayatri Chakravorty Spivak, whose scholarship has become increasingly focused on gender, race, and politics. For some time, feminist critics and scholars in various disciplines had been using (and often adapting) the work of Foucault, Derrida, Lacan, and other important postmodern/poststructuralist theorists. At least one woman (arguably a feminist) was often grouped with these "great (white) masters" of theory: Julia Kristeva. Moreover, feminist scholars began to realize that women had been not only making and using postmodern theory but also producing postmodern art, film, and literature, as figures such as Barbara Kruger, Angela Carter, and Laurie Anderson (but few women of color) began to receive the attention they deserved.

Since the mid-1980s, such collections as Linda J. Nicholson's *Feminism/Postmodernism* (1990), Henry A. Giroux's *Postmodernism, Feminism, and Cultural Politics* (1991),and Margaret Ferguson and Jennifer Wicke's *Feminism and Postmodernism* (1994) have appeared; scores of articles have analyzed feminism's and/or women's relation to poststructuralist and postmodern theory, postmodern fiction or other arts, and postmodernity itself. But for many feminists the question remains: Is postmodernism compatible with or useful for feminism? We might also ask: Is feminism good for postmodernism? [12]

Henry A. Giroux—who shares hooks's (and my) interests in feminism, postmodernism, liberatory pedagogy, and politics—has recently argued that perhaps postmodernism needs feminism even more than feminism needs postmodernism, since "feminism provides postmodernism with a politics, and a great deal more" (33). I would add that postmodernism needs theorists of race, for this reason and others. Jane Flax, a postmodern feminist political philosopher and psychoanalyst, believes that feminist theory has much to gain from postmodern critiques of Enlightenment rationality and essentialism, since de-essentializing gender is a crucial strategy for many feminists.

Yet, for other feminists, this very de-essentializing of gender, welcomed by hooks as by other postmodern feminists, is the *problem,* not a solution to pressing social and political concerns. The feminist political theorist Christine Di Stefano, for instance, argues that feminism requires the very notions of rationality and subjectivity that postmodernism has decentered or discarded. The feminist literary critic and theorist Margaret

Homans notes that "time and again, discussions of postmodern feminist politics founder on the question of how to act politically without using totalizing categories such as 'women'" (80).

Yet, feminists *can* resist totalizing, universalizing, and essentializing "women" and still be able to act. For instance, women can join together to act politically, based on their similarities—even contingent or temporary ones—of interest, need, or position, rather than of essence. Judith Butler, a preeminent feminist philosopher and queer theorist who has been influenced by Derrida and Foucault, argues that effective political action is not only *possible* but more *likely* if we refuse to totalize or essentialize "woman." For Butler, as for both Foucault and hooks, "identity categories are never merely descriptive, but always normative, and as such, exclusionary." Butler suggests that feminists would be better off seeing "women" as "an undesignatable field of differences" rather than as a totalized "identity category" so that the term can become "a site of permanent openness and resignifiability" ("Contingent Foundations" 16).[13] Such "permanent openness" provides a space for postmodern feminist politics.

But can postmodernism, or even postmodern feminism, really contribute to a broader emancipatory politics, including the struggles to end racism, imperialism, and other forms of oppression? Explicit analyses of postmodernism and *race* have emerged even more recently than those of postmodernism and *gender,* and hooks has been one of the major voices in these developing dialogues (as has Cornel West)[14]—dialogues only now becoming audible to some white scholars. In 1990 hooks noted, "There is too little work which seeks to examine the impact of postmodernism on contemporary black culture" (*Yearning* 8). I would add that there has been even less work analyzing the impact of black culture and thought on postmodernism or as integral *parts* of postmodernism. In her chapter "Postmodern Blackness," hooks acknowledges "the resistance on the part of most black folks to hearing about real connection between postmodernism and black experience" and notes that "very few African-American intellectuals have talked or written about postmodernism" (*Yearning* 25, 23).

Some of hooks's recent work is *about* postmodernism; some of it *is* postmodern. She describes some of her own creative writing as "reflective of a postmodern oppositional sensibility, . . . abstract, fragmented, non-linear" (*Yearning* 29), and she says her book *Yearning* "could be seen as postmodern" in its "polyphonic vocality," which emerges from a "postmodern social context . . . expressive of those postmodern conditions of homelessness, displacement, rootlessness, etc." (*Yearning* 229).[15]

Interestingly, hooks's theoretical discussions of postmodernism have probably found a larger (if still too small) audience among white academics than among "black folks" or black intellectuals (perhaps overlapping categories). But maybe it is time to think about not only postmodern blackness but "postmodern whiteness" and to realize that what used to be called (plain old) postmodernism may have been not only *male* but also *white* postmodernism.

White scholars studying postmodernism often find ourselves in a difficult position when we try to analyze its relations with black culture (which we don't know "from the inside" anyway). We must negotiate our way between the Scylla of "commodification of 'blackness' that is so peculiar to postmodern strategies of colonization" (hooks, *Yearning* 8) and the Charybdis of neglecting and/or marginalizing the perspectives and contributions of people of color.[16] Perhaps that is one reason why I find so appealing hooks's call for and belief in the possibility of respectful dialogue between white scholars and scholars of color on these issues and her deconstruction of essentialized racial identity.[17]

Yet the relationship between postmodernism and issues of race, gender, and politics is perceived in widely divergent ways. Many conservative critics of a sort of "lumpen postmodernism" have long associated postmodernism with radical politics, multiculturalism, and feminism, while many on the left have accused postmodern art and postmodern theories (such as deconstruction) of being ahistorical and apolitical (and for some, also blind to race and gender).[18] Until rather recently, the latter criticism was much closer to the mark, in my view. For instance, even though in some of his earliest texts (such as "Structure, Sign, and Play," a lecture first presented in 1966) Derrida had critiqued the principle of ethnocentrism, his own work has been decidedly Euro- and androcentric.[19] Even though a focus on *difference* is often viewed as central to postmodernism, it has been feminists and theorists of race who have insisted that *racial* and *sexual* differences do matter.[20]

For some feminists and theorists of race, including hooks, an especially attractive aspect of postmodernism has been what Lyotard calls its "incredulity toward meta-narratives." These meta-narratives are modernity's grand stories or theories that explain and legitimate human history (*Postmodern Condition* xxiv). Postmodernists, many feminists, and many postcolonial and critical race theorists are understandably suspicious of meta-narratives, which, as Madan Sarup notes, are "master narratives—narratives of mastery, of *man* seeking *his telos* in the *conquest* of *nature*" (132, emphasis added).[21] In an interview by Bill Moyers, Toni Morrison also critiques such "master narratives" that entrench cultural hegemony and oppression and efface differences. Modernity's master narratives inevitably reflect the imperialist, patriarchal, and racist order that spawned them.

For many postmodernist thinkers, the turn *away* from universal, to-tal theories and master narratives is accompanied by a turn *toward* local narratives and acknowledgment of particularity and difference. In prin-ciple, this paradigm shift from the totalizing to the localizing would seem to be welcomed by theorists of gender and race; yet the shift in paradigms has not always been accompanied by a shift in practices. Even now, it sometimes appears that all the postmodernist writers and theo-rists are white men and most of the feminists are white women.[22]

One could respond to this critique by suggesting that postmodern practice will eventually catch up to postmodern theory. Women of color, including hooks, have justly criticized and begun to remedy white feminists' blindness to issues of race and class. Feminists of all colors have begun to remedy postmodernists' blindness to gender. (Lesbian, gay, and queer theorists have begun to remedy feminists' and postmodernists' blindness to heterosexism.) And, largely through the interventions of feminists and theorists of race, "First World reflections on postmod-ernism have recently become more consciously historical, social, politi-cal, and ideological" (West, "Black Culture" 90).

Yet some feminists and theorists of race remain skeptical about post-modernism, especially given its ostensible deconstruction of stable identities, foundations, and truth itself. Those committed to radical so-cial and political change wonder how postmodernism can be liberatory if there is "no one" to liberate and if there are no foundations on which to base arguments for or assessments of justice or liberation.

But, I would argue, reconceiving subjectivity, as hooks and other feminists and postmodernists do, is not the same as rejecting it. Aban-doning a quest for absolute foundations need not mean ceasing to act out of conviction; even "contingent foundations" (Butler) can ground practices. De-essentializing gender and race does not require abandon-ing the interests of real oppressed people. Such de-essentializing may en-able acknowledgment of differences among women (class, race, sexual orientation, religion) and of gender and other differences within racial and ethnic communities, while encouraging local and flexible alliances and coalitions among women and between women and men.

The debates sketched thus far have primarily occurred among those committed to theory but also concerned about whether *postmodern* the-ory can be helpful in developing effective feminist and antiracist prac-tices. There has also been a contemporaneous debate about whether *theory itself* is necessary for either these political practices or for discipli-nary practices.[23] For example, hooks discusses the "antagonism toward theory that has been pervasive throughout contemporary feminist movement" (*Talking Back* 37). The "theory debates" have been especially heated in feminist literary studies, in which many apparently believe that they must choose between doing literary *criticism* and doing literary *theory* and that "real feminists" will choose the former. Particularly important are hooks's contributions to these "theory debates" because she is both a major feminist theorist (or, more accurately, a theorist of race/gender/class/culture) and a prolific critic (writing on literature, film, music, and art, with special attention to their representations of race and gender).

As theory came to have an ever stronger influence on literary and cultural studies in the 1970s and 1980s, many white feminists began to debate the values and risks of "doing theory." Nina Baym's often reprinted (and later revised) 1984 essay, "The Madwoman and Her Languages: Why I Don't Do Feminist Literary Theory," suggests at least a basic familiarity with many then-current theories that Baym nonetheless rejected. Not all subsequent critics of theory have been as well acquainted with the work being rebuffed. Baym argues that "perhaps the central issue in academic literary feminism right now is theory itself" but that the dominant current theories (e.g., psychoanalytic) are androcentric and "irretrievably misogynist" (45). Yet, indicative of the blind spots of that time for many white feminists, she does not criticize these theories for being Anglo- or Eurocentric, nor does she cite any theorists or critics of color.[24]

Shortly before Baym's essay appeared, the white feminist critic Jane Marcus had published "Storming the Toolshed" (in *Signs* in 1982). Marcus argues, "It is no historical accident that the hegemony of the theoreticians and the valorization of theory itself parallels [*sic*] the rise of feminist criticism," whose very materiality and particularity, she argues, (male) theorists wish to flee (624).[25] Yet Marcus believes that feminist literary critics' "first target" should be "the shed where the power tools of literary theory have been kept" (628), although she seems more in favor of stealing these tools to keep them out of the "masters'" hands than of actually using them.

Although Marcus barely discusses them, black feminists had already explored this dilemma of the "master's tools." In fact, Marcus's title and essay echo Audre Lorde's "The Master's Tools Will Never Dismantle the Master's House," first presented at a 1979 conference and later published in *Sister Outsider* (1984). Lorde's comments are less well known than the title of the piece (which hooks aptly calls "that much quoted yet often misunderstood cautionary statement" [*Talking Back* 36]). In my view, Lorde's essay is more a critique of the all-too-typical failure of the conference organizers to include women of color in any significant way and a call to embrace differences, so that women can "make them our strengths" (112) than it is a critique of using the "master's" theories. Although Lorde does not couch her remarks in the language of post-modern theory, I think her work anticipates—and helped enable—the embracing of difference, alterity, and heterogeneity so crucial to some recent versions of postmodernism and to many versions of feminism.

For many, Lorde's titular assertion has been taken to mean that those interested in effecting social and political change cannot and should not use (or even refashion) any existing "man-made" (or white-made) intel-lectual tools, including theory, since these are corrupted by sexism, racism, homophobia, and so on; instead, we must create new ones.[26] Yet, as hooks argues, there is "a grave difference between that engagement with white [or male] culture which seeks to deconstruct, demystify, challenge, and transform, and gestures of collaboration and complic-ity." She believes that black thinkers, including feminists, "cannot par-ticipate in dialogue that is the mark of freedom and critical agency if we dismiss all work emerging from white western traditions" (*Yearning* 110). I believe those of us interested in effecting social change should storm the toolshed, use the tools that work, reshape or discard the ones that don't, and also create new ones for new tasks.

Some black feminist critics—like some white, Chicana, Asian Ameri-can, and Native American feminists—still question both the need for and the political usefulness of theory. In two essays in *New Literary His-tory* (1987 and 1991), Joyce A. Joyce argues that male African American critics, such as Henry Louis Gates Jr. and Houston A. Baker Jr., who use poststructuralist theory (the "master's tools"?) thereby divorce them-selves from their own literary traditions and from their own blackness ("Black Canon" 337–41; "Black Woman Scholar" 552).[27] I would argue, however, that Gates's and Baker's work has encouraged more attention to issues of race by white literary critics and by other postmodern and poststructuralist theorists. Joyce also asserts that "all of the best-known Black women [literary] critics . . . have so far produced work that resists any indoctrination in deconstruction" (although she admits that Hor-tense Spillers's work displays a "poststructuralist sensibility"), while "their male peers . . . now champion the poststructuralist play with lan-guage over critical analyses that attempt to transform societal values" ("Black Woman Scholar" 552). By sharply distinguishing male from fe-male critical practices and by conflating deconstruction with all other forms of poststructuralism (e.g., the more political work of Foucault),

Joyce neglects much recent work by feminists (including black feminists such as hooks) who use and transform poststructuralist and postmodern cultural theories precisely because of a desire "to transform societal values."

The influential black feminist critic Barbara Christian expressed strong reservations about "The Race for Theory" in her essay of that name, which first appeared in 1987 in *Cultural Critique* and has been revised and reprinted several times. In Christian's view, recent (postmodern) theory is hegemonic, monolithic, and monologic, abstracted from the diversity of actual human, including literary, practices. Yet, in my view, if a postmodern theory were all of these things, it would cease to be a "postmodern" theory, at least as I use the term—which is not to deny that *some* theoretical work in the last few decades has been all of the things that Christian and other critics suggest. But much has not. Christian is troubled by what she sees as theory's support of "constructs like the *center* and the *periphery*," yet most recent theory, including hooks's work, *deconstructs* these categories rather than reinforces them.

While Christian's criticisms of contemporary theory's "linguistic jargon" and "emphasis on quoting its prophets" are apt, her comments on theory's "preoccupations with mechanical analyses of language, graphs, algebraic equations" (227) seem directed at structuralist work of the 1950s or early 1960s more than at any theories popular when she wrote the essay. She argues that theorists have "political control" and "have the power . . . to determine the ideas which are deemed valuable"; but even within the academy, such control seems at best indirect and incomplete. Yet, Christian argues that theorists have had the power to influence and even co-opt "black, women, Third World" critics into "speaking a language and defining their discussion in terms alien to and opposed to our needs and orientation" (226). As Michael Awkward notes, Christian "cannot even conceive of the possibility that these critics *choose* to employ theory because they believe it offers provocative means of discussing the texts of non-hegemonic groups" (240).[28]

hooks's belief in the importance of theory perhaps moved her to respond directly to Christian's essay. She is dismayed by the antitheoretical stance of feminists of color such as Christian, and finds it "profoundly disturbing to see how little feminist theory is being written by black women and other women of color" (*Talking Back* 38). To Christian's argument that "people of color have always theorized—but in forms quite different from the Western form of abstract logic" (226), hooks responds that this claim is "simply inaccurate" and that "had it been made by a white person . . . many more people would be disturbed by its message," which would seem racist. She notes that the Dogon people of Africa, for instance, have "very abstract logical schemas to support rituals that focus on creating gendered subjects" (*Talking Back* 39). And hooks astutely notes how often we all use abstract language (and even theory) in everyday life.

Christian makes some valuable points, nonetheless, about theory. She suggests that theorizing by people of color, especially African Americans, "is often in narrative forms, in the stories we create, in riddles and proverbs, in the play with language, since dynamic rather than fixed ideas seem more to our liking" (226). Like other feminists' (including white ones') theoretical work, hooks's writing often makes use of narrative and autobiography, for instance, but it *also* uses abstract philosophical and political language. Christian suggests a useful distinction between "theorizing" as process and "theory" as a fixed system. Perhaps it is time to rethink what we mean by theorizing and what counts as a theory, as hooks also suggests (*Talking Back* 36–37). For example, Alice Walker's speculative, narrative, poetic, autobiographical essay "In Search of Our Mothers' Gardens" (in her book of the same title) is certainly a work of both theory and theorizing, as I see it. Moreover, so is Christian's own antitheory essay, which is full of theoretical terms such as "binary," "hegemonic," and "deconstruct" and is devoted to speculation about the nature of things—past, present, and future—and thus fits my basic definition of "theory/theorizing."

I agree with hooks (and think Christian would, too) that we need "multiple theories emerging from diverse perspectives in a variety of styles." Moreover, hooks justly criticizes those for whom "only one type of theory is seen as valuable—that which is Euro-centric, linguistically convoluted, and rooted in Western white male sexist and racially biased frameworks" (*Talking Back* 37, 36). Yet this does not mean that we should *reject* rather than *reform* theory. Christian herself suggests, in "The Highs and Lows of Black Feminist Criticism" (which draws on Walker), that both the "highs" ("discourse, theory, the canon") and the "lows" ("stories, poems, plays. The language of the folk") have a place in black feminist criticism (50–51). Certainly, hooks is no friend of inaccessible and alienating jargon or of the academic hierarchies growing up around certain privileged theories. Yet, hooks's own work testifies to the possibility of accessible, illuminating, complex theory drawing on both the highs and the lows.

Rethinking Identity, Agency, and Ethics

hooks is one of the few black feminist critics/theorists who use, write about, and also critique postmodern theories; Valerie Smith, Hazel

Carby, and Hortense Spillers are some others.[29] The more political strand
of poststructuralism associated with thinkers such as Foucault and Stuart Hall runs through much of hooks's work, and she frequently uses the
concepts and strategies of "deconstruction" and "decentering." She
even deconstructs the often posited opposition between theory and
practice when she suggests that "critical practices in everyday black life
are most often deconstructive; they aim to unpack, take apart, dismem-
ber" ("Dialectically Down" 52).

Yet, hooks does not embrace poststructuralism or postmodernism
uncritically; as West notes, she "creatively appropriates" them (hooks
and West 62), refashioning them into useful tools. Nonetheless, hooks
criticizes postmodern theorists (and theorists *of* postmodernism) for
rarely acknowledging the theoretical or artistic productions and experiences of black people, particularly black women (*Yearning* 24), a point
West also makes ("Black Culture" 91–92). Moreover, hooks notes that
postmodern theory, so interested in "heterogeneity, the decentered subject . . . [the] recognition of otherness, still directs its critical voice primarily to a specialized audience that shares a common language rooted
in the very master narratives it claims to challenge" (*Yearning* 25).

In spite of her criticisms, hooks believes that postmodernist thinking
can have a "transformative impact" if it makes a "critical break with the
notion of 'authority' as 'mastery over'" (*Yearning* 25) and if it breaks
with white supremacist thinking. Her own work in theory and cultural
analysis exemplifies this kind of transformative, accessible postmodernism. By contrast, critics who do not distinguish among the various
strands of postmodernism and poststructuralism see all of them as
equally authoritarian and elitist, as denying reality in favor of language
and negating the possibility of human agency and thus of political
change. Yet, if we criticize postmodern theorists' failure to theorize adequately about differences and particulars, we should not replicate this
failure in our theorizing about theory.

hooks has repeatedly stressed the need for theory in both antiracist
and feminist struggles. She argues that "without liberatory feminist theory, there can be no effective feminist movement" (*Talking Back* 35). I
think hooks would agree with Stanlie M. James that, particularly for
black feminists, theorizing itself "is a form of agency" that can transform
the individual, the community, and the broader society (2). James's observation that "black feminism's theorizing is rooted in Black communities and nourished by them even as it challenges those very communities to address issues of internal oppression" (2) is confirmed by hooks's
own work. This sense of rootedness and responsibility may partially explain why hooks feels it is so crucial that theory "be directed to masses of

women and men in our society," not just written by and for academics (*Talking Back* 35).

As I often tell my students who are resistant to theory, all practice is embedded in theory: becoming aware of and explicit about our theoretical assumptions enables us to reflect critically on them—individually and socially—and to imagine alternatives to them. hooks and many other theorists committed to liberatory politics believe that any theory—including feminist and postmodern—must be able to meet the test of practice. In her essay, "Essentialism and Experience," hooks discusses how postmodernism's "totalizing critique of 'subjectivity, essence, identity' can seem very threatening to marginalized groups, for whom it has been an active gesture of political resistance to name one's identity" (172–73). She understands why some critics suspect it is no coincidence that postmodernists' deconstruction of the subject, voice, and identity has taken place just at the "historical moment when many subjugated people feel themselves coming to voice for the first time." Yet, hooks argues that "this sense of threat and the fear it evokes are based on a misunderstanding of the postmodernist political project" (*Yearning* 28). And she does see postmodernism as *having* a political project, unlike some of its critics.

Postmodern critiques of both gender and racial essentialism can themselves grow out of and contribute to political practices. As hooks notes, "Individual black women . . . have persisted in our efforts to deconstruct the category 'woman' and argued that gender is not the sole determinant of woman's identity" ("Essentialism" 172). The monolithic category of "woman" has been critiqued at least since the early 1980s by many feminists of color, who have argued that race and class, among other factors, intersect with gender in the construction of identity and can no longer be ignored by white feminists (see, for example, many essays in Moraga and Anzaldúa; Anzaldúa). The totalizing category of "woman" has also been called into question explicitly by some white postmodern feminists, including Kristeva (e.g., "Women's Time") and Butler.

Certainly, the differences within the category of "woman" can be established by historical or sociological work and not only by deconstructive or other postmodern approaches. Yet, hooks's view of multiple subjectivity, like Kristeva's of the "subject in process," draws on (and contributes to) the discourses of postmodernism, psychoanalysis, *and* feminism.[30] Many feminists *and* postmodernists would agree that more fluid ideas and performances of gender can enable us to move beyond binary thinking, to embrace more fully our own and the world's complexities, and to create new and more just social arrangements.[31]

Postmodern critiques of essentialism, universalism, and "static over-determined identity" can be as useful for rethinking *race* as they have been for rethinking *gender*—and for rethinking the intersections of race, class, and gender (hooks, *Yearning* 28). One of hooks's major contributions to postmodern theory has been her analysis of the relations between theories of subjectivity and theories of race. She asserts that "abandoning essentialist notions would be a serious challenge to racism" by allowing a more complex view of racial identities, including white ones (*Yearning* 28). As she argues in *Black Looks,* crucial to whites' "unlearning white supremacist attitudes and values is the deconstruction of the category 'whiteness' " (12). Scholars including hooks have recently begun to analyze whiteness, as it is conceptualized and experienced by both whites and people of color.[32]

For hooks, postmodernist antiessentialism is compatible with theories and practices of what she calls "radical black subjectivity" (*Yearning* 19). She argues that "critiques of essentialism"—most often made by postmodern and some feminist theorists—"have usefully deconstructed the idea of a monolithic homogenous black identity and experience" ("Essentialism" 172). Indeed, hooks herself has been a crucial agent in this deconstructive activity. As she argues, a monolithic or homogenous view of blackness can (like other claims about essence) result in a narrowing of possibilities and a belief that there is *one* black experience, which she sees as harmful whether this belief is held by whites seeking "*the* black perspective" or by blacks regulating the boundaries of acceptably black behavior by accusing some of not being " 'authentically' black" (*Black Looks* 52).[33]

hooks's own view of subjectivity and identity leads her, as it does other postmodernists (including postmodern feminists), to critique "identity politics" on theoretical grounds, but she is unwilling to abandon the notion of identity altogether. She recognizes "the primacy of identity politics as an important *stage* in liberation process" (*Yearning* 19, emphasis added) but also argues that "narrowly focused black identity politics do a disservice to black liberation struggle because they seek to render invisible the complex and multiple subjectivity of black folks" (*Killing Rage* 247).[34]

Moreover, hooks sees the idea of an essential, monolithic black identity as both modernist and imperialist. She believes *post*modernism can open new spaces, both real and theoretical, in which "to affirm multiple black identities, varied black experience" (*Yearning* 28). Just as she wants to complicate rather than abandon notions of *identity,* hooks is "unwilling to relinquish the power of *experience* as a standpoint on which to base analysis or formulate theory" ("Essentialism" 181–82, emphasis added). Yet, de-essentializing "experience" can allow us to account for the varieties and particularities of experiences.

Not everyone who critiques essentialism or unified subjectivity must abandon notions of "identity," "experience," "reality," or "history." As hooks argues, there may be "no normative black identity," but "there is a shared history that frames the construction of our diverse black experiences. Knowledge of that history is needed by everyone as we seek to construct self and identity" (*Killing Rage* 247). Her view of subjectivity may be part of what Avery Gordon and Christopher Newfield see as "a major development in cultural theory in the past decade": the effort to "render the use of individual and group identity fully antiessentialist *and* social" (744).[35] Certainly, hooks's model of identity is primarily a social one that retains an emphasis on lived (and shared) experience rather than essence. Her view of racial identity is similar to Michael Omi and Howard Winant's concept of "racial formation," which "emphasizes the social nature of race, the absence of any essential racial characteristics, the historical flexibility of racial meanings and categories" (4). Many feminists, including hooks, seem to posit a similar "*gender* formation," since they believe that gender identity is also socially constructed.

hooks's own theory of identity seems to have developed not only from her engagement with feminist, postmodern, postcolonial, critical race, and psychoanalytic theories but also out of her personal experience. For instance, she says she realized while a college student that her self and voice, like other African Americans', were "not unilateral, monologist, or static but rather multi-dimensional" (*Talking Back* 12). Cheryl A. Wall, also discussing the relationship between identity and experience, makes a similar point: "Appeals to experience need not be essentialist and ahistorical, because the experience of Afro-American women is unmistakably polyvalent. The simultaneity of oppression in their lives resists essentialist conclusions" (10).[36] Homans praises hooks's ability to negotiate the difficult territory between "essentialism and experience," to find ways to critique the former concept while retaining the latter (85).[37]

Perhaps any attempt, including hooks's, to reconcile postmodern deconstructions of the subject with the need of black women and others to see themselves as—and to *be,* or at least to act as though they *are*—agentic subjects of experience and history can be at best only partially successful. Even if we are willing to accept the multiplicity and diversity of the *experiences* that shape postmodern/black subjectivity as well as the heterogeneity and "split-ness" of the *subject,* we still need to theorize more fully *who* or *what* is this (heterogeneous) subject of (heterogeneous) experience. What is it in the subject that experiences something capable of being perceived, described, or analyzed *as* a discrete experience? Such questions are central to the ongoing conversations, especially among feminists and other politically minded theorists, about agency, identity, and change—dialogues to which hooks has much to contribute.

Yet, some critics of postmodernism claim that, by problematizing identity and rejecting essence, postmodernism eliminates the possibility of agency (both individual and collective) and thus cannot be useful for feminist or antiracist struggles. Agency has been a special concern in much recent feminist theory. I define "agency" as the power to choose, to act, to change oneself and/or the world. Since most versions of postmodern theory assume the social, ideological, psychoanalytic, and/or linguistic construction or determination of the subject, the argument runs, how can such theory include the possibility of not-always-already-determined acts and choices? Linda Hutcheon argues that postmodernism *has* no theory of agency, whereas feminism must (*Politics* 22). Linda Alcoff critiques poststructuralists for neither theorizing nor allowing for agency since they believe in "a total construction of the subject" that eliminates "the subject's ability to reflect on the social discourse and challenge its determinations" (417).

Although these may be apt criticisms of some postmodernist and poststructuralist theories, they certainly do not apply to hooks's work or to that of most other *feminist* postmodernists (or other politically oriented postmodernists). I agree with hooks that "postmodern critiques of essentialism . . . can open up new possibilities for the construction of self and the assertion of agency" (*Yearning* 28). She defines "agency" as "the ability to act in one's best interest" (hooks and West 11), and she believes that, among other things, critical consciousness can enable one to achieve agency. Agency is also, as Kristeva puts it, the ability to "speak in a different manner than our familial and social determination" (qtd. in Clark and Hulley 175), an ability she, too, thinks we have or can attain.[38] For feminist postmodernists like hooks and Kristeva, we can speak *and* be differently, act in our own *and* others' best interests; thus, agency is possible, even though we must struggle to achieve it.

For hooks, theorizing about and engaging in critical analyses of culture are crucial forms of agency. So is any form of "talking back." Such talking back or "true speaking is not solely an expression of creative power; it is an act of resistance, a political gesture that challenges politics of domination that would render us nameless and voiceless." As hooks sees it, such "speaking becomes both a way to engage in active self-transformation and a rite of passage where one moves from being object to being subject" (*Talking Back* 8, 12).

Transgressive, counterhegemonic artistic practices provide another means of "talking back." Part of hooks's project is to "create work that shares with an audience, particularly oppressed and marginalized groups, the sense of agency artistry offers, the empowerment" (*Yearning* 111). Alice Walker makes a similar argument in "In Search of our Mothers' Gardens" that creativity is necessary to express both spirit and agency. For hooks, creating art and theorizing about art can both be agentic practices. Critical analysis of aesthetic experience can contribute to (rather than impede) one's pleasure in it and can also enhance art's ability to be counterhegemonic (*Yearning* 111).

But can art, especially postmodern art, be politically effective, or is this a utopian (or academic) dream?[39] hooks asserts that art in African American communities has always been seen as inherently political (*Yearning* 105). She believes that even postmodern art (literature, music, film, etc.)—whether by artists of color or white artists—can have socially and individually transformative power. Terry Eagleton and others have argued that postmodern art is too ironic, depthless, and self-reflexive to be political. Yet many critics' very definitions of postmodern art have been developed from generalizing about works that exhibit these qualities (e.g., Donald Barthelme's fiction or Andy Warhol's paintings).[40] If one decided, instead, that Toni Morrison's recent novels were paradigmatically postmodern, one's definition would not include depthlessness or irony as central features of postmodernism but might include, instead, stylistic and temporal experimentation linked to political and moral vision.

As hooks sees it, many black writers, artists, and cultural critics who work "on the margins" (a group in which she places herself) are "avantgarde" (and, implicitly, postmodern) in that they "eschew essentialist notions of identity, and fashion selves that emerge from the meeting of diverse epistemologies, habits of being, concrete class locations, and radical political commitments" (*Yearning* 19). I believe that this idea of *positional, situated self-fashioning* provides a welcome alternative to the binary choice (often implicit in feminist critiques of postmodernism) between the postmodern subject (totally constructed and determined) and the Enlightenment subject (individual, rational, and self-willed). For many theorists (including many Marxists), the subject's construction is *not* total, since the system (language, patriarchy, the base) that constructs the subject is itself not total but riddled by gaps and contradictions. What hooks adds to postmodern and feminist theories of the heterogeneous, nonunified "subject in process" (Kristeva's term) is a crucial reminder that the construction of subjectivity also occurs in the context of real material conditions and experiences that are shaped not only by gender but also by race, class, sexual orientation, geography, and so on. For hooks, subjects are neither disembodied and purely textualized nor unified and self-contained.

Subjects inhabit a world full of other subjects. It is the subject's relation to the "other"—and choice to treat the other as subject or object—that is the concern of ethics as well as politics. Ethical practices, too, are a form of agency and, like aesthetic and political practices, can be socially transformative. In the rejection of ethical meta-narratives and abstract principles in favor of an ethics of *practice,* hooks's ethics is postmodern. Kristeva, another postmodern feminist thinker on ethics, defines the ethical simply as "reaching out to the other" ("Stabat Mater" 182), embracing and respecting the alterity of both others and oneself.[41] The ground of hooks's ethics is this *"mutual recognition* (what I call the 'subject-to-subject' encounter, as opposed to 'subject-to-object')" (hooks, *Outlaw Culture* 241). As hooks asserts, "positive recognition and acceptance of difference is a necessary starting point" for any ethical human relationship and especially for eradicating white supremacy as well as maintaining black community (*Black Looks* 13).[42] But one cannot only see the *otherness* of the other; it is important to seek grounds of *commonality,* too.

One relationship that acknowledges both difference and similarity is love. For hooks, love is a crucial part of ethics and agency; it is necessary for individual and communal psychological health (as she discusses in *Sisters of the Yam*) and for effective politics. She believes in the power of love, which for her is linked to dialogue, empathy, and respect. As hooks puts it, Paolo Freire, who strongly influenced her, "always says that it is dialogue that is the true act of love between two subjects, and points out again and again, drawing on Che Guevara and others, that there can be no revolution without love" (hooks and West 2–3). She also shares Martin Luther King's "conviction that it is in choosing love, and beginning with love as the ethical foundation for politics, that we are best positioned to transform the society in ways that enhance the collective good." Without an "ethic of love" informing our political work, "we are often seduced . . . into continued allegiance to systems of domination—imperialism, sexism, racism, classism" (*Outlaw Culture* 247, 243). Cornel West, with whom hooks has often been in dialogue (both literal and figurative), also argues that a "love ethic" is necessary for what he calls a "politics of conversion" that can provide hope and agency to oppressed people (*Race Matters*). Both hooks's and West's emphasis on love—especially love expressed as recognition of and service to others—is influenced by religious discourses about love: Christianity, liberation theology, and, for hooks, Buddhism. But in their linking of love and politics, the personal and the political, hooks and West have also been influenced by feminism and postmodernism.[43]

Yet hooks would acknowledge that "recognition of the Other" (*Outlaw Culture* 241) is a *necessary* but not *sufficient* condition for eradicating oppression and domination. She concurs with Barbara Smith's criticism "of people thinking that oppression is only a matter of how we treat one another." Nonetheless, "how we treat one another socially and in our theories about the world affects political life" (Childers and hooks 73). For hooks, theories have real-world import, and ethical practices have political consequences.[44]

How *feminists* treat each other is an important concern for hooks as well, since such interpersonal relations can determine the future political directions and successes of antisexist and antiracist struggles. She argues that "one of the most important dimensions of feminist struggle" is feminist ethics, which means "acting out an ethical commitment to feminist solidarity that begins first with our regarding one another with respect" (*Yearning* 99, 92). Feminist ethics—and ethical feminism—entails the embracing of particularities and differences, the multiple and shifting identities that postmodernism also stresses. hooks's very choice to drop the definite article when describing "feminist movement" reflects her belief that feminism, like emancipation, is a *process* (Childers and hooks 68).

Indeed, hooks has long stressed the importance of acknowledging and respecting differences—among and within women, political projects, communities, theories, and all subjects. She thinks that even the "category 'women of color' works to erase class and other differences among us" (Childers and hooks 78), differences that require feminists'— and everyone's—attention.[45]

Nonetheless, in addition to seeing and valuing differences, feminists and all of us concerned with eradicating racism, sexism, and other forms of domination must find common grounds, even if shifting ones, in order to effect change. In one of her early books, *Feminist Theory: From Margin to Center,* hooks argues that political solidarity is crucial for feminists, but, "rather than bond on the basis of shared victimization or in response to a false sense of a common enemy [men], we can bond on the basis of our political commitment to a feminist movement that aims to end sexist oppression" as well as racism (47). Her recent work, influenced by postmodernism, suggests that neither can women bond solely on the basis of shared identity or essence *as* women, since both "women" and "identity" are heterogeneous, multiple, shifting sites. Yet, in lieu of "identity-based bonding, we might be drawn together by a *commonality of feeling*" (*Outlaw Culture* 217) or by shared interests, goals, experiences (when these indeed are shared), and commitments.

We often talk about postmodernism with metaphors of loss, rejection, abandonment—of meta-narratives, foundations, absolutes, faith. Yet it is also possible to see postmodernism as a moment of regeneration, as a time of proliferating possibilities: new discourses, media, voices, identities, and social and political relationships. Thus, like hooks, I would stress respect, love, and commitment to emancipatory struggles as necessary corollaries (or complements) to postmodern dispersion, deconstruction, and difference.

As hooks both theorizes about and engages in postmodernly transgressive, counterhegemonic, avant-garde aesthetic practices, her work performs a typically postmodern blurring of boundaries: between "creative" and "critical" writing, between academic and everyday discourses, between "high" and popular culture, and between personal and political analyses. Her discussions of both individual cultural artifacts and broader cultural formations reveal her awareness of the power of representation(s) to shape and not merely to reflect the sociopolitical order. In all of her work, she explores questions of difference, discourse, and power—questions at the forefront in at least *some* versions of both feminism and postmodernism. By her willingness to draw on a wide repertoire of theoretical and practical approaches to analyze domination and support the struggles against it, hooks seems to exemplify postmodern heterogeneity and boundary crossing.

Postmodernism is itself subject to the boundary crossing, heterogeneity, and change that it often explores. Perhaps we have always had not one unitary postmodernism but many *different* postmodernisms, with different relationships to *issues* of difference and different political, theoretical, and aesthetic agendas. hooks's recent work enables—and requires—a rethinking of postmodern theories and practices; it suggests new ethical, aesthetic, and political possibilities for postmodernism, as her earlier work did for feminism. hooks illuminates the relations between postmodern and oppositional cultural practices, between practice and theory, between women of color and white women, between women and men, and between our desires for community and our awareness of particularity and difference. Through a feminist postmodernist practice, bell hooks enables us to reimagine postmodernism as resistant, radical, and capable of contributing to emancipatory struggles.

NOTES

1. In her chapter "Postmodern Blackness," hooks uses the term "postmodernism of resistance," which I have borrowed for my title (*Yearning* 30).

2. hooks has written more than ten books and numerous articles (in both scholarly and popular periodicals) on feminism and feminist theory, contemporary culture, progressive politics, and race and racism. In *Talking Back* (1989), *Yearning* (winner of the American Book Award in 1991), *Breaking Bread* (1991; with Cornel West), *Black Looks* (1992), *Sisters of the Yam* (1993), *Teaching to Transgress* (1994), *Outlaw Culture* (1994), *Art on My Mind* (1995), and *Killing Rage* (1995), her diverse topics have included "gangsta rap," films by Spike Lee and Wim Wenders, the Clarence Thomas hearings, Zora Neale Hurston, Madonna, sex, spirituality, black self-love, and African American art.

3. For broader analyses of black women's relationship to feminism, historically and currently (a vast topic outside the scope of this essay), see Collins, *Black Feminist Thought;* V. Smith, "Black Feminist Theory and the Representation of the 'Other' "; James and Busia, *Theorizing Black Feminisms;* and hooks, *Ain't I a Woman.*

4. In this essay, I focus primarily on the debates about theory and postmodernism among white and African American feminist scholars. But, as the other essays in this collection attest, women of color other than African Americans have also debated the need for and desirability of engagement with postmodern and/ or poststructuralist discourses. Among feminists of color who have engaged with and thus helped to reshape these discourses are Paula Gunn Allen, Norma Alarcón, Trinh T. Minh-ha, and subjects of and contributors to the present volume.

5. For histories of the term "postmodernism"—its meaning, applications, and trajectory—see Hassan, "Toward a Concept of Postmodernism" in his *Postmodern Turn;* Hutcheon, *Poetics of Postmodernism* (esp. chap. 1); Hoesterey, introduction to *Zeigeist in Babel;* and Huyssen, "Mapping the Postmodern," in his *After the Great Divide.*

6. Ihab Hassan, probably the first scholar in the United States to theorize about and advocate postmodern literature and art, often provided long lists of names of those he considered "postmodern" when he wished to define postmodernism; see, for example, his essays, written from the late 1960s through the late 1980s, collected in *The Postmodern Turn.*

7. For example, see Hoesterey, *Zeitgeist in Babel* (xi) and Suleiman, "Feminism and Postmodernism" (183–84). As Suleiman notes (184), Lyotard himself credits Hassan for the term "postmodernism" (Lyotard 85). Huyssen cites both Lyotard and Kristeva for importing the term from the United States to Europe (184), although I would argue that Kristeva generally uses "postmodernism" to refer to artistic/literary avant-gardes and not to an entire cultural condition (e.g., Kristeva, "Postmodernism?").

8. Fredric Jameson, an influential figure in recent debates about postmodernism, views it as the "cultural logic of late capitalism" ("Postmodernism" 53; see also Lyotard, *Postmodern Condition*). Meta-narratives of modernity and postmodernity, as of modernism and postmodernism, have been based almost exclusively on Euramerican white, elite intellectual and social history, with some recent attention to Japan. We may need more local narratives and fewer meta-narratives of postmodernism as we move into the twenty-first century.

9. But see Huyssen, who argues that "poststructuralism is primarily a discourse of and about modernism" (207). His versions of poststructuralism and postmodernism, though, are primarily those of the 1970s and 1980s, before work by feminist, postcolonial, and critical race theorists had begun to change their direction.

10. Although many who write *about* postmodernism maintain a traditional academic style, in other work these two categories overlap; for example, Hassan has often written experimental, postmodern texts *about* postmodernism (e.g., *Paracriticisms*). Like hooks's work, some feminist writing on both postmodernism and other topics is postmodern in its blurring of generic categories (e.g., autobiography and theory), its multiple styles and voices, and its open-endedness.

11. In 1983, Craig Owens lamented "the absence of discussions of sexual difference in writings about postmodernism, as well as the fact that few women have engaged in the modernism/postmodernism debate." But rather than claiming this was because feminism and postmodernism were at odds, he argues that "women's insistence on difference and incommensurability may not only be compatible with, but also an instance of postmodern thought" (61–62). A few years later, Huyssen said he found it "baffling" that feminists had not been more involved in discussions of postmodernism (198). It is interesting that two male writers on postmodernism would be among the first to notice and begin to remedy the then-current lack of dialogue between feminism and postmodernism.

12. And if feminist theorists and critics often feel obliged to familiarize themselves with postmodernism and poststructuralism, shouldn't (male) postmodernists and poststructuralists feel similarly obliged to familiarize themselves with feminism?

13. Owens makes a similar point. Flax's essay and Tress's reply (both in *Signs*) provide a good overview of the debates between feminist critics and feminist advocates of Enlightenment rationality and individualism. Fraser and Nicholson suggest that a *cautious* alliance between feminism and postmodernism can be productive for both but also believe that feminists need not forswear metanarratives and grand theory. They argue that postmodern-feminist critique must be historically specific, pragmatic, cross-cultural, nonuniversalist, and based on a politics of alliance rather than on shared identity or essence (34–35).

14. For hooks, as for many feminists, it is crucial to analyze the *intersections* and *interactions* of race, gender, class, and other facets of identity and social experience (e.g., sexual orientation, geographic location).

15. hooks's collaborative book with West, *Breaking Bread,* may also be postmodern, as Collins suggests, in its very format as primarily a collection of dialogues between hooks and West, who "maintain the postmodern notion of multiple voices by alternating chapters" (178).

16. I am trying to avoid these dangers, as well as those analyzed in recent essays by Homans, V. Smith, and duCille. I am trying to speak in dialogue *with* (rather than *for* or *to*) the "other" (whose other I am). Thus, hooks's own voice and words play a large role in this essay. I take to heart hooks's warning that "when we write about the experiences of a group to which we do not belong, we should think about the ethics of our action, considering whether or not our work will be used to reinforce and perpetuate domination." Nonetheless, hooks believes in "cross-ethnic feminist scholarship" when it is undertaken with an awareness of one's motives and of the limits of one's "authority" (*Talking Back* 43, 48). I have thought much about my own positionality and my motives in

writing this essay. I think I was moved to write about hooks's work for many of the same reasons that I have written about Kristeva's work (and probably as many differences separate me from Kristeva as from hooks—albeit *different* differences): I respect hooks's work, find that it engages many of my own concerns, and believe that it moves me—and can move others—toward new ways of thinking. hooks addresses many of the critical issues of our time, and I hope to see more academics—especially those interested in postmodernism, contemporary theory, and postmodern feminism—seriously reading, discussing, and writing about her work (and not just mentioning or footnoting her once or twice, as many white feminists and some feminists of color now do; indeed, very few white postmodern theorists or theorists of postmodernism do even that). As far as I've been able to discover, apart from interviews and book reviews, there is not yet a scholarly article or book devoted entirely to hooks.

17. Perhaps as a Jew in the United States, I am especially open to a deconstruction of racial identity, since I believe Jews occupy a liminal space—neither truly white (ask any white supremacist) nor people of color, since most of us would acknowledge our white skin privilege and, in America at least, *relative* economic privilege and lack of overt discrimination against us. Yet we may recall that, even during the era of the civil rights movement, there were still some opportunities closed to Jews, too, in this country (in jobs, housing, college admissions, etc.). And it is worth noting the increasing number of anti-Semitic incidents in the United States and around the world. Some might see "Jewishness" not as *racial* but as religious. The Nazis, though, certainly viewed Jewishness as racial, as a matter of blood, not of religious choice. Perhaps most American and European Jews "pass" as white—until times get tough or people get mean (or anxious). (Obviously, there are also Jews of color, e.g., Ethiopian Jews and African American converts to Judaism.) I have taken to calling myself and other (white) Jews "beige"—a shade between whiteness and other colors. And I believe that if I ever visit the town in Latvia from which all four of my grandparents hailed, I would not be welcomed as a Latvian but seen as a Jew, a foreigner, a racial other. We legitimately call what has happened, since slavery, to so many people of African descent a "diaspora," but we must also remember the diaspora of Jews centuries earlier.

After I had written this note, I discovered that in her just-then-published *Killing Rage* hooks discusses the complexities of black-Jewish relations within feminism and in culture as a whole. In "Keeping a Legacy of Shared Struggle," hooks notes the "global development of anti-Semitism and anti-black racism" (204). A true relationship of mutual recognition and solidarity and the potential for effective "shared struggle" can only be realized if (white) Jews and blacks (and all people of color) recognize their specific positionalities and histories as well as their commonalities within white supremacy (204–14). See Bulkin, Pratt, and Smith's germinal feminist analyses of the relations between Jews and blacks, racism and anti-Semitism in *Yours in Struggle*.

18. Terry Eagleton, for example, criticizes postmodernism for effacing history (68) and for being, among other things, "a sick joke at the expense" of what he sees as the truly "revolutionary art of the twentieth-century avant garde" (60). For a useful survey of the debates about postmodernism (primarily postmodern art and literature rather than theory), see Hutcheon, *Politics* (esp. chap. 1). Hutcheon views postmodern texts as political primarily in their ability to problematize cultural representations but thinks that postmodernism is engaged in

both "complicity" with and "critique" of the dominant social and political orders. For broader overviews of the "can postmodernism be political?" debate, see
Huyssen, *After the Great Divide;* Jameson, *Political Unconscious;* and Edelstein, "Toward a Feminist Postmodern *Poléthique."*

19. West argues that Derrida, Lyotard, and even Foucault work largely within
"Eurocentric frameworks and modernist loyalties"; for West, Lyotard's theories
of postmodernism are "a kind of European navel-gazing in which postmodernism becomes a recurring moment within the modern." West also believes
postmodernism should be viewed as "a social category" rather than, as it often is,
an aesthetic one ("Black Culture" 88–89).

20. Giroux praises postmodernism for its "opening up of the world to cultural
and ethnic differences" (40). Flax argues that "as much as, if not more than postmodernism, the writings of women of color have compelled white feminists to
confront problems of difference and the relations of domination that are the
conditions of possibility for the coherence of our own theorizing and category
formation" (*Disputed Subjects* 145).

21. Owens, too, notes the similarity between master and meta-narratives:
"*Master narrative*—how else to translate Lyotard's *grand récit?"* (65). The term
"master narrative" is Jameson's, who uses it to refer to "allegorical narrative
signifieds" that are "deeper, underlying . . . hidden," inscribed both in texts and
in "our collective thinking and collective fantasies about history and reality" (*Political Unconscious* 34, 28).

22. It still often seems that scholarly work on feminism is likely to be about
white feminism—without saying so—when it isn't specifically *about* or *by* feminists of color (or focused on the relations between white feminists and feminists
of color). My thanks, or apologies, to Gloria (now Akasha) T. Hull, Patricia Bell
Scott, and Barbara Smith for this paraphrase of their book's title.

23. While some white feminist *theorists,* such as Flax (a political scientist and
psychotherapist) and Butler (a philosopher), use and challenge postmodern theory, many white and black feminist *literary critics* (like many feminist practitioners and activists) are suspicious of theory in general and postmodern theory in
particular. As I note below, hooks is both a theorist and a critic (of literature and
other cultural "texts"), as well as an activist. I invoke here a traditional distinction between literary criticism (analyses or interpretations of specific literary
works) and literary theory (speculations on the nature of interpretation, literature, language, etc.). But criticism and theory inevitably overlap. How can there
be a literary criticism not based on at least unconsciously held theoretical assumptions or any literary theories not derived at least in part from the reading of
literary texts? And what political practices are not based on theories (even if
unarticulated or unconscious ones) about the way things have been, are, might
be in the future—and why? Can any theory survive if it is not at all accountable
to or useful for practice?

24. Perhaps the most direct response to Baym's essay is Finke's insightful
"Rhetoric of Marginality: Why I Do Feminist Theory." Finke argues that theory is
crucial for developing the "subversive, demystifying potential of feminist criticism" (252) and for enabling feminists more effectively to "deconstruct—subvert—the hierarchical center/margin dichotomy, unmasking the reified categories that underwrite gender distinctions" (266). Yet, she does not address the
center/margin dichotomies in feminism itself that were being revealed at the
time of her essay's publication (1986); for example, hooks's *Feminist Theory* came

out in 1984. And, as was typical of most work by white feminists until rather recently, Finke does not discuss any feminists of color. I do not exempt myself from
this criticism; many of us white (and beige) academics were taught (from K–12
through graduate school) little or nothing about or by people of color and have
only recently begun both to educate ourselves and to realize how crucial it is to
interrogate and reimagine notions of "race" and our own racial identities and
racist socialization. I think (hope?) I am avoiding what duCille calls the "dangerous strategy, but one that seems to be popular among white readers of 'black
texts,' who feel compelled to supplement their critiques with exposés of their
former racism (and/or sexism) in a kind of I-once-was-blind-but-now-I-see
way"—especially when what that "I" sees is "you," the racialized "other" (610).
We must remember that everyone and every group is somebody's or some group's
other.

    25. Marcus credits Annette Kolodny (a white feminist critic) for the martial
metaphors Marcus extends in this essay (623), but Marcus seems to be borrowing
Lorde's title and metaphor without actually citing her (although she does cite
another essay of Lorde's (622n. 2) and may be assuming her audience will recognize her title as paying homage to Lorde).

    26. For example, McKay argues that "most women of color readily agree with
Audre Lorde's astute pronouncement that it is impossible to destroy the master's
house with the master's tools," although McKay notes that this pronouncement
is primarily directed at white feminists who have often replicated—and should
learn to avoid—the "master's" way of doing business (162).

    27. Both Gates and Baker were asked to respond to Joyce's essay in the same is-
sue of the journal; she also responded to their responses. These debates have become infamous, especially for their intensity and personal attacks. Gates defends
himself by saying he has "tried to work through contemporary theories of literature *not* to 'apply' them to black texts, but rather to *transform* by *translating* them
into a new rhetorical realm" (351). He believes using extant theories will enable
black critics to develop "indigenous black principles of criticism" to apply to
black literary traditions (352). I agree with Gates that many of "those who are
'against theory' and believe in common sense are merely in the grip of another
theory" (359; see also Baker, "In Dubious Battle").

    28. Awkward argues that full understanding and canonical acceptance of
literature by black women "will require that its critics continue to move beyond
description and master the discourse of contemporary literary theory" (243). He
further argues that African American critics should "appropriate" the "master's
tools" just as African American novelists and poets have successfully appropriated "putatively superior Western cultural and expressive systems—Christianity,
the English language, Western literary genres" by "transferring them into forms
through which we expressed our culturally distinct black souls" (244).

    29. I mention only some well-known black feminists who write both literary
criticism and about theory. Some black feminist critics draw on poststructuralist
theory in their analyses of literary texts. See, for example, some of the essays in
Wall, *Changing Our Own Words.* V. Smith suggests that black feminist criticism
has recently entered a more theoretical "third stage," "increasingly self-conscious
and self-reflexive, examining ways in which literary study—the . . . meaning of influence, . . . tradition, . . . literature itself—changes once questions of race, class,
and gender become central to the process of literary analysis" (46). Wallace,
whose recent work on popular culture uses postmodern theory extensively, says

she is "firmly convinced that if black feminism, or the feminism of women of color, is going to thrive on any level as cultural analysis, it cannot continue to ignore the way that Freud, Marx, Saussure, Nietzsche, Lévi-Strauss, Lacan, Derrida, and Foucault have forever altered the credibility of obvious truth, 'common sense,' or any unitary conception of reality. Moreover, there are many feminists who are practicing cultural studies, postmodernist, deconstructive, and psychoanalytic criticism who can contribute to our formulations if we read them against the grain" ("Negative Images" 658).

Wallace included an essay by hooks in her collection *Black Popular Culture.* Wallace's and hooks's work seemed quite compatible, especially in their commitments to (black) feminism and to theory, as well as their mutual interest in popular culture. Thus, many were quite surprised to see, in late 1995, Wallace's scathing—and very personal—attack on hooks's *Art on My Mind,* in which Wallace accuses hooks of being "self-righteous," "self-indulgent," and of engaging in both political sloganeering and "relentless guilt-mongering" ("Art"). Wallace sees herself as the first black feminist brave enough to challenge the "one-woman black feminist cottage industry" that is hooks, in her view. Wallace also reiterates some not uncommon criticisms of hooks's work: that hooks eschews footnotes and traditional scholarly documentation, that her books are largely compilations of already published and often brief essays and reviews, that she (over)indulges in "autobiographical reveries," that she is repetitive, and that she overuses jargon and political catchphrases (e.g., "counterhegemonic," "white supremacy"). hooks has occasionally addressed such criticisms and certainly can "defend" herself. But I would like to note that I think Wallace's review not only takes some crucial quotations from *Art on My Mind* out of context but also decontextualizes hooks's work as a whole. While I do think that it would be nice to see hooks expanding and doing more to link previously published essays when she puts them into book form, I think that many of the "sins" Wallace accuses hooks of committing are actually part of hooks's effort to create a new discursive space on the thresholds between scholarly and popular writing, between the theoretical and the practical, between the personal and the professional. Repetition is a time-honored and often effective device in religious and political rhetoric intended to spur change in the audience and in society. White supremacy continues to exist and should be named. While it is true that far fewer white than black feminists have criticized hooks's work (for a complex set of ideological, personal, and other reasons—including respect for and appreciation of hooks's work), many black feminists, scholars, activists, and writers find hooks's work invaluable. See, for example, Hixon, who, in the *Black Collegian,* calls *Killing Rage* a "must-read" and finds hooks's anger empowering and productive of hope.

30. One can see the influence of contemporary psychoanalytic theory when, for example, hooks notes that, "psychoanalytically, it is clear that the unitary self is sustained only by acts of coercive control and repression" (*Killing Rage* 249). Her belief in the importance of analyzing psychological dimensions of racial identity and of racism—a belief I share—is apparent in much of her work, especially *Sisters of the Yam.*

31. Butler persuasively argues for the political usefulness of moving beyond essentialist "identity politics" (see esp. the conclusion of *Gender Trouble*). Giroux also notes that the various postmodernisms share a "rejection of absolute essences" (18). See also Fuss, *Essentially Speaking,* and hooks's insightful review of it, "Essentialism and Experience."

32. See hooks's chapters "Representations of Whiteness in the Black Imagination" (*Black Looks*) and "Representing Whiteness: Seeing Wings of Desire" (*Yearning*). On the interdependence of the concepts of whiteness and blackness, see Morrison, *Playing in the Dark*. Some white theorists, too, are beginning to explore whiteness, no longer seeing it as normative or as the "unmarked case." See Keating, "Interrogating Whiteness," for a perceptive analysis of the complexities of rethinking whiteness and race itself.

33. hooks's nonessentialist view of race and gender also opens a space for entering "the discourse of the other." In a 1994 seminar at Stanford University, hooks said she rejects the claim that one cannot possibly understand something one has not experienced (e.g., being black or being a woman), because to accept that claim relieves one of accountability for even *trying* to understand others' experiences. I agree with hooks that there are ways (e.g., studying others' historical experiences, reading literary or cultural texts by those unlike ourselves) to develop our ability to imagine the other and thus both to respect and empathize with that other ("Essentialism" 182). Those of us whose vocation is teaching must have faith that learning is possible, that there are ways to know (even if only partially, and, as hooks says, *differently*) what others have thought and experienced. For many of us, feminist, multicultural, critical, and liberatory pedagogy is an important form of feminist and antiracist activism.

34. As Alexander puts it, while hooks "critiques again and again the narrow politics of identity that would deny black diversity," she actually "wishes not to discard subjectivity but to multiply black subjectivities in a way that still somehow encourages unification" (182).

35. Gordon and Newfield also note that such "antiessentialist uses of identity have been pioneered by feminist thought, race and postcolonial studies, and lesbian and gay studies" that have "emphasized the variable, indeterminate, shifting boundaries of any group identity" (744). I would add that postmodernism and poststructuralism have also influenced these antiessentialist views of identity.

36. Some might see this "polyvalence" of experience as true for all "postmodern subjects." For instance, Bordo argues that hooks and Flax take seriously the poststructuralist " 'decentering' of the subject—*not,* however, as a methodological or theoretical dogma (according to which any articulation of identity, of the 'we,' is a totalizing fiction) but as part of the lived experience of acting, thinking, writing in fragmenting times. For neither of them is this decentering wholly positive" (283).

37. See also duCille, who asks, "How do we [black feminist academics] negotiate an intellectually charged space for experience in a way that is not totalizing and essentializing—a space that acknowledges the constructedness of and the differences within our lived experiences while at the same time attending to the inclining, rather than the declining, significance of race, class, culture, and gender?" (607).

38. For Kristeva, the speaking subject, although always "in process," can nonetheless "get pleasure from . . . [and] even endanger" the sociosymbolic system ("System" 29, 30). As Friedman has argued, agency is among those once legitimized, then taboo concepts (along with identity and experience) coming back into play in "post/poststructuralist" discourses, largely through the interventions into poststructuralist theorizing by feminists and theorists of race and postcoloniality.

39. As Felski notes, "One of the most important achievements of the women's movement has been to repoliticize art on the level of both production and reception" (175). I think that white women writers and writers of color have also repoliticized postmodern art.

40. For example, in "POSTFACE 1982," Hassan provides almost a full page of names "to adumbrate postmodernism" in both the arts and theory (*Dismemberment* 260). That list includes only one (white) woman theorist (Kristeva) and one (white) woman writer (Christine Brooke-Rose). Although he includes three (male) Latin American writers (Cortázar, Borges, and García Marquez), there are no U.S. writers or theorists of color on his list.

41. I develop this point in "Toward a Feminist Postmodern *Poléthique.*" Giroux also notes the inextricability of ethics and politics, both of which concern the "relationship between the self and the other" (48). So does teaching, about which both Giroux and hooks, like their mentor Freire, have written (see hooks, *Teaching to Transgress*).

42. hooks warns of the "commodification of difference," particularly by white theorists, who may consume, decontextualize, and dehistoricize "the other" (*Black Looks* 31). Yet she also argues that "whenever there's the possibility for exploitation, what intervenes is *recognition of the Other* . . . that seems to disrupt the possibility of domination." Kristeva believes that psychoanalysis can help us see that "the other is in me. It is my unconscious" (qtd. in Clark and Hulley 164). Heeding Kristeva's call for us to recognize ourselves as other to ourselves and as someone else's other (*Nations without Nationalism; Strangers to Ourselves*) may also help whites avoid the trap hooks notes of seeing only people of color as other.

43. Clearly, hooks and West do not reject all meta-narratives or foundations but interrogate, adapt, and appropriate those that seem vital. In their work, faith, love, and emancipation are foundational beliefs. I believe that one can be eclectically and selectively, rather than devoutly, postmodern. Actually, "impure" postmodernism may be the *most* postmodern.

44. See also West, who stresses the need to address both values and institutional structures in efforts to combat racism, "lived nihilism," and poverty (*Race Matters*).

45. Spivak also critiques the term "women of color" for effacing real differences among women around the world.

WORKS CITED

Alcoff, Linda. "Cultural Feminism versus Post-Structuralism: The Identity Crisis in Feminist Theory." *Signs* 13 (1988): 405–36.

Alexander, Natalie. "Piecings from a Second Reader." Review of *Yearning: Race, Gender, and Cultural Politics,* by bell hooks. *Hypatia* 7 (1992): 177–87.

Anzaldúa, Gloria, ed. *Making Face, Making Soul/Haciendo Caras: Creative and Critical Perspectives by Feminists of Color.* San Francisco: Aunt Lute Books, 1990.

Awkward, Michael. "Appropriative Gestures: Theory and Afro-American Literary Criticism." *Gender and Theory.* Ed. Kauffman. 238–46.

Baker, Houston A., Jr. "In Dubious Battle." *New Literary History* 18 (1987): 363–69.

Baym, Nina. "The Madwoman and Her Languages: Why I Don't Do Feminist Literary Theory." *Feminist Issues in Literary Scholarshop.* Ed. Shari Benstock. Bloomington: Indiana University Press, 1987. 45–61.

Bordo, Susan. *Unbearable Weight: Feminism, Western Culture, and the Body.* Berkeley: University of California Press, 1993.

Bulkin, Elly, Minnie Bruce Pratt, and Barbara Smith. *Yours in Struggle: Three Feminist Perspectives on Anti-Semitism and Racism.* Brooklyn: Long Haul Press, 1984.

Butler, Judith. "Contingent Foundations: Feminism and the Question of 'Postmodernism.'" *Feminists Theorize the Political.* Ed. Judith Butler and Joan W. Scott. New York: Routledge, 1992. 3–21.

———. *Gender Trouble: Feminism and the Subversion of Identity.* New York: Routledge, 1990.

Childers, Mary, and bell hooks. "A Conversation about Race and Class." *Conflicts in Feminism.* Ed. Marianne Hirsch and Evelyn Fox Keller. New York: Routledge, 1990. 60–81.

Christian, Barbara. "The Highs and Lows of Black Feminist Criticism." *Reading Black, Reading Feminist: A Critical Anthology.* Ed. Henry Louis Gates Jr. New York: Meridian/Penguin, 1990. 44–51.

———. "The Race for Theory." *Gender and Theory.* Ed. Kauffman. 225–37.

Clark, Suzanne, and Kathleen Hulley. "An Interview with Julia Kristeva: Cultural Strangeness and the Subject in Crisis." *Discourse* 13 (1990–91): 149–80.

Collins, Patricia Hill. Review of *Breaking Bread: Insurgent Black Intellectual Life,* by bell hooks and Cornel West, and *Segregated Sisterhood: Racism and the Politics of American Feminism,* by Nancie Caraway. *Signs* 20 (1994): 176–79.

———. *Black Feminist Thought: Knowledge, Consciousness, and the Politics of Empowerment.* Boston: Unwin Hyman, 1990.

Derrida, Jacques. "Structure, Sign, and Play in the Discourse of the Human Sciences." *The Structuralist Controversy: The Languages of Criticism and the Sciences of Man.* Ed. Richard Macksey and Eugenio Donato. Baltimore: Johns Hopkins University Press, 1970. 247–72.

Di Stefano, Christine. "Dilemmas of Difference: Feminism, Modernity, and Postmodernism." *Feminism/Postmodernism.* Ed. Nicholson. 63–82.

duCille, Ann. "The Occult of True Black Womanhood: Critical Demeanor and Black Feminist Studies." *Signs* 19 (1994): 591–629.

Eagleton, Terry. "Capitalism, Modernism and Postmodernism." *New Left Review* 152 (1985): 60–73.

Edelstein, Marilyn. "Toward a Feminist Postmodern *Poléthique:* Kristeva on Ethics and Politics." *Ethics, Politics, and Difference in Julia Kristeva's Writing.* Ed. Kelly Oliver. New York: Routledge, 1993. 196–214.

Felski, Rita. *Beyond Feminist Aesthetics: Feminist Literature and Social Change.* Cambridge, Mass.: Harvard University Press, 1989.

Ferguson, Margaret, and Jennifer Wicke, eds. *Feminism and Postmodernism.* Durham, N.C.: Duke University Press, 1994.

Finke, Laurie. "The Rhetoric of Marginality: Why I Do Feminist Theory." *Tulsa Studies in Women's Literature* 5 (1986): 251–72.

Flax, Jane. *Disputed Subjects: Essays on Psychoanalysis, Politics and Philosophy.* New York: Routledge, 1993.

———. "Postmodernism and Gender Relations in Feminist Theory." *Signs* 12 (1987): 621–43.

Fraser, Nancy, and Linda J. Nicholson. "Social Criticism without Philosophy: An Encounter between Feminism and Postmodernism." *Feminism/Postmodernism.* Ed. Nicholson. 19–38.

Friedman, Susan Stanford. "Post/Poststructuralist Feminist Criticism: The Politics of Recuperation and Negotiation." *New Literary History* 22 (1991): 465-90.

Fuss, Diana. *Essentially Speaking: Feminism, Nature, and Difference.* New York: Routledge, 1989.

Gates, Henry Louis, Jr. "'What's Love Got to Do with It?' Critical Theory, Integrity, and the Black Idiom." *New Literary History* 18 (1987): 345-62.

Giroux, Henry A., ed. *Postmodernism, Feminism, and Cultural Politics: Redrawing Educational Boundaries.* Albany: State University of New York Press, 1991.

Gordon, Avery, and Christopher Newfield. "White Philosophy." *Critical Inquiry* 20 (1994): 737-57.

Hassan, Ihab. *The Dismemberment of Orpheus: Toward a Postmodern Literature.* Madison: University of Wisconsin Press, 1982.

———. *Paracriticisms: Seven Speculations of the Times.* Urbana: University of Illinois Press, 1975.

———. *The Postmodern Turn: Essays in Postmodern Theory and Culture.* Columbus: Ohio State University Press, 1987.

Hixon, Mamie Webb. Review of *Killing Rage: Ending Racism,* by bell hooks. *Black Collegian,* Feb. 1996, p. 11.

Hoesterey, Ingeborg. "Introduction: Postmodernism as Discursive Event." *Zeitgeist in Babel: The Post-Modernist Controversy.* Ed. Ingeborg Hoesterey. Bloomington: Indiana University Press, 1991. ix-xv.

Homans, Margaret. "'Women of Color' Writers and Feminist Theory." *New Literary History* 25 (1994): 73-94.

hooks, bell. *Ain't I a Woman: Black Women and Feminism.* Boston: South End Press, 1981.

———. *Art on My Mind: Visual Politics.* New York: New Press, 1995.

———. *Black Looks: Race and Representation.* Boston: South End Press, 1992.

———. "Dialectically Down with the Critical Program." *Black Popular Culture.* A Project by Michele Wallace, ed. Gina Dent. Dia Center for the Arts Discussions in Contemporary Culture 8. Seattle: Bay Press, 1992. 48-55.

———. "Essentialism and Experience." Review of *Essentially Speaking: Feminism, Nature, and Difference,* by Diana Fuss. *American Literary History* 3 (1991): 172-83.

———. *Feminist Theory: From Margin to Center.* Boston: South End Press, 1984.

———. *Killing Rage: Ending Racism.* New York: Henry Holt, 1995.

———. *Outlaw Culture: Resisting Representations.* New York: Routledge, 1994.

———. *Sisters of the Yam: Black Women and Self-Recovery.* Boston: South End Press, 1993.

———. *Talking Back: Thinking Feminist, Thinking Black.* Boston: South End Press, 1989.

———. *Teaching to Transgress: Education as the Practice of Freedom.* New York: Routledge, 1994.

———. *Yearning: Race, Gender, and Cultural Politics.* Boston: South End Press, 1990.

hooks, bell, and Cornel West. *Breaking Bread: Insurgent Black Intellectual Life.* Boston: South End Press, 1991.

Hull, Gloria T., Patricia Bell Scott, and Barbara Smith, eds. *All the Women Are White, All the Blacks Are Men, But Some of Us Are Brave.* Old Westbury, N.Y.: Feminist Press, 1982.

Hutcheon, Linda. *A Poetics of Postmodernism: History, Theory, Fiction.* New York: Routledge, 1988.

———. *The Politics of Postmodernism.* London: Routledge, 1989.

Huyssen, Andreas. *After the Great Divide: Modernism, Mass Culture, Postmodernism.* Bloomington: Indiana University Press, 1986.

James, Stanlie M. "Introduction." *Theorizing Black Feminisms: The Visionary Pragmatism of Black Women.* Ed. Stanlie M. James and Abena P. A. Busia. London: Routledge, 1993.

Jameson, Fredric. *The Political Unconscious: Narrative as a Socially Symbolic Act.* Ithaca, N.Y.: Cornell University Press, 1981.

———. "Postmodernism, or The Cultural Logic of Late Capitalism." *New Left Review* 146 (1984): 53–92.

Joyce, Joyce A. "The Black Canon: Reconstructing Black American Literary Criticism." *New Literary History* 18 (1987): 335–44.

———. "Black Woman Scholar, Critic, and Teacher: The Inextricable Relationship between Race, Sex, and Class." *New Literary History* 22 (1991): 543–65.

Kauffman, Linda, ed. *Gender and Theory: Dialogues on Feminist Theory.* New York: Basil Blackwell, 1989.

Keating, AnnLouise. "Interrogating 'Whiteness,' (De)Constructing 'Race.' " *College English* 57 (1995): 901–18.

Kristeva, Julia. *The Kristeva Reader.* Ed. Toril Moi. New York: Columbia University Press, 1986.

———. *Nations without Nationalism.* Trans. Leon S. Roudiez. New York: Columbia University Press, 1993.

———. "Postmodernism?" *Romanticism, Modernism, Postmodernism.* Ed. Harry R. Garvin. Special issue of *Bucknell Review* 25 (1980): 136–41.

———. "Stabat Mater." Trans. Léon S. Roudiez. *Kristeva Reader.* Ed. Moi. 160–86.

———. *Strangers to Ourselves.* Trans. Léon S. Roudiez. New York: Columbia University Press, 1991.

———. "The System and the Speaking Subject." Trans. Toril Moi. *Kristeva Reader.* Ed. Moi. 24–33.

———. "Women's Time." Trans. Alice Jardine and Harry Blake. *Kristeva Reader.* Ed. Moi. 187–213.

Lorde, Audre. *Sister Outsider: Essays and Speeches.* Freedom, Calif.: Crossing Press, 1984.

Lyotard, Jean-François. *The Postmodern Condition: A Report on Knowledge.* Trans. Geoff Bennington and Brian Massumi. Minneapolis: University of Minnesota Press, 1984.

Marcus, Jane. "Storming the Toolshed." *Signs* 7 (1982): 622–40.

McKay, Nellie Y. "Response to 'The Philosophical Bases of Feminist Literary Criticisms.' " *New Literary History* 19 (1987): 161–67.

Moraga, Cherríe, and Gloria Anzaldúa, eds. *This Bridge Called My Back: Writings by Radical Women of Color.* Watertown, Mass.: Persephone Press, 1981.

Morrison, Toni. *Playing in the Dark: Whiteness and the Literary Imagination.* New York: Vintage, 1993.

———. "A Writer's Work, with Toni Morrison." *World of Ideas.* Pt. 2. Interview by Bill Moyers. PBS, videocassette, 1990.

Nicholson, Linda J., ed. *Feminism/Postmodernism.* New York: Routledge, 1990.

Omi, Michael, and Howard Winant. *Racial Formation in the United States: From the 1960s to the 1980s.* New York: Routledge, 1986.

Owens, Craig. "The Discourse of Others: Feminists and Postmodernism." *The Anti-Aesthetic: Essays on Postmodern Culture.* Ed. Hal Foster. Seattle: Bay Press, 1983. 57–82.

Sarup, Madan. *An Introductory Guide to Post-Structuralism and Postmodernism.* Athens: University of Georgia Press, 1989.

Smith, Barbara. "Between a Rock and a Hard Place: Relationships between Black and Jewish Women." *Yours in Struggle.* Ed. Bulkin, Pratt, and Smith. 65–87.

Smith, Valerie. "Black Feminist Theory and the Representation of the 'Other.'" *Changing Our Own Words.* Ed. Wall. 38–57.

Spivak, Gayatri Chakravorty. "Imperialism and Sexual Difference." *Oxford Literary Review* 8 (1986): 225–40.

Suleiman, Susan Rubin. *Subversive Intent: Gender, Politics, and the Avant-Garde.* Cambridge, Mass.: Harvard University Press, 1990.

Tress, Daryl McGowan. "Comment on Flax's 'Postmodernism and Gender Relations in Feminist Theory.'" *Signs* 14 (1988): 196–200.

Walker, Alice. *In Search of Our Mothers' Gardens: Womanist Prose.* New York: Harcourt Brace Jovanovich, 1984.

Wall, Cheryl A., ed. *Changing Our Own Words: Essays on Criticism, Theory, and Writing by Black Women.* New Brunswick, N.J.: Rutgers University Press, 1989.

Wallace, Michele. "Art for Whose Sake?" Review of *Art on My Mind: Visual Politics,* by bell hooks. *Women's Review of Books,* Oct. 1995, p. 8.

———. "Negative Images: Towards a Black Feminist Cultural Criticism." *Cultural Studies.* Ed. Lawrence Grossberg, Cary Nelson, and Paula A. Treichler. New York: Routledge, 1992. 654–71.

West, Cornel. "Black Culture and Postmodernism." *Remaking History.* Ed. Barbara Kruger and Phil Mariani. Dia Art Foundation Discussions in Contemporary Culture 4. Seattle: Bay Press, 1989. 87–96.

———. *Race Matters.* Boston: Beacon Press, 1993.

TOMO HATTORI

5 ◇ Psycholinguistic Orientalism in Criticism of *The Woman Warrior* and *Obasan*

As U.S. culture moves into the next century under the decentered yet oddly consolidating rubric of cultural studies, the greatest pitfall in theorizing the literature of U.S. women of color remains the assumption that "literature" and "theory" exclude each other: that women of color who feel, act, and write are not theorists, that theory is not a development that concerns women of color, and that the conjoining of the two categories requires an anthology of critical essays, since such an event is novel in the cultural work of U.S. women of color. My conviction that there is a uniquely *psycholinguistic orientalism* at work in recent feminist criticism of Maxine Hong Kingston's *Woman Warrior* (1976) and Joy Kogawa's *Obasan* (1981) rests on a deeper belief that these two women's texts present elaborate and careful theories of Chinese and Japanese North American female subjectivity as much as they tell complex stories of ethnicity, identity, struggle, and remembrance. I also believe that theoretical approaches in literary criticism should examine the cultural base out of which the theory in question emerges so that the writing called "theory" can reveal its own cultural and literary dimensions. The current practice of designating which texts are "theory" and which are "literature" forecloses interpretive possibilities by enforcing one-way readings in which the theory is the glorified necessary apparatus for transforming the raw experience of (in this case) ethnic literature into legitimate, usable knowledge. I take to task recent critical essays on *The Woman Warrior* and *Obasan* for not clarifying the cultural bases of their

own interpretive theories and for reinscribing what I call a psycholinguistic orientalism into their readings of these two significant Asian
American texts.

The Woman Warrior is at the center of the longest running controversy in Chinese American literature. This debate regards the charge by
Frank Chin, Benjamin Tong, and other mostly male Chinese American
critics that Kingston presents stereotypical and even racist descriptions
of her own ethnic community. Robert G. Lee, King-Kok Cheung, and
Sau-ling Cynthia Wong have described this issue as related to the issue
of "orientalism" (Cheung, Woman 235; Lee 52; Wong 35). Orientalism
to Cheung and Lee means the general cultural process that either mis-
represents Asian American identity as "the silent and passive Other"
(Cheung 235) or erases that identity entirely as "alien, ahistorical, and
without voice" (Lee 52). Neither Lee, Cheung, nor Wong delve extensively into the academic, imaginative, and institutional sense of the
term elaborated by Edward Said in Orientalism (1978), but their use of the
word connects The Woman Warrior to one of the most influential and
misapplied postcolonial theories to appear in the United States in the
last twenty years. While Orientalism deals specifically with French and
British nineteenth-century scholarship on the Middle East, Said's critique of orientalist discourse has been welcomed by David Henry Hwang
and King-Kok Cheung as an important element in the analysis of Chinese American self-representation (Hwang x; Cheung 247n. 3).

Despite this cursory approval of Said's cultural theory as an interpretive tool within Chinese American literary culture, the most crucial elements of the controversy over The Woman Warrior involve categories of
analysis that are absent in Said's discourse. The debate over Kingston's
potential orientalism is centrally concerned with gender and autobiography—the antifeminist doubt that a woman can be a successful bard
for the Chinese American community and the question of whether this
female author's personal memoirs can, or must, adequately represent
her entire ethnic community.[1] The orientalist controversy over The
Woman Warrior is, to depart from Said's main interests, not about how
the writer represents the other but how the the writer represents herself
and her cultural identity. The unique case here of auto-orientalism necessitates an approach that can examine the relationship between the
subject and her own linguistic construction of herself as a Chinese
American female subject. The consideration of Kingston's orientalism is
thus a consideration of the psycholinguistic process through which she
articulates her gendered and ethnic subjectivity.

A critique of masculinist bias in readings of The Woman Warrior has
been diplomatically forwarded by Elaine H. Kim (198–99) and more dis-

tinctly enunciated by King-Kok Cheung (235–38). Kingston herself has exposed the more prominent instances of stereotyping and misrepresentation in her article, "Cultural Mis-readings by American Reviewers" of *The Woman Warrior*. What has not been adequately discussed is the extent to which orientalist discourse unconsciously inhabits the sympathetic and celebratory criticism of *The Woman Warrior*. Revealing this form of orientalism is especially important because it occurs in literary readings that attempt to be culturally sensitive in exploring Kingston's text. Furthermore, orientalist typologies and narratives are difficult to trace in psychoanalytic discourses that do not reflect on the orientalism of their own conceptual origins.

My discussion of Kingston's novel will also consider Joy Kogawa's *Obasan,* a contemporary novel that has been subject to the same kind of literary criticism and the same kind of insufficiently contextualized psycholinguistic theory as *The Woman Warrior*. Both *Woman Warrior* and *Obasan* have the distinction of being possibly the best-known and most critically acclaimed literary works to emerge from their respective communities in the last two decades.[2] As novels by and about women that deal with the intensely personal relationship between mothers and daughters, *Obasan* and *The Woman Warrior* coincide with the recent American feminist critical and theoretical interest in mother-daughter relationships as exemplified by the work of Adrienne Rich, Dorothy Dinnerstein, and Nancy Chodorow.[3] The fluid autobiographical narrative style of both novels also invites comparison with recent U.S. academic feminism's interest in the writings of Monique Wittig, Julia Kristeva, and Hélène Cixous.[4] Not surprisingly, there have been several critical analyses of the two novels based on U.S. and French women's psychoanalytic theories. Without exception, however, existing psychoanalytic readings of *The Woman Warrior* and *Obasan* do not adequately recover the ground of their own theories and thus inadvertently replicate the orientalist interpretive gestures they seek to resist.

Gender has always been a central issue in the Chinese American debate over *The Woman Warrior*. The most vehement critiques of Kingston's text came from the Chinese American male critics Jeffery Paul Chan, Benjamin Tong, and later, Frank Chin, who attacked the novel from a strongly masculinist perspective (Kim 198–99).[5] The main problem with the early Chinese American charges against Kingston's book was that the critique of orientalism and stereotyping was blended with a distinct and ingrained misogyny (Lim, "Japanese" 289). This history makes it difficult to revisit the question of Kingston's orientalism (especially for a male critic) without becoming embedded in the sexism of earlier male critics of *The Woman Warrior*. Despite the depth and detail of Said's scholarship, the androcentric cultural basis of his theory threatens to reproduce, albeit with more academic sophistication, the masculine bias of the earlier critique. Said's account of orientalism is therefore not as useful in looking at Kingston's novel as that of the analysis developed by Asian American women theorists who make the category of woman central to their critique of orientalist representation.

The earliest and still most powerful critique of orientalism within feminist theory is Gayatri Chakravorty Spivak's 1981 essay, "French Feminism in an International Frame" (in *In Other Worlds*). In that article, Spivak criticizes the orientalism of Julia Kristeva's *About Chinese Women*.[6] Other later Asian American theorists have since revisited Spivak's discussion of Kristeva's orientalism. Rey Chow discusses Spivak's critique in a chapter on the orientalism of Bernardo Bertolucci's 1987 film *The Last Emperor* (3–33). Lisa Lowe surveys the poststructuralist orientalism of Kristeva, Barthes, and the Tel Quel group as part of a study of different historical episodes of orientalist discourse in Europe (136–89). Lowe contends that "orientalism is not a single developmental tradition but is profoundly heterogeneous" (ix) and that "each orientalist situation expresses a distinct range of concerns with *difference*" (x). Although Spivak never mentions Said's term orientalism in her article, both Chow and Lowe clearly perceive Spivak as one of the key critics of orientalist discourse. Spivak's response to Kristeva's *About Chinese Women* is not only thematically related to the orientalist controversy over *The Woman Warrior* but also shares the same historical time as *The Woman Warrior* and the controversy surrounding it. *About Chinese Women* (translated from the original French *Des Chinoises* written in 1974) appeared in the United States in 1977, a year before Said's *Orientalism*. Spivak's critique of Kristeva in 1981 is also contemporary to the Japanese Canadian author Joy Kogawa's *Obasan*. *Obasan* and *The Woman Warrior* are both highly acclaimed literary texts that offer profound meditations on poetic and literary self-creation, motherhood, and East Asian cultural ancestry. Kristeva's examination of the maternal basis of Chinese language and identity intersects with both literary texts in their common use of the Asian female autobiographical voice. Within current U.S. feminist theory, *About Chinese Women* is a neglected work relative to Kristeva's other achievements; however, as a specifically cultural text that immerses itself in the racial, sexual, and psycholinguistic concerns shared by *The Woman Warrior* and *Obasan, About Chinese Women* is a uniquely and uncannily homologous parallel text to the two North American texts.

The notable aspect of Kristeva's orientalism in *About Chinese Women* is that it is "positive," that is, it valorizes Chinese culture as superior to the West. *About Chinese Women* holds Chinese women and the sup-posedly maternal basis of their language above the patriarchal, mascu-line cultural and philosophical models of the European intellectual tra-dition. Kristeva is interested in the Orient as an oppositional site from which to base a critique of the West and is not fundamentally concerned with Chinese social realities. China is useful in Kristeva's sociosymbolic typology because she envisions in Chinese culture the maternal, pre-oedipal, and prelinguistic qualities of nurturance, play, and rhythm that she feels are missing in the West. However, as Chow points out, "Kristeva's critique is complicated by the fact that it is sexualized: China is counterposed to the West not only because it is different, but also be-cause it is . . . feminine" (5). The typological binary of East versus West is also gendered along the lines Said describes in his characterization of orientalism as a concept influenced by "the male conception of the world" in which the East is defined as a sexually feminine space (208).

The gendering of Kristeva's orientalism is qualitatively different from Said's concept of orientalism. China is neither feminized nor sub-ordinated to the superior masculine procedures of the West but is rather valorized for preserving its ancestral female culture. Kristeva claims that "ancient China was . . . the best known and most highly developed ma-trilinear society" ("Woman" 139). Kristeva finds evidence of this in mod-ern Chinese writing that she claims has "maintained the memory of matrilinear pre-history (collective and individual) in its architectonic of image, gesture, and sound" (*About* 57). In what Spivak describes as one of "the most stupendous generalizations about Chinese writing," Kristeva claims that the life of the speaking and writing individual in China cherishes the "pre-Oedipal phase" with its "dependency on the maternal," its "absence of clear-cut divisions between the order of things and the order of symbols," and its "predominance of the unconscious impulses" (*About* 56).

Clearly, Kristeva is describing China in terms of her concept of the "chora" as "an essentially mobile and extremely provisional articulation constituted by movements and their ephemeral stases" (Kristeva, *Revolu-tion* 25). The chora, as a process that occurs in a psychic realm analogous to Jacques Lacan's imaginary, "is pre-oedipal, chronologically anterior to syntax, a cry, the gesture of a child," and manifests itself in adult dis-closure as "rhythm, prosody, pun, non-sense, laugh" (Hirsch 210). The chora is thus characterized as "rupture and articulations (rhythm)," "rhythmic space," and is "analogous only to vocal and kinetic rhythm" (Kristeva, *Revolution* 26). According to Kristeva, the "mother's body is . . . what mediates the symbolic law organizing social relations and becomes the ordering principle of the semiotic *chora*" (27). The figure of the mother occupies a central place in both Kristeva's theory of the chora and her theory of Chinese women.

Chow argues correctly that "Kristeva's idealization of the 'maternal' order in China in terms of an 'empty and peaceful center' " reduces both the maternal and China to silence (8). Kristeva relegates maternal space, Chinese culture, and Chinese language to a prelinguistic realm of infantile incoherence that is problematic because it is identified with a specific and actually existing culture. Chinese people in actual Chinese society are generally capable of speech and politics; in China, as elsewhere, people, including mothers, are organized contemporary subjects who conduct daily lives of speech and action without dissolving into choric pun and nonsense. Furthermore, Kristeva's chora is an astonishingly and conveniently arbitrary sociosymbolic concept. She writes that although "the *chora* can be designated and regulated . . . it can never be posited: as a result, one can situate the *chora* and, if necessary, lend it a typology, but one can never give it axiomatic form" (*Revolution* 26). In social and political terms, this means that the chora can be used in an orientalist typology but its position in that typology need never be explained, justified, or defined.

At this point, I would like to clarify my own theoretical position: I am not necessarily averse to the use of the semiotic or other psycholinguistic concepts for cross-cultural literary interpretations. Kristeva's account of the process of linguistic subjectivity offers many insights into the intellectual traditions of Europe and is potentially of great value to other cultural contexts. What is problematic is the typing of whole cultures and genders into what (in Kristeva's more careful accounts) is an exclusively psycholinguistic function. The problem occurs when concepts formed to describe psychic and linguistic functions within the subject are projected onto social space to describe the collective subjective processes of entire nations, genders, and cultures. If China is cast as the semiotic or choric realm of a subject, then it is in a sense confined within a psychic ghetto. If this relationship is then cast back out as an interpretive model of social relations, the result is the expression of a psychoanalytic colonialism of a symbolic "United States" over a semiotic "China."

Under those misapplied conditions, China's relevance lies only in its primitivism as a contemporary culture that manages somehow to exist as a fixed and separate entity outside of the march of Western historical time. Kristeva's project is "not to *deconstruct* the origin, but rather to *re-cuperate,* archaeologically and formulaically, what she locates as the potential originary space *before* the sign" (Spivak 146). As a result, China becomes the other, situated "in an ideal time that is marked off taxonomically from 'our' time" (Chow 6). Spivak observes that in Kristeva's typology China is fractured by the Western gaze so that, "reflecting a broader Western cultural practice, the 'classical' East is studied with primitivistic reverence, even as the 'contemporary' East is treated with realpolitikal contempt" (138). Since the uniqueness of China is cast simply as the other of Western discourse, Kristeva's representation of Chinese women bears no resemblance to actual women in China and in fact obscures the social conditions under which Chinese women exist.

In *Revolution in Poetic Language,* a landmark text of psycholinguistic theory published in the same year as *About Chinese Women* (1974), Kristeva defines the semiotic as connected to the modality known in Freudian psychoanalysis as *primary processes,* wherein "discrete quantities of energy move through the body of the subject who is not yet constituted as such" (25). According to Kristeva's theory, those people and identities typed as the semiotic do not in a strict sense exist as subjects. Since the semiotic chora is the precondition of the thetic phase in the symbolic order (Kristeva, *Revolution* 50), anyone typed as the semiotic is only a potential subject who is dependent on passage into the symbolic for her or his status as a subject. However, the typing of people and cultures as "semiotic" or "choric," as Kristeva does in *About Chinese Women,* is not entirely consistent with her own definition of those terms in *Revolution in Poetic Language.* In *Revolution,* she admits "there are non-verbal systems that are constructed exclusively on the basis of the semiotic (music, for example)" but also maintains that the two modalities, the semiotic and the symbolic, "are inseparable within the *signifying process* that constitutes language" (24). Furthermore, Kristeva states that "because the subject is always *both* semiotic *and* symbolic, no signifying system he [*sic*] produces can be either 'exclusively' semiotic or 'exclusively' symbolic, and is instead necessarily marked by an indebtedness to both" (24). Kristeva's elaboration of the semiotic in *Revolution in Poetic Language* suggests that her cultural assignment of China and Chinese women as whole sites of semiotic and choric motility is a practice that contravenes her own otherwise carefully defined theoretical position on the subject.

Recent criticism on Kristeva tacitly confirms that her analysis of Chinese culture, which introduced her to North American readers in the 1970s, is no longer credible. As editor of *The Kristeva Reader,* Toril Moi, aware of Spivak's critique of Kristeva's ethnocentrism, ironically enough chose not to excerpt any of the passages from *About Chinese Women* that are about Chinese women. Kelly Oliver's *Reading Kristeva,* the first book-length analysis of Kristeva's corpus, similarly omits extensive references to *About Chinese Women,* which [she] refers to as "one of Kristeva's 'lesser' works" and which [she] judges to be a "most questionable and often offensive text" (7). In her more recent work, Kristeva herself does not emphasize the semiotic or choric capacity of non-European cultures.

A contemporary orientalism in the Kristeva style does, however, persist in the positive criticism of *The Woman Warrior.* While Kristeva's theory about Chinese women may have waned in popularity among theorists, what is commonly referred to as French feminist theory has had a significant influence among U.S. feminist literary critics in the last two decades.[7] This feminist race for theory coincides with the rise of *The Woman Warrior* as a popular and critically respected U.S. feminist text.[8] The two movements inevitably come together in readings of *The Woman Warrior* inspired by the French feminist trio: Julia Kristeva, Hélène Cixous, and Luce Irigaray.

The most significantly developed reading along these lines is Leslie W. Rabine's "No Lost Paradise: Social Gender and Symbolic Gender in the Writings of Maxine Hong Kingston" (1987). The promising aspect of Rabine's approach is that she is determined to expose the ways in which "an exclusive theoretical focus on language structure can lead to strategies that seek to liberate the 'feminine' while leaving intact the oppression of social women" (473). Rabine conceptualizes her project as one of countering the overly symbolic theory of Cixous, Irigaray, Kristeva, and Sarah Kofman with the direct social experience presented by Kingston's writing. Rabine's choice of Kingston's *Woman Warrior* and *China Men* is an innovative way to interrogate the theoretical grounds of Cixous's and others' symbolic feminism, but I question why this analysis does not include an interrogation of the theoretical grounds of symbolic feminism using the social texts of the symbolic theorists themselves. *About Chinese Women,* after all, contains much of the same central thematic concerns as *The Woman Warrior,* such as Chinese maternality, women's language, and the relation of these to Western cultural and conceptual practices.

Rabine nevertheless maintains the qualitative distinction between the social text and the theoretical text and uses these categories to differentiate the Chinese American text from the French text. In so doing, she produces a model where the designated theory is applied to the designated writing instead of considering the social and theoretical resonances of both Kristeva's French and Kingston's U.S. texts. Indeed, the practice of using Cixous and Kristeva to read Kingston obscures the subjective textual quality of Cixous's and Kristeva's work as well as the linguistic, speculative, and theoretical qualities of Kingston's writing. In the case of Kristeva, the repression of the social dimension of gender is more the result of Rabine's omission of the text in which Kristeva locates theory in an actual social site. By not considering Kristeva's *About Chinese Women,* Rabine misses an opportunity to establish comparative links between the social grounding of Kristeva's theory and the creative prose experiments of Kingston's social text.

Rabine's interpretive model for *The Woman Warrior* replicates the conditions that Lowe identifies in *About Chinese Women,* in which the "Chinese woman is fetishized and constructed as the Other of western psychoanalytic feminism" (Lowe 152). This is a significant and delicate point to make because Rabine's analysis is motivated by a desire to overcome misreadings of *The Woman Warrior.* In her introduction to *Asian American Literature,* Kim remarks, "Even the strengths of *The Woman Warrior,* such as its portrayal of ambiguity as central to the Chinese American experience, are misconstrued by some critics" (xvi–xvii). Rabine sets as her challenge the disciplining of this enigmatic Asian strength into the frame of an orderly and explanatory critical discourse. To do this, she establishes a psychoanalytic typology to construe sympathetically the Chinese American ambiguity that Kim claims is elusive to outsiders. Rabine positions herself in subtle defiance to the equally oblique warning posted by Kim against those who think they can easily penetrate the ambiguity of Chinese American experience. Rabine is nevertheless determined to get to the heart of the cultural mystery, and this very desire for the ethnic other is what exposes the orientalism of her project.

Confronting Kim's passage directly, Rabine writes:

> Kim sees the "portrayal of ambiguity as central to the Chinese American experience." . . . This ambiguity . . . is . . . the result of love/hate relationships to the immigrant Chinese culture and to the childhood myths and memories experienced in that culture. Without a childhood imaginary realm and the access to the unconscious it opens up, we would be little more than robots. The power of the childhood imaginary realm also increases the power of marginalized cultures in the United States to resist a social order that turns us all into robots. But its very necessity to us constitutes its danger since it can also draw one back into paralytic unity with the mother, as well as accommodate one to the limits of patriarchal institutions. Kingston's ambiguity shuttles between the necessity and the danger of this childhood imaginary realm. (482)

Central to Rabine's explanation of the ambiguity of Chinese American experience is the idea that this experience is located in "the immigrant Chinese culture" and "the childhood myths and memories experienced in that culture." The narrator/daughter in *The Woman Warrior* has no experience of Chinese culture other than through her immigrant parents.

This unique situation allows Rabine to form the basis of a psychoanalytic model of ethnic acculturation that assumes that Chinese identity remains limited to childhood myth and memory.

Much to the contrary, Kingston's narrative concludes with the presentation of Chinese identity in the United States as the inheritance that marks the narrator's entry into a coherent adult speaking subject. At the end of the last section of *The Woman Warrior,* the narrator declares the modernity of her Chinese identity and the maturity of her relationship to her mother's stories: "Here is a story my mother told me, not when I was young, but recently, when I told her I also talk-story" (206). While the memory of the past culture and the mythic frame of its narration persist, the novel's concluding story of Ts'ai Yen argues that Chinese identity is the enduring center that persists after assimilation and is in fact enriched by contact with outsiders. In Kingston's novel, the Chinese culture that was the basis of the narrator's childhood experience is refashioned into a space that the narrator can return to as a final achievement. *The Woman Warrior* traces the emergence of a woman and a culture into the fabric of modern American life.

In Rabine's analysis, the narrator's experience of childhood becomes synonymous with the experience of the immigrant Chinese culture. The "childhood imaginary realm and access to the unconscious it opens up" becomes the child's total potential for Chinese ethnic identity in America. Rabine associates the childhood imaginary realm with the marginalized cultures of the United States. The orientalist psychoanalytic typology of Rabine's interpretation of Chinese American ambiguity appears in the implication that Chinese identity is a premodern experience lodged in unconscious childhood memory. Both the redemptive and regressive aspects of ethnic experience are characterized as infantile in origin.

Describing ethnic experience and subjectivity as an aspect of childhood naturalizes the ideological dominance of the nation's majority culture over its ethnic minority cultures. Such a depiction allows the majority to justify its oppression of others as an expression of a concerned desire to see the child/minority mature in a healthy and responsible way. In Rabine's interpretive typology, the Chinese mother is the implicit symbol of the artistic reformulation of maternality and Chinese identity as a prior, pre-oedipal space. The disturbing thread in this interpretation is Rabine's willingness to relegate the Chinese mother to the maternal, preverbal realm of Kristeva's semiotic. Pursuing the implicit oppositions of this symbolic arrangement, America is established as the father's land, ruled by his law and articulated in terms of U.S. ideologies of nationalism and civil society. The existence of Chinese masculinity in

America is absent from this model in which the woman is Chinese and the man is, by implication, white American.

Rabine's orientalist psychoanalysis reconstructs Chinese ethnic identity as a partial identity that is completely subsumed by the dominant national culture. The only socially useful Chinese identity is that which can be used in the political struggle to "increase the power of marginalized cultures in the United States" (Rabine 482). "China" and "Chinese" do not signify outside of Western frames of reference. In Rabine's analysis, "Chinese Americans" exist only within the context of an American autobiographical struggle for self-identity. The general process of immigrant naturalization and cultural assimilation in the United States constrains Chinese identity to the past, to an exclusively feminine and maternal identity, insisting that the orientalizing of oneself is often the price Chinese Americans must pay to fit into the U.S. cultural landscape.

A feminist psycholinguistic orientalism also surfaces prominently in readings of Joy Kogawa's *Obasan.* Shirley Geok-lin Lim, Donald C. Goellnicht, and Robin Potter invoke the French theorists Cixous, Irigaray, and Kristeva for the project of establishing both a "women's poetics" (Lim, "Japanese" 291) and an interpretive model that addresses the doubly marginal condition of the character Naomi Nakane as woman and ethnic minority (Goellnicht, "Minority" 298). Lim supports her approach to the mother-daughter relationship in *Obasan* with the work of feminist cultural theorists such as Chodorow, Dinnerstein, and Rich who have made this relationship central to their analyses of human development (Lim "Japanese" 293). Lim's literary feminism is based on "a poetics, arguably a women's poetics, that values instead of disparages ambiguities and fluid boundaries in writing" (291). Her aim is to develop a reading of Asian American women's texts that does not dismiss their "multiple presences, ambivalent stories, and circular and fluid narratives" (290–91).

The phrase "amniotic deep," from the opening prose poem of *Obasan,* provides the point from which Goellnicht and Lim explore Kogawa's poetic language as a maternal process. Both critics observe the similarity between Kogawa's "amniotic deep" and the term "amniotic bliss" used by Adrienne Rich to describe the daughter's life in the mother's body before birth (Goellnicht, "Minority" 297–98; Lim, "Japanese" 300; "Asian" 242). Lim's interpretation, that the poetic language in *Obasan* "gives to the expression of racial memory the power of the semiotic," is based on her understanding of Kristeva's term "semiotic" as the way in which " 'repressed consciousness'—all that is left out of Obasan's silence and Emily's documents—erupts and disturbs the narrative" (Lim, "Asian" 245). Goellnicht describes the "semiotic" more

simply as "Kristeva's term for pre-oedipal, mother-child communication" ("Minority" 298). Lim insists that in *Obasan* "the writing project is
inseparable from the reconstruction of the maternal" ("Asian" 241). For
these critics, Kristeva's concept of the semiotic provides vital interpretive links among the narrative and psychic processes in *Obasan* because
it describes the articulation of poetic language within the process of a
prelinguistic, pre-oedipal, maternal realm.

From these theoretical suggestions of the link between poetic and
maternal creation arise orientalist typologies that are unwarranted by
the text. On the basis of the Japanese Canadian narrator's absorption
with the silent pre-oedipal language of her Japanese mother, Goellnicht
concludes that the struggle for balance in the novel lies between the old
Japanese "mother culture" and the new Canadian "father land" ("Minority" 298; see also "Father Land"). There is little in the novel that
definitively suggests, as Goellnicht does, that silent, pre-oedipal language is characteristically maternal or that figurative, symbolic language
in the novel is paternal ("Minority" 298; "Father Land" 124). The most
significant wielders of textual and verbal language in the novel—
Grandma Kato, Aunt Emily, and Naomi—are women. On the other
hand, the men of the family are "rendered voiceless, stripped of car, ra-
dio, camera and every means of communication" (Kogawa 132) by the
internment. Deprived of public voice, Naomi's father and Stephen (her
brother) become absorbed in music, an activity that Kristeva identifies
as a nonverbal signifying system "constructed exclusively on the basis of
the semiotic" (*Revolution* 24). The commonplace orientalism of conveniently sexualized oppositions between the masculine West and the
feminine East is especially out of place in a novel where all the living female characters are Canadian and where there are no functional living
Canadian father figures worth mentioning (whether of Japanese ancestry or not). I am not suggesting that discursive roles for women and men
in the novel's Japanese Canadian family are the reverse of the "mother
tongue/culture" and "father land" opposition that Goellnicht establishes ("Minority" 298–99; "Father Land" 121–22), but I am arguing that
the novel's varied representations of gendered Japanese Canadian speech
and silence do not definitively type pre-oedipal communication as femi-
nine-Japanese and figurative language as masculine-Canadian.

Lim's reading relies on the secondary characters of Aya Obasan and
Aunt Emily to enforce the distinctive characterization of the culture of
the East as opposed to that of the West. Her interpretation of the female
voice in *Obasan* is based on a dialectic structure that presents Aya
Obasan as a representative of the mode of "recessive silence" in contrast

to Aunt Emily who is dedicated to "sociopolitical fact" (Lim, "Japanese" 305). Lim uses Aya and Emily to represent discursive methods that are plotted on a line marking the evolutionary progress of the Japanese Canadian female voice to the completed stage represented by Naomi, whose poetic language "encompasses the two negative mirrorings of aunts Aya and Emily and exceeds them" ("Asian" 245). In Lim's analysis, Aya and Emily represent linguistic prototypes for Naomi's voice as the voice of the fully achieved Japanese Canadian female subject of the novel.

Aya and Emily occupy specific positions on an evolutionary ladder within Lim's narrative of female discursive progress: "The novel encompasses and moves through the stages of muteness or aphasia (Obasan's character); logocentric documentation (Emily's character); and a speaking subject (the narrator's poetic voice)" ("Asian" 245). The least articulate female character, Aya Obasan, is the one most closely associated by Lim and other critics with the ancestral culture, Japan, and "Oriental" tradition; Emily is the stridently vocal but unachieved "Canadian" voice. While Aya and Emily are both "negative mirrorings" to Naomi, "Aunt Emily appears to be the positivist occidental inscription to Obasan's negative oriental circumscription" (Lim, "Japanese" 304). Emily's "limited and ineffectual mode" remains superior to Aya's "recessive silence" and shows that the ostensibly equitable multiculturalism of Naomi's finally achieved voice rests on a narrative of assimilationist progress. Emily, with her allegedly "Canadian" habit of democratic self-assertion, is still higher on the evolutionary ladder of the Japanese Canadian subject-in-process than Aya who, as the least assimilated Canadian, is the least progressive speaking subject.

Lim is not simply claiming that Naomi has a better grasp of the English language than Emily or Aya; she is arguing that Naomi has a better capacity for language. This gesture marks Lim's ethnocentrism. By narrowing the performance of subjectivity to the category of speech, Lim erects a symbolic order located in Canada that casts Japan as the site of the semiotic. This semiotic/symbolic split falls conveniently along the lines of an East/West cultural demarcation that has been the basis of orientalist conceptions of the world. That the semiotic and symbolic orders are not parallel but qualitatively incommensurable and that the semiotic is the realm before language places the psycholinguistic typology in perfect line with orientalist ideologies of the inscrutable, pre-Western (and therefore premodern) East.

The arbitrariness of this typological construction can be easily revealed if, for example, we change our focus from speech to writing as the defining performance of the subject. Under this criteria we could see that Naomi rarely writes but mostly narrates, reads, and remembers, thus marking her underdevelopment in this regard. Emily writes copiously but mostly in a dry documentary fashion that does not connect to deep feeling. Grandmother Kato, on the other hand, writes powerful letters from Nagasaki that deliver the "freeing words" to Naomi, and she is thus clearly the master at embodying the subject in writing. Rather than claiming that there is a Japanese-based symbolic textual order running parallel to the Canadian-based verbal one, I am insisting that one can make a variety of culturally self-serving conclusions out of the text, depending on what kinds of performances one looks at and who one chooses as the representative of those performances.

The readings of both Goellnicht and Lim rely heavily on dualistic patterns of orientalist interpretation based on the racial and cultural impermeability of East and West as analytic categories. In the most extended reading to date of *Obasan* from the perspective of Kristeva's theories (in this case through Kristeva's concept of abjection from her *Powers of Horror*), Robin Potter repeats the symptomatic flaw of representing the semiotic through cultural character types:

> When attempting to contextualize the absence and sublimated presence of Naomi's mother, I am confronted with ambiguous associations. On the one hand, the mother is firmly rooted as a second generation Canadian to Canada and to her family in that country. On the other hand, she is drawn by love or a sense of tradition or obligation to the mother country, Japan, to take care of her own aging grandmother. This choice places her neither here nor there, since Naomi is constantly calling forth her presence, and leads me to believe that the mother in this story belongs to what Kristeva would call the semiotic. The semiotic refers to the "actual organization or disposition, within the body, of instinctual drives as they affect language and its practice in dialectical conflict with the symbolic" (Roudiez 17). (Potter 132)

In Kristeva's proper terms, the mother in Kogawa's novel cannot ever "belong" to the semiotic. Naomi's mother is a mature, articulate speaking subject. She writes fluent, coherent letters to Aunt Emily. While Naomi's distant childhood memories of her mother shroud her mother in an atmosphere of mystical silence, there is never a suggestion that the mother is incapable of audible, sensible, human language.

Potter's consignment of the mother to the semiotic is plausible only if we accept "nation" as the substitute for "language" as the basis of the Lacanian and Kristevan symbolic order. This arbitrary social typing of the symbolic order over the social order consigns the mother to the "semiotic" realm of absence, where her existence depends entirely upon her daughter's privilege within the symbolic order as the agent of the mother's recovery into language. Potter deems the mother suitable for incarceration into the semiotic for the simple activity of identifying with two countries at the same time. In the actual world, people with two passports who shuttle frequently between countries do not lose their capacity for speech or their ability to cohere as human subjects (beyond seasickness or jet lag) any more than Chinese women are inherently semiotic. In any case, the state of being "neither here nor there" is not a matter of dispersal or differentiation that reaches into psychic or bodily essence, as Potter suggests when she emphasizes Léon Roudiez's statement that the semiotic refers to the "actual organization or disposition, within the body, of instinctual drives."

Concerned as Rabine, Lim, Goellnicht, and Potter are with what Lim calls "the thematics of internment, maternality, race, and gender" in *Obasan* ("Japanese" 291), their evocations of Cixous, Kristeva, and Irigaray are curiously uninformed by any critique of the way in which the first two of these theorists bring race, gender, and, in Cixous's case, colonialism together in the analysis of the subject.[9] When critics apply Kristeva's semiotic to explain female Asian identity in *Obasan* or *The Woman Warrior* without knowledge of the critical controversy that has exposed Kristeva's own typing of the semiotic as a "Chinese" process, we have to wonder if critics are not projecting an orientalist understanding of Asian women's identity through the semiotic in the same way as Kristeva's *About Chinese Women*. We have, after all, noticed so far a disturbingly common thread to psychoanalytic readings of *The Woman Warrior* and *Obasan,* in the willingness of critics to relegate the Asian mother to the maternal, preverbal, pre-oedipal realm of the semiotic.

The psycholinguistic orientalism at work in recent feminist criticism of *The Woman Warrior* and *Obasan* labors under the burden of being a theory that claims to explain ethnic women's experience. The ground of this theory includes an early explication that is clearly bent on absorbing China as a function within a Western process of psychic, cultural, and no doubt moral redemption. Under these conditions, we must question whether the feminist psycholinguistic readings considered here can actually read Kingston's and Kogawa's texts in any way other than as appropriations of minority culture by dominant U.S. cultural theory. The very articulation of U.S. women of color *and* literary theory opens the potential for a dualism that has no reason to form. The failure of literary critics to consider orientalism as embedded in the very reflex of their sympathetic concerns—the method of their feminist and ethnic psycholinguistic readings of texts—shows that the theory of situating one's explanations of self in the surroundings of a familiar culture is not a

paroxysm of ethnic essentialist narcissism but a method of circumscrib-
ing oneself from the universalizing hubris that attends cultures that
deny the grounds and legacies of their own explanatory discourses.

NOTES

1. Said deals occasionally with the sexualized nature of orientalist discourse
but only from the perspective of the male orientalist scholar and the feminized
representation of the Orient (138, 188).

2. *The Woman Warrior* won the National Book Critics Circle Award for nonfiction in 1976 and was named by *Time* magazine as one of the top ten nonfiction
books of the 1970s. *Obasan,* Kogawa's first novel, rose to prominence quickly in
Canada and the United States in the first decade of its publication. It received the
1981 Books in Canada First Novel Award, the 1982 Canadian Authors' Association Book of the Year Award, the 1982 American Book Award, and the Periodical
Distributors of Canada award for the best fiction book of 1983. In 1986, Kogawa
was named a member of the Order of Canada. *Obasan's* appearance in 1981 had a
great influence on the progress of the Japanese Canadian Redress Movement that
gained momentum through the 1980s and was settled in 1988 (Davidson 14).
When the settlement was finally announced, parts of *Obasan* were read aloud in
the Canadian House of Commons (Goellnicht, "Minority" 306). In the United
States, Kogawa has become one of the most well-known Japanese *American* novelists despite the fact that she is Canadian. *Obasan* is often anthologized and
studied within the rubric of Asian or Japanese American literature (as in Cheung,
Articulate Silences; Lim, "Japanese American Women's Life Stories"; and anthologies such as Chan, Chin, Inada, and Wong, *The Big Aiiieeeee!,* and Hagedorn,
Charlie Chan Is Dead). Ronald Takaki borrows a phrase from *Obasan* for the subtitle of his introduction to *Strangers from a Different Shore* (3, 496n. 11).

3. *The Woman Warrior* shares its year of publication (1976) with the classic
American feminist analyses of mother-daughter relationships: Rich, *Of Woman
Born;* Dinnerstein, *The Mermaid and the Minotaur;* and Miller, *Toward a New Psy-
chology of Women* (1976). Chodorow, *The Reproduction of Mothering,* and Flax,
"The Conflict between Nurturance and Autonomy," followed shortly afterward
in 1978.

4. The first texts of feminist cultural psychoanalysis from France (what would
come to be popularly known in the United States as French feminist theory)
also arrived in North America around this time: Wittig's *Les guérillères* (1969)
was translated into English and made available in the United States in 1973, and
Kristeva's *Des chinoises* (1974) was translated as *About Chinese Women* in 1977.
The experimental fiction about women warriors in Wittig's *Les guérillères* pre-
figures with considerable similarity the styles and metaphors Kingston uses
in her narrative of empowered Chinese and Chinese American women, as do
Kristeva's *About Chinese Women* and Hélène Cixous's essay "Sorties" (published
in 1975 in *La Jeune Née* in France). Like *The Woman Warrior,* Cixous's essay is also
partly autobiographical, partly mythical, and partly about women warriors (the
Amazons).

5. The most persistent critic of Kingston's representation of Chinese Americans over the years has been Frank Chin. Chin and other members of the edito-

rial collective of *Aiiieeeee!: An Anthology of Asian American Writers* articulated their critique against so-called "fake" Chinese American autobiography even before the appearance of *The Woman Warrior*. After its publication, *The Woman Warrior* drew considerable criticism from Chin, Chan, and Tong. In "To Maxine Hong Kingston: A Letter," Fong represents an exception to the mostly male Chinese American animosity toward *The Woman Warrior*. Chin's attacks on *The Woman Warrior* continued in "The Most Popular Book in China," "This Is Not an Autobiography," and "Come All Ye Asian American Writers of the Real and the Fake" (in Chan et al., *Big Aiiieeeee!*). As a member of the *Aiiieeeee!* editorial collective, Chin's invective against Kingston resurfaced in *The Big Aiiieeeee!* as well as in the new preface to the 1991 Mentor edition of the original *Aiiieeeee!* Shirley Geoklin Lim discusses the masculine prejudice of the *Aiiieeeee!* editorial collective in relation to Kogawa's *Obasan* in "Japanese American Women's Life Stories."

6. In referring to Spivak as an Asian American woman (which is to say a woman of South Asian descent living and working primarily in the United States), I wish to challenge the conventional organization of Asian American studies, which tends to look at Asian American scholars only in so far as they write about Asian American culture. Critics and theorists such as Spivak, Chow, and even Lowe tend to be relegated to the category of "postcolonial" rather than "Asian American" along a conceptual and disciplinary partition that conceals the hybrid processes out of which racial and national identity are formed.

7. I am aware of the inaccuracy of the term "French feminists" when referring to Kristeva, Irigaray, and Cixous. I accept Oliver's point that calling these theorists French feminists is odd considering that "none of them were born in France and none of them claim any kind of unqualified relation to feminism" (163–64). However, the term has acquired some coherence in the United States in identifying the three theorists as a group. My essay is concerned precisely with the use of their theories in this generalized fashion by American critics of *The Woman Warrior*.

8. S. Smith goes so far as to say, "For me at least, no single work captures so powerfully the relationship of gender to genre in twentieth-century autobiography as Maxine Hong Kingston's *The Woman Warrior*" (150). Significantly, Smith's chapter on *The Woman Warrior* from her book *A Poetics of Women's Autobiography* is anthologized in Warhol and Price Herndl, *Feminisms* (1058–78). *The Woman Warrior* has become such an instant feminist classic that Kingston herself has expressed some displeasure at the disproportionate popularity that it has gained in relation to her later novels about Chinese American men: "I don't like all this overpraising of my daughter and rudeness towards my sons" ("Personal Statement" 24).

9. Three of Cixous's plays, *La Prise de l'école de Madhubaï* (1986), *L'Histoire terrible mais inachevée de Norodom Sihanouk roi du Cambodge* (1985), and *L'Indiade ou l'Inde de leurs rêves* (1987), reflect her preoccupation with the East "as a metaphorical site of values excluded by western modernity" (Shiach 120). Shiach describes *La Prise de l'école de Madhubaï* as echoing "many of the arguments of nineteenth-century Romanticism, which looked to primitive cultural forms to provide the space for a critique of contemporary culture" (122) and sees Cixous in this play as "placing herself within a tradition of western appropriation of the narratives and metaphors of the East" (122).

WORKS CITED

Chan, Jeffery Paul, Frank Chin, Lawson Fusao Inada, and Shawn Wong, eds. *The Big Aiiieeeee!: An Anthology of Chinese American and Japanese American Literature.* New York: Penguin, 1991.

Cheung, King-Kok. *Articulate Silences: Hisaye Yamamoto, Maxine Hong Kingston, Joy Kogawa.* Ithaca, N.Y.: Cornell University Press, 1993.

———. "The Woman Warrior versus the Chinaman Pacific: Must a Chinese American Critic Choose between Feminism and Heroism?" *Conflicts in Feminism.* Ed. Marianne Hirsch and Evelyn Fox Keller. New York: Routledge, 1990. 234–51.

Chin, Frank. "The Most Popular Book in China." *Quilt* 4 (1984): 12.

———. "This Is Not an Autobiography." *Genre* 13.2 (1985): 109–30.

Chin, Frank, Jeffery Paul Chan, Lawson Fusao Inada, and Shawn Wong, eds. *Aiiieeeee!: An Anthology of Asian American Writers.* 1974. New York: Penguin, 1991.

Chodorow, Nancy J. *The Reproduction of Mothering: Psychoanalysis and the Sociology of Gender.* Berkeley: University of California Press, 1978.

Chow, Rey. *Woman and Chinese Modernity: The Politics of Reading between West and East.* Minneapolis: University of Minnesota Press, 1991.

Cixous, Hélène. *L'Histoire terrible mais inachevée de Norodom Sihanouk roi du Cambodge.* Paris: Théâtre du Soleil, 1985.

———. *L'Indiade ou l'Inde de leurs rêves; et quelques écrits sur le théâtre.* Paris: Théâtre du Soleil, 1987.

———. "Sorties." *The Newly Born Woman.* By Hélène Cixous and Catherine Clément. Trans. Betsy Wing. Minneapolis: University of Minnesota Press, 1986. 63–132.

———. *Théâtre: Portrait de Dora et La Prise de l'école de Madhubaï.* Paris: des femmes, 1986.

Davidson, Arnold. *Writing Against the Silence: Joy Kogawa's Obasan.* Toronto: ECW Press, 1993.

Dinnerstein, Dorothy. *The Mermaid and the Minotaur: Sexual Arrangements and the Human Malaise.* New York: Harper and Row, 1976.

Fishkin, Shelley Fisher. "Interview with Maxine Hong Kingston." *American Literary History* 3 (1991): 782–91.

Flax, Jane. "The Conflict between Nurturance and Autonomy in Mother/Daughter Relationships and within Feminism." *Feminist Studies* 2 (1978): 171–89.

Fong, Katheryn M. "To Maxine Hong Kingston: A Letter." *Bulletin of Concerned Asian Scholars* 9.4 (1977): 67–69.

Goellnicht, Donald C. "Father Land and/or Mother Tongue: The Divided Female Subject in Kogawa's *Obasan* and Hong Kingston's *The Woman Warrior.*" *Redefining Autobiography in Twentieth-Century Women's Fiction: An Essay Collection.* Ed. Janice Morgan and Colette T. Hall. New York: Garland, 1991. 119–34.

———. "Minority History as Metafiction: Joy Kogawa's *Obasan.*" *Tulsa Studies in Women's Literature* 8 (1989): 287–306.

Hagedorn, Jessica, ed. *Charlie Chan Is Dead: An Anthology of Contemporary Asian American Fiction.* New York: Penguin, 1993.

Hirsch, Marianne. "Review Essay: Mothers and Daughters." *Signs* 7 (1981): 200–222.

Hwang, David Henry. *FOB and Other Plays.* New York: New American Library, 1990.

Kim, Elaine H. *Asian American Literature: An Introduction to the Writings and Their Social Context.* Philadelphia: Temple University Press, 1982.

Kingston, Maxine Hong. *China Men.* New York: Alfred A. Knopf, 1980.

———. "Cultural Mis-readings by American Reviewers." *Asian and Western Writers in Dialogue: New Cultural Identities.* Ed. Guy Amirthanayagam. London: Macmillan, 1982. 55–65.

———. "Personal Statement." *Approaches.* Ed. Lim. 23–25.

———. *The Woman Warrior: Memoirs of a Girlhood among Ghosts.* 1976. New York: Random House, 1989.

Kogawa, Joy. *Obasan.* 1981. New York: Doubleday, 1994.

Kristeva, Julia. *About Chinese Women.* Trans. Anita Barrows. London: Marion Boyars, 1977. [Trans. of *Des Chinoises*].

———. *The Kristeva Reader.* Ed. Toril Moi. New York: Columbia University Press, 1986.

———. *Powers of Horror.* Trans. Léon S. Roudiez. 1980. New York: Columbia University Press, 1982. [Trans. of *Pouvoirs de l'horreur*].

———. *Revolution in Poetic Language.* Trans. Margaret Waller. Intro. Léon S. Roudiez. 1974. New York: Columbia University Press, 1984. [Trans. of *La révolution du langage poétique*].

———. "Woman Can Never Be Defined." *New French Feminisms.* Ed. Marks and Courtivron. 137–41.

Lee, Robert G. "*The Woman Warrior* as an Intervention in Asian American Historiography." *Approaches.* Ed. Lim. 52–63.

Lim, Shirley Geok-lin, ed. *Approaches to Teaching Kingston's* The Woman Warrior. New York: Modern Language Association, 1991.

———. "Asian American Daughters Rewriting Asian Maternal Texts." *Asian Americans: Comparative and Global Perspectives.* Ed. Shirley Hune, Hyung-chan Kim, Stephen S. Fugita, and Amy Ling. Pullman: Washington State University Press, 1991. 239–48.

———. "Japanese American Women's Life Stories: Maternality in Monica Sone's *Nisei Daughter* and Joy Kogawa's *Obasan*." *Feminist Studies* 16 (1990): 289–312.

Lowe, Lisa. *Critical Terrains: French and British Orientalisms.* Ithaca, N.Y.: Cornell University Press, 1991.

Marks, Elaine, and Isabelle de Courtivron, eds. *New French Feminisms: An Anthology.* 1980. New York: Schocken Books, 1981.

Miller, Jean Baker. *Toward a New Psychology of Women.* Boston: Beacon Press, 1976.

Oliver, Kelly. *Reading Kristeva: Unravelling the Double-bind.* Bloomington: Indiana University Press, 1993.

Potter, Robin. "Moral—In Whose Sense? Joy Kogawa's *Obasan* and Julia Kristeva's *Powers of Horror*." *Studies in Canadian Literature* 15.1 (1990): 117–39.

Rabine, Leslie W. "No Lost Paradise: Social Gender and Symbolic Gender in the Writings of Maxine Hong Kingston." *Signs* 12 (1987): 471–92.

Rich, Adrienne. *Of Woman Born: Motherhood as Experience and Institution.* New York: W. W. Norton, 1976.

Roudiez, Léon S. "Introduction." *Revolution in Poetic Language.* By Julia Kristeva. New York: Columbia University Press, 1984. 1–10.

Rubenstein, Roberta. *Boundaries of the Self: Gender, Culture, Fiction.* Urbana: University of Illinois Press, 1987.

Said, Edward W. *Orientalism.* New York: Random House, 1978.

Shiach, Morag. *Hélène Cixous: A Politics of Writing.* London: Routledge, 1991.

Smith, Sidonie. *A Poetics of Women's Autobiography: Marginality and the Fictions of Self-Representation*. Bloomington: Indiana University Press, 1987.

Spivak, Gayatri Chakravorty. *In Other Worlds: Essays in Cultural Politics*. 1981. New York: Routledge, 1988.

Takaki, Ronald. *Strangers from a Different Shore: A History of Asian Americans*. New York: Penguin, 1989.

Warhol, Robyn R., and Diane Price Herndl, eds. *Feminisms: An Anthology of Literary Theory and Criticism*. New Brunswick, N.J.: Rutgers University Press, 1991.

Wittig, Monique. *Les guérillères*. Trans. David Le Vay. 1969. New York: Viking, 1971.

Wong, Sau-ling Cynthia. "Kingston's Handling of Traditional Chinese Sources." *Approaches*. Ed. Lim. 26–36.

6 ◇ Who Speaks, Who Listens?

Questions of Community, Audience, and Language in Poems by Chrystos and Wendy Rose

> My purpose is to make it as clear & as inescapable as possible, what the actual, material conditions of our lives are.
>
> —Chrystos, *Not Vanishing*

> The bottom line is contributing to our communities and adding to the total strength that makes for survival.
>
> —Wendy Rose, interview with Carol Hunter

The self-described political poets Chrystos and Wendy Rose share important assumptions with other contemporary women whose poetry works toward political dialogue and change. The epigraphs I have chosen for this essay, however, both identify major sources of strength for Chrystos and Rose and imply the limits of their commonality with Euramerican writers such as Adrienne Rich and Denise Levertov. In an essay focusing on Rich and Levertov, Lorrie Smith describes their work as exemplifying a women's political poetry grounded in the belief "that shared meaning and a common language are . . . necessary and empowering to their audiences, that the enterprise of imagining our relation to politics can be a collective one," and that "poetry is an active form of social communication, hence a potential agent of revolutionary change." Thus, contemporary women's political poetry aims to "restor[e] the authority of collective values" and "mend . . . the conventional division between the lyric self and others in the world" (156); crucial to this project is the poets' anticipation of "a participatory audience receptive to change" (158). Smith's description is appropriate not only to Rich's and

Levertov's work but also to that of predecessors such as Muriel Rukeyser and younger poets such as Carolyn Forché.

Smith's characterization of this politically committed writing is broadly applicable, too, to Chrystos's and Rose's poetry, as well as to the work of other politically oriented Native writers who are similarly committed to dialogue and collective empowerment for change. However, if we wish to attend fully to their work, we must acknowledge the complications created by race and ethnicity and by sexuality, class, and other historical/cultural factors—as Chrystos insists, we must pay attention to *"the actual material conditions"* that compel the poetry (*Not Vanishing*, preface). The meanings of a collaborative relationship with the audience become problematic for Rose and Chrystos because of the multiple and divergent audiences they address and the complex relationships among those audiences and between the poets and some of their readers. Likewise, "restoring the authority of collective values" may be a conflicted, and contested, endeavor for poets whose relationships to tradition are complex. Such complications result from and reflect borderland experience: how does the Native address the non-Indian, the mixed blood address the traditional community, the feminist woman of color speak to white feminists, the oppressed speak to the oppressor, the "object" of study speak to the academic?[1]

Rose (whose background includes Hopi, Miwok, and Euramerican ancestors) and Chrystos (Menominee and Euramerican) respond to and create fluid, sometimes ambivalent, relationships with audience and community. For both writers, these relationships derive from the complex dynamics of ancestry and affinity and contribute energy, power, and tension to their acutely dialogic poetic languages. Both live on multiply defined borders that their poems recreate as margins, in relation both to Native cultures and communities and to the dominant culture. Both come from mixed backgrounds, speak from urban experience, and are distanced from the languages of their tribal ancestors. Each identifies herself in terms of pan-Indian affiliation. Chrystos is a lesbian; Rose often speaks of herself in terms of her relationships to the academy. Both affiliations, as reflected in their writings, are experienced as doubly marginalizing.

Karl Kroeber illuminates the challenge in concepts of community and audience for contemporary poets like Rose and Chrystos when he observes that the status of traditional Indian poems as "socio-cultural synecdoche[s]" implies both the centrality of performance and the identity of "the total group, tribe, or nation as the appropriate 'audience' for each individual poet-singer" (104–6). Their access to traditional communities rendered problematic by geography, mixed parentage, and other factors, the poets must simultaneously create and negotiate relationships with community and audience that will accommodate their needs for connection (or distance) and empower them to, in Rose's words, add *"to the total strength that makes for survival."* Border politics, border consciousness, and multiple marginalizations inflect their efforts to locate themselves in relation to communities and audiences, and in turn concerns with community and audience foreground heteroglossia and dialogism in their poetry.[2]

Each poet identifies herself variously within her work and expands the meanings of her multiple identities by implicitly or explicitly speaking for similarly situated others. Each voices her identity as an Indian variously—for example, in terms of collective experience, in sorrow and anger, or in celebration. For Rose, the fact of mixed blood is unavoidably bound up with her Indian, particularly her Hopi, ancestry. Concerns about mixed origins seem less important in Chrystos's poetic self-identifications; rather, she names herself a woman of color, a lesbian, and a political activist. Such self-identifications, often overlapping, hardly represent the full range of either poet's self-conceptions; they are the facets of claimed identity most noticeable in poems that foreground issues of community and audience. All together, these multiple, interwoven aspects of identity clearly convey the fluid dynamics of identity (and hence of relation to audience, community, and language) that Rose and Chrystos create.

Wendy Rose's "If I Am Too Brown or Too White for You" (GW 63–64)[3] exemplifies the quality of fluidity implied by these poets' multiple self-images and voices:

> remember I am a garnet woman
> whirling into precision
> as a crystal arithmetic
> or a cluster . . .
> . . .
> . . . my body is blood
> frozen into giving birth
> over and over in a single motion

Rose's figurative language evokes the possibilities of joy and pain as well as a whole spectrum between them. The poem ends by affirming the voice-giving effects of multiplicity:

> . . . you always see
> just in time
> . . .
> there is a small light

in the smoke, a tiny sun
in the blood . . .
. . .
so pure
it is
singing.

Their multiple self-identifications might be taken as instances of poststructuralist, postmodernist representations of the nonunitary self but, at least as importantly, they reflect the border consciousness that Rose and Chrystos share as a given of contemporary Native American experience. Likewise, the realities of life in the borderlands inevitably imply that these self-identifications will be associated with conflict. Further, their multiple self-conceptions sharpen their awareness that their audiences are also multiple: from their shifting border locations, Chrystos and Rose recognize and address different audiences as they seek to influence, and sometimes to join, diverse communities. Among the dilemmas created by their awareness of the marginalizing effects of border experience are questions about how and to whom one may speak and what may be said.

Both Rose and Chrystos respond to the potential for conflict inherent in borderland conditions. Rose's poems often expose conflicts among components of her mixed identity and between her academic and Indian affiliations. Chrystos, on the other hand, is more likely to draw attention to how her various identities and affinities can cause conflict with the communities with which she would affiliate herself (e.g., Native and lesbian, white feminists and women of color). Again, border conditions exacerbate, and border consciousness clarifies, such conflicts. Their complex self-conceptions and multiple conceptions of audience and community assure that heteroglossia will surface audibly and the dialogic will become a defining characteristic in their poetic language. These multiplicities also assure that the conflict of competing intentions (Bakhtin 294), the "serious contest of codes" (Saldívar 259), will be foregrounded—as both consequence and means of the struggle to establish collectivity with their various audiences and communities.

Who constitutes the audiences and communities that Chrystos and Rose address? This is where the need to modify Smith's description of the politically engaged woman poet and her audience is most evident: Rose and Chrystos do not necessarily assume commonality with those whom they address; rather, they acknowledge and emphasize the need to create commonality through struggle, sometimes even with audiences "like them" (e.g., women, Indians). When they identify a primary audience, it is often an audience of others, characterized in opposition to the poet or speaker: "You" may be racist white feminists, superficially sympathetic non-Indians, academics engaged in various kinds of appropriation or presumption—and the poem's effort may be to shake, shame, or persuade "you" into new recognitions and behaviors. On the other hand, both poets directly address audiences less clearly "other": Native resisters, elders, or ancestors, for example. Each also addresses the communities with which she would ally herself, from which she seeks nurture and recognition, in order to make common cause. (Again, I note that I am not discussing many poems—including the whole body of Chrystos's love poetry—in which audience is conceived quite differently from what I see in these border-inflected, overtly political poems.)

For many Native American writers, issues of audience and community are vexed by the question: "What is ethical to tell?"[4] Can tradition be offered as a means to commonality with an eclectic audience? These writers may find themselves torn between what might be thought of as contradictory ways of honoring tradition. On the one hand, they might honor, by acknowledging in their writing, the stories that are their sources and in so doing continue the oral tradition that is the ground of Native cultural survival. Or, on the other, cognizant of the opportunities for misunderstanding, misrepresentation, and appropriation offered by every translation and sharing of tradition, they might honor by protecting the old stories and alluding to sacred or otherwise culturally vital materials cryptically, indirectly, partially, or not at all. Together, Rose and Chrystos represent the range of contemporary approaches to this issue.[5]

Their somewhat ambiguous relationships to traditional Native communities complicate both poets' work. Chrystos is adamantly silent about traditional stories and spirituality; as she says in the prefatory statement to *Not Vanishing,* "Our rituals, stories & religious practices have been stolen and abused, as has our land. I don't publish work which would encourage this—so you will find no creation myths here" (n.p.). On the other hand, Rose alludes, often cryptically or indirectly, to traditional Hopi lore, sometimes adapting such material as a way of claiming her place (as in "Builder-Kachina: Home-going"); she responds to questions about non-Native readers' access to Indian poetry by referring to the context of U.S. society in general: "I think that a person does need to stretch the imagination a little bit, perhaps, or to learn something about Native American cultures or Native American thought systems or religion, or philosophy. Just a little bit. . . . This is a plural society and all of us have to work at it a little bit to get the full flavor of the society" (qtd. in Bruchac 263). Chrystos resists the self-censorship that would keep her silent about contemporary conflicts within her communities.

As she confronts these issues, she illuminates the problematical relationship to community that she shares with Rose. "What is ethical to
tell? This is especially complex when one is part of oppressed groups,
who stand to have any negative information used against them." Chrystos continues:

> I've been relatively silent about a number of issues that concern me be-
> cause I've feared alienating Native People and/or Lesbians. These issues
> include . . . the full implications of being a person not really welcome in
> either group. . . . What do these silences mean? How can I break out of
> them respectfully? . . . In opening these areas to scrutiny, am I violating
> my culture? Is that culture the actual tradition or merely a mirror of colo-
> nization? ("Askenet" 241, 242)

Rose writes from the outsider's need to redefine community in ways
that will enable her to heal the isolation and hostility engendered by her
marginalizations. She speaks of feeling "alien" among whites yet knows
that she "wouldn't really fit easily into Hopi society" and that she is also
cut off from her mother's Miwok people: "When I think of my mother's
people, I think of confusion, tragedy, death, fragmentation, bones, and
things that are gone forever." Thus, while she urges writers "to look
within our own communities" and to "be more responsive to our own
people," she is also, like Chrystos, committed to "acknowledging and
identifying with . . . the struggle of indigenous people the world over."
Coming from Rose, what might seem a fairly simple statement about
"roots" becomes, if not problematical, at least multiply suggestive: "The
vehicle for finding my Hopi and my Miwok roots has been existing
within a community in which these things are important and are
known, being part of contemporary Indian life" (qtd. in Hunter 49, 53,
46, 55, 43).[6] This statement contains simultaneously regret for the loss
of community, resolve to survive that loss, and affirmation of the community that is now being created and sustained by contemporary Indian people, those who are or are not tribally affiliated.

For both poets, then, relationships with Native communities are
complex, potentially problematic, and marked by tensions that may be
either productive or debilitating. Such multivalenced realities produce
parallel complications vis-à-vis their audiences, who, unavoidably, are
implicated in questions of community: both poets, after all, speak to
and about those with whom they would align themselves; both, too, address others who are variously defined but who almost always include
white Euramericans with a whole history of responses to indigenous
cultures and communities. For Chrystos and Rose, the audience encompasses conceivably both those with whom the poet would affiliate her-

self most deeply and those against whom she feels compelled to protect her chosen or inherited communities.

This means that Chrystos and Rose often address audiences at whom they are angry. Their poems may then raise questions about anger's uses and effects—questions that arise most immediately, perhaps, if we recognize ourselves among the recipients of the anger. Chrystos is often given to single-minded expressions of outrage; Rose, too, sometimes opts for this approach.[7] In the context of their political agendas, beginning with the imperative of survival, such poems remind us that acknowledging and articulating anger in and of itself is a step toward solidarity and survival. But poets and critics of many origins remind us that voicing anger can only be a step, if the aim is to empower the dispossessed and change the world. Thus, whoever we are, we may look to politically engaged writers to use their anger creatively, to show us how to move beyond the static knowledge of either guilt or oppression. Both Rose and Chrystos offer many lessons.

Rose demonstrates how powerful anger can orient the poem toward revision and redefinition in works such as "I Expected My Skin and My Blood to Ripen" (LC 14–15), "Three Thousand Dollar Death Song" (LC 26–27), and "Notes on a Conspiracy" (GW 11–13). Each begins with an epigraph from the written records of the long assault on Native peoples; in the body of each poem, a Native-identified voice speaks of the physical and emotional realities denied by the epigraphs that come from the world of anthropological collecting—auction catalogs and museum invoices. Rose's anger hits home as each poem shocks readers into recognizing that its two voices refer to the same events or facts that are veiled and marginalized by the objectifying prose of the epigraph but that the body of the poem brings to the center of attention: rape, massacre, robbery, grief. Any reader who has, in museums or galleries, casually or studiously observed Native "artifacts" must be drawn into complicity by the juxtaposition of epigraph and poem: we have on some level benefited from some of the practices implied, for our aesthetics or "appreciation" have been "enriched" by the collecting and cataloging of the objects on which we gaze. But each poem's "body" forces us to acknowledge the bodies and lives of Native peoples and the horrors that made some of these artifacts "available" to collectors.

Among the effects of such poems is an all-pervasive dialogism and dialogue. The contrasting discourses of epigraph and poem embody the competing intentions and meanings of heteroglossia and open the possibility of conversation as the reader responds. Thus, the poems succeed both in condemning reprehensible actions and attitudes and in engaging perhaps historically implicated readers in change. Importantly, the poems facilitate engagement through reflection and questioning that encompass both mourning the dead and damaged and struggling to reimagine and reclaim Indian history and lives. For example, in "Notes on a Conspiracy," the spirit of the dead, referring to the colonizers, exclaims, "How little we knew! We should have asked / where is the dust of your mothers? / What happened to your own land? / Why did you come so far from your homes?" The questioning continues, "And we. Where is our strength that was acorn and blue jay . . . When will we dance—you remember the one— / where we bring up the sun with a shout?" The poem foregrounds dialogism by pointing out how language was and is used as a tool of oppression—"They blame us for their guilt. / They say we are now a privileged few"—but dialogism is complicated by questions that, recalling the title, invite us to consider whether the Natives themselves, in some terrible way, might have been implicated in the "conspiracy" or in its continuing effects. Even so and without softening the sharp knowledge of death and loss, the poem's shifts among past, present, and future imply the possibility of a revitalized Indian present and future—this spirit of the dead is not dead, after all: it is speaking.

Poems such as "Notes on a Conspiracy" establish part of the context of the struggle that is a major source of the concerns with audience and community in Rose's and Chrystos's work. The experiences of invasion, destruction, and oppression that such poems directly recall underlie the struggles for relationship, recognition, and authority and the questions of how and to whom to speak.

These questions and struggles are present powerfully, if implicitly, in a poem by Chrystos that reflects the concerns of her essay "Askenet" as it confronts the difficulties of community and illuminates the conflicts potential within identity politics, when identities collide.

Ya Don Wanna Eat Pussy

that Chippewa said to that gay white man who never has
Ya don wanna eat pussy after eatin hot peppers   he laughed
I stared   in the white sink memorizing rust stains
He nodded in the general direction of the windows behind us
   Two Native women chopping onions & pickles
   to make tuna fish sandwiches
   for these six men helping to move   (NV 36)

Repetition of the title line draws attention to the offensive language; the succeeding lines emphasize its divisive power:

He said   *Ya didn hear that did ya*   Good
She answered   *I chose to ignore it*
I muttered   *So did I*
Ya don wanna take offense at an Indian man's joke
     no matter how crude
in front of a white man
Close to my tribe   he probably guessed we're lesbians
said that   to see what we'd do
which was to keep on doin what we had been doin

The situation effectively silences the women. Yet the poem allows Chrystos, by mimicking the Chippewa's speech, to draw attention to the dialogic doubleness of her own language and thus to reempower herself as an offended woman. On the one hand, her explanation indicates her desire to protect the possibility of community with the Indian man; on the other, she distances herself from him and mocks him, by using his speech only here. At the same time, "close to my tribe" offers painful dialogic possibilities: In what sense is he close? Is the speaker herself close to her tribe? Does his closeness give him the power to exclude her, or does it imply that there should be a bond between them?

That gay white man stopped talking about how much he loved
hot peppers
That Chippewa said   *Not too much for me*   *Don eat fish*
probably another joke we ignored   I said
The grocery was fresh out of buffalo & deer

With "probably another joke," Chrystos again draws attention to heteroglossia and the divisions it implies; in the next line's rejoinder, she implies the doubleness of "we ignored." The poem ends with the gay man's direct entry into the uneasy searching of the multiply oppressed for community, or at least recognition, across the dividing lines:

Much later that gay white man called that Chippewa a drunk
we both stared at a different floor
in a different silence   just as sharp
& hot

In Rose's earlier poetry, collected in *Lost Copper,* the desire for connection with Native communities often awakens tensions identified with mixed origins. The individual in search of community is marginalized by her ambiguous identity, which may be seen as endangering the community's integrity and survival. Images of fragmentation are common, as are suggestions that voice and song—hence, language— are problematic for the person whose connections to community are

ambiguous or broken.[8] Thus, "It is I . . . who vanishes, who leans under-
balanced / into nothing; it is I . . . without song / who dies and cries the
death-time" ("Vanishing Point: Urban Indian," LC 12). And "Builder-
Kachina: Home-going" (LC 126–27) figures the poet-speaker as "a shred
of brown cotton" blown west from the Hopi village of Hotevilla to California. Though it was thirty years ago,

> . . . the scars are still fresh
> in me. They speak in my flesh,
> they rasp and shake in my bones,
> they circle like buzzards
> in my soul.
>
> Must I explain why
> the songs are stiff and shy?

In both poems, the speaker feels shut out by language, "without song"
in the first and in the second unbearably divided between California,
which "moves my pen," and "Hotevilla dash[ing] through my blood." In
"The Endangered Roots of a Person" (LC 50–51), Rose navigates between
fragmentation and the possibility of healing through language and ritual. The poem begins, "I remember lying awake / in a Phoenix motel . . .
coming apart accidentally / like an isolated hunk of campfire soot / cor-
nered by time into a cave." "Sometimes," she acknowledges, "Medicine
People shake their hands / over you," and she recalls, "The Hand-
trembler said / I belong here. I fit in this world." Yet the ending may
imply only a tenuous reassurance:

> On some future dig
> they'll find me like this
> uncovered where I knelt
> piecing together the flesh
> that was scattered in the mesa wind
> at my twisted-twin birth.[9]

In "The Day I Was Conceived" (LC 48–49), images of splitting, carving, and scarring are associated with the creation of life by a silversmith
"Badger-father." Numerous allusions to the father's Hopi identity offer a
grounding that shifts slightly as Rose refers, too, to her mother's Miwok
people: "acorn-tongues, cedar lodges, . . . shells still wet / from the sea."
Such references to a double inheritance might be construed as enriching; in the contexts of Rose's comments about her own experience, however, they should probably be read as equally disruptive. "The Day I Was
Conceived" reappears in *Going to War with All My Relations* as "Honani
Chunta" (14–15); the new title, translated as "faithless badger," compli-

cates the poem by raising questions that can be answered, if at all, only by inference and speculation. The poem's ending, though, unchanged except for the line breaks, suggests that mixed origins remain painfully problematic: "I sing / but do not carve. . . . I dance but do not pray. . . . I grow but do not live" (LC 49).

"The Well-Intentioned Question" (LC 6–7; GW 55–56) might be thought of as elaborating on the consequences of the conception and inheritance described in "The Day I Was Conceived"/"Honani Chunta." Its structure recalls the defeating balances of the latter poem's conclusion: the "Indian name soars" and is "stopped," "catapults" and then "bumps," "howls" and then listens. When asked her "Indian name," surely by a non-Indian, the poet responds by drawing attention to the multiple, competing meanings of an apparently simple but in fact heavily dialogized question. Rather than answering in the manner undoubtedly expected by the asker, she characterizes her unrevealed and perhaps literally nonexistent "Indian name" in ambiguous terms that subtly draw attention to her vexed relationship to the community, the source of names. Her Indian name seems to signal her marginalized status: she is observed by "obsidian-hard women / sighting me with eyes / Coyote gave them"; and the final lines imply a permanent isolation, as her "Indian name listens / for footsteps / stopping short of my door / then leaving forever." In the course of the poem, "Indian name" becomes dialogized: the asker's expectations, the traditional implications, and the meanings of both to the speaker all come into complex conflict. Her Indian name does not include her in an Indian community; further, the asker of the "well-intentioned question" and the reader, also awaiting the answer, may be implicated—not having received the expected exotic or picturesque answer, do we leave forever, believing that the speaker is neither "really Indian" nor worthy of further interest?[10]

In some of these poems Rose moves toward imagining reintegration into a sense of Hopi or Indian identity and community. Thus, in "Vanishing Point," the urban Indian's urgent repetitions of "It is I" (repetitions that render the statement and identity itself dialogic) culminate as she claims a role that might be construed as protective, heroic, ironic, or all three simultaneously:

> . . . It is I who die
> bearing cracked turquoise & making noise
> so as to protect your fragile immortality
> O Medicine Ones.

Most reassuring is the final stanza of "Builder-Kachina: Home-going." Here the badger-father speaks:

> Carefully
> the way we plant the corn
> in single places, each place
> a hole just one finger around.
> We'll build your roots
> that way. . . .
>
>   . . .
>
> What we can't find
> we'll build but
> slowly,
> slowly.

Referring to "Builder-Kachina . . . invisible / yet touching me all over / with his sound," Rose at once demonstrates the poem's promise and exposes the heteroglossia latent even in a word like kachina (of course, simply transliterating this concept into a word pronounceable in English has already implied that potential). Builder-Kachina, as she notes (LC 127), represents not a traditional conception of the Hopi spirit people but her own creative response to a "somewhat flexible" tradition. The tradition, she implicitly affirms, gives her a means of connecting with the community. Yet the last three lines, "we'll build but / slowly, / slowly," remind us of the need for care and caution and of the likelihood that disruptions and uncertainties will recur.

Among Rose's earlier poems, perhaps the most confident evocation of community comes in "Walking on the Prayerstick" (LC 4). The poem speaks with the serenity of a people who know themselves at one with the natural world: "We map our lives this way: trace our lineage / by the corn." Past and present are continuous; the speaking voice is communal; the audience is invited: "Imagine you float / to those white scar marks / on the granite where . . . we first learned to sing / on ancient mornings." The poem's placement early in *Lost Copper* suggests that it offers a grounding for those that follow, yet the many poems that express tension and ambivalence about community also suggest that it might be as nostalgic as it is affirmative: in a sense the poem voices an ideal from which Rose's mixed-blood speakers are excluded. The image of "scar marks . . . where water / drains breaking open the rocks" echoes in other poems where scars and splittings are ambiguously associated with the pain of breaking as well as the possibility of mending.

Chrystos might be thought of as trying to circumvent or break through tensions like those Rose represents, when she claims community by simply asserting that it exists. Thus, "I Walk in the History of My People" (NV 7) begins:

> There are women locked in my joints
> 　　for refusing to speak to the police
> My red blood full of those
> 　　arrested　　in flight　　shot

Community is founded on a history of cultural and physical pain, realized by the speaker in her own body's ills and in her memory, and confirmed by difference: "In my marrow are hungry faces / who live on land the whites don't want." Similarly, in "Going Through" (DO 90–91) Chrystos claims kinship with those who are gone:

> These are the hills where bear hunted sweet berries
> We women rubbed our hair with their grease
> 　　This was a song requiring many harmonies
> a sky blue as a drum　　flute sweet as spring.

Again, community implies pain, founded as it now is in loss felt not only by the human speaker but also by bereaved nature. Native traditions have the capacity for introducing into heteroglossia and dialogism an element probably unforeseen by M. M. Bakhtin, the speaking voices of nature: the voices of trees, a river, and wild roses are layered into the lament that is this poem's most effective claim of community ("River turns in her sleep / *Where are my sweet salmon?*"). Another dialogic element is Chrystos's allusion to the rhythms and repetitions of traditional song in "A Song for My People" (DO 70) and "We Cut Off Our Hair" (DO 103). Each concludes with a song or prayer that, by implicitly invoking the cultural community that created and has sung such expression through generations, grounds the written English of the present claim in a spirit of ongoing resistance.

That community, continuity, and resistance demand complex effort is the burden of "I Like to Think" (DO 68), in which Chrystos engages her audiences on several levels:

> I Like to Think
> of the Black miners in south africa
> continually
> I like to remember that they are always
> Black
> 　. . .
> I need to remember their wages
> aligned with the price of diamond & gold jewelry
> & so do you
> I need to know
> they plunder what is their own land
> I like to think about the days they spend in total darkness

> . . .
> I like to remember the misery of death
> under the gleam of necklaces   rings   cars   knives   spoons
> I like to think how much we have in common
> . . .
> I like to remember all the white owners
> of Navajo rugs   Zuni jewelry   Lakota shirts   Pueblo pottery
> . . .
> & the price of those things when whites sell them
> to each other after buying them from us for dimes
> or taking them

The poem's repetitions become a chant with transformative power. The repeated "I like to think" seems to insist on the dialogic nature of the sentence and of language, without doing us the favor of translating—*we* need to think. Simultaneously, the nine repetitions of "like" may push the comparative meaning through the verb: "we" are *like* other exploited peoples. This is made explicit as "they" (the black miners) become "we" in the middle of the poem ("how much we have in common"), while the third-person plural comes to refer to the "white owners." But the contrast between solidarity and exploitation is complicated by Chrystos's use of spacing: "I need to remember that the Native design towels / I want to buy at Macy's   fill a white man's pocket." The temptation to complicity is not only verbally acknowledged but also visually represented, conveying a brief shock to the reader. It is this recognition of possible betrayal that justifies the simplicity of the immediately following final lines and complicates the ending:

> I like to think of our relationship
> boiled to a simple phrase
> They take   We give
> They take more

While the poem ends by sharply distinguishing "us" from "them," it does not merely articulate anger. I think this is in part because its address to the audience is inclusive. If in the end it speaks most directly to an Indian audience, exhorting them to recognize the grounds of solidarity and the dividing lines, as those of race and exploitation for profit, its first direct address to the reader—"& so do you"—does not identify that "you" and is not preceded by qualifiers that exclude any from those who "need to remember." While different readers' relationships to the poem change, as the meanings of "we" and "they" shift and separate, the non-Native and white readers have still been given the work of remembering. We may not be invited into the community of color-based resistance to oppression the poem seeks to build, but we are all, I think, asked to consider how we wish to align ourselves in relation to that community: Will we listen, remember, learn how to support, exploit . . . ?

If, by the end of "I Like to Think," Chrystos intimates the possibilities of creating common cause within and across communities of color, even the possibility that white readers might be engaged in supportive solidarity, Indians' ongoing marginalization by the dominant culture remains a pressing reality for both poets. Rose brings consciousness of such marginalization into sharp relief in early poems that draw on her experience as an anthropology student. Issues of community, audience, and language remain problematic in the university, which arouses both anger and ambivalence as the aspiring student recognizes herself as the exploited "object" of others' scholarly gazes. In "The Anthropology Convention" (LC 22), the speaker identifies with the anthropologists' objects of study: "From the day we are born / there are eyes all around / to watch . . . for exotic pots of words / spilled from our coral and rawhide tongues. / O we are / the Natives." Other poems indicate the consequences, for a Native student, of aspiring to participate in the academic project. "Matriculation" (LC 32–33) shows her compelled to test and disrupt the language and stories she hears:

> They really got mad
> when I picked up the books
> and like laundry began
> to shake them clean.

She likens her instructors' lectures to earlier colonizing adventures:

> The rattles and groans
> of the speeches you give
> might in another time have been
> the wood and rope of tallships
> . . .
> You discover me
> again and again.

Yet, she soon realizes, "You don't / see me." She becomes "a red ghost" ("Handprints," LC 36–37), searching in the university for "a woman / built from earthen blocks / who is not / specimen" or "evidence / for 'affirmative / action'"—searching for herself. Not surprisingly, becoming an "Academic squaw" (LC 30), like being of mixed origins, subjects her to splitting and breaking:

> Like bone in outer space
> this brain leans to a fierce break;
> with crooked muscles and names mis-said
> we ethno-data heroically bend
> further and further, becoming born
> from someone else's belly.

She knows splitting and division equally painfully in "Indian Anthropologist: Overhanging Sand Dune Story" (LC 39):

> They hope, the professors,
> to keep the keyhole blocked
> where my mind is pipelined
> to my soul; they block it
> with the shovel and pick
> of the pioneer spirit,
> the very energy that made
> this western earth turn over
> and throw us from her back

Rose notes that the word "squaw" is, "in modern usage, a derogatory term" (LC 30); using it ironically, she underlines her awareness of the high stakes involved in dialogism's competing intentions—a recognition that comes painfully to the "red ghost" and is implicit in all her confrontations with the academy's stories of Native lives. One consequence, the silencing of the Natives' own stories, is realized with personal immediacy in "How I Came to Be a Graduate Student" (LC 38): "It was when my songs became quiet. / No one was threatened." The Indian who would enter the academy, these poems tell us, becomes vulnerable to and implicated in tensions and ambivalences analogous to those that confront the mixed-blood person. Both the Indian academic and the mixed blood experience discomfort and alienation as internal realities and as externally imposed conditions, as borders drawn by history and politics are reinforced and reflected internally, with devastating effects. In both contexts, her identity as an Indian is contested, and she must respond defensively to influences that would undercut her affiliation with living Native communities.

Reading the university poems in *Lost Copper,* together with Chrystos's poems of struggle for a multiracial activist community, throws into clear relief behaviors Chrystos's intended audience might not recognize in themselves but from which she attempts to shake us. We may not be anthropologists "collecting" stories or curators preserving cultural "artifacts," but, academics or not, those who would support oppressed peoples' struggles for power, recognition, or redress are hardly immune to behaving in appropriative, stereotyping, and otherwise oppressive ways.

"I Am Not Your Princess" (NV 66–67) responds to a non-Native audience romantically eager to know, honor, and help "the Indians." Insisting that we acknowledge her individual identity and integrity, Chrystos at once distances herself from generalizations and affirms solidarity with Native peoples and communities by insisting that she cannot speak for them, only for herself. She begins by drawing attention, uncharacteristically, to her own mixed origins: "Sandpaper between two cultures which tear / one another apart I'm not / a means by which you can reach spiritual understanding." She makes clear that it is not mixed origins as such but history, culture, and the limits of individual experience that make her unable—and unwilling—to fulfill her implied interlocutor's desires. Thus, while she offers a recipe for fry bread, it is accompanied by a language lesson, but not the lesson of an "Indian name" or prayer for which the listener might have hoped: "This is Indian food / only if you know that Indian is a government word / which has nothing to do with our names for ourselves." Rather it is a lesson about heteroglossia's angrily contested meanings, which are brought into visible dialogic conflict along the borders between "the government's" and "our own" names—and between Indian individuals and communities and those who wish to exoticize or homogenize them. Refusing to "chant for you . . . sweat with you or ease your guilt with fine turtle tales," she refuses to collaborate in the appropriation of Native language, voices, and stories—as she does, too, when she warns us, "Don't assume . . . that I even know names of all the tribes / or can pronounce names I've never heard." She insists that we not impose our stories and needs on her, in effect appropriating her, as a Native person, to our agendas: "Look at my heart   not your fantasies   Please don't ever / again tell me about your Cherokee great-great grandmother."

While voicing anger and frustration, Chrystos also conveys a desire to reach and instruct the audience, despite her doubts: "I don't think your attempts to understand us are going to work." Yet she is not advising us to give up, so much as indicating that our expectations are wrong: she would rather, I think, that we recognize her as a human individual and respectfully leave her alone or support her own self-determination. And she conveys this hope in a way that allows the audience their own self-respect, a way of revising expectations by claiming the common ground of "human weakness   like your own . . . work to do," washing "the same things / you wash," and by repeating the fry bread ingredients at the end, with a disclaimer, both modest and assertive: "Remember this is only my recipe   There are many others." The poem thus acknowledges an important, though limited commonality that can be the basis of respect without smoothing over anger or pain.

In "Just Like You" (DO 48–49), Chrystos challenges her audience to extend the recognition of commonality and share a particular political perception. Where the audience is, by the end of this provocative poem, may be open to question but that, one might argue, is the necessary nature of work that truly challenges things as they are. The poem takes off from the common fact that, like her reader, the speaker gets "a lot of junk mail." As she peruses the newly arrived "american eagle outfitters catalogue," her response defines her in ways that may separate her from her readers. In the first place, she admits that she has "many complex bitter feelings about the words / american & Eagle in conjunction"; still, she opens the catalog and proceeds to read it in a way that suggests that the dialogism at work in the preceding lines may also be latent in the visual images. In "romantic patagonia / four spray-starched ken and barbie dolls" are depicted, "icons . . . so clean . . . [in] bright blue, red & yellow . . . ready to go sailing on someone's rosewood & brass yacht." Juxtaposed to this "beach ball collage," she sees "four brown-skinned women," three of them shoeless. "I'm sure they were unpaid," she states and then focuses on "the only person looking straight at the camera," a small girl in this group of brown-skinned women. The child holds a slingshot; the poem concludes, "She looks as though she'd like to put a rock / right through the camera lens / just like me." By the end, the title's statement has become a question—are poet and audience "just alike" in their assessments of the junk mail that linked them? Are their ties any more substantial than junk mail? The poem's judgments and contrasting images create gaps that readers must negotiate. In the process, they must engage in dialogue and recognize dialogism. If they end by agreeing with Chrystos, then poet and readers together may have built a small piece of the foundation of an activist community. However, the indeterminacy of the readers' responses highlights some of the difficulties of establishing such alliances.

Chrystos's strategy in "Just Like You" is to foreground realities that the dominant discourse generally admits only as background, contrast, or atmosphere for the images and messages of a white "Western" culture of consumption: what has been marginalized is brought to the center and allowed to displace the catalog's brightly colored "icons," challenging the exploitative gaze of the camera. Similarly, in "I Like to Think," she brings the black miners of South Africa up from underground in order to incite a critique of the institutions that marginalize them for profit. Any reclamation of suppressed stories implicitly questions assumptions about what is worthy of the center (what is "centrally important") and what is of only "marginal importance." That is also one of the effects of Rose's early university poems (as I discuss below, Rose's more recent work develops complex modes of bringing the "marginal" into the center).

In "The Women Who Love Me" (DO 104–5) and "Lesbian Air" (DO 142–43), respectively, Chrystos redresses with engaging energy and evident joy the marginalization documented in "Ya Don Wanna":

> They're the Lesbians mothers don't want to meet
> who make shy girls blush from their feet up
> They're out here on the same razor I walk shouting
> the goddam emperor is naked & so is the empress
> . . .
> Just remember when you open your mouths to trash us
> we're the ones carving out the tunnels
> so you'll have room to breathe

and

> Ah the theory of Lesbianism is a lot of words that not
> all Lesbians understand or want to   It is the wanting
> of women we share . . . Our tongues meet we can never
> have too much of each other as we speak on palestinian
> land rights, as we march against racism, as we demand
> abortion rights for women who might hate us as we
> stand for them . . . as we breathe Lesbian air . . . as we
> write Lesbian traffic tickets, as we predict Lesbian
> earthquakes . . . We are our mother's infinite variety   We
> are Lesbian redwoods   We are Lesbian rain forests . . .
> we are Lesbian lizards . . . we are the Lesbian sky

These poems draw attention to language in a way that challenges borders by foregrounding and enriching the heteroglossia of "lesbian." Addressing "the women who love [her]" and those who are nervous, homophobic, or not lesbians, they affirm and celebrate lesbians' presence and challenge us to recognize that presence in struggles and mundane events that involve all of our lives, however we might define ourselves. Thus, in the project of bringing the marginalized into the center, Chrystos engages an inclusive audience. (I want to suggest, though economy prevents enlarging upon the idea here, that she may also be implicitly questioning the exclusivity of "the center," inviting us to consider the validity of acknowledging multiple, coexisting centers.) Though "Lesbian Air" ends with affirmations that suggest Native American cultures' emphasis on connection with nature, neither of these poems draws attention to a specifically Indian context. Yet reading them in conjunction with poems that do directly address issues of relationship to Indian communities, we can see "Lesbian Air" and "The Women Who

Love Me," too, as working toward inclusiveness in specifically Native contexts.

Like Chrystos, Rose redefines margins and centers, both to empower self and community and to instruct her audiences. Her engagement with these issues is evident in poems from *Lost Copper,* such as "I Expected My Skin and My Blood to Ripen" and "Three Thousand Dollar Death Song," as well as in the early university poems. In *Going to War with All My Relations,* Rose voices a more complex, less defensive ambivalence about the academy, but what predominates is the voice of authority—the voice of one who will no longer allow herself to be appropriated as an object of study, because she no longer assumes that such appropriation is inevitable for herself or others. While this authority does not exempt her from soul-searching or from difficult encounters, it does empower her to respond effectively to people and assumptions that earlier paralyzed or simply angered her.

Again, "If I Am Too Brown or Too White for You" (GW 63–64) seems to embody Rose's creative vision of an empowering alternative to the complicity in self-marginalization commonly imposed by mixed origins and abetted by the academy.[11] As such, it may be read as enabling her to claim and exercise the authority manifest in later poems. In "If I Am," she celebrates the dynamic possibilities of being both vividly alive and undefinable—imperfect, "clouded," and "pure" all at once. This capacity for affirming integrity in the midst of flux, or even integrity *as* flux— as the "small light / in the smoke," the "tiny sun / in the blood" becomes a "pure" singing—allows Rose to take the stance she does in the poem that follows it in *Going to War,* "Margaret Neumann" (65–69). Here she approaches her complex relationship to her German great-great grandmother from a meditative position in which a Native identity is both a given, assumed without needing to be defended, and fluid, "clouded" by history. Her relationship to the audience, mediated by the figure of her ancestor, is similarly complicated and rendered collaborative.

Margaret Neumann, a participant in the California gold rush and inevitably implicated in the shedding of "Bear Creek blood, blood of Mariposa, / Yosemite blood, Ahwahnee blood," is introduced as a "wild girl" with "dangerous dreams," a characterization that associates her with some of Rose's own self-depictions. Not only "wild" but "transformed . . . at the border," Margaret is recognized, too, as a fluid identity, an ancestor in the process of becoming, for whom experience might be imagined as dialogic—hence an audience (Rose addresses her directly) who might hear the dialogic layers of language and with whom dialogue might be imaginable.

> Into the muscle and flesh
> of what you called wilderness
> you drove the brown horses
> . . .
> You brought to life
> the anxious temblor
> in my heart.

Language and its layers of intentions both justify and expose invasion and cataclysmic disruption. Single-minded condemnation, then, would be inadequate linguistically and emotionally. If Margaret has "brought to life" that "anxious temblor," it is because she has also brought to life the speaker's heart. Rose imagines her ancestor as a living spirit, a participant in the process of imaginative creation and recreation:

> Are you the astonished one
> or am I? . . .
> . . . that you
> are my ancestor
> learning to imagine me.

Meeting Margaret in mythic time, where present and past coincide in transformative simultaneity, Rose recognizes her ancestor's complex reality—which is her own truest inheritance—and imagines this distant relative into dialogue.

The relationship she creates is one of reciprocity, a balance that implies an ongoing rhythm of recognition and recreation:

> If you are a part of me
> I am also that crazy acorn
> within your throat
> around which pioneer stories
> rattle and squirm
> If you are the brave heritage
> of Gold Rush California,
> I am also the bone
> that buzzes behind your breast.
> If I am the tongue made indigenous
> by all the men you would love,
> I am also the ghost
> of the pioneer's future.

The poet imagines an embrace of contraries, a resolution provisional in its commitment to difficult emotional realities and to dialogic processes, yet convincing in its empowerment of the multiply identified speaker. These lines, after all, both compellingly imagine the European

ancestor's discomfort and give precedence to the speaker's present indigenous and mixed reality—implying both an ongoing discomfort and
the restorative power of revision and recreation. Again, Rose draws attention to the contested meanings that constitute heteroglossia as "pio-
neer stories / rattle and squirm" and the speaker becomes "the tongue
made indigenous"; and her images make concrete, and concretely disturbing, the acute dialogism compelled by border consciousness.

Yet "touching the silver / at the center" of both of them, Rose is
moved to an imaginative act of faith ("I believe you would understand")
founded on an implicit confidence in the power of her and her ancestor's historically grounded imagination:

> Do you remember
> the sacred signs
> . . .
> in the German Black Forest?
> Do you remember the tribes
> that so loved their land
> before the roll
> of Roman wheels?

The poem ends successfully on these two questions, not because the answer is a foregone conclusion, but because Rose has imagined an ancestor and by extension a contemporary audience capable of hearing and
responding. Having created the possibility of dialogue by imagining her
ancestor as a participant, she can leave the poem's ending truly open.
She has not transcended ambivalence, but she has conceived of a dialogic process in which she need not be trapped or paralyzed by any of
the components of her multiple identities. This enables a more creative,
more productive, because less defensively reactive, relationship with her
various communities and audiences than was evident in the earlier
poems on mixed-blood and/or academic experiences. Such an accomplishment also grounds the poems about the academy and others that
question and redefine margins and centers in *Going to War with All My
Relations*.

"Excavation at Santa Barbara Mission" (GW 6–8) bears the following
epigraph: "*When archaeologists excavated Santa Barbara Mission in California, they discovered human bones in the adobe walls.*" In the course of the
poem, the artist-archaeologist must confront the (literal) foundation of
her expectations about the dig and her relationship to the site; she can
deny neither her position as a "hungry scientist" nor her kinship with
the bones she unearths. The process of self-recognition raises questions
of complicity that the poem cannot evade. The possibility of conflict is

implicit from the first lines: "My pointed trowel / is the artist's brush / that will *stroke and pry* . . . the old mission wall" (emphasis added). The poet explains her eagerness: she "wanted to count [herself] / among the ancient dead / as a faithful neophyte . . . in love / with the padres / and the Spanish hymns." As the "excavation," proceeds, she discovers the problematic and conflicting meanings of such counting and replaces the Spanish hymns with a different song. She finds "so many bones / mixed with the blood / from my own knuckles," the bones' fragility matched by her own growing helplessness as, "crouching in white dust," she hears "the whistle / of longbones breaking / apart like memories." Her hands "empty themselves / of old dreams"—her own? those of dead Indians?—even as she knows herself "a hungry scientist / sustain[ed] . . . with bones of / men and women . . . who survived in their own way." The limits of that survival, though, and the anguish of her own realizations are evident in her final, chanting lines:

> They built the mission with dead Indians.
> They built the mission with dead Indians.
> They built the mission with dead Indians.
> They built the mission with dead Indians.

The fourfold repetition (itself reminiscent of much traditional Native American poetry) asserts the literal centrality of the Indian dead in the walls and confirms the poem's primary accomplishment, placing them in the center of consciousness for the speaker and her audience. Doing this, she has redefined the Santa Barbara Mission, excavated its buried history, and revised the way we must speak of it in the future. In its creation of a process of self-recognition and acknowledgment, this poem recalls "Margaret Neumann"; in both poems, the discovery of multiple identities is arduous, and the implications for community complex.

The multiple meanings Rose finds in "bones" link "Excavation at Santa Barbara Mission" to other poems that question or revise margins and centers. Bones are more than the remnants of victimization or appropriation found in the earlier university poems and in "Three Thousand Dollar Death Song." At Santa Barbara, bones are fragile and broken yet not simply dead remnants. They are "scattered like corn." Mixed with the speaker's blood, "breaking / apart like memories," they are intimately evocative of physical and spiritual connection and loss; "shivering into mist," they transform the poet's vision even as they dissolve; brittle and crumbling, they are yet a strong foundation, for they *are* the walls of the mission. The poem exposes "bones" as dialogic, infused with past and present intentions that imply future possibilities. The walls made of bones figure both the brutalities inherent in colonialism's borders and the difficult revisions that may be possible in the border-lands of the present.

The revisions of "Excavation" affect most immediately Rose's knowl-edge of herself in relation to the past; "Muskogee" (GW 48–49) affirms her relationship to the past and to the "Mother Ground" through the creation of a contemporary multiethnic Indian community. "Musko-gee" is a Creek word that names both a people and their language. In this poem, Rose uses the cultural differences between herself, "this desert girl," and the people of the Roundhouse, the oaks, and the Trail of Tears to emphasize strength and continuity: "there is still / the song that carried me east to sacred ground," a song of earth, history, and relation-ship, as she has been taught by the Muskogee "elder" she addresses. Singing, she remembers the people's affirmation of their own center through fidelity to memory, ritual, and dream:

> . . . when they made you walk away from your land
> she only rolled over, tricked them good,
>
> for the center is still the center, the fire
> carefully kept, Mother Ground still alive.

Strong in this song and her memory, she sees bones as the intimate signs "of how we are related through the red earth here" and of "Mother Ground's" continuing protection. (She thus realizes an organic relationship analogous to that affirmed in "Walking on the Prayerstick" but in a way that accommodates cultural difference within a pantribal community.)

Perhaps partly enabled by the self-recognition (albeit ambivalent) of "Excavation at Santa Barbara Mission" and by the empowering knowl-edge of relationship in "Muskogee," Rose speaks with authoritative assurance in two poems that redefine margins and centers in the con-text of the academy: "For the Campus Committee on the Quality of Life" (GW 57–58) and "For the Complacent College Students Who Don't Think People Should 'Live in the Past'" (GW 61–62). The first rep-rimands with morally grounded energy; in the second, Rose reaches out to help her students see their own possible connections to those they would criticize. "For the Campus Committee" is prefaced by a lengthy epigraph that forcefully catalogs the indignities visited upon the speaker's diversely identified students, indignities presumably ig-nored in the committee's proposal of *"coffee hours and bowling teams."* The contrast between such projects and *"sickle cell crises . . . rocks thrown at . . . mixed-blood children,"* sterilization *"merely for crossing a border,"* struggles against alcohol, and BIA checks that don't arrive demonstrates the marginalization of the oppressed and the heteroglossia of "Quality of Life" as it is understood by the relatively comfortable and by the students for whom Rose speaks. Epigraph and poem work together, for while the epigraph lists the literal indignities, the poem itself identifies in viscerally concrete terms the effects of institutionalized disregard for the disenfranchised:

> . . . we have stripped ourselves bare for you
> and you eat, just that simple thing
> unable to taste the sweet blood or feel
> against your teeth the bone . . .

In the poem's second half, Rose does with "bones" what Chrystos does with "lesbian" in "Lesbian Air." Bones become literally and figuratively the lives of the ignored, oppressed, and marginalized, which Rose brings back into the center by giving them ubiquity and dialogic vitality.

> O we are the bones
> a forest of bones
> . . .
> bones of clay, obsidian, redwood
> . . .
> . . . weak and hurting bones,
> . . .
> bridges of bones, fences, horizons, barriers
> of bones . . .
> bone prisons, bone colleges, encampments
> of bones, we are the bones
> of what you forget, of what
> you thought were just lies
> we are the bones
> that stop you from feeling better
> . . .
> the bones forever
> floating out of reach.

These "bones" signal, too, both the futility of improving "the quality of life" unless those in power attend to the students' grievances and the students' own refusal ("floating out of reach") to have their needs or identities defined by campus committees. Their implicit appeal to the audience is grounded in a claim of a relationship that is as persistent as it is uncomfortable for all—"you" consume and ignore "us"; "we" "follow . . . you home . . . direct . . . your dreams" and will not let "you" rest. The audience is left, as in Chrystos's "Just Like You," without the comfort of a formula or a promise, to consider, to choose, perhaps to act.

In "For the Complacent College Students," Rose reaches out to offer her audience the possibility of dialogue (and dialogic understanding), if the students will accept her invitation to consider imaginatively the implications of their own experiences. The provisional quality of the offer is evident in the beginnings of the poem's four sections: "do you see," "and if someone thinks," "and you wonder," and "and now you wonder." Rose first takes us adroitly through a demonstration in which the killing of ivy "on the old brick wall" becomes an analogy for cultural genocide: the roots are severed in "one lethal cut," the flowers "pressed and dried . . . catalogued, thoroughly studied, / or thrown away . . . as if they had never lived / except on display."

The poem's second, more directly personal half depends entirely upon our willingness to imagine ourselves as similarly vulnerable to being cut off at the roots—or perhaps already cut off: "and you wonder at the name / your mother's mother wore." To reach the inheritors of the westward expansion, Rose evokes the vehicles of her own Native people's dispossession: "you wonder . . . at the wagon or the sailing ship she rode." Perhaps she is able with equanimity to offer such likely touchstones of her students' dreams and uncertainties because she has wondered similarly about herself and her ancestors, not only in "Notes on a Conspiracy" but also in "Margaret Neumann." Indeed, Rose invites her students and readers to engage in such questioning exploration for themselves, as she suggests: "and now you wonder / if you are she and she is you, . . . prayer or prophecy or mere suggestion . . . the woman's face / you never knew that you rub with warm water / in the morning." As befits so suggestively intimate an ending, Rose asks of her "complacent" students an undertaking somewhat analogous to her own "excavations" at Santa Barbara and her poetic conversation with her German great-great grandmother. In so doing, she addresses the assumptions perhaps unstated in the students' critique of those who "live in the past": that such people and their pasts are insignificant to and less real than the students' immediate present—that in fact they deserve to be marginalized. As she revises the implications of living in the past, subtly playing on the power differentials inherent in the phrase's dialogic layers, she also reveals the commonality of our need to know ourselves in terms of our pasts; thus by imagining the students' own concerns, she recenters the issue and the unnamed people whose efforts to recover their pasts presumably prompted the students' objections.

"To Make History" (GW 79–80) similarly engages and instructs its audience in a process of creation that is also a process of establishing related-

ness. While it does not explicitly address marginalization, by juxtaposing it to poems that resist the dominant "historical" versions of Indians'
lives we can read it as redressing such impositions, as it creates a concept
of history that involves the integration of the maker, the story, and the
natural world. "To Make History" thus destabilizes margins and centers,
by emphasizing the making, and not just the reception, of history. The
poem marks a shift from Rose's early university poems, where she and
her readers could only react angrily or sadly to versions of history imposed on them by finished texts. Now Rose offers an alternative image to
the walls of Santa Barbara; making history is figured here as making a
blanket: "The strongest memory is the warp / carrying structure and order to the sky." This process requires delicacy and care, for the product
and the maker are both fragile:

> Take care not to go too fast
> or the body of the blanket
> will burst like breaking bones.
>
> Your hands get wilder, bleed and blister.

Reminiscent of the images in "Excavation at Santa Barbara Mission,"
these lines imply that to aim at the objectivity assumed by anthropology and conventional academic history would be self-deluding, even
harmful. What the poem offers instead is participation in the interwoven and dialogic layers of natural, human, and visionary realities. Eras-
ing the lines between the codifiers and the objects of history, it offers an
ethos in which people tell their own stories. With the spider's web, the
mesa, and the four directions, the final lines might suggest Hopi origin
myths and surely imply a promise of order and connectedness: [12]

> Backlit spider webs encircle the day
> fragile and tough as morning. Listen
> to the singing, the mystical thing
>
> finished and folded and spinning away.
> Lie face down on the mesa, hands and feet pointing
> to the four corners of everything
>
> and now it is done
> now it is done.

Invoking mystery and ritual, continuity and completion, Rose renders
"history" dialogic. Most radically, I believe, she invites her audience—
an unusually inclusive audience for her—to participate in the ongoing
creation of history: if "now it is done," still "the mystical thing" is "spin-
ning away." Ritual offers both closure and the promise of continuity.

Chrystos offers a similar invitation to participate in the remaking of history (and of the world) in "Urban Indian" (DO 151):

> I drum an old song on the hood of an abandoned stripped car
> . . .
> calling down horses   calling down deer   calling down loons
> calling down turtles
> . . .
> as green our mother takes herself back   fine dust is all
> that's left of these prisons & pain
> I am dreaming on this
> Dream on with me

Her dream-song is analogous to Rose's blanket-web; as Rose does in "To Make History," here Chrystos affirms a community of creative continuity and invites all who would, to join.

"Ceremony for Completing a Poetry Reading," the final poem in *Not Vanishing* (100), is perhaps Chrystos's most sustained evocation to date of an inclusive, desired community. Like "To Make History" and "Urban Indian," it uses Native cultural references to evoke the poet's spiritual and historical ground but without implying exclusivity. Chrystos is certainly not reversing her criticism of non-Native appropriations of Indian spirituality. But at least within this poem's hopeful invitation to reciprocity, she suggests that cultural specificity need not mean borders that strangle, distort, or cut off the realization of common joy, mutually sustaining engagement. For once, at least, the desired community and the desired audience may be both unified and diverse. The poem's double premise is stated in its opening lines: "This is a give away poem / You've . . . made a circle with me of the places / I've wandered." From these premises, the poet invites us to "Hear / the stories . . . Let me give you ribbonwork leggings . . . Come closer." She details the gifts and asks our permission to bestow them—which, by reading on, we grant and receive thereby the "seeds of a new way . . . the sound of our feet dancing . . . the sound of our thoughts flying . . . the sound of peace moving into our faces & sitting down." As in many other poems, repeated phrases create the effect of incantatory efficacy, evoking the forms and aesthetics of traditional Native song and thus revealing the dialogism of the poem's language—realizing rhythmically the speech and intentions of indigenous singers in the language of colonizers and their descendants (among them, many of her readers).

It would be a mistake to read "Ceremony for Completing a Poetry Reading" (or "To Make History") as replacing or softening the anger, resistance, and challenges voiced in poems such as "For the Campus Committee," "Just Like You," "I Walk in the History of My People," or "Three

Thousand Dollar Death Song." What this "Ceremony" does, rather, is to intimate the possibilities that justify the poets' sometimes impatient challenges to their diverse readers, the possibilities for community that our more adequate, active responses might welcome into being. Not only a justified and self-defending anger at the continuing destructions but also a vision of life-sustaining alternatives move Chrystos and Rose to words of resistance.

Chrystos and Wendy Rose speak in distinctive voices of the history and experiences shared by Native peoples; when addressing concerns that do not so evidently unite them, they are still linked by their desires for community, interrogations of their various audiences, foregrounding of the dialogic, and activist impulses. Juxtaposing their work creates the possibility of a dialogue that might clarify and enlarge the power of each voice. Their differing emphases, modes of speaking, and manners of addressing community and audience—Chrystos's propensity for the "raw" ("Askenet, Meaning 'Raw' in My Language"), visceral challenge and direct assertion, Rose's more indirect, meditative, or suggestive approach—complement and illuminate each other. Thus, Rose's sometimes difficult syntax and images may in effect be opened up by Chrystos's incisive assertions. Likewise, Chrystos's single-minded indignation, her resistance sometimes to acknowledging fine distinctions, may be complicated by Rose's attention to nuances intellectual or emotional. The voice of each is strengthened in dialogue with the complementary powers of the other. Here we should recall that Native American oral cultures—which Rose and Chrystos invoke and honor—traditionally integrate storyteller/singer, community, and language. Membership in community is fundamental to integrity, to voice, and to power; one speaks most fully and truly in and with one's community. Both Chrystos and Rose aspire to such relationships, even if in contexts that revise tradition. Reading their poems together, then, as mutually clarifying and empowering reveals the potential for a contemporary activist community to come together in keeping with traditional conceptions.

NOTES

1. I use Native American, Native, American Indian, and Indian interchangeably to acknowledge different Native people's practices and preferences and to draw attention to the political-cultural contests and the heteroglossia involved in self-naming and naming by others. I use specific tribal names when referring to particular communities or cultures.

2. As defined by Bakhtin, heteroglossia, the internal, inherent, and socially/historically conditioned stratification of language, continuously brought about by the fact that "every socially significant verbal performance has the ability . . .

to infect with its own intention certain aspects of language" (290), means that
language "represents the co-existence of socio-ideological contradictions between the present and the past . . . between different socio-ideological groups . . .
between tendencies, schools, circles and so forth. . . . These 'languages' of heteroglossia . . . do not *exclude* each other, but rather intersect with each other in
many different ways" (291). As a consequence, language "is not a neutral
medium"; rather, "it is populated—overpopulated—with the intentions of others. Expropriating it, forcing it to submit to one's own intentions and accents, is
a difficult and complicated process" (294). Language dominated by heteroglossia
is dialogic; in Bakhtin's editors' words, it is marked by "a constant interaction between meanings" (426). "A word, discourse, language or culture undergoes 'dia-
logization' when it becomes relativized, de-privileged, aware of competing
definitions for the same things" (427). Among the treatments of border culture
and border experience most useful for illuminating Native American experience and literature are Anzaldúa, *Borderlands/La Frontera;* Hicks, *Border Writing;*
Rosaldo, "Politics, Patriarchs, and Laughter"; and Saldívar, "The Limits of Cultural Studies."

   3. Parenthetical references to books are as follows: Chrystos, DO—*Dream On,*
NV—*Not Vanishing;* Rose, GW—*Going to War with All My Relations,* and LC—*Lost
Copper.*

   4. Chrystos asks this question in a slightly different context ("Askenet" 241).

   5. The most direct evidence of disagreement among writers that I have encountered is Allen's criticism of Leslie Marmon Silko's use of sacred stories in *Ceremony.* For varied responses to such questions, see comments in Bruchac, *Survival
This Way* (esp. those by Maurice Kenny [152], Elizabeth Cook-Lynn [69], Gerald
Vizenor [302, 309], Harold Littlebird [160, 163, 166], and Lance Henson [109,
115]).

   6. In her interview with Bruchac, Rose affirms that her "community is urban
Indian and is *pan* tribal" (254). To Coltelli, she said that pantribalism is not opposed to tribal identity (129).

   7. I have in mind poems such as Chrystos's "White Girl Don't" (NV 74), "Table
Manners" (NV 73), "I Was Minding My Own Business" (DO 56), and "In the
Ritzy" (DO 51), and Rose's "The Mormons Next Door" (GW 42–43) and "Dear
Grandfather Webb from England" (GW 46–47).

   8. In general, I assume that when Rose and Chrystos use first-person singular
pronouns they are speaking, at least in part, autobiographically. This is consistent with their remarks in essays or interviews and need not imply that the poems are either limited by or directly expressive of the writers' literal experiences.
Hermann supports a similar critical assumption, arguing that "the distinction
between author and narrator, so important in Western literary theory, is much
less relevant for literature written by Indians. . . . This can be explained by the
influence of the oral tradition . . . since the function of the storyteller is to act
as a link in the chain of perpetuating traditional material which is decidedly
not . . . created by an individual" (189n. 2). Though neither Rose nor (apparently)
Chrystos grew up in traditional communities, their evident interest in such affiliation and their commitments to community, variously defined, lend validity to
Hermann's argument.

   9. In a note to "The Endangered Roots," Rose says that she uses "the *feeling*" of
the "twisted-twin" reference, which traditionally denotes one who was supposed
to be born twins but was united just before birth, as a "persona."

10. Rose comments about the fact that she has no Indian name and about what a name confers (Hunter 54–55).

11. *The Halfbreed Chronicles,* in which "If I Am" was first published, marks an important transition in Rose's understanding of the meaning of mixed origins and the term "half-breed," which contributes to the power of many of the *Going to War* poems and to her surer sense of relationship to variously characterized communities. See interviews with her by Bruchac, Hunter, and Coltelli.

12. Sources for Hopi origin myths include Yava, "Way Back in the Distant Past," in which he notes that Hopi tradition accommodates multiple versions of history: "Different villages and clans have their own special details, and different explanations" (11). See also Mullett, *Spider Woman Stories* (esp. 1–6), and Tyler, *Pueblo Gods and Myths* (esp. 95–97).

WORKS CITED

Allen, Paula Gunn. "Special Problems in Teaching Leslie Marmon Silko's *Ceremony.*" *American Indian Quarterly* 14.4 (1990): 379–86.

Anzaldúa, Gloria. *Borderlands/La Frontera: The New Mestiza.* San Francisco: Aunt Lute, 1987.

Bakhtin, Mikhail M. *The Dialogic Imagination.* Trans. Michael Holquist and Caryl Emerson. Austin: University of Texas Press, 1981.

Bruchac, Joseph. *Survival This Way: Interviews with American Indian Poets.* Tucson: University of Arizona Press, 1987.

Chrystos. "Askenet, Meaning 'Raw' in My Language." *Inversions: Writing by Dykes, Queers, and Lesbians.* Ed. Betsy Warland. Vancouver, B.C.: Press Gang, 1991. 237–47.

———. *Dream On.* Vancouver, B.C.: Press Gang, 1991.

———. *Not Vanishing.* Vancouver, B.C.: Press Gang, 1988.

Coltelli, Laura. *Winged Words: American Indian Writers Speak.* Lincoln: University of Nebraska Press, 1990.

Hermann, Elizabeth. " 'Academic Squaws': Some Aspects of Culture Contact in the Literature and Criticism of Paula Gunn Allen and Wendy Rose." *Minority Literatures in North America: Contemporary Perspectives.* Ed. Wolfgang Karrer and Harmut Lutz. Frankfurt: Peter Lang, 1990. 175–91.

Hicks, Emily D. *Border Writing: The Multidimensional Text.* Minneapolis: University of Minnesota Press, 1991.

Hunter, Carol. "An Interview with Wendy Rose." *Coyote Was Here: Essays on Contemporary Native American Literature and Mobilization.* Ed. Bo Schöler. Aarhus, Denmark: Seklos, 1984. 40–56.

Kroeber, Karl. "The Wolf Comes: Indian Poetry and Linguistic Criticism." *Smoothing the Ground: Essays on Native American Oral Literature.* Ed. Brian Swann. Berkeley: University of California Press, 1983. 98–111.

Mullett, G. M. *Spider Woman Stories: Legends of the Hopi Indians.* Tucson: University of Arizona Press, 1979.

Rosaldo, Renato. "Politics, Patriarchs, and Laughter." *Cultural Critique* 6 (Spring 1987): 65–86.

Rose, Wendy. *Going to War with All My Relations.* Flagstaff, Ariz.: Northland-Entrada, 1993.

———. *The Halfbreed Chronicles.* Los Angeles: West End, 1985.

———. *Lost Copper.* Banning, Calif.: Malki Museum Press, 1980.

Saldívar, José David. "The Limits of Cultural Studies." *American Literary History* 2 (1990): 251–66.

Smith, Lorrie. "Dialogue and the Political Imagination in Denise Levertov and Adrienne Rich." *Word, Self, Poem.* Ed. Leonard Trawick. Kent, Ohio: Kent State University Press, 1990. 155–62.

Tyler, Hamilton A. *Pueblo Gods and Myths.* Norman: University of Oklahoma Press, 1964.

Yava, Albert. "Way Back in the Distant Past." *The South Corner of Time: Hopi Navajo Papago Yaqui Tribal Literature.* Ed. Larry Evers. Tucson: University of Arizona Press, 1980. 8–13.

PART 2

*Issues of Gender, Class,
Race, and Sexuality*

7 ◇ Of Men and Men

Reconstructing Chinese American Masculinity

For all the advances in gender and ethnic studies challenging traditional notions of manhood and womanhood and unsettling stereotypes about people of color, as social beings we continue to react to or be shaped by sexually and racially coded characteristics. Judith Butler, in refining her theory of performativity, insists that the social construction of identity is far from free: "The 'performative' dimension of construction is precisely the forced reiteration of norms. In this sense . . . constraint calls to be rethought as the very condition of performativity. Performativity is neither free play nor theatrical self-presentation; nor can it be simply equated with performance" (*Bodies* 94–95). But if we construe performativity as the stereotypical roles assigned to a particular group, there is then a discernible connection between theatrical and cinematic performance and performativity for people of color in the United States. After all, the limited social representations they see of themselves in cultural media—both "high-" and "low-" brow art—interfere with their formation of identity. In this essay, I would like to focus on the difficulty of self-definition—that is, the limits set on one's performance—resulting from historical inequality and cultural imperialism. Using examples from literature and cinema, I will show how often Chinese American men, and Asian American men in general, who are seldom allowed by the dominant culture to *perform* "masculine" roles, are self-driven to rehearse gender norms. Constraint in this instance is not only "that which sets a limit to performativity" but "that which impels and sustains performativity" (Butler, *Bodies* 95). Before we can go "beyond gender binarism" and liberate ourselves from dominant scripts for masculinity and femininity, we need to ascertain the anxieties and aspirations that are at stake behind these repetitive performances.[1]

What rights and motives have I as a female critic to deliberate on manhood? That men of different cultures have for centuries prescribed feminine ideals comes to mind as a quick rejoinder.[2] More seriously, in the Asian American (as in the African American and Mexican American) cultural domain, feminism and nationalism have taken on the appearance of a split between women and men. Feminists intent on exposing Asian sexism have been attacked by cultural nationalists who complain that female writers reinforce the denigrating stereotypes about Asian males; the effort of some male writers to reconstruct manhood and instill cultural pride by reviving an "Asian heroic tradition" has also caused consternation among feminists (Kim; Lim; Ling; S. Wong, "Ethnicizing Gender"). Elsewhere I have stressed the dual allegiance of Chinese American women who wish to dismantle Chinese patriarchy on the one hand and redress the invisibility of Asian American men on the other ("Woman Warrior"). I have also discussed contradictory cultural inscriptions of masculinity in the works of three East Asian American female writers (*Articulate Silences*). In this essay, I would like to obviate further the opposition between Asian American women and men by examining differences among male writers and uncovering alternative expressions of masculinity. Just as Maxine Hong Kingston in *China Men* and *Tripmaster Monkey* attempts to identify with her male protagonists, critics too can traverse gender lines. I hope my analysis of Asian American masculinity will encourage greater empathy and less truculent exchange between the sexes.[3]

"Emasculation" and the "Asian Heroic Tradition"

The editors of *Aiiieeeee!* and *The Big Aiiieeeee!*—Jeffery Paul Chan, Frank Chin, Lawson Fusao Inada, and Shawn Wong—refer to the history of Asian Americans as one of "emasculation." Although terms such as "emasculated" and "effeminate" presume and underwrite the superiority of the masculine over the feminine (hooks 76; Ling 313), emasculation evokes multiple injuries and carries a special poignancy with regard to Asian American experience. According to Edward W. Said, "the Orient was always in the position both of outsider and of incorporated weak partner for the West" (208).[4] Historical circumstances also consigned many early Chinese immigrants to virtual bachelorhood, since

Chinese laborers who came to the United States in the late nineteenth century were forbidden to bring their wives or to marry white women and were consequently denied paternity. Because of unequal employment opportunities, these men were forced to be cooks, waiters, laundry workers, and domestics—jobs traditionally considered "women's work."

Cultural and political factors further contribute to their feminization. Socialized to respect authority and to exercise verbal restraint, many people of Asian ancestry seem submissive and passive in the eyes of non-Asians. Such cultural difference is deepened by racist politics, insofar as Asians are granted limited acceptance as long as they refrain from "making waves" in American society (Chin and Chan; Chin et al.). The more recent stereotype of Asian Americans as the model minority, whereby they are praised for their ability to assimilate and comply with dominant ideologies, further undergirds the domesticated image of Asian Americans. This assignation, which came into currency in the wake of the civil rights movement, has provoked an insidious comparison between Asian Americans and African Americans—the intractable minority that should follow the Asian American example. Ironically, as noted by the editors of *Aiiieeeee!* (Chin et al. xxvi), the African American presence in the United States—in music and literature as well as politics—has been as strongly felt as the corresponding Asian American absence, at least until very recently. Where were the Asian jazz and blues, Langston Hughes and James Baldwin, Martin Luther King and Malcolm X? Because cultural and political visibility has been a male prerogative traditionally, such absence casts yet another shadow on Asian American manhood.

These legacies have produced repercussions in the film and publishing industry. As Gina Marchetti observes, "Images of ethnicity and race always conjure up images of masculinity and femininity" ("Ethnicity" 288; see also E. Wong). Marchetti describes how Hollywood maintains racial and ethnic hierarchies through gendering: "Thus, fantasies of threatening Asian men, emasculated eunuchs, alluring Asian 'dragon ladies,' and submissive female slaves all work to rationalize white, male domination" (289). Elaine H. Kim similarly observes, "Asian men have been coded as having no sexuality, while Asian women have nothing else. . . . Both exist to define the white man's virility" (69). Focusing on the movie imagery of Asian men, Richard Fung divides their roles into "two categories: the egghead/wimp, or . . . the kung fu master/ninja/samurai. He is sometimes dangerous, sometimes friendly, but almost always characterized by a desexualized Zen asceticism . . . defined by a striking absence down there" (148). In the bitter words of the *Aiiieeeee!* cohort, "the white stereotype of the acceptable and unacceptable Asian is utterly without manhood. Good or bad, the stereotypical Asian is nothing as a man" (xxx). Furthermore, in Hollywood movies Asian women often fall in love with Caucasian men, whereas Asian men are almost never presented as desirable partners for either Caucasian women, Asian women, other women of color, or other Asian men (Fung; Marchetti, *Romance;* Tajima).[5]

Despite the new cultural awareness in the wake of the civil rights movement and the increasing variety of roles Hollywood has granted Asian women, little has changed in popular portrayals of Asian males other than that Asian American writers and directors are now accused of complicity in disfiguring Asian men (e.g., Moy 115–29). It is unfair to expect any one writer or director to represent a culture, but one cannot help registering that the most popular books and films by Asian Americans have one element in common: the marginalization of Asian American men. One is hard-pressed to find positive male models in the Chinese American literary texts that have won the largest readership, such as Kingston's *Woman Warrior,* David Henry Hwang's *M. Butterfly,* and Amy Tan's *Joy Luck Club* and *Kitchen God's Wife.* Indeed, Asian men are all but absent in *The Woman Warrior* and *The Joy Luck Club;* they are presented as the epitome of deception and cruelty in *M. Butterfly* and *The Kitchen God's Wife.* Asian American writers should no doubt continue to expose and combat Asian sexism, but they must also guard against internalizing and reproducing racial stereotypes, thereby reinforcing the deep-seated biases of the American reading and viewing public.

Is the fact that Asian men are marginalized in the most widely circulated works by Chinese American writers merely a coincidence? Kingston wrote both *The Woman Warrior* and *China Men; The Woman Warrior* is now one of the most widely taught texts in American colleges and universities, while the critical silence surrounding *China Men,* which uses similar narrative strategies, is deafening by contrast. The highly uneven reception of the two books by the same author surely has to do more with subject matter than with literary merit.[6] The lukewarm reception accorded *China Men* (or even *Tripmaster Monkey*) suggests a certain apathy toward Asian men; indeed, a more recent example, Wayne Wang's film adaptation of *The Joy Luck Club,* suggests antipathy. In Tan's novel two of the daughters are trapped in failed marriages with Caucasian men. In the movie not only is one of the Caucasian husbands ultimately idealized but the most obnoxious white husband in the book—the one who forces his wife to draw separate grocery lists for herself and himself and who makes her pay more than her fair share—is reincarnated as Asian (on the movie, see Hagedorn, "Asian"; Nakayama; Payne).

Given the history of skewed representation of Asian American men (as being either absent, "unmanly," or villainous) in American public discourse, it is understandable that the editors of *Aiiieeeee!* and *The Big Aiiieeeee!* set out to redefine "Asian American manhood." In *Aiiieeeee!* they link the crisis in masculinity to the deprivation of history, language, and a literary heritage. In *The Big Aiiieeeee!* they attempt to refashion Asian American masculinity by espousing an "Asian heroic tradition." They glorify the martial heroes featured in Chinese and Japanese epics, such as *Water Margin, Three Kingdoms, Journey to the West,* and *Chushingura,* implicitly presenting renowned heroes for contemporary Asians to emulate.

I am sympathetic to the editors' effort to reformulate Asian American masculinity. I particularly appreciate their determination to revive an alternative history and literary tradition. The emphasis on loyalty, honor, wisdom, courage, and resistance in these works helps to combat established stereotypes of Asian deviousness and conformity. What I find problematic is their unthinking resuscitation of manly codes that require violence. I believe that it is in part because Asians first settled and are still concentrated in the American West, where the frontier myth of conquest has been especially pervasive, that the editors (themselves from the West Coast) are in thrall of heroism that takes a "Western" form despite their announced intent to forge an Asian heritage. The fact that Asians have been "feminized" historically has no doubt also spurred the editors' masculinist quest.[7]

In an essay at the beginning of *The Big Aiiieeeee!,* entitled "Come All Ye Asian American Writers of the Real and the Fake," Chin foregrounds a Chinese ethos that at once contradicts orientalist perceptions of Chinese culture and aligns Chinese masculinity with white masculinity. He distills the following essence from *The Analects* by Confucius: "We are born to fight to maintain our personal integrity. All art is martial art. Writing is fighting. . . . Living is fighting. Life is war" (Chan et al. 35). Such a worldview is less reflective of Confucius—famous and notorious for his abiding respect for hierarchy—than of the American "national character" that, according to Richard Slotkin, embraces "the myth of regeneration through violence" (*Regeneration* 5). Confucius would also be shocked to hear his teaching summarized as the "ethic of private revenge [and] the ethic of popular revenge against the corrupt state" (Chan et al. 34–35). Chin's drive to counter orientalist constructions thus generates an equally singular interpretation of Chinese culture. Despite his avowed intention to combat white supremacy, his selective and tendentious invocation of Chinese ethos echoes Euramerican ideologies of masculinity, and his nationalist gesture is marred by an apparent counterinvestment in patriarchal prescriptions.

The literary revival of the Asian heroic tradition coincides with the fetishization of the kung fu fighter in American cinema. The only "positive" Asian male image that has made its way to Hollywood is the Bruce Lee figure; the box office success of *Dragon* (a movie based on Lee's life) and the popularity of action movies from Hong Kong—notably those directed by John Woo and Jackie Chan—attest to the continual appeal of that profile. The larger society may enjoy these movies simply as oriental variations on Hollywood gore and mayhem, but for many Asian Americans these films provide images of Asian heroism not previously encountered in American popular culture. One cannot overestimate the magnetic hold these heroic figures have on Asian Americans who seldom see themselves in leading roles in the white media. Because these movies are also eagerly consumed by non-Asians, Asian Americans (who must still grapple with racial slurs and hate crimes outside the cinema) can derive a sense of vicarious acceptance as the larger audience roots for the on-screen Asian fighters. Like some of the martial heroes exalted in *The Big Aiiieeeee!*, these fighters only fortify the association of manhood with violence. Both the literary and cinematic interventions blast effeminate stereotypes by merely reinstating and legitimizing machismo.[8]

Donald Duk and China Boy

The tenets set forth in *Aiiieeeee!* and *The Big Aiiieeeee!* are fleshed out in Frank Chin's *Donald Duk,* in which the eponymous teenage protagonist struggles to overcome his racial self-contempt by learning about the Chinese heroic tradition and the history of his predecessors in America. As one of the few works by Asian Americans that contain sympathetic father figures, the novel also addresses a concern first articulated in *Aiiieeeee!:* "the failure of Asian American manhood to express itself in its simplest form: fathers and sons" (xlvi).[9] Both Donald's father, King Duk, and his namesake, Uncle Donald Duk, are unusually patient in teaching Donald about his Chinese legacy. King Duk initiates the project of building 108 paper airplanes for the Chinese New Year to commemorate the 108 outlaws in the Chinese classic *Water Margin.* As the man who invites and cooks for an entire opera troupe of three hundred people and distributes rice to every household in Chinatown during the New Year, he himself exemplifies the bounty of Soong Gong, one of the most respected heroes in the epic. When Donald mischievously burns one of the airplanes, named after Lee Kuey, Uncle Donald Duk gives him a lesson about his real name: "Your Chinese name is not Duk, but Lee. Lee, just like Lee Kuey" (23). This passing reference to names is one of the many details in the novel that provoke Donald to learn more about his ancestors and the fabled outlaws.

Chin thus skillfully interweaves the history of Chinese immigrants with legendary characters. The heroes in *Water Margin* are mostly righteous men victimized by a corrupt government; they become rebels with a price on their heads and live separately as a fraternity away from society. Similarly, because of the Chinese exclusion laws in the late nineteenth century, many early immigrants came to the United States as "outlaws"—illegally, by forging immigration documents (hence Donald's fake last name). The strategies by which these men defied racist American legislation were not unlike those adopted against Chinese officialdom by the heroic characters. Furthermore, like the outlaws, the immigrants—ghettoized in various Chinatowns—were also segregated from mainstream America. For Chin, bent on refiguring Asian American manhood, *Water Margin* is a resonant literary source. By linking the Chinese forefathers in America with the fabled outlaws, he recasts those abused "Chinamen" who built the trans-Pacific railroad as undaunted pioneers. The epic also provides Chin with Chinese characters that match well with Euramerican worthies. According to Uncle Donald Duk, "the Water Margin was a place like [Sherwood Forest]. . . . All the good guys who want better government are badmouthed by the [bad] guys in charge, and they go outlaw. . . . Just like Robin Hood. But in the Chinese book, there are 108 Robin Hoods" (22).

Yet some of the Chinese rebels are far more savage than Robin Hood and the Merry Men. It is especially surprising to see that of the 108 colorful outlaws who appear in the Chinese classic, including some very civil ones, Lee Kuey—one of the most brutish and ruthless—should soar to greatest prominence in *Donald Duk*. In the words of Uncle Donald Duk, who introduces the character to Donald: "Lee Kuey . . . gets mad very easily. . . . He goes naked and runs into a fight with a thirty-pound battle axe in each hand. He loves to fight and kill people. When he runs out of the other side of a battle, his body is covered with layers of other peoples' drying blood" (22–23). The implication is that this famous ancestor should inspire the young Donald with awe, though one similarity between Lee Kuey and Donald is that they both lack good judgment. Another figure celebrated in *Donald Duk* is Kwan Kung, whom King Duk describes as "the most powerful character" (67). Power here is again construed as the ability to kill: "One look into your Kwan Kung eyes and he's dead" (67). Although the book effectively explodes the myth of the passive and submissive oriental, it conflates lethal fury with fortitude.

Yet the novel also gives us a glimpse of other ways to fight. Donald provides an alibi for a man falsely accused of murder; he and his friend

Arnold Azalea openly challenge and rectify the distorted representation of Asianness in their American classroom. Their newfound knowledge about the Chinese and Chinese Americans has goaded them to action. Through these youngsters Chin (like Kingston in *The Woman Warrior*) has transformed traditional Chinese fighters into Chinese Americans battling racism with words rather than with actual weapons.

I have argued elsewhere that a pacifist strain is no less pervasive in Chinese literature and culture than the heroic heritage presented as dominant by the editors of *The Big Aiiieeeee!* ("Woman Warrior" 242–43). A reader unaware of these incongruities would be nonplussed by the opposite pronouncements about Chinese beliefs in *Donald Duk* and in Gus Lee's *China Boy*. Donald is taught by his father and uncle about war and revenge in the Chinese heroic tradition, whereas the protagonist in Lee's novel—Kai Ting—is taught by his mother to abstain from fighting under all circumstances; war, according to this narrator, violates the essence of an "ancient, classical education and the immutable humanistic standards of Chinese society" (4). Juxtaposing the two books illuminates the degree to which subjectivity enters into the remaking of a cultural tradition. As Lee Yu-cheng observes, Chin's revisioning of the Chinese American tradition is motivated by a desire to discover a "usable past," which in this case disproves the orientalist stereotype of the effete Asian (115). Gus Lee's rendition of the Chinese tradition, on the other hand, serves to emphasize the protagonist's difficult struggle to become an all-American boy. Despite such dramatic differences in the depiction of Chinese culture, both works argue the need to fight one's way to manhood.

In Lee's autobiographical novel, seven-year-old Kai must negotiate between the pacifist teaching of his immigrant mother and the street violence in America, not to mention the abusive behavior of his Irish American stepmother. His mother, who has told him that hurting people will damage his *"yuing chi,* [his] balanced karma" (4), dies when Kai is only six, whereupon he is exposed to the blows of his stepmother Edna and the punches of the Panhandle, a rough neighborhood in San Francisco. Thanks to Colonel Ting, his "Westernized" father, Kai is soon sent to take boxing lessons at the YMCA.

The narrator who lives to tell his tale has fully accepted physical combat as a way of life: "Fighting was the final test of life on the street. It measured a boy's courage and tested the texture of his guts, the promise of his nascent manhood, his worthiness to live and bear friends on poor streets" (90). The climactic ending of the novel occurs in a scene of unmitigated gore. The reader is expected to cheer when Kai finally beats down his vicious opponent on the street, without reflecting on his equally relentless method of revenge or that Kai is the one who provokes that fight in the first place. This ending recalls a telling simile introduced at the beginning of the book: "Streetfighting was like menstruation for men" (3). The letting of blood by physical assault is thereby sanctioned as a biological passage into adulthood.

The book also suggests that for men of color the demonstration of strength through force has an extra hold beyond the traditional initiation into manhood. The streetfighting takes place in a predominantly black and Hispanic neighborhood. Toussaint LaRue, Kai's African American friend, explains how African Americans come to see physical combat as a privilege: "in ole days, no Negro man kin hit or fight. We belongs to da whites, like hosses. . . . Man fight 'notha man, be damagin white man goods. So he get whipped. . . . Now . . . we kin fights, like men" (98). This passage implies that black men who have been demeaned by whites take up the means of the masters with a vengeance. But in making up for past subjugation by being belligerent toward others, they simply remake themselves in the image of their oppressors. Asian American men may be similarly misguided.

Kai takes Toussaint's remarks to mean that "fighting [is] a measure of citizenship. Of civilization" (98). Ironic as his interpretation may sound, it is not wide of the mark, for the book leaves us with a sobering reflection that street violence is not so different from institutionalized violence.[10] The narrator informs us that "some who survived [the Panhandle] became cops, but more became crooks. . . . Almost to a man, or boy, the children of the Panhandle became soldiers" (4–5). The interchangeability or affinity of cops, crooks, and soldiers is unsettling. As readers discover in *Honor and Duty*—the sequel to *China Boy*—Kai himself, after his training at the Y and on the street, completes his education in violence by entering West Point, though he eventually rejects its military ethos. If the lurid descriptions of brutal hand-to-hand combat in *China Boy* are meant to parody the process by which boys are inculcated in violence and to shock one into pacifism, the novel also capitalizes on what it seeks to undermine.

In light of Lee's description of Chinese culture as being averse to bloodshed, the bodily injuries that mark the protagonist's progression into American manhood also signify the violence of assimilation and the need to obliterate the mother tongue along with its attendant precepts. In the narrator's mind, the two cultures are personified by his two mothers. We are told that "China, like [his] mother, had grown in modern times to distrust men who accomplished things with muscles and swords" (204) and that marrying Edna is "a major-league step toward cementing [his father's] American assimilation" (58). The nonviolent teaching of Kai's Chinese mother is presented as an obstacle to Kai's adjustment to American life: "This is America! And *she does not exist!*" cries Edna (85). The Chinese mother must literally be dead for Kai to become a self-made American man under Edna's aegis.

Cultural Revolution and *Pangs of Love*

Where inherited notions of gender are concerned, the linking of virility and violence in *Donald Duk* and *China Boy* is sadly at odds with the challenges posed by feminist and gay studies (though I will later show how it is possible to read against the grain of the two novels to discern alternative models). And the nationalist agenda in *Aiiieeeee!* and *The Big Aiiieeeee!* comes close to reestablishing an Asian patriarchy that excludes dissident voices and discounts sexual differences. The Asian American recourse to a heroic past, like so many other (cultural) nationalist struggles, underplays the contributions of those who do not fit the profile of a warrior, notably women and gays.[11] Chin's preoccupation with manhood as traditionally defined, for example, often translates as homophobia: "It is an article of white liberal American faith today that Chinese men, at their best, are effeminate closet queens like Charlie Chan and, at their worst, are homosexual menaces like Fu Manchu. No wonder David Henry Hwang's derivative *M. Butterfly* won the Tony. . . . The good Chinese man, at his best, is the fulfillment of white male homosexual fantasy" (Chan et al. xiii). Chin is merely articulating here a widespread presumption in American society at large that a gay person is less than a man, particularly if he happens to be Asian. But in this instance homophobic sentiment is couched as a cultural nationalist discourse against racism. Chin, so sensitive about the "emasculation" of heterosexual Asian men, nevertheless joins the dominant culture in vilifying gay Asians, who are doubly marginalized by racism and heterosexism. In his afterword to *M. Butterfly,* Hwang elaborates on the invidious construction of the gay Asian even within homosexual circles:

> Gay friends have told me of a derogatory term used in their community: "Rice Queen"—a gay Caucasian man primarily attracted to Asians. In these relationships, the Asian virtually always plays the role of the "woman"; the Rice Queen, culturally and sexually, is the "man." This pattern of relationships had become so codified that, until recently, it was considered unnatural for gay Asians to date one another. Such men would be taunted with a phrase which implied they were lesbians. (98)

It is only fitting, then, that a provocative challenge to established notions of masculinity appears in *Cultural Revolution* by Norman Wong, a gay Chinese American. Though billed as short stories, the book is a series of interrelated episodes tracking the history and dynamics of an immigrant family. Two stories in particular, "Robbed" and "Ordinary Chinese People," demonstrate how patriarchal beliefs hurt both the daughter and the son—not to mention the mother—in the family. "Robbed" is told from the point of view of Julia, a toddler who witnesses her mother undergo a painful abortion because the parents do not want to have another girl. The night before the abortion, the family is robbed by a thief who enters the house by breaking a window. After the broken pane has been replaced, the father writes the words "NOTHING INSIDE" (105) on a piece of paper and pastes it over the new glass. Julia, who is inside all this time, "stares at her father's sign. It reads: EDISNI GNIHTON" (105). Julia imagines that the burglar reenters the house by shattering the window again: "The white sign rips in half. . . . The burglar . . . sees nothing inside . . . *except for her.* . . . He hoists her on his back. She holds tight. He . . . takes her away" (108, emphasis added).

Julia's fantasy reveals not only her resentment at being apparently "nothing" to her parents but also her inventiveness at revaluating herself.[12] The "father's sign," already drained of meaning earlier by her focus on its mirror image, virtually goes to pieces in her mind. She further defies patriarchal order by redefining herself as valuable—as worthy of being stolen. The fact that she "holds tight" to the thief underlines her wish to escape from her father's house, from its sexist disregard for daughters and its preference for sons.

The full irony of this story emerges only when read against "Ordinary Chinese People," a story told from the point of view of Julia's younger brother, Michael, the wished-for son. The Chinese preference for boys is predicated largely on the fact that sons can perpetuate the family name by producing male offspring. But Michael is gay, and his homosexuality thwarts his parents' expectations. Because the Chinese qualifications for masculinity are thus inextricably tied to the reproductive role, Michael's "manhood" is under siege.

The title of the story also calls attention to the distance between Michael's working-class family and the white middle-class family depicted in Robert Redford's movie *Ordinary People* (1980). People of color, laborers, and homosexuals are not among the movie's "ordinary people." But Michael is seduced by the images in the film, which he "secretly watched five times over a weekend": "Michael wished his family were more like the Jarretts. They talked about their problems, problems that seemed real, dramatic, important" (137). The parents of Michael and Julia are too busy working to spend any time with their children, let

alone figure out their problems. By implication, the problems in his
family are unreal, mundane, and trivial.

Haunted by both Chinese and American norms, Michael is kept
from coming out. He does, however, try to discuss his sense of alienation
with his track coach, with whom he is infatuated. But the coach, white
and presumably straight, offers cold comfort. "Don't be afraid," he tells
Michael. "We all feel lonely sometimes. It's all a part of growing up, of
becoming a man" (138). Yet "becoming a man" has radically different
meanings for the coach and for Michael. The coach draws on a cliché
that arises out of the "universal" experience of growing up as a white
heterosexual male. His definition of "man" is precisely responsible for
isolating Michael. Unable to communicate with either his family or his
coach, he tries—in line with the script of the film—to commit suicide.

Michael's attempted suicide can be variously interpreted. It may simply be a desperate way to attract the coach's attention, as the narrator
suggests: "It occurred to Michael that if he did to himself what Conrad
had done to himself, then his coach would fall in love with him" (138).
Instead, the attempt backfires and confirms his "abnormality" to the
coach, who pushes him away completely: "This is out of my hands," says
the coach. "There are people out there who can help you" (139). For the
coach's heterosexual center to hold, Michael must be cast "out there." In
light of the story's insistent refrain of Michael's "responsibility as the
number-one and only son" (146), however, the attempted suicide can
also be seen as self-punishment. Regarding the social prohibition against
sexual "deviance," Judith Butler observes: "When the threat of punishment wielded by that prohibition is too great . . . it may be that we effectively punish ourselves in advance" (*Bodies* 100). The concept of advance self-punishment to forestall societal condemnation evidently
informs Wong's story. Michael's attempted suicide, like Gallimard's suicide in *M. Butterfly,* can be seen as a self-sentencing for an unspeakable
"crime." [13] In Redford's film, Conrad Jarrett tries to kill himself because
of his unresolved guilt at failing to prevent his older brother from
drowning—a hidden cause that surfaces only after repeated sessions of
psychotherapy. Michael's attempted suicide reflects his unspoken shame
for violating the expectations of both his parents and society at large.
Wong thus exposes the extent to which patriarchy regulates sexuality
and blames both patriarchal Chinese culture and white culture for cast-
ing Michael as out of the ordinary—as queer, deviant, and delinquent.

Incisive as Wong is in his critique of Chinese and American gender
norms, however, he fails to offer any positive models of Asian men, heterosexual or gay. All the Chinese men in Michael's family are depicted as
diffident and physically weak, in stark contrast to the invariably defiant

and strong women. Although Wong thus calls attention to the arbitrariness of gender constructions by reversing gender roles, his use of three generations of frail and lethargic Chinese men to symbolize a debilitating cultural heritage is disturbing. When Michael tells his mother he doesn't feel well, she scolds: "Just like your father. Always sick. Sick in the head. Well, I'm ... sick and tired of both of you" (143). Even Michael's homosexuality is presented as an "abnormal product of his Chinese parents" (147)—one more manifestation of a general malaise passed down through the generations.

Such a presentation may accurately reflect the depth of self-contempt instilled by racism and compulsory heterosexuality, but it also lends credence to debasing stereotypes about Asian men. Michael himself finds Asian males physically repugnant in general and is attracted to whites almost exclusively on a racial basis, though race and class are often linked in his mind: "Sometimes he imagined his mother marrying a rich white man. They would be living in Kahala, the most expensive neighborhood in Honolulu" (147). His coach, described as "handsome, sensitive, tall," is referred to by race rather than by name: "The white man's voice was like a pair of warm arms around Michael" (138). Michael is also in love with the character Conrad Jarrett, and he fantasizes about becoming involved with him. Both his off-screen and on-screen romances are imagined, unilateral, and consequently unrequited, leading to the triangular fantasy behind his attempted suicide: "His coach would fall in love with him as he had fallen in love with Conrad" (138). Inundated with and dazzled by white images, he aspires to be what he is not, an aspiration that amounts to self-annihilation. His attempt to slit his wrist in the exact manner of Conrad—a mimesis of a mimesis—reveals his fatal wish to be a dead ringer for the white character.

Ironically, this story ends with the reality of a dreaded resemblance: Michael's father lying next to Michael in bed—one infirm Chinese man next to another. His father lectures him on the responsibility of being a number-one son. But Michael knows already that "like his father, he would fail. . . . They were number-one sons in appearance only" (147). Their common physical illness bespeaks their shared weakness in character. The narrator seems to have internalized the colonialist stereotype of the Chinese as the "sick man of the East" and the American image of Asian men as devoid of manhood.

Like Wong's "Ordinary Chinese People," the title story in David Wong Louie's *Pangs of Love* explores the interplay of race, gender, sexuality, and generational differences. "Pangs of Love" recounts the tension between an immigrant Chinese mother and her American-born sons, which results from a language barrier and changes in family structure.

When the narrator, heterosexual himself, is asked by his mother—Mrs. Pang—why his gay brother has no girlfriends, he becomes tongue-tied. One is reminded of a similar scene in "Ordinary Chinese People" when Michael cannot begin to tell his mother about the motives behind his suicide attempt: "Michael knew that his coach was speaking too quickly for his mother to comprehend. Michael would have to explain it all again to her in Chinese. Explain what?" (139). The narrator's speechlessness in "Pangs of Love" also has as much to do with the language barrier (his mother does not speak English and his Chinese is at best that of "a precocious five-year-old") as with the concept of homosexuality, which he believes is incomprehensible to his mother, a woman from another time and another culture. Mrs. Pang is eager to see her sons married so she can have grandchildren. Like Michael's parents, however, she is unlikely to have her wishes fulfilled. One son is gay; the other—the narrator—seems likewise unable to carry on a conventional family. His fiancée, Mandy, has left him for another lover; he is currently dating Deborah, a "rebound among rebounds," whom he has no intention of marrying (84). The traditional Chinese household is on shaky ground; even heterosexuality does not guarantee patrilineage.

As in Wong's "Ordinary Chinese People," the subversive potential of Louie's story in decentering the patriarchal family is achieved at the expense of impugning Chinese American manhood. The narrator, who sees his mother as backward and unsophisticated, is himself riddled with insecurity, especially in dealing with Japanese men and white women. He works for a corporation that manufactures fragrances, under a Japanese boss named Kyoto: "Every time we meet he sizes me up, eyes crawling across my body, and lots of sidelong glances. *Who is this guy?* It's the same going-over I get when I enter a sushi joint, when the chefs . . . take my measure, colonizers amused by the native's hunger for their superior culture" (79). The narrator, acutely aware of his difference from Japanese men, expresses a combination of resentment at their condescending gaze and discomfiture at being gazed upon as a Chinese American fazed by Japan's former conquest of China and present economic strength.

Mandy and Deborah further unhinge his sense of masculinity: "Deborah wants me to move out of my mother's place, says I'm a mama's boy, calls me that even as we make love" (85). Although it is not uncommon in Chinese homes for adult sons and daughters to live with their parents, the narrator does not dispute Deborah's Eurocentric bias. His manhood was called into question earlier by Mandy. He and Mandy used to make love with the aid of a gamy musk perfume, "each drop equal in potency to the glandular secretions of a herd of buck deer" (81). They would use the perfume "whenever Mandy was feeling amorous but needed a jump start" (81), as though the narrator needed to shore up his sex appeal and potency with the synthetic fragrance. Still, he could not make the relationship last: "Within a year, about the time Sony purchased Columbia Pictures, she fell for someone named Ito, and broke off our engagement" (80).

"Pangs of Love" presents the narrator as a man unsure of his attractiveness and adequacy. His masculine anxieties vis-à-vis Japanese men and white women converge in Mandy's selection of a new lover. Already feeling self-conscious about being Kyoto's "right-hand slave" (84), the narrator must take special umbrage at Mandy's preference for a Japanese man. Worse still, Mandy's departure coincides with Kyoto's request that the narrator alter the composition of the musk perfume; he infers from the request that the "manly scent of musk is no longer manly enough" (82), no doubt spoken with a sniff at his own sexuality. Although Mandy simply leaves one Asian man for another, Japanese men, with their imperial past and superior economic present (not to mention their samurai icon), have often been perceived as more dominating and more sexy (and sexist) than Chinese and Chinese American men. In the reductive words of Bernardo Bertolucci (on the differences between the Japanese and Chinese members of his film crew for *The Last Emperor*): "They are very different. . . . The Japanese have this myth of virility. They are more macho. The Chinese are the opposite, more feminine. A bit passive" (qtd. in Chow 5).[14]

The narrator, who is daunted by the myth of Japanese puissance, seems to share Bertolucci's questionable assumption. His sense of being less potent than Mandy's lover is hammered home when he tries to convey that lover's ethnicity to his mother by pointing at a Japanese wrestler—whom he describes as a "Samurai Warrior"—on television (94). We have already been told earlier that the entire Pang family used to watch wrestling on Saturday nights: "It was myth in action. The American Dream in all its muscle-bound splendor played out before our faithful eyes" (94). The linkage of brute force with success runs deep in America (Slotkin, *Gunfighter*). (One is reminded of the China Boy's initiation). The narrator, in equating manhood with physical, financial, and imperial power, short-circuits his own masculinity. "Pangs of Love" thus undermines Chinese patriarchy only to reimpose patriarchal norms. It also accentuates the precariousness of Chinese American manhood, which stands trial before both Caucasian women and Japanese men.

This impression is borne out by several other stories in Louie's collection. Although these stories feature male protagonists who are romantic and imaginative, if somewhat eccentric, in contrast to the stereotype of the insipid or misogynist Asian male, many of the male characters betray a sense of deficiency vis-à-vis non-Asian women and men.[15] For instance, the protagonists in "Birthday," "Social Science," and "The Mover" have all been abandoned by a Caucasian wife or lover; they all try to gain a sense of vicarious power by assuming the role of a white man. In "Birthday," Wallace Wong is deserted by his lover. But he clings to the role of her son's father by trying to displace the biological father, a Caucasian. In "Social Science," Henry is a jilted husband threatened with eviction because the landlady has decided to sell. A prospective buyer, Dave Brinkley, is interested in Henry's ex-wife. In a fantastic subterfuge, Henry impersonates Brinkley so as to win back his wife but succeeds only in giving the escrow papers to another buyer.

This theme of impersonation—out of both envy and rivalry—is especially pronounced in "The Mover." The narrator and his girlfriend, Suzy, have just moved into a new apartment. But Suzy, after cataloging "all that was wrong" with the narrator, walks out on him (120). As he languishes in the dark on the floor of his new apartment, without heat, electricity, furniture, or lover, he pretends that he is "dead, lying in a morgue in China" (122). A teenager named George—apparently the son of the former resident—and his girlfriend Phyllis enter the apartment and proceed upstairs to a room the narrator and Suzy "had designated as [their] bedroom" (124), unaware that the new tenant has already arrived. The narrator surreptitiously follows the couple upstairs and through a keyhole watches them make love: "I saw plenty through my sharpshooter's squint. . . . At once, my intruders looked like a spirited heap of laundry and an exotic form of torture. But . . . who could mistake the sounds of the wondrous suction of love" (124). Just as Michael wishes to be Conrad, the narrator here wishes to be George; each desires to be an active (white) participant instead of a lonely (Asian) spectator in front of a screen or at a keyhole.

Meanwhile, Phyllis's father comes looking for his daughter. On an impulse, the narrator pretends to be the father of the boy: " 'I can assure you,' I began, 'your daughter's safe with my boy.' . . . I was astonished by my daring, and certain, despite my thirty years, that my voice lacked the easy authority of a parent" (125). After Phyllis's father has left, the narrator, who fantasizes a resemblance between Suzy and Phyllis, also tries to find himself in George: "All I wanted was to see his face, to see myself there as I had seen Suzy in the girl's face" (134).

The narrator's impulse to assume successively the roles of George's father and of George reveals his desire for the paternal authority and sexual bravado these non-Asian men possess. He registers the voice of Phyllis's father as "full, confident, mature" (125). The narrator, on the contrary, is told that he doesn't "sound like anyone's father" (131). George's escapade with Phyllis heightens the narrator's sense of deprivation and inadequacy: "My heart needed massage; in my stomach a little man was trying to punch his way out" (134). It is as though the positions of the thirty-year-old speaker and teenage George were inverted: the older man is the one still groping for his manhood. He tries to alter the situation by voicing paternal solicitude: "I asked [George] if he had gloves, a hat, a scarf. I told him zip up tight" (136). George, instead of taking the part of the son or apologizing for trespassing, tells the narrator upon leaving the house: "Thanks for the visit. . . . I think you'll like it here" (136). With remarkable self-possession and speaking like a man, George reassures the narrator.

"The Mover" thus highlights the narrator's difficulty in establishing his manhood—as a lover and as a father. Although one need not assume that the narrator is Chinese American to appreciate the humor and pathos of this story, the peculiar insecurities that waylay the protagonist clearly recall the predicament of Chinese American men, who were denied fatherhood historically and are still stigmatized as sexually deficient by U.S. popular culture. As Claude Steele has shown in his study of female and African American students in educational testing, those who suffer from "stereotype threat" invariably exhibit anxiety during performance: "Performing in domains where prevailing stereotypes allege one's inferiority . . . creates a predicament in which any faltering of performance threatens to confirm the stereotype as self-characteristic. This predicament . . . can cause an apprehension and self-consciousness that directly interferes with performance in that situation" ("Threat"). The male characters in Louie's fiction are all too conscious of this threat, albeit in a sexual terrain; they cannot avoid scrutinizing themselves through the lens of the stereotyping majority.

James S. Moy has castigated contemporary Asian American playwrights such as David Henry Hwang and Philip Kan Gotanda for allegedly creating Asian (American) men who are just as disfigured as established stereotypes. What Moy calls "flawed self-representations" (115) in drama has a certain parallel in the Asian American fiction analyzed here, in which the problem lies as much in deliberate inversions of stereotypes as in unintentional reinscriptions. Unlike the plays criticized by Moy, however, these literary texts successfully capture a range of individual difference and revitalize Asian American male images. The teenage and adult protagonists in these works all possess personality and sexuality, in contrast to the faceless and desexed Asian figures that populate Hollywood cinema. Still, none of them can disentangle from the prevailing ideology of manhood or escape its hegemonic hold. The male protagonists in *Donald Duk* and *China Boy* try to measure up to American notions of manliness by valorizing physical aggression; those in *Cultural Revolution* and *Pangs of Love* are conditioned by the dominant culture to see Chinese American men as subordinate to their Euramerican counterparts. All four works attest to the power of cultural imperialism in gendering ethnicity and in "ethnicizing gender" (S. Wong).

Alternative Models

Michele Wallace argues that

> blacks had been systematically deprived of the continuity of their own African culture not only by the oppression of slavery . . . but also by integration and assimilation, which had denied them the knowledge of their history of struggle and the memory of their autonomous cultural practices. In the process of assimilation, integration and accommodation, blacks had taken on the culture and values of whites in regard to sexuality and gender. (xix)

The same holds true for many Asian Americans. To find a concept of masculinity that is not already implicated in U.S. cultural hegemony and racial hierarchy, that is compatible with both the nationalist impulse to reclaim an Asian legacy and the feminist desire to combat machismo, I turn first to Chinese classics and drama. My intention is not to substitute one template for another but to furnish counterexamples to the pantheon of martial heroes erected by the editors of *The Big Aiiieeeee!*

I grew up in Hong Kong where I was exposed to one of the most irresistible Chinese male images—that of a *shushen* or poet-scholar. This ideal is propagated in Chinese romance and opera (e.g., *Peony Pavilion, The Western Chamber, Butterfly Lovers,* and *The Flirting Scholar*). The poet-scholar, far from either brutish or asexual, is seductive because of his gentle demeanor, his wit, and his refined sensibility. He prides himself on being indifferent to wealth and political power and seeks women and men who are his equals in intelligence and integrity. (True shushen are not to be confused with the elitist literati or Mandarins, who could be quite corrupt.) If reviving the image of the martial hero can counteract effeminate stereotypes of Asian American men, surely reclaiming the ideal of the poet-scholar will combat their cultural invisibility.

This model of the poet-scholar belies popular perceptions of Asian men as inarticulate, unromantic, and unimaginative, fit only to become computer nerds, engineers, or kung fu fighters. It further offers an ideal of masculinity that is at once sexy and nonaggressive and a mode of conduct that breaks down the putative dichotomy of gay and straight behavior. I retrieve this image not out of any nostalgic longing for a specific historical type, however. What comes to mind when I think of the poet-scholar is not whether he is actually a poet or a scholar but the attributes associated with him: attentiveness, courtesy, humor, personal integrity, indifference to material and political interest, and aversion to violence. To me, these are qualities that very much become a man.

Although I locate the poet-scholar in Chinese classics, he is still alive and well. I personally know a number of Asian American men—both heterosexual and gay—who embody that ideal. In American society, it is unfortunately an underrated one. Hence, many of these men—like the male protagonists in *Cultural Revolution* and *Pangs of Love*—still strive to be more "American-masculine." [16] I may thus be presenting Asian American men with a double bind in criticizing the martial hero while advocating the poet-scholar model. If they try to emulate the martial hero, they risk valorizing brute force and perpetuating patriarchal mores. If they pattern themselves after the poet-scholar, they risk appearing "unmanly" to Americans steeped in the New World configuration of gender, thereby reinforcing the popular perception of Asian men as effeminate—as befitting the model minority. Yet to live according to the "Western" ideal, to live in acute awareness of the white gaze, Asian American men may constantly find themselves falling short. It is especially ironic that contemporary Chinese American male writers, who correspond to the traditional shushen by race, gender, and profession, should endorse physical violence or express ethnic self-contempt for not having a piece of the American beefcake. [17]

I do not mean to belittle the valiant attempts by Asian Americans to challenge prevailing perceptions about Asian masculinity and femininity. But it takes even greater courage to defy the Euramerican norms and to refuse to be held hostage to them. Asian Americans can resist one-way adaptation and turn racial stereotypes into sources of inspiration by demonstrating that what the dominant culture perceives as "feminine" may in fact be a transgressive expression of masculinity. If African Americans can recodify black as beautiful, Asian Americans, and perhaps non-Asians as well, can learn to see "effeminacy" (for want of a better word) in men as desirable. From both nationalistic and feminist standpoints, a quest for Chinese American manhood should allow us to reclaim an alternative repertoire rather than simply reproduce clones of Western heroes.

Masculinity, like femininity, is multiple. The fact that the cherished ideal of the poet-scholar—an exemplar of Chinese masculinity—may strike most Americans as unmanly is sufficient to point to the arbitrariness of gender construction. But I am not suggesting that the poet-scholar is man par excellence nor trying to proffer a foolproof formula for manhood. Quite the contrary, I wish to contest any monolithic standards of gender—especially those of masculinity that have vitiated the self-worth of men with different cultural or sexual preferences. My invocation of the poet-scholar, like Chin's summons of the Chinese outlaws, is meant to conjure images of Asian American masculinity that contradict popular representations.

Nevertheless, I recognize that for any positive Asian images to take hold in the United States, they must first contend with cultural hegemony. About a year ago, a Hong Kong movie entitled *Flirting Scholar* was shown in a Los Angeles theater that frequently screens Chinese action movies. At first pleasantly surprised that a film featuring a Chinese poet-scholar had finally made its way to California, I was soon disabused. *Flirting Scholar* is based on a well-known Chinese story, which is in turn based on a real Chinese poet's life. But the famous story had been drastically altered to turn the traditional scholar into a deadly kung fu fighter in disguise. The changes undoubtedly heighten the movie's appeal to an American audience. Thus, the globalization of the movie industry, instead of fostering greater diversity, can in fact accelerate cultural imperialism.

The incident also reminds us that "performativity is neither free play nor theatrical self-presentation" and suggests that one cannot simply transplant a paragon from another culture regardless of the existing conditions on American soil. The icons of both the martial hero and the poet-scholar are quite remote and removed from the concerns of Asian Americans here and now. The martial hero underwrites physical aggression in an already all-too-violent society. Although there is much to admire in the poet-scholar, he is too detached from worldly politics to inspire those whose very consciousness as "Asian Americans" emerged in the wake of the civil rights movement. Advocating such a model may further smack of elitism in view of the high drop-out rates of underprivileged youngsters in high schools and colleges.[18]

Let us return, then, to the American environs of *Donald Duk* and *China Boy*. If we can stop thinking about manhood as embodying the American ideal of rugged individualism, or what Wallace calls "superficial masculine characteristics—demonstrable sexuality; physical prowess; the capacity for warlike behavior" (xix–xx), we can begin to discern different contours of masculinity even in these two novels that spotlight machismo. Both works contain male characters who embody what Nel Noddings, following Carol Gilligan, describes as "caring." Although

Noddings proclaims caring to be a "feminine approach to ethics," she adds that "there is no reason why men should not embrace it" (2). Indeed, male exemplars of this ethic can be found in both novels. King Duk in *Donald Duk* demonstrates it on collective and individual levels. What makes him an admirable figure is not so much his ability to play the menacing Kwan Kung as his unusual capacity to minister to the many less fortunate members of his community and to instill ethnic pride in his son by countering dominant perceptions of the Chinese. In explaining Chinese customs to Donald and imparting to him a sense of communal responsibility, King Duk also plays the role of a cultural transmitter, a role often reserved for strong mothers in Asian American literature. As mentioned earlier, Donald Duk's own courage in disputing the stock Chinese images presented in the classroom and in standing up for a wrongly charged suspect is evidence of valor that is life-affirming rather than life-threatening.

The ethic of caring, enacted by men of diverse racial origins, also softens the poverty and violence depicted in *China Boy*. Uncle Shim, who resembles the classical Chinese poet-scholar, helps Kai against great odds to retain a vestige of Chinese culture and a sense of self-esteem after his mother's death. Hector Pueblo, a Mexican auto mechanic, rescues Kai from a ferocious beating, tends him in his garage, and alerts Kai's father to his son's plight. Tony Barraza, Kai's Italian American boxing teacher, ensures that the hungry boy is well fed. Barney Lewis, his African American boxing teacher, on discovering that Edna has removed all the photos of Kai's beloved mother from the house, goes out of his way to obtain one for Kai. All these surrogate fathers "share their life gifts" with him (147); they nurture and succor him when his own father seems oblivious to his tribulations. But the character Kai most cherishes is his peer Toussaint (Toos), who, despite his dubious equation of fighting and manhood, literally extends his hand to Kai when all the other boys are engaged in the ritual of China boy bashing. Kai recalls, "My primary bond to him was for the things he did not do. He did not pound or trap me. He never cut me down. Or laughed with knives in his eyes. Then he opened his heart by explaining things to me, giving me his learning, and taking me into his home" (97). The passage turns around the dominant conception of masculinity as (aggressive) activity. Kai is forever drawn to Toos because he refrains from the cocky and blustering acts associated with boys. Toos also inspires in Kai reciprocal caring: "I had never had a friend before, and I cared for him as few lads have for another" (99).

In a book that centers on male mentoring, it is important to remember that Kai learns about caring as well as fighting from men. If their efficacy as martial or pugilistic instructors enables Kai to survive physically, their caring is what makes him wish to continue to live. Noddings remarks, "When the attitude of the one-caring bespeaks caring, the cared-for glows, grows stronger, and feels . . . that something has been added to him" (20). For Kai, who has felt abandoned by his biological mother and abused by his stepmother, and who at one point wished to "evaporat[e]" (290), this something is nothing short of the courage to go on. Caring women such as Kai's sister Janie, Angelina Costello, and Mrs. LaRue are equally important to Kai. But in shifting Noddings's emphasis from feminine to masculine caring, in showing how well the male characters manifest a nurturing behavior traditionally associated with women, I wish to underline precisely how *dis-arming* such behavior is in men and how attainable it is for men of all ethnicities and classes.

Conclusion

It may seem retrogressive to reinvoke the notion of masculinity at a time when scholars in ethnic, gay, and feminist studies are repeatedly stressing the arbitrariness of gender construction and the radical indeterminacy of categories such as sex and race. I have tried to show in this essay how these categories still govern our everyday lives and determine social hierarchies. I have also argued that the subjugation and reconstruction of Asian American manhood are legitimate feminist concerns. In turning a deaf ear to the grievances of Asian American men, feminist scholars risk homogenizing patriarchy on the one hand and enabling masculinist projects to proceed apace on the other. "Men in feminism" have for some time confronted the concerns of women (Jardine and Smith); women can likewise empathize with the predicament faced by men, attend to the differences among men, and participate in the process of rethinking masculinity. Only by engaging in such reciprocal investigations can we move beyond the conflicts within and between feminism and (cultural) nationalism to arrive at new kinds of connections.

No amount of academic theorizing can immediately undo a history of inequity and insidious representation. To this day, masculinity and power—both physical and political—still figure in conjunction. Men who have always enjoyed masculine perquisites may well be able to afford to ignore gender expectations. Men of color looking for equality may still aspire to play roles that have been associated with domination. Because racism toward Asians has traditionally been couched in gendered terms, many Asian American men have either internalized racist stereotypes of Asians as lacking in masculinity or rebelled against the stereotypes by assuming pugnacious roles to prove their manliness. Nevertheless, to try to understand the motives for such repetitive performances and to begin to entertain alternative scripts will, I hope, prepare the stage for a brave new cast.

NOTES

An earlier version of this essay was delivered in a session entitled "Beyond Gender Binarism" at the Modern Language Association convention in San Diego, 1994. I thank Russell Leong and Jinqi Ling for their comments on an earlier draft. I am also grateful for the support provided by the Center for Advanced Study in the Behavioral Sciences at Stanford University and by the Andrew W. Mellon Foundation.

1. While most of my examples are drawn from Chinese American fiction, the challenges faced by Chinese American men in the United States are confronted by many other Asian men as well, though the stereotypes associated with different national groups can be contradictory. For instance, whereas Chinese men are considered asexual, Filipino men are often represented as oversexed. The different perceptions about Chinese men and Japanese men will be discussed later in the text.

2. All the paragons of womanhood, be they Homer's Penelope and Helen of Troy (as well as her reincarnation in Marlowe's *Dr. Faustus* and Goethe's *Faust*), Ruth in the Old Testament, the Virgin Mary in the New Testament, Shakespeare's Cleopatra, Spenser's Faerie Queene, Samuel Richardson's Pamela and Clarissa, Puccini's Madame Butterfly, or her contemporary Miss Saigon, have been created by men, not to mention those myriad counterparts created by Asian men.

3. In an interview by Kay Bonetti, Kingston likened herself to Tang Ao in *China Men*. Just as the character Tang Ao is made to feel what it means to be of the other gender, so the author enters the realm of men and becomes "the kind of woman who loves men and who can tell their stories" (interview for the American Audio Prose Library, Columbia, Mo., 1986). For various perspectives on the interplay of nationalisms, feminisms, and sexualities, see Parker, Russo, Sommer, and Yaeger, *Nationalities and Sexualities;* see also Wallace, *Black Macho.*

4. In the words of Song Liling in Hwang's *M. Butterfly,* "The West thinks of itself as masculine—big guns, big industry, big money—so the East is feminine—weak, delicate, poor . . . but good at art, and full of inscrutable wisdom—the feminine mystique" (3.1).

5. *Eat a Bowl of Tea* and *The Lover,* two popular films based on novels, feature attractive Asian men. But the male protagonist in *Tea* is impotent; the one in *Lover* is, in Jessica Hagedorn's words, a "pathetic Chinese millionaire boy-toy" dominated by a French adolescent girl (xxii).

6. Kingston is herself upset by the unequal attention given to her first two books: "I don't like all this overpraising of my daughter and rudeness toward my sons—especially since my writing has gotten better" ("Personal Statement" 24). Reluctance to confront the racist treatment of early Chinese immigrants has probably also contributed to the slighting of *China Men.* See R. Lee, "Claiming Land," for further discussion of the marginalization of this work.

7. See Cunningham, "Between Violence and Silence," and Lane, "Homosexuality," for the dialectic of emasculation and masculinist response across different racial groups.

8. It should be noted that Hong Kong movies, unlike the traditional epics (which contain few heroines), frequently feature female fighters, so that physical prowess is not strictly associated with masculinity. Just as Asian American men who endure effeminate stereotypes find the Asian male heroes uplifting, so many Asian American women, often stereotyped as demure "China dolls," find themselves drawn to the Asian heroines on screen. When the emphasis is on acrobatics and swordsmanship, I too enjoy these movies. But, partly as a result of Hollywood influence, the more recent movies have zoomed in on bloodshed and violence.

9. Unfortunately, the mother and daughters in *Donald Duk,* who all endorse assimilation into Euramerican culture, are little more than caricatures, as though Chin wishes to counter Kingston's and Tan's detailed delineation of mothers and daughters and sketchy characterization of Chinese men in *The Woman Warrior* and *The Joy Luck Club.*

10. Viet Thanh Nguyen elaborated on the thin line between criminal violence and institutionalized violence in a paper entitled "Postcolonialism and the Discourse of Violence: A Transnational Reading of Gus Lee's *China Boy,*" delivered at the Modern Language Association convention in San Diego, 1994. One need only recall the beating of Rodney King to see the continuing blurring of the line.

11. In *The Big Aiiieeeee!* Chin condemns as accomplices with white ideology any Asian American writers who do not write out of the Asian heroic tradition. His wholesale denunciation of these writers in the name of championing an authentic literary tradition unwittingly reproduces the strategy of the white literary establishment, which has traditionally censored voices that do not echo white male "universals," especially voices of women, gays, and people of color. See Chiu, "Uncanny Doubles," on how Chin "reiterates some of the exclusionary tendencies of mainstream American nationalism in his scapegoating of women" (95), and Eng, "In the Shadows," on "the need to refrain from seeking homophobic solutions to racism" (110).

12. I thank my student Kelly Jeong for her insights on Julia's ability to reset her own worth and on the ironic tropes around manhood in "Ordinary Chinese People."

13. See Eng, "In the Shadows," for a probing analysis of *M. Butterfly,* especially with regard to Gallimard's "advance self-punishment purchased in exchange for a promise of sexual impunity" (95).

14. Early Japanese immigrants were also more fortunate than their Chinese counterparts in that they were allowed to bring their wives and "picture brides" to the United States.

15. Louie, my colleague at UCLA, has repeatedly told me and my students that even though the ethnicity of his protagonists is not always explicit, he invariably has Asians or Asian Americans in mind.

16. Kingston distinguishes between "Chinese-feminine" and "American-feminine" in *The Woman Warrior* (172).

17. On this point see also S. Wong's critique of the *Asian Pacific Men* calendar ("Subverting Desire"). One may argue that the masculine ideal privileged by the editors of *The Big Aiiieeeee!* is influenced more by African American than by Caucasian models. But African American men too have been indoctrinated in white

America's ideal of masculinity. Of course, the "occidental" ideal takes many forms other than those inspired by frontier heroes—including the courtly lover, the knight errant, the debonair intellectual, and the "Mr. Smith" idealist who goes to Washington. But Asian American men, in order to counter stereotypes, tend to favor the more aggressive "Western" models.

I should also add that the Chinese poet-scholar found in classics and opera is typically pale and emaciated; he could certainly benefit from some martial training. In fact, yet another kind of Chinese masculine ideal is embodied by someone who is *wen wu shuang quan*—"accomplished in both the literary and martial arts" (S. Wong, "Ethnicizing Gender," 127n. 3).

18. I thank Russell Leong and Jinqi Ling for alerting me to this point.

WORKS CITED

Butler, Judith. *Bodies that Matter: On the Discursive Limits of "Sex."* New York: Routledge, 1993.

———. *Gender Trouble: Feminism and the Subversion of Identity.* New York: Routledge, 1990.

Chan, Jeffery Paul, Frank Chin, Lawson Fusao Inada, and Shawn Wong, eds. *The Big Aiiieeeee! An Anthology of Chinese American and Japanese American Literature.* New York: Penguin, 1991.

Cheung, King-Kok. *Articulate Silences: Hisaye Yamamoto, Maxine Hong Kingston, Joy Kogawa.* Ithaca, N.Y.: Cornell University Press, 1993.

———. "The Woman Warrior versus the Chinaman Pacific: Must a Chinese American Critic Choose between Feminism and Heroism?" *Conflicts in Feminism.* Ed. Marianne Hirsch and Evelyn Fox Keller. New York: Routledge, 1990. 234–51.

Chin, Frank. "Confessions of the Chinatown Cowboy." *Bulletin of Concerned Asian Scholars* 4.3 (1972): 58–70.

———. *Donald Duk.* Minneapolis: Coffee House, 1991.

Chin, Frank, and Jeffery Paul Chan. "Racist Love." *Seeing through Shuck.* Ed. Richard Kostelanetz. New York: Ballantine, 1972. 65–79.

Chin, Frank, Jeffery Paul Chan, Lawson Fusao Inada, and Shawn Wong, eds. *Aiiieeeee! An Anthology of Asian American Writers.* 1974. Washington, D.C.: Howard University Press, 1983.

Chiu, Jeannie. "Uncanny Doubles: Nationalism and Repression in Frank Chin's 'Railroad Standard Time.' " *Critical Mass* 1.1 (1993): 93–107.

Chow, Rey. *Woman and Chinese Modernity: The Politics of Reading between West and East.* Minneapolis: University of Minnesota Press, 1991.

Cunningham, Chris. "Between Violence and Silence: Is There a Site for a Masculinist Discourse on Race?" Ph.D. dissertation, University of California, Los Angeles, 1995.

Eng, David L. "In the Shadows of a Diva: Committing Homosexuality in David Henry Hwang's *M. Butterfly.*" *Amerasia Journal* 20.1 (1994): 93–116.

Fung, Richard. "Looking for My Penis: The Eroticized Asian in Gay Video Porn." *How Do I Look? Queer Film and Video.* Ed. Bad Object-Choices. Seattle: Bay Press, 1991. 145–68.

Hagedorn, Jessica. "Asian Women in Film: No Joy, No Luck." *Ms.,* Jan/Feb 1994, pp. 74–79.

———, ed. *Charlie Chan Is Dead: An Anthology of Contemporary Asian American Fiction*. New York: Penguin, 1993.

hooks, bell. *Yearning: Race, Gender, and Cultural Politics*. Boston: South End Press, 1990.

Hwang, David Henry. *M. Butterfly*. New York: Plume, 1988.

Jardine, Alice, and Paul Smith, eds. *Men in Feminism*. New York: Methuen, 1987.

Kim, Elaine H. " 'Such Opposite Creatures': Men and Women in Asian American Literature." *Michigan Quarterly Review* 29.1 (1990): 68–93.

Kingston, Maxine Hong. *China Men*. 1980. New York: Vintage, 1989.

———. "Personal Statement." *Approaches to Teaching Kingston's* The Woman Warrior. Ed. Shirley Geok-lin Lim. New York: Modern Language Association, 1991. 23–25.

———. *Tripmaster Monkey: His Fake Book*. 1989. New York: Vintage, 1990.

———. *The Woman Warrior: Memoirs of a Girlhood among Ghosts*. 1976. New York: Vintage, 1989.

Lane, Alycee. "Homosexuality and the Crisis of Black Cultural Particularity." Ph.D. dissertation, University of California, Los Angeles, 1996.

Lee, Gus. *China Boy*. New York: Dutton, 1991.

———. *Honor and Duty*. New York: Alfred A. Knopf, 1994.

Lee, Rachel C. "Claiming Land, Claiming Voice, Claiming Canon: Institutionalized Challenges in Kingston's *China Men* and *The Woman Warrior*." *Reviewing Asian America: Locating Diversity*. Ed. Wendy L. Ng, Soo-Young Chin, James S. Moy, and Gary Y. Okihiro. Pullman: Washington State University Press, 1995. 147–59.

Lee Yu-cheng. "Politics of Memory in *Donald Duk*." *Wen-hua shu-hsing yu hua-yi mei-kuo wen-hsueh* [Cultural identity and Chinese American literature]. Ed. Shan Te-hsing and Ho Wen-ching. Taipei: Institute of European and American Studies, Academia Sinica, 1994. 115–32.

Lim, Shirley Geok-lin. "Japanese American Women's Life Stories: Maternality in Monica Sone's *Nisei Daughter* and Joy Kogawa's *Obasan*." *Feminist Studies* 16 (1990): 289–312.

Ling, Jinqi. "Identity Crisis and Gender Politics: Reappropriating Asian American Masculinity." *An Interethnic Companion to Asian American Literature*. Ed. King-Kok Cheung. New York: Cambridge University Press, 1997. 312–37.

Louie, David Wong. *Pangs of Love*. 1991. New York: Plume, 1992.

Marchetti, Gina. "Ethnicity, the Cinema, and Cultural Studies." *Unspeakable Images: Ethnicity and the American Cinema*. Ed. Lester D. Friedman. Urbana: University of Illinois Press, 1991. 277–307.

———. *Romance and the "Yellow Peril": Race, Sex, and Discursive Strategies in Hollywood Fiction*. Berkeley: University of California Press, 1993.

Moy, James S. *Marginal Sights: Staging the Chinese in America*. Iowa City: University of Iowa Press, 1993.

Nakayama, William. "The Minority Syndrome." *Transpacific*, Oct. 1993, pp. 86–87.

Noddings, Nel. *Caring: A Feminine Approach to Ethics and Moral Education*. Berkeley: University of California Press, 1984.

Parker, Andrew, Mary Russo, Doris Sommer, and Patricia Yaeger, eds. *Nationalisms and Sexualities*. New York: Routledge, 1992.

Payne, Robert. "A Divisive Debate." *Rafu Shimpo*, Dec. 9, 1995, p. 3.

Said, Edward W. *Orientalism*. New York: Vintage, 1979.

Slotkin, Richard. *Gunfighter Nation: The Myth of the Frontier in Twentieth-Century America.* New York: Maxwell Macmillan International, 1992.
———. *Regeneration through Violence: The Mythology of the American Frontier, 1600–1860.* Middleton, Conn.: Wesleyan University Press, 1973.
Steele, Claude M. "A Threat in the Air: How Stereotypes Shape Intellectual Identity and Performance." *American Psychologist* 52.6 (1997): 613–29.
Tajima, Renee E. "Lotus Blossoms Don't Bleed: Images of Asian Women." *Making Waves: An Anthology of Writings by and about Asian American Women.* Ed. Asian Women United of California. Boston: Beacon, 1989. 308–17.
Tan, Amy. *The Joy Luck Club.* New York: Putnam, 1989.
———. *The Kitchen God's Wife.* New York: Ballantine, 1991.
Wallace, Michele. *Black Macho and the Myth of the Superwoman.* 1978. London: Verso, 1990.
Wong, Eugene Franklin. *On Visual Media Racism: Asians in American Motion Pictures.* New York: Ayer Press, 1978.
Wong, Norman. *Cultural Revolution.* New York: Persea, 1994.
Wong, Sau-ling Cynthia. "Ethnicizing Gender: An Exploration of Sexuality as Sign in Chinese Immigrant Literature." *Reading the Literatures of Asian America.* Ed. Shirley Geok-lin Lim and Amy Ling. Philadelphia: Temple University Press, 1992. 111–29.
———. "Subverting Desire: Reading the Body in the 1991 Asian Pacific Islander Men's Calendar." *Critical Mass* 1.1 (1993): 63–74.

8 ◇ Rethinking Class from a Chicana Perspective

Identity and Otherness in Chicana
Literature and Theory

Refiguring Identity, Recapturing Totality

In her essay "Feminism on the Border: From Gender Politics to Geopolitics," Sonia Saldívar-Hull interrogates the effectiveness of Marxist and
feminist theories and methodologies for comprehending the Chicana
experience and providing a viable model for liberation. "Is it possible,"
she asks in her two-pronged attack, "for Chicanas to consider ourselves
part of this 'sisterhood' called feminism? Can we assume that our
specific interests and problems will be taken care of by our Marxist com-
pañeros?" Because the Chicana has "a specific history under racial and
sexual and class exploitation," Saldívar-Hull argues that the theoretical
matrix of Marxism and feminism must be further problematized with
categories of race and ethnicity. Nonetheless, her cogent approach
strongly resembles, while deepening and complicating, a Marxist historical materialist method. She eschews poststructuralism, arguing that
"the Chicana feminist does not present 'signifying spaces' but material
geopolitical issues that redirect feminist discourse" and that "Chicana
feminism develops from an awareness of specific material experience of
the historical moment" (203, 208, 217).

Similarly, Norma Alarcón critiques dominant feminist paradigms for
their isolating emphases on sexual difference, for their desire to construct
feminist theory solely on the basis of gender, resulting in a "gendered
standpoint epistemology that leads to feminism's bizarre relationship

with other liberation movements, working inherently against the interests of non-white women and no one else" ("Theoretical Subject[s]" 30). The Chicana lesbian writer and critic Cherríe Moraga also questions versions of feminism—and by extension identity politics—that lack a material basis to their approach and that isolate or autonomize central categories of socioeconomic organization, such as race, class, and gender, instead of recognizing their dialectical relationships. She writes:

> "Radical Feminism," the ideology which sees men's oppression of women as the root of and paradigm for all other oppressions allows women to view ourselves as a class and to claim our sexual identity as the source of our oppression and men's sexual identity as the source of the world's evil. But this ideology can never then fully integrate the concept of the "simultaneity of oppression" as Third World feminism is attempting to do. For, if race and class suffer the woman of color as much as her sexual identity, then the Radical Feminist must extend her own "identity" politics to include her "identity" as oppressor as well. (To say anything of the having to acknowledge that there are men who may suffer more than she.) This is something that for the most part, Radical Feminism has refused to do. (*Loving* 128)

These Chicanas effectively critique the impoverished theoretical underpinnings of the contemporary politics of organizing around a putative shared identity, a politics correspondent with the theoretical dominance of the race/class/gender trinity. These writers call into question a feminism premised on the mythological possibility of a female consciousness derived from some organic "women's position" in society, pointing up the acute and material differences between working-class and middle-class women or third world and first world women that undermine the notion of a shared identity and even point up the exploitive relations within that mythic shared identity. They indict a Marxism that theorizes class as a pure and primary category, ignoring that the uneven experiences of class condition one's race and gender, that race and gender condition one's class positioning, and that a first world working class might be complicit with the exploitation and oppression of a colonized or internally colonized third world working class. Likewise, the Chicana perspective of these writers, as we will see, also challenges the construction of national identity to underwrite a national liberation movement against a colonial or internal colonial situation that ignores the specific conditions of colonized women and their sexuality.

Conversely, the Chicana perspective of these writers promotes a theoretical approach both sensitive to the dialectical interaction and relationship between the categories of race, class, gender, and nation and cognizant that these categories are not pure and do not exist apart from one another, that one's racial and gender identities are inflected by one's class position and vice versa, and that race and gender have historically conditioned the positioning of individuals differentially within the global colonial and class system. Indeed, while this dialectical approach, articulated most forcefully by Saldívar-Hull, might historically be associated with Marxist methodology—and it certainly is the defining element of Marxism—it has been most strenuously worked out, I think, in the province of Chicana criticism and theory. Yvonne Yarbro-Bejarano has laid out most clearly the objectives of Chicana theoretical practice to which I refer when she writes, "Perhaps the most important principle of Chicana feminist criticism is the realization that the Chicana's experience as a woman is inextricable from her experience as a member of an oppressed working-class racial minority and a culture which is not the dominant culture. Her task is to show how in works by Chicanas, elements of gender, race, culture, and class coalesce" (139). While certainly, as Yarbro-Bejarano notes, "this may seem painfully obvious," she correctly reiterates the content of this critical task because, in fact, despite the seeming obviousness, this dialectical method has fallen out of use in contemporary critical practice, particularly in poststructuralist and post-Marxist varieties, as I will discuss.

Indeed, as seen most clearly in Saldívar-Hull's formulation above, it is through the Chicana perspective that a Marxist method is being reasserted, deepened, and complicated as a more genuine historical materialism. While poststructuralism and post-Marxism reject out of hand the concept of totality at the center of Marxism, Chicana theory restores the concept of totality (what Gloria Anzaldúa terms "a more whole perspective"), combatting poststructuralism's and post-Marxism's delight in a fragmentation that disables rather than fosters a dialectical method. As Yarbro-Bejarano writes, "By asserting herself as Chicana or *mestiza,* the Chicana confronts the damaging fragmentation of her identity into component parts at war with each other" (170). The Chicana perspective, in fact, produces a comprehensive class consciousness that includes race, gender, and culture as class determinants, as "the very term 'Chicana' or 'mestiza' communicates the multiple connotations of color and femaleness, as well as historical adumbrations of class and cultural membership within the economic structure and dominant culture of the United States" (Yarbro-Bejarano 140). Thus, Chicana cultural practice refigures identity by recapturing totality, that is, by understanding the total set of forces and factors that historically construct and position one's identity. In this essay, through a study of Lorna Dee Cervantes's poetry and Chicana cultural theory, I will explore the way in which Chicana literary practice constructs this "more whole" class consciousness.

Lorna Dee Cervantes's poetry offers in practice an expression of this third world feminism theorized by Moraga and Saldívar-Hull. Like other Chicana literature of the 1980s that has repositioned the Chicano political class and through its feminist intervention "given new life to a stalled Chicano movement" (Alarcón, "Chicana" 249), Cervantes's poetry challenges the unity of the Chicano class and of the working class at both the literary and political levels. Indeed, the accomplishment of her two volumes of poetry, *Emplumada* and *From the Cables of Genocide: Poems on Love and Hunger,* lies in Cervantes's poetic construction of a revolutionary class-conscious subjectivity, a task that involves not only a reformulation of class and class consciousness (that takes into account race, gender, and nation and challenges poststructuralist and post-Marxist identity politics) but also includes a reterritorialization of the imaginative geography of Chicano and working-class culture. Thus, considering these calls for a Chicana historical materialist method, I will examine the possibilities produced by an encounter between Marxist literary theory and Chicana literature and theory. My analysis focuses on an evaluation of how Chicana theory can help us rethink class in a way that foregrounds the recognition that components of a class are produced historically and may be composed of different genders and diverse races.

In the case of Chicano/a literature, the proletarian underpinnings have always been present. Indeed, as Rosa Linda Fregoso and Angie Chabram point out, the very term "Chicano" "signified both the affirmation of our working-class and indigenous origins, and the rejection of assimilation, acculturation, and the myth of the American melting pot. Implicit in the term Chicano was a strategic relation and a strategy of struggle which thematized the Chicano community and called for social struggle and reform" (205). But the encroachment of poststructuralist theories of identity in ethnic, racial, and gender studies has effaced the dialectical entwinement of race, class, and gender as determinants of identities or subject positions. Thus, interpellating Chicano/a literature into a class-based literary theoretical model is meant to rearticulate the "displaced" yet interrelated class determinants of Chicano/a identity. With contemporary criticism obscuring the originary radical politics of third world movements and literatures, the search for identity that has dominated not only Chicano but also other third world cultural politics is defined according to narrow conceptions of ethnicity, race, and nation underwritten by the "schizophrenizing" (Gilles Deleuze and

Felix Guattari's term) critical approach of post-Marxism and poststructuralism. This approach effectively buys into and reproduces the fragmentation of consciousness wrought by the mechanisms of late capitalism, thus preventing rather than enhancing a coherent comprehension
of the global colonial system as a whole. In the context of post-Marxism,
informed by "the cultural logic of late capitalism," the categories of race,
class, gender, and nation are unrelated rather than dialectical determinants of identity, as we can see in Chantal Mouffe's representative statement of post-Marxist identity theory:

> Within every society, each social agent is inscribed in a multiplicity of
> social relations—not only social relations of production but also the so-
> cial relations, among others, of sex, race, nationality, and vicinity. All
> these social relations determine positionalities or subject position and
> cannot be reduced to only one. Thus, someone inscribed in the relations
> of production as a worker is also a man or a woman, white or black,
> Catholic or protestant, French or German, and so on. A person's subjec-
> tivity is not constructed only on the basis of his or her position in the re-
> lations of production. (90)

Implicit in this account of social identity is the notion that one's race
or gender do not determine one's position within the global system of
production, ignoring the reality that people of color have historically
been targeted for economic oppression and that race and gender are determinants of class identity. The workers' "identity" as women and
people of color is different from a white male working-class identity.
Race, class, and gender are not strands of identity that can be neatly separated from one another into a "democratic chain of equivalencies," to
use Mouffe's language. One is not black, female, and a worker but rather
a black woman worker; one has not multiple identities but a composite
identity overdetermined by factors such as race, class, gender, nation,
generation, and so on. Here Moraga's concept of the simultaneity of oppression can be invoked. Indeed, W. E. B. Du Bois opens *Black Reconstruction* with a chapter each on the black worker and on the white worker,
providing two distinct histories to account for their differential and unequal incorporation into the labor market and effectively demonstrating the interrelatedness of racial and class formation. Splitting or fragmenting these determinants of social and political identity distorts and
narrows our understanding of racial and gender dynamics within the
global class structure.

The fragmenting tendencies of post-Marxism and poststructuralism
are in many ways complicit with a liberal pluralism that ignores the real
socioeconomic contradictions on which Marxist analysis focuses. The
result is a problematic celebration of political diversity (that may in-

clude hostile antagonisms) without recognizing contradictions or establishing a coherent platform for long-term social transformation. For example, in her essay "Heterogeneity, Hybridity, Multiplicity: Marking Asian American Differences," Lisa Lowe theorizes an Asian American identity that accounts for the term's heterogeneity. She explores a "conception of ethnicity as heterogeneous" because it can create "a position for Asian Americans that is both ethnically specific, yet simultaneously uneven and unclosed" (32), putatively allowing for greater political flexibility. Lowe writes that with such a theory of heterogeneity "Asian Americans can articulate distinct group demands based on our particular histories of exclusions, but the redefined lack of closure—which reveals rather than conceals differences—opens political lines of affiliation with other groups (labor unions, other racial and ethnic groups, and gay, lesbian, and feminist groups) in the challenge to specific forms of domination insofar as they share common features" (30). Observing that "the most exclusive construction of Asian American identity . . . is at odds with the formation of important political alliances and affiliations across racial and ethnic, gender, sexuality, and class lines" (31), Lowe asserts that she is not arguing "against the strategic importance of Asian American identity, nor against the building of Asian American culture," but that she is instead suggesting "that acknowledging class and gender differences among Asian Americans does not weaken us as a group; to the contrary, these differences represent greater political opportunity to affiliate with other groups whose cohesions may be based on other valences of oppression" (32). Underwriting Lowe's argument is, as we see in Mouffe's writing, a postmodern theory of multiple inscription and positionality: the notion that within society each social agent is inscribed in a multiplicity of social relations—relations of production as well as those of race, sex, nationality, and others. Thus, the theory goes, each individual inhabits a variety of subject positions, each of which in turn supposedly corresponds to a particular set of political interests. For Lowe, this means "that it may be less meaningful to act exclusively in terms of a single valence or political interest—such as ethnicity or nation—than to acknowledge that social subjects are the sites of a variety of differences" (31).

The problem with this poststructuralist account of identity politics is that in "marking Asian American differences" it effectively leaves the marker of "Asian American" itself in a vacuum; the term is evacuated of any meaningful content—political, cultural, or otherwise—and defined only by difference. Like Mouffe's, Lowe's approach prevents rather than enhances a coherent comprehension of the racial, patriarchal, global colonial system as a whole. Again, the categories of race, class, gender, and nation become unrelated rather than dialectical determinants of identity. Given Lowe's account, we might ask what she finally sees as the political interest that corresponds to the valence of nation, race, or ethnicity for Asian America. As a political category, it has no particular class content for Lowe: we see this, for example, in her eschewing of "an essentialized identity" because "it can discourage laboring Asian Americans from joining unions with workers of other colors" (31). By the same token, it forgoes any particular gender politics, leaving unclear what ethnic or national political content defines the marker Asian American. These identities, for Lowe, exist and express themselves outside of racial and national contexts, through external political affiliations. Lowe neglects the fact that one's racial and national politics are conditioned by the way one experiences racial and national identity through class and gender. The national interests as perceived by the neoconservative Asian American professional, for example, may not be the same as that of "laboring Asian Americans," nor the middle-class reformist's the same as the Maoist's. It seems doubtful that such class differences, for example, would strengthen rather than weaken the Asian American collective by creating greater political opportunity to affiliate with other groups. Asian America is far from strengthened when Asian American capital allies with other capital and the Asian American working class allies with other workers. The contradiction is in fact highlighted. The concept of heterogeneity isolates race and ethnicity from the material circumstances of their articulation and is unable to deal with these contradictions. Instead of celebrating differences as mere diversity, we need to move beyond this liberal pluralist fetish of postmodernism and restore the concept of contradiction to problematize in fruitful ways the neat delineation of political identities.

It is here that I want to take my cue from Chicana feminist criticism, which has vigorously combatted the narrowly defined and constrictive identity politics informing dominant feminist and Chicano critical discourses. In spite of the call for a Chicana feminist criticism by Chicana critics, criticism of Cervantes's work has been restricted to analyzing her poems as privileging either the ethnic or feminist aspect of Chicana identity. Class as a category is generally ignored as an aspect or determinant of that identity. Lynette Seator, for example, argues that *Emplumada* "is poetry that defines a Mexican-American identity and so carries an 'ethnic' denomination." Although she tempers the particularity of this statement with the qualification that, "for Cervantes, the role of ethnic writer intent on affirming a personal and group identity within a clearly defined temporal and spatial context is complicated by the fact that her sense of self as woman does not conform to the traditions of her ethnic heritage" (83), Seator still reduces the struggles expressed in the poems to those against and within her ethnic heritage. Similarly, Marta Ester Sánchez asserts, "Cervantes' identity as woman is inextricably bound to her Chicana self. The central tension in her poetic voice is between her identity as Chicana and her role as poet." She belongs to a "generation that inscribes its own cultural identity in writing and thus gives value to the words and actions of her ancestors" (8, 130). Juan Bruce-Novoa, on the other hand, writes that *Emplumada* is primarily feminist "in its process and structure" and that, although it is a Chicana text, "the essential problematic is not ethnic, but rather sexual" ("Bernice Zamora" 573). Each of these critics explores a crucial aspect of Cervantes's work, but their analyses are impoverished by their failure to fuse dialectically race and gender and to incorporate them into an analysis of inequality that would provide a deeper and more historical understanding of not only the Chicano and women's movement but of class itself.

Identity and Otherness

In opposition to Mouffe's "questioning [of] the totality of social relationships," to the schizophrenizing critical methods of post-Marxism, I thus reinsert the category of totality in examining how Cervantes's poetry provides a dialectical understanding of the relation between race, class, and gender in its construction of a revolutionary Chicana working-class subjectivity. From *Emplumada* (1981), which is rooted in yet offers a critique of the Chicano movement, to *From the Cables of Genocide* (1991), which rethinks poetic and political consciousness and identity, Cervantes's poetry radically retheorizes identity and identity politics through a poetic reconceptualization of the relations between identity and otherness in terms of race, class, and gender, experience and totality, and nationalism and internationalism. Her poetry offers a version of Chicana Marxism that goes beyond writing Chicanas "into the movement script" (Chabram-Dernersesian) and instead writes them into, by rewriting, the master narrative of global anti-imperialist class struggle.

Cervantes's poetic recasting of identity and political agency represents a significant intervention into the Chicano literary genre that for the most part has been thematized and cast as the cultural search for identity underwriting the Chicano movement of the 1960s, which was itself "a quest for a new identity and for political power" (Muñoz 15). Indeed, as Bruce-Novoa wrote in 1982, "*Chicano literature,* as most people use the term, is that which is associated with a new consciousness of political, social, and cultural identity linked to the Chicano movement" (*Chicano Poetry* 3). The literary works that explored and defined this new political and cultural identity, however, were predominantly centered on the experience of the Chicano male, such as Ernesto Galarza's *Barrio Boy,* José Antonio Villareal's *Pocho,* Oscar Zeta Acosta's *The Autobiography of a Brown Buffalo,* Rudolfo Anaya's *Bless Me, Ultima,* and Tomas Rivera's . . . *Y No Se Lo Tragó la Tierra.*

Cervantes reconceives Chicano literature and its linkage to the identity politics of the Chicano movement in two significant ways. First, she introduces a strong feminist component that forces a reconsideration of the explicitly masculinist underpinnings of the Chicano identity ratifying the movement's political agendas, a masculinism perhaps most blatantly advertised in Corky Gonzalez's statement at the Chicano Youth Conference in Denver in 1969: "Look at the Congressional Medals of Honor our people have. It shows that when it comes to machismo there is no match for La Raza" (qtd. in Steiner 327). Cervantes's poetry redraws the boundaries of the Chicano/a nation: if the traditional corrido, or border ballad, dramatizes the conflicts between Mexicans and Anglos at the border of the two nations, Cervantes's poetry demarcates additional borders within the Chicano/a nation, much as Moraga and Anzaldúa do in theorizing a Chicana national resistance consciousness. Moraga, for example, recently noted, "Chicanos are an occupied nation within a nation, and women and women's sexuality are occupied within the Chicano nation" (*Last Generation* 150). Anzaldúa conceptualizes this metaphorization of the borderlands most recognizably in the preface to her by now well-known *Borderlands/La Frontera: The New Mestiza,* in which she writes:

> The actual physical borderland that I'm dealing with in this book is the Texas-U.S. Southwest/Mexican border. The psychological borderlands, the sexual borderlands and the spiritual borderlands are not particular to the Southwest. In fact, the Borderlands are physically present wherever two or more cultures edge each other, where people of different races occupy the same territory, where under, lower, middle and upper classes touch, where the space between two individuals shrinks with intimacy. (Preface, n.p.)

As I will discuss later, while Anzaldúa theorizes the *mestiza* consciousness as "developing a tolerance for contradictions" such that "not only does she sustain contradictions, she turns the ambivalence into something else" (79), Cervantes's poetry figures these other contradictions as overdetermining the more general systemic contradiction between the forces and relations of production. Anzaldúa's writing, it must be noted, falls prey to the postmodernist fetish of heterogeneity, turning contradiction into "something else." Cervantes's aesthetic insists on mapping the relays among race, class, gender, and nation within the international colonial system of domination and subordination. Thus, even though, in Louis Althusser's theory of overdetermination, the "vast accumulation of 'contradictions' " are "radically heterogeneous—of different origins, different sense, different levels and points of application," nevertheless "the basic contradiction dominating the period . . . is active in all these 'contradictions' and even in their 'fusion' " (100). Cervantes's poetry enacts such a fusion.

Second, what is perhaps most poetically and politically innovative about *Emplumada* and *From the Cables of Genocide* is Cervantes's reconceptualization of the relation between identity and otherness and of the very meaning of identity and its political implementation. Identity and otherness for Cervantes are not opposites defined against each other. Rather, establishing or discovering identity for Cervantes involves and requires the reclaiming of otherness, of that outside world and that distant history beyond one's experienced world and history. While identity politics has traditionally located its authority and sought its validation in the experience of its constituency—just as the political identity of the Chicano movement was developed out of the "representative" biographical experiences of its cultural practitioners—Cervantes's cultural practice effectively constructs a poetic consciousness alienated from these politically informing experiences or else takes license in inhabiting the consciousness of other subject positions outside the range of her own biographical experiences. Indeed, although Cervantes speaks of "bringing out images that are uniquely Chicana" and of creating in her poems a "definition of what it is to be Chicana" (qtd. in Monda 105-6), this notion of a Chicana identity is not necessarily based on experience, for Cervantes views poetry, she noted in my recent interview of her, as "an alternative to experience" (July 30, 1993). Indeed, Moraga strongly echoes this sentiment in her autobiographical political manifesto *Loving in the War Years,* in which she writes, "It seemed I had to step outside my familia to see what we as a people were doing suffering. This is my politics. This is my writing" (ii).

From the opening poem of *Emplumada,* "Uncle's First Rabbit," both of these elements are strikingly present, making immediately evident Cervantes's implicit challenge to, or attempt to expand the coordinates of, the agenda of Chicano literary nationalism. The poem deals critically yet sympathetically with the masculinist socialization of a young Chicano, delineating his rite of passage into a destructive manhood as he ventures out to shoot his first rabbit. The experience daunts, even repulses, the boy: "As he leveled the rifle, / and the terrible singing began / . . . He had dreamed of running, / shouldering the rifle to town, / selling it, and taking the next / train out" (3). He cannot escape the situation, and the "keening" of the dying rabbit "under the butt of his rifle" haunts him. It is later associated with the voice of his dead baby sister, who dies in a premature labor instigated by his father's "drunken kicking," and with his brutalized mother, whom he remembers "softly, keening" after the incident.

Throughout his life the boy attempts to escape the socially reproduced violence and values of manhood but is unsuccessful. "When the war came," Cervantes writes, "he took the man's vow. He was / finally leaving and taking the bastard's last bloodline with him." The legacy of violence bequeathed to him by his father, however, does not end, as he awakens from the war "to find himself slugging the bloodied / face of his wife." The socially and culturally transmitted values of machismo continue despite his attempts and desire to redirect or alter the destructive protocols of masculine behavior. At the end of the poem, he is still thinking "how he'll / take the new pickup to town, sell it, / and get the next train out." Just as the Chicano in the poem cannot fulfill his utopian vision of breaking out of the socially constructed gender identity that imprisons him and leads to his brutalization of women, the poem suggests that the cultural nationalism of the Chicano movement cannot achieve complete liberation until it both becomes conscious of the gender inequality informing Chicano culture and overcomes it by creating cultural forms capable of the utopian expression sought by the boy/man in the poem.

Interestingly, while Cervantes introduces this crucial gender dimension to the liberation project of Chicano nationalism, she suggests that Chicano males must achieve a self-consciousness of this inequality and realize that they too, even if not to the same extent, are victims of sexual inequality. She does not narrate the poem from a woman's point of view but instead attempts to represent the Chicano male consciousness and to narrate the process by which a male achieves this gender consciousness—indeed, this higher form of Chicano class consciousness. While she could easily have written the poem from her own experience as a Chicana (she does, in fact, write of women's oppression from a Chicana perspective in later poems in *Emplumada*), she strategically exits the realm of personal experience and attempts to imagine an experience and enter a consciousness other than her own. The poem effectively militates against a feminist politics rooted necessarily in a "female" identity and instead demonstrates the efficacy of understanding gender as a social construction for any politics of Chicano resistance to racial patriarchal capitalism, ackowledging, as Anzaldúa observes, that "men, even more than women, are fettered to gender roles" (84). The male must recognize that a genuine class consciousness involves a consciousness of the operations of gender ideologies in constructing and positioning identities and political interests.

Indeed, from a perspective of totality that understands the interrelatedness of race, class, and gender oppression within the global colonial class structure, gender oppression, while experienced uniquely and most severely by women, is not the result of an isolated set of forces operating autonomously within the capitalist system but rather one part of the complex totality of forces that sustains that system and its methods of exploitation as a whole. Indeed, here we might fruitfully apply to the category of gender Barbara Jeanne Fields's analysis of "race" as an ideological construct that those in power "constantly reinvent and re-ritualize to fit our own terrain," to meet the requirements of exploitation in a specific socioeconomic system or context. She adds, "Probably a majority of American historians think of slavery as primarily a system of race relations—as though the chief business of slavery were the production of white supremacy rather than the production of cotton, sugar, rice and tobacco" (99). Understanding gender as a categorical deployment in the context of a totality of social relations and power dynamics counteracts positing an automatic correspondence between a particular political set of interests and a social position or identity. "Uncle's First Rabbit" shows clearly that male liberation demands a feminist political solution, that the ideological dictates involved in the social construction of "manhood" overall make the Chicano male complicit in the patriarchal structures (his fighting in the war, for example), informing the racial capitalist system in ways that countertend his economic and human interest.

Thus, Cervantes's poem illustrates that feminism, here a specifically Chicana feminism, does not constitute a political ideology or program that comprehends or corresponds to exclusively women's interests but rather to Chicano working-class men as well. The stress is not on a gender-informed identity politics but rather on a decoding or comprehension of the whole complex of mutually reinforcing race, class, and gender relations that comprise the concrete social totality of the capitalist system so that a properly strategic and comprehensive political identity and movement can be formulated. So, in fact, as Moraga writes, the enemy or opposition can be identified:

> I remain amazed at how often so-called "Tercermundistas" in the U.S. work to annihilate the concept and existence of white supremacy, but turn their faces away from male supremacy. Perhaps this is because when you start to talk about sexism, the world becomes increasingly complex. The power no longer breaks down into neat little hierarchical categories, but becomes a series of starts and detours. Since the categories are not easy to arrive at, the enemy is not easy to name. (*Loving* 108)

Indeed, Moraga's intention is not to a define a specifically women's politics but rather to insert sexuality into a Chicano politics already founded on an antiracist, anticapitalist, working-class ideology. She continues,

> The one aspect of our identity which has been uniformly ignored by every existing political movement in this country is sexuality, both as a source of oppression and a means of liberation. Although other movements have dealt with this issue, sexual oppression and desire have never been considered specifically in relation to the lives of women of color. Sexuality, race, and sex have usually been presented in contradiction to each other, rather than as part and parcel of a complex web of personal and political identity and oppression. (*Loving* 109)

Decoding this "complex web" demands precisely the analytical concept of totality, such that the categories of race, class, gender, and nation, which may be insufficient in themselves when developed and applied in isolation, may be dialectically transformed into those very complex categories that "are not easy to arrive at." In the next section, I explore this mapping among and overlapping of political subjectivities or categories of identity traditionally held apart, in order to see how Cervantes's poetry and Chicana theory achieves this theoretical fusion.

Nationalism and/versus Feminism

"Uncle's First Rabbit" effectively underwrites a politics based on comprehension of the concrete social totality, as expressed by Moraga, in opposition to a politics organized around a narrowly construed and autonomized aspect of identity (race, class, or gender) divorced from its articulation and deployment in specific historical and material contexts. Read politically in the context of the Chicano movement, the poem voices Cervantes's critique of the masculinism of the movement ideology and attempts to foster in the general Chicano consciousness a realization of the way in which the machismo ideology works against the interests of the movement as a whole. The poem suggests a critique of Chicano nationalism without dismissing the category of nation as a political subject. Rather, it revisions a nationalism analogous to that Moraga imagines in her chapter "Queer Aztlan: The Re-formation of Chicano Tribe":

> The nationalism I seek is one that decolonizes the brown and female body as it decolonizes the brown and female earth. It is a new nationalism in which la Chicana Indigena stands at the center, and heterosexism and homophobia are no longer the cultural order of the day. I cling to the word "nation" because without the specific naming of the nation, the nation will be lost (as when feminism is reduced to humanism, the

woman is subsumed). Let us retain our radical naming but expand it to meet a broader and wiser revolution. (*Last Generation* 150)

Such a position avoids theoretically throwing the baby out with the bath water, advocating instead the refining of viable political models rather than dismantling them wholesale in the spirit of some post-colonial thinking that argues that "the notion of the three worlds ... flattens heterogeneities, masks contradictions, and elides differences" (Shohat 101). For Moraga, the global vision can be maintained but must be adjusted to treat comprehensively issues of gender, sexuality, and class. Similarly, for Cervantes, feminism and nationalism are compatible—indeed feminism can enhance and deepen the nationalist agenda—but the two demand some theoretical work. What follows from this realization is a deconstruction of the concept of an "identity politics," for, theoretically, in terms of the objective interests of each, Cervantes's poem suggests that there are not different sets of political interests that would automatically correspond to male or female subject positions. Thus, when considering the question raised by Diana Fuss in her discussion of identity politics, "Is politics based on identity, or is identity based on politics?" (100), we have to see her query as misposed through the erroneous presumption of an implicit equation of the two; or at the least we have to recognize that traditional accounts and practices of identity politics have construed identity in theoretically suspect ways that partialize and ahistoricize identities, thus yielding political perspectives that inaccurately comprehend the political interests growing out of the historical and material underpinnings of any subject.

To measure the effectiveness of Cervantes's strategy of constructing poetic and political consciousness, it is useful to counterpoint the representation of the male consciousness of racial, gender, and class exploitation in "Uncle's First Rabbit" with that in the work of the Chicano poet Gary Soto. While in "Uncle's First Rabbit" Cervantes effectively critiques masculinist ideology by demonstrating the oppressiveness of gender inequality for both women and men, the male consciousness in Soto's poetry comprehends the middle-class woman as somehow the symbol and source of the inequality and exploitation that the racialized worker suffers. In his poem "The Underground Parking," for example, Soto depicts the middle-class woman as mediating between the exploited racialized worker and the dominant male oppressor as well as the object of his revenge for the oppression he suffers. The poem begins:

> A man who holds fear
> Like the lung a spot of cancer,
> Waits for your wife.

He is already listening for her whimper
To stop echoing and to break
Against concrete, listening
For the final fist at her ear

(*Elements* 5)

Here the poet addresses his male oppressor, threatening him with violence against his wife as a way of seeking justice or exacting revenge for
his own suffering. Interestingly, as Soto makes clear, the poet takes out
the pain of his exploitation and poverty on women, such that the violence inflicted by racial patriarchal capitalism results only in more violence against women, not in a serious challenge to the socioeconomic
system or ideology that structures that inequality. The poem continues:

The woman who gets it in a car
Or on the hard earth of a vacant lot,
Is under the heaviness of a toilet flushing,
Of Out of a job and Why change
Bedsheets? She is under arms of tattoos,
Kick in the mouth, shitted shorts,
An ice pick at the throat.
She faces No rent money, Alice,
And not a single tear or a multitude could pull him off. (5)

In this poem, the ideology of machismo motivates the racially oppressed and economically exploited Chicano to resist racial patriarchal
capitalism by reasserting his "manhood" to the white male through a
violent sexual transgression of the white man's sexual property. The
poem unselfconsciously figures the bourgeois woman as an abstract
value of exchange between men in the international heterosexual economy. I borrow this formulation from Luce Irigaray who, drawing on the
language and analysis of Marx, sees the subjection of woman as institutionalized through her reduction to an object of economic exchange between men, to the status of a commodity. Irigaray writes:

Just as commodities, despite their resistance, become more or less autonomous repositories for the value of human work, so, as mirrors of and
for man, women more or less unwittingly come to represent the danger
of a disappropriation of masculine power: the phallic mirage;—just as a
commodity finds the expression of its value in an equivalent . . . that
necessarily remains external to it, so woman derives her price from her
relation to the male sex, constituted as a transcendental value: the phallus. (188)

This analysis of sexual exchange has particular explanatory power with
regard to the relations of uneven development that persist between the

U.S. nation and the third world Chicano nation internally colonized in this country. Irigaray sees "masculine hom(m)osexuality" as ubiquitous but, because its practice is socially prohibited, "played out through the bodies of women, matter, or sign"; thus, "heterosexuality has been up to now just an alibi for the smooth workings of man's relations with himself, of relations among men" (172). The white woman is denied to the Chicano worker because the success of white patriarchal imperialism is contingent upon the emasculation of its colonized nation. Just as "men make commerce of [women], but do not enter into any exchanges with them" (172), so the United States exploits the Chicano nation rather than evenly exchanging with it.

In Soto's poetic conception, the Chicano male nation, as mirror of and for U.S. masculine imperialism, comes to represent the U.S. phallic mirage that represents "the danger of a disappropriation of [white] masculine power" (Irigaray 172). Soto's conception of revolutionary action centers on attacking the woman ensconced in patriarchy rather than the male power structure that positions her (as well as his Chicano worker). In his poem "After Tonight," for example, Soto begins menacingly:

> Because there are avenues
> Of traffic lights, a phone book
> Of brothers and lawyers,
> Why should you think your purse
> Will not be tugged from your arm
> Or the screen door
> Will remain latched
> Against the man
> Who hugs and kisses
> His pillow
> In the corridor of loneliness? (8)

Soto's poetry figures the bourgeois woman as the quintessential consumer expropriating the surplus value of the Chicano worker's labor, again bypassing the patriarchal configuration referred to in the opening lines of the poem:

> There is a window of light
> A sprinkler turning
> As the earth turns,
> And you do not think of the hills
> And of the splintered wrists it takes
> To give you
> The heat rising toward the ceiling. (8)

Figuring the woman as the central enemy whose body should be the site of racial and class struggle, Soto's poetry is actually complicit with

patriarchal masculinist ideology, expressing not so much a desire for total social transformation as for entrance into the elite patriarchal society
in which he can enjoy the privileges that should "rightly" accrue to his
masculine status. His resentment, it should be stressed, is not against the
"brothers and lawyers" of the woman's class who also live off the fruits
of his labor but only against the woman. Soto's revolution calls not for
the institution of a society without classes but for a class society overdetermined by gender in which women alone comprise the exploited
class.

The figuration of class consciousness in Soto's poetry, informed by a
misogynist *resentiment,* participates in capitalist patriarchal ideology
and offers only a partial understanding of class because of its inability
to encode gender as a central feature of class; but in "Uncle's First Rabbit," Cervantes decodes the male psyche and attempts through the
poem to create the discursive conditions necessary to "engender" a Chi-
cano/a class consciousness that comprehends sexual oppression as
part and parcel of the system of oppressive and exploitive class relations.
Cervantes inhabits her ideological other, the Chicano male and poetically constructs a Chicano consciousness endowed with the possibility
of achieving this deeper, more genuine sense of class consciousness.
Georg Lukács argues that "the superiority of the proletariat must lie exclusively in its ability to see society from the centre, as coherent whole,"
a superiority that derives from the fact that the worker's "consciousness
is the *self-consciousness of the commodity;* or in other words it is the self-
knowledge, the self-revelation of capitalist society founded upon the
production and exchange of commodities" (69, 168). So the Chicana's
ability to inhabit or represent her male other derives from her superior
perspective conditioned by her self-consciousness as a commodity in
both the heterosexual patriarchal economy (in Irigaray's terms) and
the capitalist economy (in Marxist terms). Through this dual self-
consciousness (like Du Bois's double consciousness) of the commodity,
the Chicana occupies within the system of racial patriarchal capitalism
a superior position from which to comprehend the totality of capitalist
society's operations "as a coherent whole."

Toward a Poetic Typology of Consciousness

Cervantes's Chicana identity can potentially allow her, by virtue of the
superexploitation and oppression she systematically endures, a privileged perspective if and only if her experience fosters a realization or
consciousness of that totality. This consciousness of one's position
within the concrete social totality is not automatically inscribed in one's

identity. Thus, identity does not automatically authorize politics. In conceptualizing the relation between identity and politics, then, we might state the case as this: one's "identity," defined here as a function of one's position in the racial, patriarchal, capitalist system, can potentially provide one with a more or less privileged comprehension of the social totality—and by extension with a politics responsive to one's objective interests—but that one's identity (as male or female, worker or capitalist, African American, Euramerican, Asian American, etc.) and experience do not necessarily or automatically register those objective interests or guarantee a political consciousness of those interests. Thus, Cervantes's poetics attempt to exceed individual experience and provide access into otherness, into perspectives provided by other social positions such that one can through inhabiting several types of consciousness begin to comprehend the totality of social relations. Lukács theorizes society as composed of or allowing for a limited "number of clearly distinguished basic types whose characteristics are determined by the types of position available in the process of production" (51). Yet his theory is too rigidly economistic, ignoring the fact that one's position in the process of production is also conditioned by such factors as race, gender, and national identity. Cervantes's poetry recasts typicality itself in a way that rethinks the class experience as lived through gender, race, and national identity as she inhabits and negotiates these types of consciousness.

These dual poetic methods of inhabiting other subjectivities and alienating one's poetic consciousness in a way that authorizes the imagining of otherness introduce the important dichotomy between knowledge and experience that dominates Cervantes's poetry. By inhabiting and exploring the putative or typical consciousness ascribed to other subject positions in the social totality, Cervantes creates throughout her poems a decentered narrator that slides back and forth, negotiating between various subject positions in an attempt to construct a single though dialogized and overdetermined consciousness of social agency that can in turn comprehend and organize these diverse positions of the concrete social totality. Cervantes's method thus proposes a poetics responsive to and comprehensive of the global colonial situation of late capitalism that has effected, in Fredric Jameson's words, "a growing contradiction between lived experience and structure," a "gap between the local positioning of the individual subject and the totality of class structures in which he or she is situated, a gap between phenomenological perception and a reality that transcends all individual thinking or experience" (353).

The problem Jameson identifies is one of space: How do we map the coordinates of a global or multinational structure of relations when it is so much larger than ourselves and when we, with our limited experience, comprehend only a small corner of that structure? Jameson proposes an aesthetic of cognitive mapping as a potential solution to this profound problem of consciousness. Working from and using as an analogue Kevin Lynch's *Image of the City*, in which Lynch suggests that "urban alienation is directly proportional to the mental unmappability of local cityscapes" (353), Jameson argues that "the incapacity to map socially is as crippling to political experience as the analogous incapacity to map spatially is for urban experience" (353). We need to develop, Jameson argues, an imaginary or imaginative sense of the global colonial system as an absent totality. We need a positive ideology (in the Althusserian sense of ideology as "the imaginary representation of the subject's relationship to his or her real conditions of existence" [353]) that can comprehend the objective totality.

Cervantes's poetry begins to map this sociopolitical space and to construct a mode of poetic consciousness capable of imagining the totality of social relations under capitalism in terms of the nexus of racial, class, and gender oppression. The persona of Cervantes's poetry is often alienated from the position it represents, as though writing from a vacuum as a mere observer; or, as in the case of "Uncle's First Rabbit," she inhabits or imagines a subjectivity different from, though certainly intertwined with, her own. One critic plausibly suggests that "the poems of *Emplumada* are not a full portrayal of the poet's life, but they do tell the whole story in the sense that she does not create a mythical other as a tabula rasa on which to write her life. Her sense of self does not emerge at the expense of loss of self by another" (Seator 134). Indeed, the poems are able to tell the whole story precisely because they are not autobiographical, because they comprehend more than her isolated experience. Cervantes in fact suppresses her autobiographical self in some of the poems or else reconceives the self in a larger collective and international as opposed to individualist sense, in order to transcend her specifically Chicana identity, allowing the persona at times to occupy sites of oppression that cross the boundaries of various oppressed cultures. The "whole story" is not contained within her life as a Chicana or within the Chicano movement. Cervantes's poems function as mediations and transitions through which specific parts and complexes of the social totality can be linked together in a dynamic set of interrelations and reciprocal determinations. As a whole, the poems construct interactively an overdetermined consciousness.

Cervantes's central self never emerges completely in *Emplumada*. Not only does she make "the experience of alienation the subject of her poems," as Marta Ester Sánchez claims (89), but she also makes alienation central to the form and structure of the narrative voice of her poetry. In a 1985 interview, Cervantes spoke about "that other persona, that other voice" of her poetry and remarked that growing up poor "you grow up as an observer, you grow up as an outsider, not really being a participant" (Binder 149–50). Even the bilingual poems, she says, do not represent "an authentic voice"; the Spanish "is almost like an outside voice coming in" (Monda 105). Through this type of alienation effect, the poems can respond to the global colonial situation with regard to which Jameson writes, "We can say that if individual experience is authentic, then it cannot be true; and that if a scientific or cognitive model of the same content is true, then it escapes individual experience" (349).

We see this technique of alienation at work representatively in Cervantes's poem "Cannery Town in August," in which she places the narrator/persona outside of the working-class experience that, biographically, was prominent in her own life. The poem begins:

> All night it humps the air.
> Speechless, the steam rises
> from the cannery columns. I hear
> the night bird rave about work
> or lunch, or sing the swing shift
> home. I listen, while bodyless
> uniforms and spinach specked shoes
> drift in monochrome down the dark
> moon-possessed streets.
>
> (*Emplumada* 6)

The poet is an outsider who can only hear and listen. Yet, when regarding the women workers, she says, "I imagine them not speaking, dumbed / by the can's clamor and drop / to the trucks that wait, grunting." It is not simply that she is an outsider. That she imagines herself as an outsider, however, constitutes the central importance of the poem and defines the basic narrative and political strategy of *Emplumada*. Alienated from this particular historically constituted working-class group to the position of observer, she has to imagine the experience of work and the stupefaction that results, the silencing or "dumbing" that exploitive work threatens for the poet. The whole process is "speechless" and she must give it voice, positioning herself the poet as an organizer who must demystify or dereify social experience through an ideological act of imagination or imaginative knowing from the outside, not through an experiential process.

This act, of course, involves the danger of appropriating the voice of others, of presuming to speak for and thus silencing others. But, then, as Moraga points out, speaking for others is the ultimate and inevitable responsibility of the "movement writer": "Sometimes," Moraga writes, "I feel my back will break from the pressure I feel to speak for others" (*Loving* iii). What Cervantes lays out in "Cannery Town" is a poetics of consciousness, a method by which we might attempt to imagine the social totality so that we can begin to map politically and formulate projects of liberation that address types of oppression outside the range of our own experiences. This relation between self and other, the tension between knowledge and experience that threatens to problematize the inevitable position of speaking for others, is dramatized forcefully in Cervantes's poem "Night Stand." The poem begins with a listing of the fruits of labor, a sort of grocery list of commodities: " 'Onions, lettuce, leeks, broccoli, / garlic, cantaloupe, peaches, plums' " (*From the Cables* 38). As if the shopping poet achieves a shock of recognition about the labor that reaped this produce, the poem then effectively dereifies it, identifying the worker at the same time that the poet diagrams her relationship to him:

> The man whose work is hard
> slides onto me glistening
> as a bass wielding the sheen
> I'm mirrored with when I
> step out of the bath.
> He wears the patch the sun
> has x-rayed to his chest.
> He's the color of work.
> I'm the color of reading. (38)

In a moment of leisure, the poet envisions herself as reflecting and understanding, though not enduring or experiencing, the life of the farm worker. Cervantes here juxtaposes a knowledge gained through experience and marked on the body ("He's the color of work") and a knowledge gained through study and research ("I'm the color of reading"). Thus, alienated from but not incognizant of this work experience, the poet justifies her speaking for the working class and expresses her political solidarity, exploding the premise of identity politics that, in Todd Gitlin's words, "anatomy is destiny" (172). In fact, though experiential knowledge can yield understanding, Cervantes exposes its limitations in terms of understanding that experience in a larger context:

> . . . although he may not know
> beyond the suicide of soul
> the poor possess, the threshing race
> machines, the names of Goerring,
> Himmler, Buchenwald, Farben . . .
> and all that written fables

> spell for us—this he knows—
> Esta gente no entiende nada.
>
> And I—am the way I had intended.
> I've come to what I wanted.
> And here, writing, wearing things
> the discarded dead have
> bought and sold: we know. (39)

The task of the poet is to derive and convey a heightened understanding of that experience by situating it within its global framework of genocide and class oppression, by subjecting it to her totalizing perspective. She has a knowledge of the past not from direct but rather vicarious experience, from "wearing things" of "the discarded dead," which approximates an historical materialist method and understanding. Indeed, as we see in a later poem in *From the Cables of Genocide,* "On Touring Her Hometown," Cervantes conceives of historical knowledge as an archival or imaginative recuperation through which she links herself to and acknowledges her difference from the historical experiences that inform her position in the present. The poem opens, "I'm going away to where I'm from" (41), expressing the paradox that the further she leaves herself for otherness, the more she understands herself in relation to larger societal structures and relationships. Her destination is that working-class historical other, as she writes:

> . . . There's a place
> in the mists of this city where a silence,
> lean as ghosts, beckons, is archaic
> in the workclothes of my otherness. (41)

Finally, for Cervantes, as at the end of "Night Stand," experiential and scientific knowledge complement each other in a collective epistemological synthesis: "we know."

Cervantes's attempt to transcend poetically her own experience suggests a recognition that, to borrow Frantz Fanon's words, "it is at the heart of national consciousness that international consciousness lives and grows" (242). In her poems in *Emplumada,* the persona is frequently bound to the subtext of Chicano history at the same time that she attempts to rise above the strictures of that history. History is at once positive in that it provides a rich cultural tradition to work with and to derive her identity from and negative in that it threatens to confine her to that idea. In her poems the poet describes herself frequently as a "hoverer," like the two hummingbirds in the title poem "Emplumada" who, "hovering, stuck to each other." "These are warriors," Cervantes writes, "distancing themselves from history" (66).

For Cervantes, movement requires this simultaneous plunging into and distancing from a history that at once grants and yet confines identity and restricts mobility (historical necessity). In "Caribou Girl," for example, Cervantes traces the development of the poet from a hooved and clumsy animal doomed to drown to a feathered animal that can soar or plunge as the occasion warrants: "I dream Quetzalcoatl, Ometeotl, the Great Manitou / who leaves me a vision to make me strong, / who lifts me to the birds / from a mere cat girl" (*Emplumada* 22). The persona distances herself from her prior condition, as she writes, "In the distance I see her slip from the rocks, / see her once more try to walk on water. / I know she can't fly. / . . . She slips from the rocks / and I know she will drown" (23). She must eventually forgo this image if she is going to accomplish her task as a poet: "but I'm / going to leave her / for another breath / before I plunge with her again" (23). The poem allegorizes what I have identified as Cervantes's revolutionary agenda and characterizes her response to the Chicano movement. The Chicano/a must be able to progress beyond nationalism and a cultural political movement to recognize the necessity of unifying other movements with his or her own in order to complete the permanent revolution on a global scale. For the Chicana, however, this plunge is a risky and dangerous move. Anzaldúa, for example, mimics the theme of "Caribou Girl" when she speaks of her "resistance to knowing, to letting go, to that deep ocean where I once dived into death. I am afraid of drowning. Resistance to sex, intimate touching, opening myself to the alien other where I am out of control, not on patrol" (48). This theme also dominates *From the Cables of Genocide,* most notably in Cervantes's trope of "the fear of going down," the title of the last section and last poem of the volume.

Yet, as Fanon points out, the national period is an essential stage on the way to internationalism. Indeed, for Cervantes in *Emplumada,* the Chicana identity becomes the very figure for this international identity. Sánchez, for example, defines Cervantes's "Chicana voice as a translating, or a mediating, voice between her community's experience and a larger audience" (185). Furthermore, the term "Chicana" itself signifies a type of nationlessness in the geographical and legal sense. As Ramón Saldívar writes, Chicano subjectivity "remains on that precarious utopian margin between [Mexican and American identities], perhaps as the very sign of marginality institutionalized in geopolitical terms by the border between the sovereign states of Mexico and the United States" (174). This duality is expressed in such companion poems as "Oaxaca, 1974" and "Visions of Mexico," which express respectively the Chicano/a's non-identity with Mexican or U.S. nationalities. The "Chicana," then, is both the source of national identity and the figure of international identity.

In *Emplumada,* Cervantes writes in a vacuum, this utopian margin that is at once the place ascribed to her by virtue of the cultural and economic alienation for which her race, class, and gender affiliations target her and also a place for utopian blueprinting. Her experience often resonates with her Chicana cultural background, but her alienation in a sense grows out of this lack of a clear identity that the label Chicana suggests. We see in both *Emplumada* and *From the Cables of Genocide,* to borrow Jameson's words again, "forms that inscribe a new sense of the absent global colonial system on the very syntax of poetic language itself" (349). This is most clear in the lyrical moments in *Emplumada.*

Cervantes's lyrical moments always straddle reality and ideality, and the boundary that divides these two spheres is temporal. The heavily imagistic lyrics have two edges. The images both anticipate the end of ideology, the end of what Marx refers to as prehistory, when they can constitute "pure art," and contain an ideological residue that resonates with social conflict and violence. This dual resonance of images is expressed most clearly in the following lines from "Poem for the Young White Man . . .": "Every day I am deluged with reminders / that this is not / my land / and this is my land" (*Emplumada* 36–37). "This" ostensibly refers to different lands—the actual landscape of the United States and the poetic landscape of her imagined world. Yet, linguistically, they do not refer to different lands. The land is hers but is not hers because of U.S. colonial occupation.

Similarly, in "Starfish," the images evoke a world fragmented by national conflict and the global colonial system and yet transcend that world. The starfish "were lovely in the quartz and jasper sand / as if they had created terrariums with their bodies / on purpose" (*Emplumada* 30). The poem opens with this expression of fantasy of self-containment, of the formation of a totality, or false totality, by exclusion. This sentiment also opens the earlier poem in *Emplumada,* "Four Portraits of Fire":

> I find a strange knowledge of wind,
> an open door in the mountain
> pass where everything intersects.
> Believe me. This will not pass.
> This is a world where flags
> contain themselves, and are still,
> marked by their unfurled edges. (28)

The utopian pass where diverse groups intersect and live harmoniously cannot "pass," is not feasible in this world of antagonistic nations. Just as these flags are consumed by flames in this poem, "Starfish" similarly ends in violence. The poet attempts to order these self-contained lives in relation to each other: "We would dry them, arrange them, / Form seascapes, geodesics . . . We gathered what we could / In the approaching darkness" (30). Poetry, however, is simply not powerful enough to comprehend completely or to alter materially real conditions:

> Then we left hundreds of
> thousands of flawless five-fingered specimens sprawled
> Along the beach as far as we could see, all massed
> Together: little martyrs, soldiers, artless suicides
> In lifelong liberation from the sea. So many
> Splayed hands, the tide shoveled in. (30)

These "five-fingered specimens," suggestive of a human hand, function metonymically for the immigrant working class. Coming in on the tide, they might represent immigrants who arrive in the United States expecting liberation but finding only bondage and death. Thus, in a time still troubled by exploitation and inequality, these images encompass powerful connotations that, in the utopian moment Cervantes writes under erasure, might surpass ideology and diffuse into pure art.

These lyrics conjure the absent global colonial system, aesthetically mapping it, at the same time that they negate that system and allow us to imagine a qualitatively different and new world. Cervantes has created a form for a utopian content that does not yet exist, but in this sense she enlarges the space of Chicano/a literature and pushes us to think beyond its limits. Indeed, as Leon Trotsky notes, "the new man cannot be formed without a new lyrical poetry. But to create it, the poet himself must feel the world in a new way" (199). In *From the Cables of Genocide*, however, Cervantes forgoes the lyric form for a poetry that overtly connects various oppressed cultures and cognitively maps through poetic allegory the geography of first world imperialist violence. Indeed, as one critic notes, the "From" in the title of the collection "suggests that these poems are part of a larger body of texts and connects them not only to Chicano but also to other Native American, African American, and Jewish lost or silenced poems" (Rayo 103). Indeed, as in "Night Stand" Cervantes connects the Chicano bracero experience in the United States with the genocide of Nazi Germany, "The threshing race / machines," so in the poem "Buckshot" she works from an old Irish folk song, again drawing from the cultural experience of another colonized nation. Cervantes's allegorical internationalism manifests itself most ingeniously perhaps in her poem "Shooting the Wren," which in many ways may be the more mature counterpart of "Uncle's First Rabbit." The poem opens:

> He sends trophies from Sunday's kill: a China
> pheasant—feathers despicable starling coal,
> backs the color of Chilean copper. They shimmer
> in the distance, *a beautiful expectancy of only 2.2*
> *years so who could feel bad about the downing*
> *of another rooster?* The species about wiped out
> for the hats of the thirties are plentiful
> game now.
>   (*From the Cables* 68)

Here the first line break indicates the allegorical conflation of the Chinese nation with the China pheasant, suggesting the hunt as an allegory of capitalist imperialist plunder. This is borne out by the symbolic connection of the birds with coal and Chilean copper, resources gathered by colonial conquests, and by the theme of genocide ("The species about wiped out"). This theme resurfaces later when she writes that the pheasant's feathers

> . . . gleam iridescence,
> what was more precious than gold to an extinguished
> race. I walk among the ghosts of history, the
> agony of the tortured condemned to their barracks
> of serene mustard slopes. In California: China
> berry manzanita, wild boar imported from Europe. (68)

The thought of the feathers compels the poet to reflect on history, specifically that of anti-Chinese racism and the U.S. colonization of immigrant Chinese who were condemned to barracks. This racist colonization is contextualized within the global economic structure of foreign trade, imports and exports, highlighting again Cervantes's poetics of totality in which race, gender, and nation are inscribed and understood within the global colonial totality of the capitalist economy and class structure.

Thus, Cervantes establishes connections between various oppressed nations, peoples, and classes in poetically constructing a *mestiza,* feminist, class consciousness—in Anzaldúa's words, "a more whole perspective, one that includes rather than excludes" (79). In many ways Cervantes's poetry begins to respond to Moraga's probing questions, "*What would a movement bent on the freedom of women of color look like?* In other words, what are the implications of not only looking outside of our culture, but into our culture and ourselves and from that place to begin to develop a strategy for a movement that could challenge the bedrock of oppressive systems of belief globally?" (*Loving* 109). For Cervantes, race and gender consciousness are shaped fundamentally by one's position in the global class structure. Thus, gender and race consciousness cannot be examined as discrete elements apart from class consciousness. In her poetics of cognitive mapping, she rewrites and complicates what Jameson calls "the single great collective story"— class struggle—in a way that incorporates and is sensitive to the related struggles around issues of race, gender, and national liberation and in a way that reconceptualizes the meaning of class itself from a Chicana feminist perspective.

WORKS CITED

Alarcón, Norma. "Chicana Feminism: In the Tracks of the Native Woman." *Cultural Studies* 4.3 (1990): 248–55.

———. "The Theoretical Subject(s) of *This Bridge Called My Back* and Anglo-American Feminism." *Criticism in the Borderlands.* Ed. Calderón and Saldívar. 28–39.

Althusser, Louis. *For Marx.* Trans. Ben Brewster. New York: Verso, 1969.

Anzaldúa, Gloria. *Borderlands/La Frontera: The New Mestiza.* San Francisco: Aunt Lute, 1987.

Binder, Wolfgang. *Partial Autobiographies: Interviews with Twenty Chicano Poets.* Berlin: Verlag Palm and Enke Erlangen, 1985.

Bruce-Novoa, Juan. "Bernice Zamora Y Lorna Dee Cervantes: Una Estetica Feminista." *Revista Ibero Americana* 51 (1985): 565–73.

———. *Chicano Poetry: A Response to Chaos.* Austin: University of Texas Press, 1982.

Calderón, Héctor, and José David Saldívar, eds. *Criticism in the Borderlands: Studies in Chicano Literature, Culture, and Ideology.* Durham, N.C.: Duke University Press, 1991.

Cervantes, Lorna Dee. *Emplumada.* Pittsburgh: University of Pittsburgh Press, 1981.

———. *From the Cables of Genocide: Poems on Love and Hunger.* Houston: Arte Publico Press, 1991.

Chabram, Angie, and Rosa Linda Fregoso. "Chicana/o Cultural Representations: Reframing Alternative Critical Discourses." *Cultural Studies* 4.3 (1990): 203–12.

Chabram-Dernersesian, Angie. "I Throw My Punches for My Race, *but* I Don't Want to Be a Man: Writing Us—Chica-nos (Girl, US)/Chicanas—into the Movement Script." *Cultural Studies.* Ed. Lawrence Grossberg, Cary Nelson, and Paula A. Treichler. New York: Routledge, 1992. 81–95.

Deleuze, Gilles, and Feliz Guattari. *Anti-Oedipus: Capitalism and Schizophrenia.* Minneapolis: University of Minnesota Press, 1983.

Fanon, Frantz. *The Wretched of the Earth.* New York: Grove Press, 1963.

Fields, Barbara Jeanne. "Slavery, Race, and Ideology in the United States of America." *New Left Review* 181 (1990): 95–118.

Fuss, Diana. *Essentially Speaking: Feminism, Nature, and Difference.* New York: Routledge, 1989.

Gitlin, Todd. "The Rise of 'Identity Politics.' " *Dissent* 40 (Spring 1993): 172–77.

Irigaray, Luce. *This Sex which Is Not One.* Trans. Catherine Porter. Ithaca, N.Y.: Cornell University Press, 1985.

Jameson, Fredric. "Cognitive Mapping." *Marxism.* Ed. Nelson and Grossberg. 347–57.

Lowe, Lisa. "Heterogeneity, Hybridity, Multiplicity: Marking Asian American Differences." *Diaspora* 1.1 (1991): 24–44.

Lukács, Georg. *History and Class Consciousness.* Trans. Rodney Livingstone. Cambridge, Mass.: MIT Press, 1966.

Monda, Bernadette. "Interview with Lorna Dee Cervantes." *Third Woman* 2.1 (1984): 103–7.

Moraga, Cherríe. *The Last Generation.* Boston: South End Press, 1993.

———. *Loving in the War Years.* Boston: South End Press, 1983.

Mouffe, Chantal. "Hegemony and New Political Subjects: Toward a New Concept of Democracy." *Marxism.* Ed. Nelson and Grossberg. 89–101.

Muñoz, Carlos, Jr. *Youth, Identity, Power: The Chicano Movement.* New York: Verso, 1989.

Nelson, Cary, and Lawrence Grossberg, eds. *Marxism and the Interpretation of Culture.* Urbana: University of Illinois, 1988.

Rayo, Agueda Pizarro. Review of *From the Cables of Genocide: Poems on Love and Hunger. Review: Latin American Literature and Arts,* July-Dec. 1991, 103–5.

Saldívar, Ramón. *Chicano Narrative: The Dialectics of Difference.* Madison: University of Wisconsin Press, 1990.

Saldívar-Hull, Sonia. "Feminism on the Border: From Gender Politics to Geopolitics." *Criticism in the Borderlands.* Ed. Calderón and Saldívar. 203–20.

Sánchez, Marta Ester. *Contemporary Chicana Poetry: A Critical Approach to an Emerging Literature.* Berkeley: University of California Press, 1985.

Seator, Lynette. "*Emplumada:* Chicana Rites of Passage." *Melus* 11.2 (1984): 83–101.

Shohat, Ella. "Notes on the Post-Colonial." *Social Text* 31/32 (1992): 99–113.

Soto, Gary. *The Elements of San Joaquin.* Pittsburgh: University of Pittsburgh Press, 1977.

Steiner, Stan. "The Poet in the Boxing Ring." *La Causa Politica: A Chicano Political Reader.* Ed. F. Chris Garcia. Notre Dame, Ind.: University of Notre Dame Press, 1974. 324–35.

Trotsky, Leon. *Literature and Revolution.* London: Redwords, 1991.

Yarbro-Bejarano, Yvonne. "Chicana Literature from a Chicana Feminist Perspective." *Chicana Creativity and Criticism: Charting New Frontiers in American Literature.* Ed. María Herrera-Sobek and Helena María Viramontes. Houston: Arte Publico Press, 1988. 139–45.

9 ◈ Theory in the Mirror

> There's something endemic to white culture or to
> American culture or to European-Anglo *genes* that says
> "It's my right, I get to have anything I want now. And
> aren't I special. And if you don't think I'm special then
> you're horrible and I'm going to kill you."
> — Paula Gunn Allen, interview (my emphasis)

Word Warriors, breaking silence, becoming speaking subjects—all are positions white women and women of color have used to resist and undermine hegemonic racial and gendered relations in the United States. Picking up the pen and writing a self, a subject position, into existence has been an effective tool for what Chela Sandoval calls "oppositional consciousness." Like any tool of resistance, the pen, breaking silence, works at some but not consistently at all levels of social and cultural consciousness. Recent mass market and literary productions reflect an escalation of violence for both the "haves," increasingly at risk of losing their privilege, and the "have-nots," increasingly at risk of losing their lives. While it seems that things are more the same—calls for "racial harmony" when people of color express outrage against racist suppression—they also remain in a constant state of change, where the balance could swing in a moment toward an empowered "other."

What happens to the male and female white bodies of the first world when confronted by the female body of the "third world" wrapped in the culturally loaded garb of revolution, talking "like a man" and taking up the gun? Is there a difference between white women taking up the gun (à la Thelma and Louise) and women of color taking up that gun, which is culturally inscribed as a white masculine subject position? I would argue that by taking up the pen and writing the gun into a text, that in turn turns the gun onto white bodies, women of color such as Leslie Marmon Silko and Paula Gunn Allen engage in what I am calling "guerrilla ethnography." Such an act of writing is a surprise attack across the borders of racial demarcation/categorization.

Ethnography is traditionally defined as a written account of a people and their culture. As James Clifford notes, ethnography is the practice of writing the culture of the other, a "serious fiction": ". . . ethnographic texts are orchestrations of multivocal exchanges occurring in politically charged situations. The subjectivities produced in these often unequal exchanges—whether of 'natives' or of visiting participant-observers—are constructed domains of truth, serious fictions" (10). Lila Abu-Lughod offers one of the more succinct definitions of the foundations of "the ambiguous term 'ethnography,' which refers both to the activity of doing anthropological research, and more commonly, to the 'written results' or accounts of the lives of other cultural groups" (8–9). What lies at the heart of this anthropological enterprise are "Western knowers and representers, and non-Western knowns and representeds" (11). To be the *prototypical* ethnographer, to write ethnography, then, means to be white, male, and educated in the Western tradition and to write about other cultures.

But how are ethnography and guerrilla warfare connected? By definition, guerrilla actions are surprise attacks committed by individuals behind enemy lines, in opposition to formal, hierarchically organized battles fought by trained, disciplined soldiers. Guerrilla ethnography, as I construct it, overturns prototypical ethnography by operating behind the "enemy" lines of ethnographic discourses, writing an informal, nonhierarchical representation of culture, instigating a reversal of ideology. So we need a Western represented and a non-Western representer to commit guerrilla ethnography, a serious fictional portrait of Western (white) cultural practice, a written account of the lives of "white" people, a picture of what it means to be culturally white by one who is not.

White

Whiteness, according to "white" folks such as Richard Dyer and Marilyn Frye, is scripted as "everything and nothing, [which] is the source of its representational power" (Dyer 45). It is "invisible" because it is *natural,* "colourless multi-colouredness," and is read as the positive pole in the binaries of modernity/backwardness, reason/irrationality, order/chaos, stability/violence, and most specifically for Dyer, masculine, not feminine. "White" masculinity has become the un/marked, naturalized category from which demarcation emanates: "One effect of colonial discourse is the production of an un/marked, apparently autonomous white/Western self, in contrast with the marked, Other racial and cultural categories with which the racially and culturally dominant category is constructed. In this context, it has also for the most part been Other, marked subjects rather than white/Western, unmarked subjects whose racial and cultural identities have been the focus of study" (Frankenberg 17). The task, then, would be to mark "white" bodies in some way, to make them "the focus of study," to denaturalize "whiteness." Frye describes what she calls "whiteliness" as not a matter of skin color but of a "deeply ingrained way of being in the world" (*Politics* 152), of being "judge . . . peacemaker . . . preacher . . . martyr" by virtue of the superiority or privilege accruing to whiteliness. "Whitely people generally consider themselves to be benevolent and good-willed, fair, honest and ethical . . . [with] a staggering faith in their own rightness and goodness, and that of other whitely people" (154). At least this is how whitely folks construct selves and each other and how whitely folks strategically maintain positions of domination.

In "Eating the Other," bell hooks points out that whiteness has been ignored as a constructed rather than a natural and essential presence; she critiques the ways in which this operation is ignored or suppressed in the debates over essentialism:

> Those progressive white intellectuals who are particularly critical of "essentialist" notions of identity when writing about mass culture, race, and gender have not focused their critiques on white identity and the way essentialism informs representations of whiteness. It is always the non-white, or in some cases the non-heterosexual Other, who is guilty of essentialism. Few white intellectuals call attention to the way in which the contemporary obsession with white consumption of the dark Other has served as a catalyst for the resurgence of essentialist based racial and ethnic nationalism. (*Black Looks* 30)

The "consumption" of the third world by the first world calls to mind the "cannibals" Columbus claims to have first encountered and his consumption of their cultural body.[1] Rather than the rational, orderly, whitely people of the myth, hooks gives us back a white culture of "cannibalism."[2]

In *Almanac of the Dead*, Leslie Marmon Silko, like hooks, holds a mirror up to white folks that reflects whiteness in its "cannibalistic" chaos. This is what I mean by guerrilla ethnography. It is the making of a picture of what it means to be culturally white by one who is not. Silko's *Almanac of the Dead* is a written portrait of whitely culture and a surprise attack, an inversion of the conventions of ethnographic writing, and a dark/red consumption of the white other—reversing hooks's formulation of white consumption of a dark other. Engaging in guerrilla ethnography, Silko challenges the underlying assumptions of anthropology's fathers Franz Boas and Bronislaw Malinowski. In holding up the mirror to "white," her fieldwork becomes (in)appropriate. She is non-Western and nonwhite. She has no legitimate access to white male privilege of the phallogocentric kind. She writes fiction on purpose, never intends an ethnographic enterprise, yet writes the cultural record of whiteliness. She is dark *and* female. Her covert operations in white backyards and bedrooms and on summer beaches (the epic/soap opera/ historical romance/thriller/apocalyptic novel form) commit guerrilla warfare in words—some seven hundred pages of hit and run. Silko's ethnographic portrait, instead of producing "constructed domains of truth, serious fictions" (Clifford 10), reverses Clifford's formulation, constructing an unequal exchange with a subjectivity produced by one presumed less powerful, one who creates a domain of fiction, playful truths in a multivocal exchange.

Binary

The binary inherent in the contemporary use of the word "race" is one of the issues I would like to call into question. The word race comes into play most frequently as it points to black/white relations and discourses, omitting any other possible categories. I am thinking here in particular of the example of the 1993 series of television commercials in the New York City area that were designed to somehow calm racial tensions in the wake of the Crown Heights riots and the burning of Los Angeles. The logo consisted of one black and one white hand clasped, enclosed in a circle of white. There is no attempt to represent a multiplicity of categories. There are only two colors here.

In *Playing in the Dark,* Toni Morrison looks at American literature and its "responses to a dark, abiding, signing Africanist presence" (5): "Why is it [the landscape] seen as raw and savage? Because it is peopled by a nonwhite indigenous population? Perhaps. But certainly because there is ready to hand a bound and unfree, rebellious but serviceable, black population against which . . . all white men are enabled to measure these privileging and privileged differences" (45). She asserts that this Africanist presence, marked as absence and "deployed as rawness and savagery, . . . provided the staging ground and arena for the elaboration of the quintessential American identity" (44). As it is for hooks and Dyer, whiteness for Morrison is scripted as "unraced" and unexamined in meaningful ways. While at crucial moments in Morrison's other textual productions binaries break down, fall apart, and fail as she works to destabilize rigid dichotomies, at this moment she seems to reinscribe the rhetoric of race as it currently operates in U.S. cultural theory and practice—a binary composed of the opposition of "black" and "white." The elision of the indigenous population "within a natural and mental landscape" of white American identity is not new, but Morrison's dismissal is surprising.

By reversing Morrison's formulation, we see an assumption of an "unbound and free" indigenous population, in opposition to the "bound and unfree . . . black population" she articulates, which buttresses both "white" and "black" notions of what constitutes "red." At the same time, in asserting the black/white binary, Morrison's formulation maintains the opposition of dominant/privileged and subordinate/ unfree. Silko's *Almanac of the Dead,* like other fictional works by Morrison herself, breaks this binary and inserts "red" as an articulating presence between the "other" two categorical imperatives. This insertion succeeds as a representation of whiteness in the "red" imagination.

Insertion

Silko, however, is not interested in simply reversing binaries and hence reinscribing them but wishes also to subvert such a dualistic value system. One of the ways in which she successfully manages this subversion is to refuse the dichotomy of bad "white" people and good "red" people; rather, *Almanac of the Dead* brings into sharp relief the struggle between opposing forces for balance. Red people sometimes do "bad" things; white people sometimes do "good" things (albeit infrequently). One of the great mistakes characters commit in *Almanac of the Dead* is to deny or forget "where they come from." Menardo, the malignant salesman of apocalypse insurance, is both Mexican and mestizo. As a child, he understands his connection to the indigenous community and his mestizo grandfather, until the Anglo Brothers separate him from his "pagan people." His life is spent becoming more and more like "white" folks or more "whitely"—he first denies his indigenous ancestry, then works to rid himself of his Mexican identity as well—denying where he comes from and becoming whitely (258). To become whitely if you are red, or to make whiteliness invisible, as if it came from nowhere, sets the condition for cultural and racial dislocation. This dislocation leaves bodies vulnerable to what Jack Forbes, in *Columbus and Other Cannibals,* calls "Wétiko psychosis"—a "disease of aggression against other living things, and, more precisely, the disease of the consuming of other creatures' lives and possessions" (10). Like hooks, Forbes identifies this cannibalism as consumption of cultural *bodies*—a whitely act. To be whitely, then, is to be diseased like Menardo, to consume *any* other, not only *the*

other. To inoculate oneself against wétiko psychosis is to remain connected to the stories and the people. Like Frantz Fanon's psychosis of
colonialism, Forbes's wétiko disease can be caught by those who are not
"white"—that is, non-Europeans can be recruited into the psychosis
(Forbes 87). The sane people stay sane by remaining connected to their
community—"remembering" their true selves. Memory is resistance.

In *Black Looks,* hooks raises questions about representations of
"whiteness" in the "black" imagination:

> Without evoking a simplistic essentialist "us and them" dichotomy that
> suggests black folks merely invert stereotypical racist interpretations so
> that black becomes synonymous with goodness and white with evil, I
> want to focus on that representation of whiteness that is not formed in
> reaction to stereotypes but emerges as a response to the traumatic pain
> and anguish that remains a consequence of white racist domination, a
> psychic state that informs and shapes the way black folks "see" white-
> ness. (169)

She goes on to describe whiteness as terrifying and terrorizing in the
black imagination: "[To] name that whiteness in the black imagination
is often a representation of terror" (172).

If white is a representation of terror in the black imagination, how
then does red "see" white? Does whiteness operate in the red imagination as terrifying, in ways similar to what hooks asserts constitutes the
black imagination? How do the stereotypes of the "savage red" and the
"rational civilized white" get turned about? I would argue that for Silko,
whiteness is not necessarily as terrifying as it is terrified. White people
use drugs, kill each other and others, and buy insurance against every
possible disaster, including "uprising" by those who terrify them most—
any and all nonwhite others. Silko's critical narrative of destruction and
convergence—white apocalypse—becomes a cultural critique of white
terror.

Silko razes completely white racist domination in *Almanac of the Dead,*
disavowing its association with autonomous intentionality. Rather,
white people are controlled by and operate under the aegis of the Gunadeeyahs, the destroyers, one of several Keresan clans; this use of the
tribal identificatory marker of clan implies that "red" begat "white." In
all three of her fictional productions, Silko retells this Keres story of the
Gunadeeyahs, a clan organized around a hunger for blood, violence,
and destruction. In *Ceremony,* Emo and his group are the tools of the destroyers, set to the task of keeping Tayo from completing his part in the
ritual of the text. Here is the version of the witches' convention Silko
tells in *Almanac of the Dead:* "Now the old story came back to Sterling as
he walked along. The appearance of Europeans had been no accident;

the Gunadeeyahs had called for their white brethren to join them. Sure enough the Spaniards had arrived in Mexico fresh from the Church Inquisition with appetites whetted for disembowelment and blood. No wonder Cortes and Montezuma had hit it off together when they met; both had been members of the same secret clan" (760). This version is shorter than the other versions we have seen, and it is desacralized, deritualized in its language and details. The witches' contest has disappeared. The appearance of white people is now a matter of calling kindred spirits rather than a creation story. A red clan creates or calls up white people, rather than the "naturalized" creation stories that are versions of a white or black god baking clay into burned, undercooked, or just right red people, or the tale of a white patriarch doing magic tricks with water and DNA.

Silko's refusal to privilege whiteness as creator, prime practitioner of evil, or even clan inventor is crucial to her representation of whiteness as terrified rather than terrifying, and in fact weak and vulnerable. Serlo, a cold-hearted, brutal, white European male virgin, brings into sharp relief this terrorizing fear. Serlo works to save the Sangre Pura of the European nobility. All of his sperm is frozen, preserved for posterity, as a genetic representative of the European monarchies. He ejaculates into a sterile vacuum pump commonly used for the artificial insemination of cattle. For Serlo, the whitest of the whites, *all* bodies are polluted and polluting, except those with Sangre Pura: "Serlo did not mind Beaufrey's cheap street boys, or the gringos, not even Eric; how could Serlo have possibly felt anything at all about them? Jealousy was out of the question. Serlo had *sangre pura;* 'blue blood' deserved 'blue blood.' In the end there could be nothing better" (*Almanac* 542). To those with Sangre Pura, the rabble is black, red, and white, all vulgar and cheap. In his paralyzing fear of apocalypse, Serlo is the one who suffers most from wétiko psychosis in this text. Without a white protector/god to save him from the apocalypse, Serlo's vulnerability makes him cruel and sadistic, behaviors that cover his fear and terror.

What ethnographic picture of white, middle-class femininity does Silko write? Are women, as part of some universal sisterhood, somehow less likely to be connected to the Gunadeeyahs? Are they less likely to be greedy, violent, selfish, racist colonialists? No. There are two white women whom we get to know fairly well in *Almanac of the Dead:* Seese, a drug-addicted stripper who has lost her child, and Leah Blue, a real estate mogul married to the mob who is more white boy masculine than even her contract killer husband, Max. Both of these women are failed mothers, first and foremost. Seese's baby is kidnapped by the father's lover, Beaufrey: "Afterward, Seese had drifted as if she were a sea-green ribbon of kelp caught in a current with a voice that accused her over and over. A less distinct voice said she had done the best she knew how. Her baby had not drowned in his bathwater. He had not been born addicted. But she could find no consolation for this loss" (*Almanac* 111). The kidnapped baby is used by Beaufrey's lover Serlo, the terrified Sangre Pure virgin, as a body for pedophilic violent pornography. The living white male baby body is mutilated and murdered for the camera, its Caucasian organs harvested (563). Genocide and violent domination is literally written onto the body. The maternal is corrupt and destructive, high on cocaine. Seese's search for the dead baby, and her decision to give up drugs, are the most she can do to nurture and mother. Like Serlo, Seese covers over her fear by her refusal to nurture.

Leah Blue, another white mother, sells real estate while her two young sons wait in the air-conditioned Cadillac. She fails to attend to her younger son, Bingo, when he has nightmares, and refuses all along to love Sonny and Bingo. They grow up on their own, mean-spirited and psychotic. Leah is cold, calculating, and unemotional. When the two boys are young and Leah is just beginning to buy and sell real estate in Tucson, she uses the boys as leverage in a deal about to be made. When Bingo finally tires of Sonny's teasing, he slumps against the wheel of the car in tears, setting off the car's horn.

> The first time it had happened, the agent representing the seller turned pale. He paused, expecting Leah to rush across the vacant lot to get the kid off the horn. And Leah might have done that except she saw the agent's discomfort. Cars on the street were slowing, and it was Leah, in her bright green mumu and matching heels standing in the center of the vacant lot, people were staring at. Leah had sensed the agent was about to give in on the interest rate; the sound of the car horn had worked like a vise. Leah never even glanced in the direction of the car. The agent broke. . . . At that moment she had felt something she had never felt before. The horn had stopped and she could hear the voices of the boys approaching behind her. But nothing could interfere or change what she had just experienced. . . . The sensation was the closest to anything sexual she'd felt since Max got shot. (360)

This vision of white, upper-middle-class motherhood and Leah's use of her sons to close a real estate deal is as disturbing as the portrait of drug-addicted, working-class Seese. These are the failed mothers.

Given Silko's cosmology, another devastating critique of these two white women centers upon their inability to tell the stories that matter to their children. Storytelling is the good that binds, a primary method for nurturing. It is in the act of remembering through storytelling that there is resistance. The one mother in the book who succeeds is Old

Yoeme, a Yaqui woman who initiates the twins Zeta and Lecha through storytelling. She tells the twins about snakes and seeing, Guzman and cottonwood trees, the family history, and Geronimo's mistaken identity. Yoeme is the one who tells the twins, *"You* are Indians" (114). Seese has no stories that could initiate her baby son, except the ones that white people in this text create—stories of greed, violence, self-gratification, pleasure in pain, and destruction. Leah's stories are also about greed, but more importantly, her land-grabbing, water-claiming stories involve the land and its rape.

Leah's stories are metonymies for what I see as the crux of Silko's reclamation effort—the land and the body are the terrains most violated and most entwined. They are also the terrains being taken back in the march north by marked and colonized bodies. The fate of the body is linked directly to the fate of the colonized land. Angelita la Escapía and Zeta operate from violent revolutionary positions to "take back the land" and "protect Mother Earth from destruction"—the same landscape Silko works to reclaim through storytelling. These two women warriors (as well as Rose the Yupik woman, later in the book) wrest a "subjectivity denied" by taking up the gun and using it against the masculinist culture they are overthrowing: Angelita "had come to the healers convention in Tucson to make contacts with certain people, the people with the weapons she needed to protect the followers of the spirit macaws from air attacks. Those amazing shoulder-mounted missiles worked as simply as holiday skyrockets. Angelita had fired one herself. . . . Angelita heard from spirits too—only her spirits were furious and they told her to defend the people from attack" (712). Zeta has been running guns back and forth across the "border" for several years, stockpiling guns for this day of redemption for the "American continents . . . soaked with Native American and African blood" (739). She agrees to sell the missiles to Angelita, and they form an alliance of women warriors—with real guns and real power.

Resistance

Sandoval and hooks posit strategies of racial resistance that emanate from positions of oppression. Of her location in the margin "as a space of radical openness," hooks says, "I am located in the margin. I make a definite distinction between that marginality which is imposed by oppressive structures and that marginality one chooses as a site of resistance—as location of radical openness and possibility. This site of resistance is continually formed in that segregated culture of opposition that is our critical response to domination" (*Yearning* 153). She clearly acknowledges the agency of choosing and using that site in subversive and disruptive ways.

Sandoval describes a "differential consciousness" that also claims some sort of subjectivity for *all* within the oppressive power structures of first world, hierarchical, racist, classist patriarchy and women's movement. There are five levels of engagement. The first four are "equal rights," "revolutionary" (different but equal), "supremacism" (different therefore better), and "separatism" (different therefore separate). The fifth level of Sandoval's map of resistance is the one that allows movement among the other four levels and beyond. Instead of discarding each tactic as it is deployed and moving up an evolutionary ladder of progressively radical action, Sandoval's "differential consciousness" allows strategies that "weave" between and among all of the possible sites of resistance: "What U.S. third world feminism demands is a new subjectivity, a political revision that denies any one ideology as the final answer, while instead positing a *tactical subjectivity* with the capacity to re-center depending upon the kinds of oppression to be confronted" (14).

Silko's scenario in *Almanac of the Dead* is just this kind of new "tactical subjectivity." The disenfranchised other (the repressed) returns to take back the land in an *assertion* of subjectivity. In an interview for the *Bloomsbury Review,* Silko hints that this is the result not of mere revolution but of the return of days in their living essence, the denouement of prophesy of the kind found in almanacs ("Past" 10). Time, circular time, is described similarly in *Almanac of the Dead:* "The days, years, and centuries were spirit beings who traveled the universe, returning endlessly. The Spirits of the Night and the Spirits of the Day would take care of people" (523). It is not relativity or linearity that controls the discourses and operations of subjectivity and identity. Rather, Mayan time is the controlling principle of motion and action. At a 1992 seminar at the University of Arizona, Silko described Mayan time as a round "tortilla, . . . like water, they're all around, we're in it, we're just in all the years, all the time that's ever been in the past and all the time that's yet to come. You can see the future. The future is here now."

The text's final empowerment is in the hands of the War Twins Ma'sewe and O'yo'yo'we of Keres tradition, embodied as El Feo and Tacho, as well as in the hands of Grandmother Spider (Old Yoeme) or Thought Woman Ts'its'tsi'nako, who sends into being two more goddesses, Naotsete and Uretsete (Zeta and Lecha). This group of psychic beings operates to balance the world, a balancing in which gender is one of the important operating principles.[3]

The portrait of whiteness that Silko paints in *Almanac of the Dead* is bleak at best. Greedy, "ruly," violent natures are assigned white status, even if blood belies this position. This ethnographic version of Eur-american cultural production and social construction, written in the interstices and between the lines of the aesthetic form and appearance of Western European fictional genres, operates to destabilize those historical and sociological versions of culture and society that buttress white supremacist internal colonialism in the Americas. As a presumed response to the ethnography of Elsie Crews Parsons and others, who were in fact revisioning Laguna cultural production and social construction for white consumption and redemption, *Almanac of the Dead* revisions contemporary white culture for red and white consumption and terror.

Grandmothers

Paula Gunn Allen commits a similar practice in *Grandmothers of the Light: A Medicine Woman's Sourcebook*. Using current Euramerican ethnographic practice, she revises previous images of indigenous peoples through "thousands of stories collected from hundreds of tribes [that] have been published in the United States" (3). By making use of these accounts, which were collected by white people for the most part, she takes up the ways in which white people have revised tribal narratives and what that means *about* whiteness. Silko steps outside of ethnographic practice into fiction in order to turn the mirror onto white folks, but Allen works in a different medium, borrowing ethnographic materials and conventions to, among other things, comment upon and highlight whiteness.

The contradictions of my reading of *Grandmothers of the Light* and of Allen's writing strategies in that text are precisely where her guerrilla ethnography is located. In her borrowing she embeds a refusal to follow even her own paradigms. In " 'Border Studies': The Intersection of Gender and Color," Allen calls for a way of reading texts that attends to "the actual texts being created, their source texts, the texts to which they stand in relation, and the otherness that they both embody and delineate" (314). As we will see, Allen both attends to and dismisses these relations.

Allen intends *Grandmothers of the Light* to be a "sourcebook" of stories for those women wishing to follow the "medicine path" or shamanic tradition as she defines it. She has collected several Native American stories from several sources. Some of her sources are oral or written versions of stories told by Native Americans: "Stories change, and the teller, the audience, the occasion, the time all combine to create a man's story from a woman's story. . . . [Eduardo] Galeano [the writer of the story being introduced] cites Joseph Bruchac's *Stone Giants and Flying*

Heads as the source of his retelling. Bruchac has, of course, retold an old story in his turn" (*Grandmothers* 38).

Many of Allen's sources, however, are written accounts of narratives told *by* tribal informants *to* white ethnographers and missionaries. Our attention, then, should be directed to the sources and versions of this and other texts and how they work to create this new text. However, nowhere does she question the context of the sources she "interprets" for what will be consumed, more than likely, by a white feminist audience.[4] In the opening chapter of *Grandmothers,* Allen recounts the relationship between Frank Linderman, a white ethnologist, and Pretty Shield, the Crow Indian woman whose life story Linderman collected and published. Where are the questions of gender and power circulating in this encounter? Allen neither asks nor alludes to them. In fact, she misses the opportunity to perform the kind of critical work that she herself calls for: attention to text, source texts, relational texts, and their embodied otherness (" 'Border Studies' " 314).

This is similar to the problem Greg Sarris sees in relation to Allen's work on "Cache Creek Pomo Dreamer and basket-weaver Mabel McKay, and in Kashaya Pomo Dreamer and prophet Essie Parrish."

> It seems that in Allen's strategy to develop and support a tribal-feminist or feminist-tribal approach to American Indian women's written literatures—an approach that can both locate an Indian (woman) presence in the texts and critique patriarchal tendencies to suppress Indian women's power and subjectivity—she replicates in practice what she sets out to criticize. Allen does not *question how she reads each of the Pomo women's words. . . . She does not examine the women's particular histories and cultures to inform her ideas.* (124–26, emphasis added)

While contextualizing the Native American content of the stories she reproduces and even at times offering citations for the source material from which she gathers them, she does not contextualize their collection. The problematics of white ethnographers, trappers, and missionaries—travelers across the landscape—writing *their* versions of what they have seen or heard as outsiders remains unexamined. Thus, Allen contradicts her own paradigm, a move that renders the text less credible.

What rescues *Grandmothers of the Light* from the problems of decontextualization is a kind of mimicry that operates throughout the text. The implication of Allen's introductory remarks to the collection is that somehow these stories and the manner in which she has collected them will be in opposition to "the rationalist world where the linear mind reigns supreme [read "white"]" (5). Yet the paradigm of growth through the medicine path is relatively chronological, with each of the "seven ways of the medicine woman" functioning in ways very similar to those of Western/white coming-of-age narratives for women. In their similarity to the female bildungsroman, these stages of growth offer a familiar ground of white cultural socialization. Her coming-of-age narrative pattern is "almost the same, but not quite," "*almost the same but not white*"; producing what Homi Bhabha calls "its slippage, its excess, its difference" (126), disrupting the authority of whiteness as represented by the white/Western paradigm. As a repetition or rearticulation of colonial (ethnographic) discourse, Allen's mimicry represents a "*metonymy of presence,*" an "ambivalence . . . [that] suggests that the fetishized colonial culture is potentially and strategically an insurgent counter-appeal" (Bhabha 131).

The stages along the medicine path are written for women, a slight shift from the male pattern most often associated with coming-of-age fiction in America. While much recent feminist work has been done on the female bildungsroman, that work, too, is a bit of mimicry that highlights the "almost the same but not quite" mirror of colonized female subjectivity. For instance, the sixth way on the medicine path is that of the teacher. While not striking in and of itself, the medicine woman becomes a teacher as a menopausal woman. Menopausal women are nearly invisible to the internal colonial apparatus of North America, and when they slip through and become visible, they are cast as abject in the extreme, (not) seen as used-up, foolish, unsightly. The slippage between the image of the young, eager, white-faced teacher bringing even younger white-faced children into the rationalist disciplines of math, science, even literature, and the figure of an older, menopausal woman with brown skin and wrinkles bringing brown- and white-skinned women into greater knowledge of the "mystical and psychic" world of women's shamanic tradition is fraught with "immanent threat" (Bhabha 126) to the production of knowledge within the economy of colonization. The medicine woman/teacher plays out a mimicry of the white version of teacher.

Allen employs ethnographic form but in so doing *becomes* the shadow, "mimicking" the colonizer, like Silko's mirroring, shadowing, following, looking back. Red returns the "look of surveillance" of colonial ethnographic practice, rearticulating the whole and threatening the stability of white identity. "The *menace* of mimicry is its *double* vision which in disclosing the ambivalence of colonial discourse also disrupts its authority" (Bhabha 129). Bhabha continues, "The ambivalence of colonial authority repeatedly turns from *mimicry*—a difference that is almost nothing but not quite—to *menace*—a difference that is almost total but not quite" (132). In *Grandmothers of the Light,* Allen reverses ethnographic practice by seeking and recording the "metaphysical," deobjectifying these stories just as the anthropologists who collected the stories objectified what was once solely metaphysical.

In the oscillation between mimicry and menace, this ambivalence presses the audience continually to ask, "But how is this *different* from the way of becoming a monk, or a priest, or a good wife?" And in the asking, white readers will see the distortion in the mirror and perhaps sense that there has been a surprise attack. The stories Allen retells are not my cultural stories but, like her novel *The Woman Who Owned the Shadows,* they uncannily draw me to them. Allen, while serious about her intent to recenter what she terms "cosmogyny," also plays trickster or clown, putting on the markings of white ethnographers—but in reverse.[5] In taking up white versions of tribal stories and then doing what poets such as Jerome Rothenberg and Mary Austin have done *to* tribal stories also collected by white observers, poetically retranslating them in their own cultural terms, without questioning authenticity or cultural context, Allen takes up the pen and commits an act of guerrilla warfare. It is a surprise attack behind the lines of academic, feminist, ethnographic, and religious discourses.

Guerrilla ethnography is a strategic response to internal colonialism. In the struggle for land rights and cultural survivance (in Vizenor's term), those who commit guerrilla ethnography pose more than a theoretical threat to the stability (such as it is) of the ruling settler classes. The response to skirmishes like *Almanac of the Dead* and *Grandmothers of the Light* by white folks tells a story not of their righteous anger over "clumsy comic book fare" (St. John 124), "self-righteousness" (Jones 36), or naïveté "to the point of silliness" (Birkerts 41), but of their fear— "white" fear of the "other," the "immanent threat to both 'normalized' knowledges and disciplinary powers" (Bhabha 126). It is the story of white fear that what Silko prophesies as the apocalyptic end of white rule of the Americas is not just a story but a serious fiction. It is an apocalyptic end *only* if you are "white/whitely." In *Almanac of the Dead* and *Grandmothers of the Light,* "[red] skin splits under the racist gaze, displaced into signs of bestiality, genitalia, grotesquerie, which reveal the phobic myth of the undifferentiated whole white body" (Bhabha 132). Not only black bodies but marked bodies—black, red, female—split, disrupt, and resist. As in Vietnam, colonial America, and South Africa, guerrilla warfare is a strategy of resistance and a place of radical openness and possibility. To paraphrase Gerald Vizenor, Silko and Allen commit guerrilla warfare in words, that is, "socioacupuncture" in a wild reversal of "the social science monologue and trope to power."

NOTES

1. See Hulme, *Colonial Encounters,* for a detailed discussion of the rhetorical and discursive systems surrounding the term cannibal as a product of first encounters in the Americas between Western and indigenous cultures and bodies.

2. Frankenberg investigates whiteness as a socially constructed racial category in *White Women, Race Matters.* Her introductory remarks offer a succinct history and contextualization of the issues at hand in relation to white matters.

3. Allen, *The Sacred Hoop,* describes these supernatural beings and their functions within Keres Pueblo traditional practice. She asserts that within this constellation a balance is maintained and that gender plays a crucial role both in the maintenance of that balance and in the ordered, circular motion of time and space.

4. Allen's audience has consistently been white feminists, particularly academic feminists. Her early work is grounded deeply in the academy, and her more recent work is often contextualized more along the lines of New Age spiritualism. Both of these audiences tend to be white. Their apparent predominance doesn't mean that Allen is not read in other communities and in other ways.

5. The closing scene of Victor Masayesva Jr.'s film *itam hakim, hopiit* plays this out. The camera focuses on a Hopi clown dancer's feet shod in hightop sneakers, rubber-soled platform shoes, and mismatched and crazily striped stockings. As the dance progresses, the director shifts the film and the clown dancer's feet to the fast forward mode of a videotape player. Western/white shoes on indigenous/red feet participating in nonwhite ritual functions operate as transgression and social commentary on the craziness of white people.

WORKS CITED

Abu-Lughod, Lila. "Can There Be a Feminist Ethnography?" *Women and Performance: A Journal of Feminist Theory* 5.1 #9 (1990): 7–27.

Allen, Paula Gunn. *The Blind Lion.* Berkeley: Thorp Springs, 1975.

———. " 'Border' Studies: The Intersection of Gender and Color." *Introduction to Scholarship in Modern Languages and Literatures.* Ed. Joseph Gibaldi. New York: Modern Language Association, 1992. 303–19.

———. *Coyote's Daylight Trip.* Albuquerque: La Confluencia, 1978.

———. *Grandmothers of the Light: A Medicine Woman's Sourcebook.* Boston: Beacon, 1991.

———. Interview by Annie O. Esturoy. *This Is about Vision: Interviews with Southwestern Writers.* Ed. John F. Crawford, William Balassi, and Annie O. Esturoy. Albuquerque: University of New Mexico Press, 1990. 94–110.

———. *Shadow Country.* Native American Series. Los Angeles: University of California Press, 1982.

———. *Skins and Bones: Poems, 1979–87.* Albuquerque: West End Press, 1988.

———. *The Woman Who Owned the Shadows.* San Francisco: Spinsters/Aunt Lute, 1983.

———. *Wyrds.* San Francisco: Taurean Horn Press, 1987.

Bhabha, Homi. "Of Mimicry and Man: The Ambivalence of Colonial Discourse." *October* 28 (1984): 125–33.

Birkerts, Sven. "Apocalypse Now." Review of *Almanac of the Dead,* by Leslie Marmon Silko. *New Republic,* Nov. 4, 1991, 39–41.

Clifford, James. *The Predicament of Culture: Twentieth-Century Ethnography, Literature, and Art.* Cambridge, Mass.: Harvard University Press, 1988.

Dyer, Richard. "White." *Screen* 29.4 (1988): 44–64.

Fanon, Frantz. *Black Skin, White Masks.* Trans. Charles Lam Markmann. New York: Grove, 1967.

Forbes, Jack D. *Columbus and Other Cannibals: The Wétiko Disease of Exploitation, Imperialism and Terrorism.* Brooklyn: Autonomedia, 1992.

Frankenberg, Ruth. *White Women, Race Matters: The Social Construction of Whiteness.* Minneapolis: University of Minnesota Press, 1993.

Frye, Marilyn. *The Politics of Reality: Essays in Feminist Theory.* Trumansburg, N.Y.: Crossing Press, 1983.

———. *Willful Virgin: Essays in Feminism, 1976–1992.* Freedom, Calif.: Crossing Press, 1992.

hooks, bell. *Black Looks: Race and Representation.* Boston: South End Press, 1992.

———. *Yearning: Race, Gender, and Cultural Politics.* Boston: South End Press, 1990.

Hulme, Peter. *Colonial Encounters: Europe and the Native Caribbean, 1492–1797.* New York: Methuen, 1986.

Jones, Malcolm, Jr. Review of *Almanac of the Dead,* by Leslie Marmon Silko. *Newsweek,* Nov. 18, 1991, 84.

Morrison, Toni. *Playing in the Dark: Whiteness and the Literary Imagination.* Cambridge, Mass.: Harvard University Press, 1992.

St. John, Edward B. Review of *Almanac of the Dead,* by Leslie Marmon Silko. *Library Journal,* Oct. 15, 1991, 124.

Sandoval, Chela. "U.S. Third World Feminism: The Theory and Method of Oppositional Consciousness in a Postmodern World." *Genders* 10 (Spring 1991): 1–24.

Sarris, Greg. *Keeping Slug Woman Alive: A Holistic Approach to American Indian Texts.* Berkeley: University of California Press, 1993.

Silko, Leslie Marmon. *Almanac of the Dead.* New York: Simon and Schuster, 1991.

———. *Ceremony.* New York: Viking, 1977.

———. *Laguna Woman.* Greenfield Center, N.Y.: Greenfield Review Press, 1974.

———. "The Past Is Right Here and Now." Interview by Ray Gonzalez. *Bloomsbury Review,* Apr./May 1992, 5, 10.

———. *Storyteller.* New York: Seaver Books, 1981.

Vizenor, Gerald. *Crossbloods: Bone Courts, Bingo, and Other Reports.* Minneapolis: University of Minnesota Press, 1990.

10 ⬧ Mothering the Self

Writing through the Lesbian Sublime in Audre Lorde's *Zami* and Gloria Anzaldúa's *Borderlands/La Frontera*

> It is impossible to *define* a feminine practice of writing, and this is an impossibility that will remain, for this practice can never be theorized, enclosed, coded— which doesn't mean that it doesn't exist. But it will always surpass the discourse that regulates the phallo-centric system. . . . It will be conceived of only by sub-jects who are breakers of automatisms, by peripheral figures that no authority can ever subjugate.
> — Hélène Cixous, "The Laugh of the Medusa"

> The abject is edged with the sublime.
> — Julia Kristeva, *Powers of Horror*

Lesbian and gay literature, long relegated to the margins or closets of academic discourse, has lately become increasingly visible in the guise of "queer theory," a marriage of lesbian and gay literature and politics with postmodern, poststructural theory. Queer theory has been de-scribed as "an in-your-face rejection of the proper response to hetero-normativity, a version of acting up" (Hennessy 967). Queer theory builds on the postmodern critique of identity politics, using such theorists as Michel Foucault, Roland Barthes, Monique Wittig, Hélène Cixous, and others to construct sophisticated analyses of the ontology, aesthetics, politics, and praxis of male and female homosexuality. In the United States, lesbian theorists have been particularly active over the past de-cade, joining forces with other marginalized women, especially women of color, and insisting on visibility within the feminist movement, as well as in academia and the public sphere in general.

The writings of lesbian women of color such as Gloria Anzaldúa and Audre Lorde have provided crucial literary platforms for the more abstract theoretical discussions of American queer theorists, such as Teresa de Lauretis, Judith Butler, and others, who critique the notion of stable, autonomous identities and argue for an understanding of lesbianism "not as an essence . . . but as a critical space within social structures" (Phelan 766). In their insistence on multiple, fluid identities and on a coalitional politics that cuts across racial, ethnic, religious, and other barriers, Anzaldúa and Lorde are, in a sense, queer theorists *avant-la-lettre* who use their personal stories as antiracist, radical feminist political weapons. In their autobiographical texts, *Borderlands/La Frontera* and *Zami: A New Spelling of My Name,* Anzaldúa and Lorde subvert the normative space of autobiography by turning it to their own radical purposes and, I argue, they use the traditionally conservative, masculine mode of sublime writing subversively as well, inscribing a lesbian sublime that, as Biddy Martin says of lesbianism in general, "works to unsettle rather than to consolidate the boundaries around identity, not to dissolve them altogether but to open them to the fluidities and heterogeneities that make their renegotiation possible" (103). In their subversive use of the normative categories of autobiography, identity, and the sublime, Anzaldúa and Lorde engage in a textual form of acting up, creating the kind of "public scandal" (Berlant and Freeman 163) that queer theory both advocates and describes.

Although the sublime has historically been the provenance of male writers, from Longinus and Kant to the postmodern sublime of Harold Bloom, there is also, as Joanne Feit Diehl has observed, a tradition of women poets who elaborate a "counter-sublime," which begins, Diehl says, with Emily Dickinson and continues through such twentieth-century women poets as Elizabeth Bishop, Marianne Moore, H.D., and Adrienne Rich. These poets, Diehl claims, inscribe "the disruption of perceived experience, the heightening of perception itself, [and] the conversion of the mind" in ways similar to those of the male poets but with an important difference: "the external transformative power is perceived as feminine," with the result that the "sublime transpires without the burden of indebtedness, the necessity for physical defensiveness, or the chill of competition" (185–86). The woman poet, says Diehl, "develops an alternative line of descent where the maternal image coincides with poetic identity" (177). In place of the Kantian primacy of reason and repression of the body, which constructs the sublime moment in terms of mental domination of a fearsome other, the female sublime rejects the separation of mind and body, insisting on a model of relatedness that is inscribed as what Patricia Yaeger, in her essay "Toward a

Female Sublime," calls the "pre-oedipal sublime." Building on Neil Hertz's reading of the Romantic sublime as "oedipal,"[1] Yaeger argues,

> If what is repressed in the "oedipal" sublime is the desire for pre-oedipal bonding with the mother's body (which in most Romantic poems is given an imaginative correlative in the chaos and blissful heterodoxy of the cosmos), in the "pre-oedipal" sublime these libidinal moments are not repressed; they break into consciousness and are welcomed as a primary, healthful part of the writer's experience, as part of the motive for metaphor. (205)

Lee Edelman, in his response to Yaeger's essay, cautions against her tendency to universalize female experience and argues that this version of the sublime "might more strategically be called a lesbian rather than a female sublime" (220). I would suggest that the sublime moments in Lorde's and Anzaldúa's autobiographical texts enact what Edelman calls the lesbian sublime, a politicized version of the female sublime that is firmly grounded in the social and historical specificity that gives this mode of writing its subversive potential.

Since the lesbian sublime is characterized by a return to pre-oedipal bonding with the mother, before we look at the sublime moments in Anzaldúa's *Borderlands/La Frontera* and Lorde's *Zami,* it is important to consider how the figure of the mother is inscribed in these texts. When we look closely at the different uses to which Lorde and Anzaldúa put the figure of the mother, an interesting dichotomy emerges: the autobiographical narrators' disappointment and even anger with their biological mothers, contrasting with the idealized images they present of the mother-goddesses who serve as models for their independent, emergent sense of self. In reimagining their mothers as powerful female goddesses, Lorde and Anzaldúa rewrite their own roles as women, transforming themselves autobiographically into the writers—or the mothers—of their own destinies.

Lorde and Anzaldúa bitterly describe their mothers as agents of the patriarchal status quo who disapproved of their daughters' independence, nonconformity, and creativity. Lorde's mother "viewed any act of separation from her as an indictment of her authority" and "a request for privacy was treated like an outright act of insolence for which the punishment was swift and painful" (*Zami* 83). Anzaldúa's mother tries to model her daughter into an obedient, self-effacing Chicanita, a socialization process that Anzaldúa stubbornly resists: "Even as a child I would not obey. I was 'lazy.' Instead of ironing my younger brothers' shirts or cleaning the cupboards, I would pass many hours studying, reading, painting, writing. Every bit of self-faith I'd painstakingly gathered took a beating daily. Nothing in my culture approved of me" (*Borderlands* 16). In trying to stamp out her daughter's difference, Anzaldúa says, her mother acted as an "accomplice to oppression by unwittingly passing on to [her] children the oppressor's ideologies" ("La Prieta" 207).[2] In my mother's eyes, says Anzaldúa, "I saw myself reflected as 'strange,' 'abnormal,' 'QUEER.' I saw no other reflection. Helpless to change that image, I retreated into books and solitude and kept away from others" ("La Prieta" 199). Significantly, Anzaldúa makes this comment in a section of her autobiographical essay "La Prieta" that deals with her premature menstruation:

> When I was three months old tiny pink spots began appearing on my diaper. "She's a throwback to the Eskimo," the doctor told my mother. "Eskimo girl children get their periods early." At seven I had budding breasts. My mother would wrap them in tight cotton girdles so the kids at school would not think them strange. . . . My mother would pin onto my panties a folded piece of rag. "Keep your legs shut, Prieta." This, the deep dark secret between us, her punishment for having fucked before the wedding, my punishment for being born. (199)

Anzaldúa's mother reinforces her daughter's fear and shame at the menstrual blood, making Anzaldúa feel "that there was something 'wrong' " with her: "The whole time I was growing up I felt that I was not of this earth. An alien from another planet—I'd been dropped on my mother's lap" ("La Prieta" 199).[3]

As Julia Kristeva observes in *Pouvoirs de l'horreur*, menstrual blood is one of the primary forms associated with the abject, which is "ce qui perturbe une identité, un système, un ordre. Ce qui ne respecte pas les limites, les places, les règles" [that which perturbs an identity, a system, an order. That which does not respect limits, places, rules] (12). The threat of the abject comes from its tendency to cross boundaries, to go beyond or escape the neatly drawn power lines of patriarchal culture: "Toute sécrétion . . . tout ce que s'échappe du corps feminin ou masculin, souille" [All secretions, everything that escapes from the feminine or masculine body, stains], says Kristeva, and this "souillure" is always the subject of strong taboos.[4] According to Kristeva, the fear and danger inspired by menstruation come, in psychoanalytic terms, from "cette autre menace pour le sujet qu'est l'engloutissement dans la relation duelle où il risque . . . d'engouffrer sans retour dans la mére son identité propre" [that other menace for the subject, which is the total absorption in the dual relation, in which it risks losing its own identity forever in the mother] (79).

Although Kristeva has been roundly criticized by queer theorists such as Teresa de Lauretis and Judith Butler for her insistence on the "psy-chotic" nature of lesbianism and her unwillingness to venture beyond the patriarchal fold,[5] her theory of the abject is useful when turned to more radical purposes than she may have intended. Rather than shun-ning the "menace" of the abject, as Kristeva might advise, Anzaldúa and Lorde embrace it in their texts, going openly to meet the figure of the mother who waits at the far side of the abject. In their texts, menstrua-tion figures as a channel through which they actively seek identity with the pre-oedipal mother, resisting the fear and shame that their biologi-cal mothers tried to instill. Lorde does this in a very direct way, ground-ing in the body her womanist rewriting of the scene of her first men-struation. Anzaldúa takes a more metaphorical approach, seeking an identification not with her biological mother, who remains unavailable to her even in fantasy, but with the pre-Aztec Mayan goddess Coatlicue, who becomes the symbol of female power and resistance in her text.

Lorde's description of her first menstruation has none of the anguish of Anzaldúa's, probably in part because it occurred at the "normal" age, when it was expected (anxiously) by both mother and daughter. Lorde's first menstruation, as she describes it in *Zami,* actually provoked a scene of unusual intimacy between the two: "There was something else com-ing from my mother that I could not define. It was the lurking of that amused/annoyed brow-furrowed half-smile of hers that made me feel—all her nagging words to the contrary—that something very good and satisfactory and pleasing to her had just happened" (77). After revealing the secret of her menstruation to her mother, Lorde takes down the mor-tar and pestle to begin helping her "pound souse" for the family dinner. Her mother leaves the house for a few moments, and as Lorde begins to pound the pestle against the mortar, the act turns into a powerful fan-tasy of female sexuality:

> I plunged the pestle into the bowl, feeling the blanket of salt give way, and the broken cloves of garlic just beneath. The downward thrust of the wooden pestle slowed upon contact, rotated back and forth slowly, and then gently altered its rhythm to include an up and down beat. Back and forth, round, up and down, back, forth, round, round, up and down. . . . There was a heavy fullness at the root of me that was exciting and dangerous.
>
> As I continued to pound the spice, a vital connection seemed to estab-lish itself between the muscles of my fingers curved tightly around the smooth pestle in its insistent downward motion, and the molten core of my body whose source emanated from a new ripe fullness just beneath the pit of my stomach. That invisible thread, taut and sensitive as a cli-toris exposed, . . . ran over my ribs and along my spine, tingling and singing, into a basin that was poised between my hips. . . . And within

that basin was a tiding ocean of blood beginning to be made real and available to me for strength and information.

... The catalogue of dire menstruation-warnings from my mother passed out of my head. My body felt strong and full and open, yet captivated by the gentle motions of the pestle, and the rich smells filling the kitchen, and the fullness of the young summer heat. (*Zami* 78–79)

This scene draws together female sexuality and menstrual bleeding with food (another object that Kristeva identifies as potentially abject),[6] as well as that most taboo figure of all, incest with the mother, which Lorde's own commentary on the scene reveals as its subtext: "Years afterward when I was grown, whenever I thought about how I smelled that day, I would have a fantasy of my mother . . . looking down upon me lying on the couch, and then slowly, thoroughly, our touching and caressing each other's most secret places" (*Zami* 78). Menstruation, female sexuality, and (female) incest with the mother: Lorde brings together these elements of what Kristeva calls the abject and turns them into a powerful scene of female relationship that takes place on the far edge of the "limits" and "rules" of conventional patriarchal culture. This edge, I would suggest, can be seen as the limen through which Lorde engages in a radical lesbian variant of what Yaeger identifies as the "pre-oedipal sublime," that is, a mode of writing that offers "a model of the self . . . where self-empowerment and intersubjective bliss entertain one another in an atmosphere free of paranoia" (Yaeger 205).

Another way to think of the female sublime is through the concept of *jouissance,* in the Barthesian/French feminist usage of the term as a sexual/textual force that breaks through conventions and limitations to stage a liberating release into a utopian space of overdetermination and ambiguity. Barthes defines the *"texte de jouissance"* as

celui que met en état de perte, celui que déconforte (peut-être jusqu'à un certain ennui), faire vaciller les assises historiques, culturelles, psychologiques, du lecteur, la resistance de ses goûts, de ses valeurs et de ses souvenirs, met en crise son rapport au langage. (25)

[one that engenders a state of loss, one that discomforts (perhaps to the point of a kind of boredom), rocks the historical, cultural, and psychological beliefs of the reader, the resistance of his tastes, his values, and his memories, brings to crisis his rapport with language.]

Lorde's celebration of the richness and power of emergent female sexuality, culminating in her uninhibited expression of the fantasy of incest with her mother, forces her readers to confront the patriarchal taboos that have long repressed the appearance of such fantasies in writing. In Lorde's version of the sublime, the powers of jouissance are used as a source of strength to break through these taboos; losing herself in the rapture of the moment, Lorde experiences a form of the sublime that gives free rein to the pre-oedipal desire for oneness with the mother, setting the stage for her emergence as a politicized lesbian writer. Becoming a woman in the rush of blood that marks her first menstrual period, she is also on her way to becoming the empowered subject who will later inscribe this moment in her autobiography as a crucial scene of self-authorization.

In contrast to the explicitly sexual and embodied character of Lorde's version of the lesbian sublime in *Zami,* Anzaldúa, in *Borderlands,* relies on metaphor and a revisionist mythology to inscribe her rejection of the taboos against female sexuality and lesbian desire. Anzaldúa leads up to her invocation of the sublime with a rewriting of Chicano/a religious history, in which she reverses Aztec and Catholic patriarchalism by resurrecting in writing the older Mesoamerican goddesses. "The male-dominated Azteca-Mexica culture drove the powerful female deities underground by giving them monstrous attributes and by substituting male deities in their place," Anzaldúa explains (27). For the older Coatlicue, the Serpent goddess of life and death, the Nahuas substituted Tonantsi, who was split from her darker attributes and who later, after the Conquest, became Guadalupe, the Mexican Virgin Mary. The Spanish, Anzaldúa says, "desexed *Guadalupe,* taking *Coatlalopeuh,* the serpent/sexuality, out of her. They completed the split begun by the Nahuas by making *la Virgen de Guadalupe/ Virgen Maria* into chaste virgins and *Tlazolteotl/Coatlicue/la Chingada* into *putas*" (27–28). Anzaldúa's rewriting of the Guadalupe/Coatlicue myth rejects "the *virgen/puta* (whore) dichotomy" (31), restoring to Coatlicue her power as the figure who "contained and balanced the dualities of male and female, light and dark, life and death" (32).

When Anzaldúa talks about the "Coatlicue state," she is referring to a return to sources of human power, later repressed, that wear a female aspect yet in fact transcend the binary oppositions of male/female, light/dark, and so on. Coatlicue, she says, "represents: duality in life, a synthesis of duality, and a third perspective—something more than mere duality or a synthesis of duality" (46). Anzaldúa is able to tap into this power source through what she calls a "fall" into the Coatlicue state, which I would characterize as an instance of the lesbian sublime.

The movement of the chapter entitled "*La herencia de Coatlicue*/The *Coatlicue* State" away from the "shame" and "fear" of her early menstruation toward the liberating release of taboos and fears that accompanies the Coatlicue state sets up the model of female empowerment that Anzaldúa will continue to elaborate in the book's subsequent chapters.

The chapter begins with a description of her premature menstruation, which she refers to through the metaphor of Coatlicue:

> I was two or three years old the first time *Coatlicue* visited my psyche. . . . By the worried look on my parents' faces I learned early that something was fundamentally wrong with me. When I was older I would look into the mirror, afraid of *mi secreto terrible*. . . . The secret I tried to conceal was that I was not normal, that I was not like the others. I felt alien, I knew I was alien. I was the mutant stoned out of the herd, something deformed with evil inside. (*Borderlands* 42–43).

Her "*secreto terrible*" is her "bleeding," which "distanced her from others" as well as from her own body, which she felt "had betrayed her" (43). Anzaldúa uses her personal story to illustrate the "agony of inadequacy" that she sees operating in the Chicanos as a people: "As a person, I, as a people, we, Chicanos, blame ourselves, hate ourselves, terrorize ourselves. Most of this goes on unconsciously; we only know that we are hurting, we suspect that there is something 'wrong' with us, something fundamentally 'wrong'" (45). Anzaldúa describes the process of breaking through this self-hatred and denial, moving from an old conception of self to a new one, as "a dry birth, a breech birth, a screaming birth, one that fights her every inch of the way" (49). Coatlicue functions as a sort of midwife in this process of self-birthing, at once coaxing and threatening Anzaldúa, forcing her to look in the mirror and confront the "truth about herself" (48). Anzaldúa connects this "truth" to her body, to her troubled attitude toward her own sexuality: looking into the mirror, she sees "resistance to knowing, to letting go. . . . Resistance to sex, intimate touching, opening myself to the alien other where I am out of control" (48). The moment at which she breaks through this resistance and confronts openly the face in the mirror is written in the embodied, sexual, relational language that characterizes the lesbian sublime:

> Suddenly, I feel like I have another set of teeth in my mouth. A tremor goes through my body from my buttocks to the roof of my mouth. . . . Shock pulls my breath out of me. The sphincter muscle tugs itself up, up, and the heart in my cunt starts to beat. A light is all around me—so intense it could be white or black or at that juncture where extremes turn into their opposites. It passes through my body and comes out of the

other side. I collapse into myself—a delicious caving into myself—imploding, the walls like matchsticks softly folding inward in slow motion. I see *oposición e insurrección*. I see the crack growing on the rock. I see the fine frenzy building. I see the heat of anger or rebellion or hope split open that rock, releasing *la Coatlicue*. And someone in me takes matters into our own hands, and eventually, takes dominion over serpents— over my own body, my sexual activity, my soul, my mind, my weaknesses and strengths. Mine. Ours. Not the heterosexual white man's or the colored man's or the state's or the culture's or the religion's or the parents'—just ours, mine.

And suddenly I feel everything rushing to a center, a nucleus. All the lost pieces of myself come flying from the deserts and the mountains and the valleys, magnetized toward that center. *Completa. (Borderlands* 51)

In this sublime moment, Anzaldúa overcomes what she calls the "blocks" that have been imposed on her from without, reaching deep inside herself to recover the repressed power that Coatlicue represents. Like Cixous's rewriting of the Western mythic figure Medusa in "The Laugh of Medusa," whose subversive laughter mocks the fears and taboos of the patriarchy, Anzaldúa's revisioning of Coatlicue turns her into an enabling model of female resistance to oppressive patriarchal and imperialist norms, ushering in the reign of what she calls "the new mestiza."

If the height of the sublime moment in Anzaldúa's text represents a moment of "completion" and "centering" of the self, this potentially essentialist understanding of subjectivity is quickly decentered and bracketed by her subsequent chapters, which elaborate her notion of the "*mestiza* self," a hybrid, multivocal form of selfhood that sets up difference and diversity as its only unifying force.[7] Unlike Cixous's dangerously universal "New Woman" in "The Laugh of the Medusa," Anzaldúa's figure of the mestiza avoids the pitfalls of essentialism and universalism by remaining steadfastly open to multiple, shifting identities. Although neither Anzaldúa nor Lorde employ the abstract language of queer theory, they participate in queer theory's critique of fixed identity in their refusal either to boil down their differences into a single overriding category or to arrange them hierarchically. "As a forty-nine-year-old Black lesbian feminist socialist mother of two, including one boy, and a member of an interracial couple, I usually find myself a part of some group defined as other, deviant, inferior, or just plain wrong," Lorde writes (*Sister Outsider* 114). She continues:

I find I am constantly being encouraged to pluck out some one aspect of myself and present this as the meaningful whole, eclipsing or denying the other parts of my self. But this is a destructive and fragmenting way to live. My fullest concentration of energy is available to me only when I integrate all the parts of who I am, openly, allowing power from particular sources of my living to flow back and forth freely through all my different selves, without the restrictions of externally imposed definitions. (120)

Anzaldúa, too, insists on the free-flowing multiplicity of selves and allegiances: "What am I? *A third world lesbian feminist with Marxist and mystic leanings.* They would chop me up into little fragments and tag each piece with a label. . . . Who me, confused? Ambivalent? Not so. Only your labels split me" ("La Prieta" 205).

In *Gender Trouble,* Butler argues that identity can be "proliferated" subversively, in a way that breaks out of binary oppositions; her privileged example of such a subversive identity is the lesbian.[8] She calls for "a thorough-going appropriation and redeployment of the categories of identity themselves, not merely to contest 'sex,' but to articulate the convergence of multiple sexual discourses at the site of 'identity' in order to render that category . . . permanently problematic" (128). Anzaldúa and Lorde take Butler's oppositional strategy even further, proliferating identity not only in terms of gender but also in terms of race, class, ethnicity, and other even more marginalized affinities, such as Anzaldúa's Chicana mysticism and Lorde's Afrocentrist mysticism.

In a section of *Borderlands* entitled *"Si le preguntas a mi mamá, '¿Qué eres?'"* [If you ask my mother, what are you?], Anzaldúa considers the complicated response that such a question entails: "We call ourselves Mexican, referring to race and ancestry; *mestizo* when affirming both our Indian and Spanish (but we hardly ever own our Black ancestry [*sic*]); Chicano when referring to a politically aware people born and/or raised in the U.S.; *Raza* when referring to Chicanos; *tejanos* when we are Chicanos from Texas" (63). One of her goals in *Borderlands* is to find a way to balance all of these identities in a way that celebrates diversity and multiplicity over homogenization. To this end she proffers the figure of the mestiza as a model: "Being tricultural, monolingual, bilingual, or multilingual, speaking a patois, and in a state of perpetual transition," the mestiza "constantly has to shift out of habitual formations" and "copes by developing a tolerance for contradictions, a tolerance for ambiguity. . . . She learns to juggle cultures. She has a plural personality, she operates in a pluralistic mode" (78–79). In order to become mestiza, Anzaldúa says, one must first undertake "a conscious rupture with all oppressive traditions of all cultures and religions" (82). The new mestiza "reinterprets history and, using new symbols, she shapes new myths. She adopts new perspectives toward the darkskinned, women, and queers. She strengthens her tolerance . . . for ambiguity. . . . She surrenders all notions of safety, of the familiar. Deconstruct, construct. She becomes a *nahual,* able to transform herself into a tree, a coyote, into another person" (82–83).

This image of the mestiza as a *nahual* is particularly interesting because it brings together Anzaldúa's political project with her identity as a writer, and it is at this intersection that we find another sublime moment embedded in the text. This time the "fall" into the Coatlicue state is triggered by writing; through a form of writing that is here explicitly linked to the body, Anzaldúa taps into the feminine power of the female sublime/Coatlicue state and symbolically gives birth to herself in her new guise as a nahual, a writer: "When I write it feels like I'm carving bone. It feels like I'm creating my own face, my own heart—a Nahuatl concept. My soul makes itself through the creative act. It is constantly remaking and giving birth to itself through my body. It is this learning to live with *la Coatlicue* that transforms living in the Borderlands from a nightmare into a numinous experience. It is always a path/state to something else" (73). Having said this, Anzaldúa inscribes the scene of writing, describing how she fights her way through a "block" and "falls" into the Coatlicue state where she can access the creative energies that fuel her writing:

> Blocks (*Coatlicue* states) are related to my cultural identity. . . . The stress of living with cultural ambiguity both compels me to write and blocks me. It isn't until I'm almost at the end of the blocked state that I remember and recognize it for what it is. At soon as this happens, the piercing light of awareness melts the block and I accept the deep and the darkness and I hear one of my voices saying, "I am tired of fighting. I surrender. I give up, let go, let the walls fall." . . .
>
> And in descending to the depths I realize that down is up, and I rise up from and into the deep. And once again I recognize that the internal tension of oppositions can propel (if it doesn't tear apart) the mestiza writer out of the *metate* where she is being ground with corn and water, eject her out as *nahual,* an agent of transformation. (74)

Emerging from the Coatlicue state, Anzaldúa-as-nahual is able, through her writing, to challenge the mainstream American devaluation of things female, Indian, and mystical. The sublime moment of the Coatlicue state hybridizes Indian and Euramerican elements into a new *mestizaje* that becomes a powerful tool of feminist, antiracist resistance.

After the sublime moment of her first menstruation, which symbolically frees her to begin exploring her emergent lesbian sexuality, Lorde's autobiography narrates a series of encounters with women that moves her steadily toward a positive vision of black women as strong and independent. In the last half of *Zami,* she tells the story of her painful love affair with Muriel, a white woman who had already undergone electroshock treatments for depression by the time she moved to Greenwich Village in the 1950s and became Lorde's lover. Lorde's love for Muriel is based in a feeling of protectiveness: "I could take care of Muriel. I could make the world work for her, if not for myself" (190). But as Lorde begins to put together the pieces of her own life, working in the New York Public Library, attending Hunter College at night, and writing poetry in her spare time, Muriel is unable to get a job and soon begins to slip back into the self-destructive patterns that eventually send her back to the mental institutions. Muriel stays out all night drinking and embarks on a series of casual affairs with other women in their circle, leaving Lorde to mourn her "in a wildness of grief" (236).

At the depths of her despair, Lorde suddenly goes through another sublime moment that represents an inner liberation that will lead to a rewriting—a rebirthing—of her self. The sublime moment takes place just as Lorde finally lets go of her disastrous relationship with Muriel. Lorde describes her and Muriel's love as "an old dance, not consciously learned, but desperately followed. We had learned well in the kitchens of our mothers, both powerful women who did not let go easily. In those warm places of survival, love was another name for control, however openly given" (214). This second sublime moment of the text marks Lorde's movement away from the type of relationship exemplified by the mother-daughter relationship, based on power, control, and possession, toward the freer, more positive, self-accepting type of relationship that she demonstrates with Afrekete, the final love affair detailed in the autobiography.

This second sublime moment is an instance of the feminine sublime in a black gospel key. The external stimulus is completely innocuous; just after resigning herself to having lost Muriel, Lorde boards a bus to go to work and, "quite suddenly, there was music swelling up into my head, as if a choir of angels had boarded the Second Avenue bus directly in front of me. They were singing the last chorus of an old spiritual of hope. . . . The physical realities of the dingy bus slid away from me. I suddenly stood upon a hill in the center of an unknown country, hearing the sky fill with a new spelling of my own name" (238–39). Here Lorde draws on and rewrites the black religious tradition, re-presenting a moment of revelation not of the name of God but of the name of a new lesbian collectivity.[9] The new spelling of her name will be, precisely, *"Zami. A Carriacou name for women who work together as friends and lovers"* (255); this

sublime moment marks the transition point at which the autobiographical protagonist Audre, who has until then merely dabbled in a non-
politicized way with her emergent lesbian identity, authorizes herself to
"bring [her] personal and political visions together" in the writing that
bears her name (197).

That *Zami* is a collective name, standing at once for Lorde as an individual and for "women who work together as friends and lovers," reveals
Lorde's brand of identity politics. Inclusive rather than exclusive, Lorde,
like Anzaldúa, envisions a community of struggle, the survival of one
dependent on the survival of all. But Lorde's vision of community is
more complex than it would seem at first; both she and Anzaldúa believe
in coalition across the lines of groups that are often pitted against each
other. "Community must not mean a shedding of our differences, nor
the pathetic pretense that these differences do not exist," Lorde maintains (*Sister Outsider* 112), adding: "You do not have to be me in order for
us to fight alongside each other. . . . What we must do is commit ourselves
to some future that can include each other and to work toward that future with the particular strengths of our individual identities" (142).

Anzaldúa presents a similar vision of coalition in her foreword to the
second edition of *This Bridge Called My Back:* "We have come to realize
that we are not alone in our struggles nor separate nor autonomous but
that we—white black straight queer male female—are connected and
interdependent," she says (Moraga and Anzaldúa n.p.). She refuses to
"let color, class, and gender separate us from those who would be kindred spirits" ("La Prieta" 206). As Lorde says, "We share a common interest, survival, and it cannot be pursued in isolation from others simply
because their differences make us uncomfortable" (*Sister Outsider* 141).
Anzaldúa's and Lorde's insistence on coalition-in-difference is similar to
Barthes's vision of the ideal community as "celle d'un monde où il n'y
aurait plus que des différences, en sorte que se différencier ne serait pas
s'exclure" [one of a world where there would not be anything but differences, so that to differentiate oneself would not be to exclude oneself]
(88). It is also similar to, and may have paved the way for, the coalitional
politics of Queer Nation, a loose alliance of gay and lesbian activist
groups whose "tactics are to cross borders, to occupy spaces," in order to
"make the national world safe for . . . full expression of difference and
rage and sexuality" (Berlant and Freeman 152, 178).

Anticipating theorists such as Butler, who criticizes separatist lesbianism "that defines itself in radical exclusion from heterosexuality"
because it "deprives itself of the capacity to resignify the very heterosexual constructs by which it is partially and inevitably constituted" (128),
Anzaldúa and Lorde deliberately site their autobiographical texts and

their political projects on the border. Anzaldúa defines this border as a space where "I with my own affinities and my people with theirs can live together and transform the planet" ("La Prieta" 209). Borders, Anzaldúa writes,

> are set up to define the places that are safe and unsafe, to distinguish *us* from *them*. . . . A borderland is a vague and undetermined place created by the emotional residue of an unnatural boundary. It is in a constant state of transition. The prohibited and the forbidden are its inhabitants. *Los atravesados* live here: the squint-eyed, the perverse, the queer, the troublesome, the mongrel, the mulato, the half-breed, the half dead; in short, those who cross over, pass over, or go through the confines of the "normal." (*Borderlands* 3)

Anzaldúa turns the borderland into a positive space of difference, reversing the stereotypes that privilege the center over the margin.[10] She uses the border as a tool for challenging the homogenizing tendencies of mainstream society, as is evident, for example, in her proliferations in *Borderlands* of the margins between Spanish and English, as well as the generic margins between autobiography, history, essay, and poetry. By writing *Borderlands* in Chicano Spanish, "a border tongue" that has hybridized English and Spanish into what Anzaldúa calls "*un nuevo lenguaje. Un lenguaje que corresponde a un modo de vivir*" [a new language. A language that corresponds to a lifestyle] (55), she practices a defiant multilingualism that sites itself on the border, at once inside and outside of the cultures that contribute to her hybrid identity.

Both Lorde and Anzaldúa insist on borders that are open, permeable, and shifting. Lorde is adamant in her refusal to let any one identity or difference dominate over the others that make up her plural personality. Despite ostracism from within the lesbian community, Lorde refuses to restrict herself to a given role: neither "butch" nor "femme," "I was given a wide berth," she says. "Non-conventional people can be dangerous, even in the gay community" (*Zami* 224). Ultimately, Lorde finds that her nonconformist position gives her strength:

> Once I accepted my position as different from the larger society as well as different from any single sub-society—Black or gay—I felt I didn't have to try so hard. To be accepted. To look femme. To be straight. To look straight. To be proper. To look "nice." To be liked. To be loved. To be approved. What I didn't realize was how much harder I had to try merely to stay alive, or rather, to stay human. How much stronger a person I became in that trying (181).

Instead of trying to hide their differences from mainstream society, as their mothers did, Lorde and Anzaldúa affirm these differences, using

JENNIFER BROWDY DE HERNANDEZ

them as sources of strength from which to combat the oppressions of the dominant culture. "Difference is that raw and powerful connection from which our personal power is forged," Lorde declares; differences can be used positively as "a fund of necessary polarities between which our creativity can spark like a dialectic" (*Sister Outsider* 111).

From this fund springs their writing, and from their writing grows their power to have an effect on the world. "A woman who writes has power," Anzaldúa says. "I have never seen so much power in the ability to move and transform others as from that of the writing of women of color" ("Speaking" 172). Lorde agrees: "Poetry is not only dream and vision; it is the skeleton architecture of our lives. It lays the foundations for a future of change, a bridge across our fears of what has never been before" (*Sister Outsider* 38).

At the end of *Zami,* Lorde tells the story of Kitty, or Afrekete, a young black mother with whom Lorde has a brief but satisfying affair. Lorde explains in the epilogue that Afrekete is the name of an African goddess, daughter of MawuLisa, "the great mother of us all"; Afrekete is "*her youngest daughter, the mischievous linguist, trickster, best-beloved, whom we must all become*" (255). The character Afrekete is both the solid and sexy woman with whom Lorde has a steamy affair and a figure for the powerful woman writer, whom Anzaldúa calls the nahual—the "mischievous linguist" and "trickster" who can take the master's tool of language and transform it into a feminist weapon in the war against racism, sexism, and homophobia.

Afrekete also stands for Lorde herself as an oppositional writer. In the prologue to *Zami,* Lorde asks, "*To whom do I owe the power behind my voice?*" and she answers her question with a listing of some of the women who have been important to her, culminating with an italicized evocation of Afrekete that ends the prologue and answers the question most completely: "*To the journeywoman pieces of myself. / Becoming. / Afrekete*" (3, 5). By beginning and ending *Zami* with the image of Afrekete, Lorde implies that she has incorporated the subversive (and sexy) trickster into her own identity in the process of writing her autobiography; she has rebirthed herself not only as the collective *Zami* but also as the mischievous, linguist/writer Afrekete, who will reach deep into the often repressed powers of female sexuality to fuel her writing, as Lorde does, for example, in writing the subversive sublime scene of her first menstruation. The figure of Afrekete brings together writing and eroticism, in Lorde's sense of the erotic as "creative energy empowered," "a well of replenishing and provocative force" (*Sister Outsider* 54, 55) and indicates the scope of Lorde's vision of the role of the lesbian writer. "Recognizing the power of the erotic within our lives can give us the energy to pursue genuine change within our world," she writes in "Uses of the Erotic: The Erotic as Power." "For not only do we touch our most profoundly creative source, but we do that which is female and self-affirming in the face of a racist, patriarchal, and anti-erotic society" (*Sister Outsider* 59).

Borderlands ends with a description of what Anzaldúa calls her "*tierra natal,*" the farmland of the Rio Grande valley where Anzaldúa and her family plant seeds that bear "fruit hundreds of times the size of the seed. We water and hoe them. We harvest them. The vines dry, rot, and are plowed under. Growth, death, decay, birth. The soil prepared again and again, impregnated, worked on. A constant changing of forms, *renacimientos de la tierra madre*" (91). Here the female sexuality that Lorde figures in Afrekete is troped through the images of Mother Earth, who must be impregnated and nurtured in order to produce fruit. Drawing on this source of female power, writing her way through the lesbian sublime toward a position of strength and authority, Anzaldúa nurtures herself and the other inhabitants of the Borderlands as she once nurtured the seeds on the land, producing the "fruit" of her own oppositional rewriting of the self.

Lorde also uses the figure of the mother to describe her search for a way of authorizing or authoring herself in a female mode. In "Eye to Eye: Black Women, Hatred, and Anger," Lorde describes her desire to "*mother*" herself, to give birth to herself in the act of rewriting herself as an empowered woman: "We can learn to mother ourselves," she writes. This means that "we must establish authority over our own definition. . . . It means that I affirm my own worth by committing myself to my own survival" (*Sister Outsider* 173). In *Borderlands* and *Zami,* Lorde and Anzaldúa use autobiography as a writerly form of survival, creating a space in which to enact their transformative vision of the self as multiple, heterogeneous, and profoundly woman-oriented. The lesbian sublime moments that punctuate the texts are indications of Anzaldúa's and Lorde's sometimes violent passages through the birth canal of feminist awakening, from which they emerge as strong, independent women capable of writing their own destinies, their own selves. "What I want," writes Anzaldúa, ". . . [is] the freedom to carve and chisel my own face, to staunch the bleeding with ashes, to fashion my own gods out of my entrails. And if going home is denied me then I will have to stand and claim my space, making a new culture—*una cultura mestiza*—with my own lumber, my own bricks and mortar and my own feminist architecture" (22). In *Borderlands* and *Zami,* Anzaldúa and Lorde not only "claim" this space, they *create* it.

NOTES

1. Yaeger paraphrases Hertz's thesis as follows: "According to Hertz . . . the oedipal moment of blockage, as it is staged within the tradition of the sublime, aims at a moment of 'conflict and structure' in which a 'disarrayed sequence is converted to one-on-one confrontation' which confirms 'the unitary status of self' ([Hertz], p. 76). But while what is being repressed, disguised and re-figured is an initial wish for inundation—a primordial desire to bond or fuse with the other—the poet-ego schooled in defending male ego boundaries reacts to this wish for inundation with ambivalence and fear. And this fear can only be mastered through a reaction formation that takes the form of oedipal aggression. This aggression, in turn, arouses anxiety, for the writer responds to his own aggressive desire to appropriate with a surge of guilt, and a feeling that is quickly followed by a gesture of reparation. This reparation is not directed toward the pre-oedipal other—who has already been disguised and denied—but to the oedipalized self/other dyad who wears the father's imago and cries out to be incorporated and internalized. In [Shelley's] 'Mont Blanc' this father-imago, this manmountain, is absorbed into the ego as an assurance (rather than a disruption) of the incorporative self's ego-boundaries" (Yaeger 205).

2. In "Age, Race, Class, and Sex," Lorde calls on women "to identify and develop new definitions of power and new patterns of relating across difference. . . . As Paulo Freire shows so well in *The Pedagogy of the Oppressed,* the true focus of revolutionary change is never merely the oppressive situations which we seek to escape, but that piece of the oppressor which is planted deep within each of us, and which knows only the oppressors' tactics, the oppressors' relationships" (*Sister Outsider* 123).

3. Lorde describes this feeling of dislocation in very similar terms in *Zami:* "I grew up feeling like an only planet, or some isolated world in a hostile, or at best, unfriendly, firmament" (34).

4. Butler's reading of Mary Douglas is also relevant here: "If the body is synechdochal for the social system per se, then any kind of unregulated permeability constitutes a site of pollution and endangerment" (132).

5. Butler, in the influential *Gender Trouble* (1990), castigates Kristeva for her "tactical dismissal and reduction of lesbian experience" (87); Butler contends that Kristeva "describes both the maternal body and lesbian experience from a position of sanctioned heterosexuality that fails to acknowledge its own fear of losing that sanction" (87). In her 1994 volume of essays, *The Practice of Love,* de Lauretis also criticizes Kristeva's work for its "homophobic, heterosexist subtext" (178); "it is difficult to see," de Lauretis concludes, "why any feminist would want to salvage something out of this dismal view of female subjectivity as structured by paranoia, exacerbated masochism, ever-lurking psychosis, and absolute dependence on the fruit of the penis" (180).

6. "Toute nourriture est susceptible de souiller. . . . La nourriture est l'objet oral (cet abject) qui fonde la relation archaïque de l'être humain à l'autre, sa mère" [All food is susceptible to defilement. . . . Food is the oral object (that

abject) which grounds the archaic relationship between the human being and the other, his mother] (Kristeva 91).

7. Edelman points out that while the pre-oedipal sublime may operate "in a theoretically regressive way to affirm identity and thereby constitute a coherent locus of subjectivity under the suspect banner of unity, idealism, and empowerment . . . what is regressive here in theory can still have, given its historical context . . . powerful and progressive force within the politics of gender" (222).

8. Butler identifies the lesbian as, at least potentially, "a being whom neither *man* nor *woman* truly describes. This is not the figure of the androgyne, nor some hypothetical 'third gender,' nor is it a *transcendence* of the binary. Instead, it is an internal subversion in which the binary is both presupposed and proliferated to the point where it no longer makes sense" (127).

9. For an interesting discussion of the relation of black Pentecostal speaking in tongues and black women's writing, see Henderson, "Speaking in Tongues." She argues that "black women writers . . . are modern-day apostles, empowered by experience to speak as poets and prophets in many tongues" (124). Also relevant is Stockton's discussion of "spiritual materialism" in poststructuralist feminist theory; she argues that when poststructuralists "bend back to bodies" they "almost always repeat a Christian spiritual problematic, since they must invest in beliefs in something real that escapes and exceeds human sign systems" (119). My own reading of a "feminine sublime" participates in this paradox, arguing for an oxymoronic "embodied discourse" that exceeds, sublimely, the constraints of language only *through* its return to, and celebration of, the female body. However, it would be unnecessarily recuperative to place Lorde and Anzaldúa in a Christian mystical tradition since they have so obviously tried to find alternative religious traditions through which to (re)construct themselves (i.e., Afrekete and Coatlicue), religion being only one of the many discourses upon which they draw in their autobiographical self-representations.

10. In "Thinking through the Boundary," Kirby offers a useful definition of the difference between "place" and "space." Place "seems to assume set boundaries that one fills to achieve a solid identity. Place settles space into objects, working to reinscribe the Cartesian monad and the autonomous ego. It perpetuates the fixed parameters of ontological categories, making them coherent containers of essences, in relation to which one must be 'inside' or 'out,' 'native' or 'foreign.' . . . If place is organic and stable, space is malleable, a fabric of continually shifting sites and boundaries" (176). Anzaldúa's invocation of the Borderlands as a homeland resists the essentialism of place that Kirby describes: "Living on borders and in margins," Anzaldúa writes, means "keeping intact [her] shifting and multiple identity and integrity" (*Borderlands*, preface, n.p.).

WORKS CITED

Anzaldúa, Gloria. *Borderlands/La Frontera: The New Mestiza*. San Francisco: Aunt Lute, 1987.

———. "La Prieta." *This Bridge Called My Back*. 2d ed. Ed. Moraga and Anzaldúa. 198–209.

———. "Speaking in Tongues: A Letter to Third World Women Writers." *This Bridge Called My Back*. 2d ed. Ed. Moraga and Anzaldúa. 165–74.

Barthes, Roland. *Le plaisir du texte*. Paris: Editions du Seuil, 1973.

Berlant, Lauren, and Elizabeth Freeman. "Queer Nationality." *Boundary 2* 19.1 (1992): 149–80.

Butler, Judith. *Gender Trouble: Feminism and the Subversion of Identity.* New York: Routledge, 1990.

Cixous, Hélène. "The Laugh of the Medusa." Trans. Keith Cohen and Paula Cohen. *New French Feminisms.* Ed. Elaine Marks and Isabelle de Courtivron. New York: Schocken Books, 1981. 245–64.

de Lauretis, Teresa. *The Practice of Love: Lesbian Sexuality and Perverse Desire.* Bloomington: Indiana University Press, 1994.

Diehl, Joanne Feit. "In the Twilight of the Gods: Women Poets and the American Sublime." *The American Sublime.* Ed. Mary Arensberg. Albany: State University of New York Press, 1986. 173–214.

Edelman, Lee. "A Risk in the Sublime: The Politics of Gender and Theory." *Gender and Theory.* Ed. Kauffman. 213–24.

Henderson, Gwendolyn Mae. "Speaking in Tongues: Dialogics, Dialectics, and the Black Woman Writer's Literary Tradition." *Reading Black, Reading Feminist: A Critical Anthology.* Ed. Henry Louis Gates Jr. New York: Meridian, 1990. 116–44.

Hennessy, Rosemary. "Queer Theory: A Review of the *differences* Special Issue and Wittig's *The Straight Mind.*" *Signs* 18 (1993): 964–73.

Hertz, Neil. "The Notion of Blockage in the Literature of the Sublime." *Psychoanalysis and the Question of the Text.* Ed. Geoffrey Hartman. Baltimore: Johns Hopkins University Press, 1978. 62–85.

Kauffman, Linda, ed. *Gender and Theory: Dialogues on Feminist Criticism.* Oxford: Blackwell, 1989.

Kirby, Kathleen M. "Thinking through the Boundary: The Politics of Location, Subjects, and Space." *Boundary 2* 20.2 (1993): 173–89.

Kristeva, Julia. *Pouvoirs de l'horreur* [Powers of horror]. Paris: Editions de Seuil, 1980.

Lorde, Audre. *The Cancer Journals.* San Francisco: Aunt Lute, 1980.

———. *Sister Outsider: Essays and Speeches.* Freedom, Calif.: Crossing Press, 1984.

———. *Zami: A New Spelling of My Name.* Freedom, Calif.: Crossing Press, 1982.

Martin, Biddy. "Lesbian Identity and Autobiographical Differences[s]." *Life/Lines: Theorizing Women's Autobiography.* Ed. Bella Brodzki and Celeste Schenck. Ithaca, N.Y.: Cornell University Press, 1988. 77–103.

Moraga, Cherríe, and Gloria Anzaldúa, eds. *This Bridge Called My Back: Writings by Radical Women of Color.* 2d ed. New York: Kitchen Table/Women of Color Press, 1983.

Phelan, Shane. "(Be)Coming Out: Lesbian Identity and Politics." *Signs* 18 (1993): 765–90.

Stockton, Kathryn Bond. "Bodies and God: Poststructuralist Feminists Return to the Fold of Spiritual Materialism." *Boundary 2* 19.2 (1992): 113–49.

Yaeger, Patricia. "Toward a Female Sublime." *Gender and Theory.* Ed. Kauffman. 191–212.

PART 3

Stretching the Boundaries
of Literary Theory

11 ◇ Like "Reeds through the Ribs of a Basket"

Native Women Weaving Stories

Parade Theory

Over morning coffee in a Michigan bookstore, we are talking about Native literature: reading it, teaching it, theorizing it, living it. We are searching for interpretive ground, a critical center. It doesn't take long to realize that the center inhabits shifting ground, borderland in motion. Mixedblood, margins, crossblood, mixed culture, frontier space. . . . We are pretty serious about the discussion, as serious as you can get about trickster territory, especially before noon. Then Patrick LeBeau talks about that old photo he saw: Indian students from Pratt's infamous Carlisle boarding school marching in a big parade at the 1893 World's Fair and Columbian Exhibition in Chicago. They all carry an instrument or emblem of the trade they have been taught. Tools of the farmer, tailor, carpenter. Carrying hammers and hoes, they are Indians marching into the new era. And here we are, we laugh. A bunch of Indians in an academic parade, marching along with our Ph.D.'s. Degrees held like banners of our own indoctrination.

Do we carry the tools of literary studies that way? Have we naively waved theory like a frat emblem? Are the current theories destructive to the essence of Native literature as were many boarding school teachings to a Native lifestyle? At the least we must admit they are at times and in important ways inhospitable. A full understanding of Native literary traditions cannot flourish when the interpretive theories, the tools of literary analysis, all stem from an other/another cultural and literary aesthetic.

Reading any literature we translate the textual symbols. We reanimate them to give them meaning. But can we translate the hieroglyphs of a Native American system with the interpretive tools of a North American or continental literary or scholastic tradition? For example, the hierograms of Indian expression, the sacred symbols, stem from a particular worldview that attributes to words and sounds a spiritual element. Can we "read" these symbols correctly in a secular literary translation? The pictures we carry of literary forms, along with our glossary of common literary terms, cause us to read in certain ways and not in others. We come to texts with preestablished interpretive systems. Contemporary theory enforces a certain reading of Native literature. It may not necessarily be a false reading. I believe, however, it is incomplete.

Since Indian texts best reflect the cultural center from which they emanate, we would do well to look to the texts themselves for essential cues to reading. As Terry Eagleton suggests, "literary texts are 'code-productive' and 'code-transgressive' as well as 'code-confirming': they may teach us new ways of reading, not just reinforce the ones with which we come equipped" (125). The works of Native American writers both inadvertently and self-consciously embody literary processes and genres unlike those of the old canon. Many Indian authors have chosen purposefully to ignore standard rules and forms ill suited to Native storytelling. They strive to introduce different codes. Their works teach readers and critics new ways of reading and interacting with voices on the page. The work of Native women writers especially carries a new vision as it refuses to separate the literary and academic from the sacred and the daily, as it brings to the text the unpaginated experiences of contemporary tribal reality. Writing by Native women remains infused with supraliterary intentions. As Linda Hogan proclaims in "Neighbors": "This is the truth, not just a poem" (*Savings* 65).

Cultural Contexts

An exploration of works by writers such as Hogan, Diane Glancy, Leslie Marmon Silko, and Marilou Awiakta demonstrates how they both theorize and enact a Native aesthetic of literature and culture. The creative and the critical coexist in contemporary works by these women, just as Dennis Tedlock suggests they do in the traditional oral performances where the "conveyer" also functions as the "interpreter." We get, he says, "the criticism at the same time and from the same person" (47–48). Acknowledging the inherent interpretive elements of much Native literature is not to claim irrelevance for separate critical readings or theoretical discussions of that literature; rather, it is to suggest an important starting point for developing a culturally accurate critical context.

Silko's comments on structure in "Language and Literature from a Pueblo Indian Perspective" provide an example of how such a context might be discovered:

> For those of you accustomed to a structure that moves from point A to point B to point C, this presentation may be somewhat difficult to follow because the structure of Pueblo expression resembles something like a spider's web—with many little threads radiating from a center, crisscrossing each other. As with the web, the structure will emerge as it is made, and you must simply listen and trust, as the Pueblo people do, that meaning will be made. (54)

Aesthetic form, she suggests, has a cultural origin. Only patience and attentiveness allow us to discern the ritual or formal patterns. Furthermore, meaning and design are linked, and no preordained order or pre-established theoretical map will suffice to unlock meaning.

Silko's notion of the web introduces an image of cyclical patterning. While this circularity is perhaps the most frequently recognized aspect of tribal literature, it might also be the most oversimplified. The circle itself takes many forms and therefore involves multiple relationships. The web whose structure Silko identifies as central to Pueblo expression illustrates this complexity, involving as it does a center as well as a complex interweaving of both "radial" and "lateral" strands. In function, the web also involves the relationship between the various elements of construction, the vibration of the web in response to contact—that is, motion.

Our explorations of Native American literature and our search for culturally accurate critical language and approaches should be informed by an understanding of the elements that make up stories but also by the motion of stories, the dynamics of literary expression. Circularity as an aesthetic form has often been examined comparatively against the Western linear model. That examination should also explore the motions these visions enact. Beginning, middle, end; introduction, body, conclusion; rising action, climax, falling action—these classic Western patterns seldom inform the designs of tribal stories. Nor do many of the visual images of Western literature—time *line,* love *triangle, parallel* universe—or the dynamics they suggest. For example, the well-known Lakota author Vine Deloria Jr. talks about the nature and function of Native American poetry: "It is hardly chronological and its sequences relate to the integrity of the circle, not the directional determination of the line. It encompasses, it does not point" (ix). The Laguna tribal writer and scholar Lee Francis proclaims that Native stories are not about "beginning, middle, end" but about "middle, middle, middle."[1] Like a poem that encompasses, a "middle, middle, middle" story has its own kind of choreography: it proceeds with a purpose other than closure and thus encourages a specific kind of audience involvement. Native stories are seldom about separate parallel existences but about intricately linked relationships and intersections. The spatial, temporal, and spiritual realities of Native people reflect a fluidity that disallows complete segregation between experiences of life and death, physical and spiritual, past and present, human and nonhuman. Thus, they are reflected in cycles that involve return, reconnection, and relationship.

Because aesthetic systems originate in cultural systems, any discussion of tribal literary forms must inevitably engage Native beliefs. Paula Gunn Allen is among those tribal writers whose work underscores the link between tribal beliefs and the circular form. She identifies the "sacred hoop" and the "medicine wheel" as central cultural symbols that inform much tribal writing: "The concept is one of singular unity that is dynamic and encompassing, including all that is contained in its most essential aspect, that of life" (56).

The Anishinaabe writer Gordon Henry also offers a rich commentary on the Native form linking the literary and the spiritual.[2] His notion of "sacred concentricity" in Native stories aptly describes the complex dynamics of circularity, whether the actual inspiration for that cyclical vision is a web, a medicine wheel, or another culturally significant image. Henry recognizes in Native life and work a sacred center from which emanate ripples of power and connection. This center (or these centers) are always dynamic, never static, and thus invoke responses that might be return, forgiveness, healing, vision, and so on. This mobile center of consciousness might be a place, a person, or an event; it might reflect the motion of the landscape, of people, of the seasons, or of families or communities.

As this brief discussion highlights, the cyclical patterning in Native American literature implies much more than shapes. The same kind of complexity arises in examinations of orality, genre classifications, and any number of other characteristics of tribal storytelling. Therefore, to develop an interpretive theory about Native literature, the patterns, physical images, and dynamics we identify must be allowed to arise from within the texts themselves, and the theoretical approaches must be flexible enough to take into account the motion of ongoing life and ongoing story. The emerging critical language of Silko, Henry, and Allen explores circularity, "sacred concentricity," or what Louis Owens calls the "centripetal" orientation of Native works (172). Their language begins to express an essential structure and a central aesthetic characteristic of Native literature because it arises from an understanding of the cultural realities of Native peoples as reflected in their own works.

Weaving Theory Story

The complications of both circular form and the critical/creative dynamic in Native literature are clearly exemplified in Marilou Awiakta's *Selu: Seeking the Corn-Mother's Wisdom.* Early in the book, Awiakta offers her readers a guide to understanding the structure and dynamics of her work, providing point blank the physical image we need to discern the movement of her text:

> A round, doublewoven basket in the Oklahoma Cherokee style is this book's natural form, arising from the thoughts themselves. As I worked with the poems, essays and stories, I saw they shared a common base— the sacred law of taking and giving back with respect, of maintaining balance. From there they wove around four themes, gradually assuming a double-sided pattern—one outer, one inner—distinct, yet interconnected in a whole. The outer side became my path to Selu, the inner one was the Corn-Mother herself. The basket image conveys the principle of composition quickly. Reading will be easy if you keep the weaving mode in mind: Over . . . under . . . over . . . under. A round basket never runs "straight-on." (34)

Just as a round basket never runs straight on, neither does the seemingly straightforward form of Awiakta's *Selu.* Although she describes the pattern for us, includes an illustration of such a basket, and follows these with a detailed explanation of the basket's construction, the "bearings" she provides do not in the least make mechanical the movement of her text. The information is not really presented to provide a static structural map on which we might overlay the parts. Instead, it adds a further dimension to our reading and conveys important cultural concepts. The description itself becomes another rich story within the text at the same time as it provides commentary on the purpose and process of storytelling.

The frame story in *Selu* is the personal story of Marilou Awiakta, an Appalachian/Cherokee woman whose childhood was spent on the nuclear reservation of Oak Ridge, Tennessee, and of her search for direction or pattern in her life. It comes to her through the Native stories of Ginitsi Selu, the Corn-Mother, and Ahw'usti, Little Deer, and through a vision that visits her as she stands before the giant model of an atom in the Museum of Science and Energy. The vision returns to Awiakta a sense of centeredness, and she begins to reconcile the multiple threads of her life and to discover the power that might come of their reweaving. She describes her condition before the vision:

> Backlash to civil rights was closing doors to many ethnic groups. The women's movement had not yet changed the general concept of "woman's place." Technology was getting bigger, language more literal and technically oriented. Pollution of the environment was a growing concern. This outer turmoil exacerbated my inner one as I tried to make harmony of my three heritages: Cherokee, Appalachian and scientific. The atom, after all, had been the companion of my childhood and youth. It was part of me, too. And high technology is a culture, with its own worldview, value system and language. I was immeshed in a tangled skein. Like a wire vine, it was shutting me up and shutting me down. Neither I nor my work had a center. (31)

Then came the vision:

> For a long time I stood in front of a giant model of an atom—an enormous, translucent blue ball with tiny lights whirling inside, representing the cloud of electrons. Stars whirling . . . whirling . . . whirling . . . drew me into an altered state of consciousness.
> Suddenly I saw Little Deer leaping in the heart of the atom.
> In that instant, as if irradiated, his story sprouted, shot up and bore fruit. The synapse in my mind electrified. With my whole being I made a quantum leap and connected Little Deer to the web of my life—at the center. The vision was clear. (32)

In the telling of both her confusion and her enlightenment, Awiakta's story reflects her understanding of linked relationships, the complicated weavings of our lives: outer turmoil and inner turmoil; Native heritage, Appalachian heritage, technological heritage; Little Deer "leaping in the heart of the atom," Little Deer "connected . . . to the web of my life." The physical images themselves embody circularity—"a tangled skein," "the web," "the center"—and motion or life—"a wire vine," "stars whirling," "sprouted . . . and bore fruit." And of course, the significant action in the telling is connecting. Awiakta connects technology and tribal story, tribal story and her own life, the physical realities with her spiritual well-being. She suddenly sees their association with one another, the important ways in which one informs the other. Indeed, relatedness is the central reality of the book as a whole. Through tribal stories and Awiakta's personal story, *Selu* addresses our involvement with the world at large: the impact our mode of living has on the health of our environment and our response-ability.

The stories of both Selu (who brings corn to her family but is not given the proper respect by her grandsons and so must leave) and Little

Deer (who devises a ceremony to encourage only responsible hunting) teach about respect, reciprocity, and balance. Awiakta realizes that the same natural law embodied in these stories can provide a guide for our relationship with nuclear energy. She also discovers her own path as a woman and a writer: her response-ability is to bring together her traditional and scientific knowledges and to advocate a reverent, responsible relationship with atomic energy. She undertakes this task not merely by protesting instances of environmental destruction but by seeking to reeducate her fellow/sister humans in their very process of thinking, by suggesting reorientation of our most basic relationships. And she approaches this Herculean task through the gentle art of storytelling.

The stories in *Selu* are about the diversity in corn, about the burning man who didn't give the proper respect to fire, about the Cherokee working to save Tellico Dam. They are also about how we think, how we tell our stories, and how we live them: like a basket with "ribs . . . centered and held in balance," like a corn seed whose "energy is concentrated and evokes a reality beyond the surface," or like a path that "weaves and spirals" through "the mountains" just as "reeds through the ribs of a basket" (35, 21, 27). Like her Cherokee elders before her, Marilou Awiakta "plants a story" and fills her book with "seed-thoughts" (15, 37). She weaves together the activity and the analysis of storytelling.

The richness of the many stories, the complexity of thought, and the intricacy of design ultimately cannot be summarized but must be discovered for themselves. Yet the central impetus behind *Selu* is readily identifiable as engagement. Awiakta invites her readers to become involved in the process of connecting her stories and ideas about stories with her life, so that ultimately they may make their own "quantum leap" beyond the book into life:

> Although this book contains my seed-thoughts about survival and the Corn-Mother, as you gather them up, please add your own. Contemplate the value of your heritage, remember the stories that are meaningful to you, underline, write responses in the margin, tuck between the pages clippings and notes of other survival wisdoms you've found. Make this *our* book.
>   . . . At the end of our journey, when we've gathered all the ears, we'll ease off beyond the confines of print and paper to a place that exists only in our minds. (38)

Awiakta begins *Selu* by describing how the story of corn has been separated from the physical reality of corn-as-food. She then immerses us in the tellings of corn as mother, enabler, transformer, and healer, and she suggests the multiple relationships among these tellings. By the time the book "eases off" the paper, few readers will ever be able to see corn as merely an "it" again. By teaching us about "the whole corn—the grain and its story, its sacred meaning," she has shown us new ways of thinking about story and the connections of story (20). This reorientation of our thinking—the reconnection of being, story, and spirit—she means us to carry into our lives, into understanding other relationships, into healing other relationships. If we truly understand connection and interdependence, we will (of necessity if not nicely) develop respect for other beings and replace our notion of it-ness. The wisdom of Selu will be ours: "Corn and all that lives are imbued with spirit and . . . a reciprocal relationship is crucial to survival" (20).

Selu launches itself by connecting with its readers who are "rushing through the high-tech world," are "used to literal language," and "want the facts—fast!" (xiv). Awiakta opens the book by playful imitation of contemporary communication. She sends her readers a fax (facsimile) invitation to read the book. She gives the reasons in two lines: "So we won't die. / Neither will Mother Earth" (xv). From that self-consciously "straightforward introduction," the book begins to weave its story about Selu, a "long and winding" story in which "essays/stories/poems interweave in a pattern" (xiv, xv). But throughout the telling it keeps circling back to its readers and their expectations. It offers explanations of its own method: "The arts are not about facts. They are about creating images and mental connections. . . . Revealing spiritual truths, not facts, is the purpose of Selu's story" (15–16). The book teases participation from readers and proclaims: "The language is intimate, for in the primal mind there is *no psychic distance* between the singer and the song; listeners share the web of context and experience" (168). Finally, Awiakta eases the story off the page assured that her vision has been shared, her readers transformed as clearly as she herself has been by Selu. She believes the stories have given the participants "a synapse in the mind, a lens in the eye, a drum in the ear and a rhythm in the heart" (326).

A reading of *Selu* teaches as much about Native literary tradition as it does about the lessons of corn. The two, after all, must exist together. As Awiakta explains, "Take away its cultural context, cut out its spiritual heart—as many people do who are unaware or unmindful of Native storytelling tradition—and . . . you have an archaic legend. . . . And a legend carries no spiritual imperative to change one's behavior" (16). The literary arts in Native tradition are woven together with the art of living. The origins of stories are as important as their performance. The outcomes of their performance are as important as the act. And the continuation of storytelling in its wholeness is one of the major goals of Native literature because only the telling ensures the continuation of proper living. Thus, the meaning in *Selu* is made not only in the story but also in the theory of story. Awiakta provides both. And we need both to access the power, to know for ourselves the ongoing life of story.

Revolve-lutions in Theory

Awiakta is but one of many contemporary Indian women to weave together story and theory in their work, but one voice trying to retain the Native contexts of stories in written form and in contemporary lives. Similarly, Leslie Marmon Silko's mixed genre collection *Storyteller* describes from many angles the tradition of Laguna storytelling and continues the art. The book contains various keys to understanding the methods and purposes of the oral tradition. Indeed, in places *Storyteller* can be read as a commentary on itself. Through the voices of the characters in "The Storyteller's Escape," Silko links story and survival: "With these stories of ours / we can escape almost anything / with these stories we will survive" (247). Whether in telling about her Aunt Susie or in remarking on her conversation with Nora, Silko explores dilemmas of moving from the oral to the written. In stories such as "Yellow Woman," the fictional situation illuminates our position as both readers and storytellers as the protagonist ponders her relationship to the old stories, their meanings and realities. As *Storyteller* weaves together poems, conversations, photos, and fiction, it becomes in many ways an examination of the issues of storytelling.

In a similar way, the Cherokee mixed-blood Diane Glancy offers a story of writing and the writing life in *Claiming Breath*. In the book, Glancy claims integrity for her own story (which is not the romantic story of a modern-day Indian princess), validity for her own mixed blood, mixed cultural understanding of the literary and creative process, and a place for her work in the larger canon of literary works. Throughout the text, which collapses the experiences of a lifetime into a journal of one year, Glancy presents various theories on writing. Her comments offer a basis for reading her work and serve to illuminate the larger Native literary tradition. In a section entitled "Enucleation," for example, she discusses "points of clarity on the subject of poetry" (74). Here she claims that "good lines" should be "epicyclic": "They should be on their own, while hinging on the larger process of the poem. The dictionary definition of epicyclic [is] 'a circle in which a planet moves & which has a center that is itself carried around at the same time on the circumference of a larger circle.' In other words, the line of a poem has its own orbit, yet moves within the purpose of the larger orbit of the poem" (74–75).

These ideas, of course, have important connections to the previously recognized Native aesthetic of circularity, both spiritual and literary. Glancy's comments on writing throughout the book reinforce a reading of the passage as applicable to writing *and* life. When she states, for example, that "the poet heals & clarifies &, yes, even creates" the "world" (75), her theoretical stance involves the supraliterary intentions of writing and a belief in the power of words. In a section entitled "Dance Lessons with the Spirit World," where Glancy again explores the purposes and processes of speech and writing, she makes a clear statement about the power of spoken words: "What I say gives meaning to what I say it to" (101). *Claiming Breath* includes many other discussions about writing and reading, including a long section on the Native oral tradition, a how-to guide to writing poetry, and comments on the migrations of a Native literary aesthetic. Glancy's territory on this literary journey clearly crosses the border into theory.

Like Glancy, Linda Hogan reclaims the interpretive privilege for Native writing within her creative work. Hogan's revolutionary voice opposes any attempt to colonize identity or literature. In "Left Hand Canyon," she decries the theft of language identity: "You can't take a man's words / They are his even as the land / is taken away." And she reclaims identity, speech, and writing: "If his words were taken from him, / I'm giving them back. / These words / if you listen / they are real. / These words, / a hand has written them" (*Red Clay* 32). Here and elsewhere Hogan insists upon the power of presence in Native literature and the prerogative both to speak and to have the speech known in its own context. In her poem "Naming the Animals," for example, she criticizes the biblical Adam's presumptuous naming of the animals "as if they had not been there / before his words, had not / had other tongues and powers / or sung themselves into life / before him" (*Book* 40). Just as clearly, she opposes the "naming" of Native people and Native literature. In "Workday," she writes:

> Now I go to the University
> and out for lunch
> and listen to the higher-ups
> tell me all they have read
> about Indians
> and how to analyze this poem.
>
> (*Savings* 43)

Hogan challenges this presumption of superior understanding and, like Awiakta, Silko, and Glancy, asserts the "stolen powers" of Native Americans: "All things know the names for themselves / and no man speaks them / or takes away their tongue" (*Book* 40–41). Indian people "speak" themselves, and their speaking carries its own cultural context. Only from within that context can we understand and accurately theorize Native voices.

Reading Indian Voices Speaking

The voice in American Indian literature is very often literally that: the sound of Indian people talking. The sound of singing. The sound of an Indian language. Conversation. Words for speaking, not for print. Or transformation into the being of other creatures. The voices of other beings. Traditional myths intermingled with contemporary story. Contemporary story told in a nonlinear fashion. The interweaving of the realities of this world and time with that of other worlds and other times. The transgressing of the boundaries of genre. The use of the circle as an aesthetic form instead of the use of a straight line. The refusal to write an end to story because story always continues. The creating of characters whose beliefs and actions violate certain standards of morality or good taste. The telling of history from a Native perspective. The telling of history from the perspective of the planet rather than the perspective of humankind. Or . . . not writing. Not writing down all the words so that the reader has a role to play in helping the story come into being. Not explaining "logically" in cause and effect but believing in the chance of life and the chance of story. Things just happen sometimes. No because.

Not writing black and white, red and white, up and down, rich and poor, good and bad, spirit and flesh. Not writing either/or because sometimes the real truth is either/and, both/and. Not writing sense. Writing reality. Not writing literature. Writing revolution. Not writing literature. Writing life.

Indian women's voices, speaking, creating, taking shape, shaping the world, coming into being. Hearing voices now wherever we go. Indian voices. Tribal voices. Weaving stories.

Voices. Writing voices speaking. Voices.

NOTES

1. From Francis's comments during a panel discussion at Wordcraft Circle conference, "Bridges to Community: From Homeplace to Cyberspace," University of Memphis, Oct. 1995.

2. From conversations with Henry about his notion of "sacred concentricity" and from his comments in a lecture at the University of Wisconsin, Milwaukee, 1992.

WORKS CITED

Allen, Paula Gunn. *The Sacred Hoop: Recovering the Feminine in American Indian Traditions.* Boston: Beacon, 1986.

Awiakta, Marilou. *Selu: Seeking the Corn-Mother's Wisdom.* Golden, Colo.: Fulcrum Publishing, 1993.

Deloria, Vine, Jr. "Foreword." *New and Old Voices of Wah'kon-tah: Contemporary Native American Poetry.* Ed. Robert K. Dodge and Joseph B. McCullough. New York: International Publishers, 1985. ix–x.

Eagleton, Terry. *Literary Theory: An Introduction.* Minneapolis: University of Minnesota Press, 1983.

Glancy, Diane. *Claiming Breath.* Lincoln: University of Nebraska Press, 1992.

Hogan, Linda. *The Book of Medicines.* Minneapolis: Coffee House Press, 1993.

———. *Red Clay: Poems and Stories.* Greenfield Center, N.Y.: Greenfield Review Press, 1991.

———. *Savings.* Minneapolis: Coffee House Press, 1988.

Owens, Louis. *Other Destinies: Understanding the American Indian Novel.* Norman: University of Oklahoma Press, 1992.

Silko, Leslie Marmon. "Language and Literature from a Pueblo Indian Perspective." *English Literature: Opening Up the Canon, 1979.* Ed. Leslie A. Fiedler and Houston A. Baker. Baltimore: Johns Hopkins University Press, 1981. 54–72.

———. *Storyteller.* New York: Seaver Books, 1981.

Tedlock, Dennis. "The Spoken Word and the Work of Interpretation in American Indian Religion." *Traditional American Indian Literatures.* Ed. Karl Kroeber. Lincoln: University of Nebraska Press, 1981. 45–64.

12 ◇ Heaven's Bottom

Anal Economics and the Critical
Debasement of Freud in
Toni Morrison's *Sula*

A Catalog of Bottoms, Toilets, and Asses:
"Good Taste Is Out of Place in the Company of Death"

The Bottom—"a nigger joke"—"that part of town where the Negroes lived, the part they called the Bottom in spite of the fact that it was up in the hills." (Morrison, *Sula* 4)

"In the toilet water [Shadrack] saw [his] grave black face." (13)

The toilets for COLORED WOMEN were not in the stationhouse but in "a field of high grass." (23–24)

Nel's mother "gazed at her daughter's wet buttocks." (27)

In the "darkness and freezing stench" of the outhouse, Eva "turned [her] baby over on her knees, exposed his buttocks and shoved the last bit of food she had in the world (besides three beets) up his ass." (34)

As "Sula ran into the house to go to the toilet," she heard her mother say that she loved but didn't like her daughter. (56–57)

"Even from the rear Nel could tell that it was Sula and that she was smiling." (85)

After catching Sula making love with her husband, Nel sought out the bathroom and "sank to the tile floor next to the toilet." (107)

"They killed, as best they could, the tunnel they were forbidden to build"; "but in their need to kill it all . . . they went too deep, too far. . . . A lot of them died [in the tunnel]." (161–62)

By 1965, "the Bottom had collapsed"; black people "who had made money during the war moved as close as they could to the valley" while whites with money had moved up into the hills to build television stations and a golf course; the blacks who moved down couldn't afford to move back up the Bottom. (165–66)

Sadistic Truthtelling: "Tucked Up There in the Bottom"

Nothing prepares for the precipice of *Sula*. Its jeopardy is an ecstasy that makes the body's excretions count for more than coins. Its terror is the tunneled, imploded delight of backing into histories that require rear views. Simply: *Sula* is fixed on the anus and the violence of piercing it.

What shall we make of this novel, in which black women in particular are portrayed as the penetrators of the novel's black men? More troubling still, this is a book—like Morrison's other books—in which cruel events are lyrically rendered, as if the most violent moments of the narrative lay plans to give pleasure. Is this lyricism sadomasochistic, and is it tied to this novel's anal bent?[1]

Inspired by her dangers, I risk two claims. Morrison dares to value "debasement." She "debases" Sigmund Freud (which means, by the altering logic I will trace, that she dares to value him). Borrowing upon investments in debasement, Morrison strains to the point of rupture Christian theology's central tenet: what the world puts "low" God raises "high." Morrison's peculiar challenge to this view runs this doctrine around the literal and metaphorical rim of the rectum. She even exposes herself to the danger of shackling blacks to representations that have dogged their determined flight from oppressions: images of a people stalled in the assholes of U.S. economies. She further risks joining hands with a master *while* she debases him. In hazarding association with Freud (I don't know how consciously), Morrison (advertently or not) cuts in on debates about critical theory's (lack of) value for reading "black" fictions.[2]

I will delay explaining these assertions and thus stall unfolding "debasement" in its rich array of positive valuations. But I can say this: To debase Freud is to respect his claims enough to bend them against the sense of the civilization(s) he embraced (though with ambivalence). To debase Freud is to credit his accounts of feces as coins but to make more sorrowful what he felt some necessity to celebrate: *how the bottom was lost.*

I am speaking, of course, as if Morrison bears intentions toward Freud. Though critical correctness would suggest that I speak of *Sula,* not Morrison, as making moves on Freudian claims, I choose, instead, to name *Sula*'s bundle of interpretive possibilities "Toni Morrison." I wish in this way to emphasize Morrison's parity with Freud as a theorist (and historian) of anal matters, thus according her the pride of place and agency still reserved for theorists but seldom now for novelists (unlike authors, theorists are not dead). "Morrison" is my name for how *Sula* confronts me in the complications of my own productions, as I am made to sift the loam of *Sula*'s history. Morrison draws us into the dark of her narrative tunnel, making us feel a powerlessness in the face of her story, so piercing of a vigilance against anality.

Here, indeed, with her fondness for the Bottom, Morrison can accomplish queer crossings—especially now, against the vivid backdrop of AIDS, which has bound together black and gay communities by disproportionately striking both (not to mention the AIDS epidemic on the African continent).[3] *Sula* is timely for salving the sorrows of those "stricken" groups most associated, in the public imagination, with the anus. Morrison even directly brings black women into this fold by portraying female orgasm (to take one example) as a species of anal erotism. In fact, it is precisely the dominant culture's stand against anality that Morrison humiliates by her rich attachment to Heaven's Bottom. This attachment seems her way of *preserving* a theology traditionally dear to black communities even while making it newly recess. But make no mistake, Morrison is clearly tucking rage into corners of her narrative, and like her old woman character Eva, who runs "her finger around the crevices and sides of the lard can," Morrison is rimming a ring of trouble, lodging us deep in the fat of her concerns.

We are ready to take our first view of the Bottom. The novel begins:

> In that place, where they tore the nightshade and blackberry patches from their roots to make room for the Medallion City Golf Course, there was once a neighborhood. It stood in the hills above the valley town of Medallion and spread all the way to the river. It is called the suburbs now, but when black people lived there it was called the Bottom. . . . Just a nigger joke. The kind white folks tell when the mill closes down and they're looking for a little comfort somewhere. The kind colored folks tell on themselves when the rain doesn't come, or comes for weeks, and they're looking for a little comfort somehow. (3–5)

The black folks in *Sula* live "up" in the Bottom, "above" Medallion—a town whose name bears the trace of "coin." These reversed relations, bottoms above medallions, comfort town conventions, nonetheless, by forming only the threat of a joke. A "nigger joke": A white farmer had tricked a slave into taking hill land, in payment for some difficult chores. This sadistic trickster had convinced the slave that the hill land was "'the bottom of heaven—best land there is'"—"'High up from us,' said the master, 'but when God looks down, it's the bottom.' . . . Which accounted for the fact that white people lived on the rich valley floor in that little river town in Ohio, and the blacks populated the hills above it, taking small consolation in the fact that every day they could literally look down on the white folks. Still, it was lovely up in the Bottom" (5). If, as Freud said, jokes tell aggressive truths, this "nigger joke" besets us at the start with Morrison's own sadistic truthtelling.[4]

What *is* the truth about the Bottom? Coyly, *Sula* claims that the Bottom is "up." This is true in a geographical sense. The Bottom also inclines up in terms of the Christian theological paradigm of downward mobility: the doctrine according to which God descends from Heaven as a servant, proclaiming to His fold that the last shall be first. The Bottom rises "up" again in terms of the sexual rise (sexual orgasm) that the novel depicts as a form of reaching bottom—a movement, downward, into the soft ecstasy of loam. Confessing caution, even so, Morrison warns that the Bottom is "not up": in relation to the white economy, it is literally downwardly mobile, and later, at the end, the Bottom collapses (becomes "white") when the land becomes valuable and rich white folks from the valley move up. In fact, even from the start, one notes how this novel positions black folks outside the white capitalist complex, linking whites to the mill but blacks to the Bottom and its anal economy. Morrison thus succeeds in displaying, unbraiding, a knot that many fail to see as a tangle: Reaching bottom is theologically enjoined, sexually pleasurable, but economically dangerous for marginalized people.

Black history, of course, has told part of this story (e.g., Franklin; Foner). Black economic progress makes for a sad tale that, if it were a novel, would be noted for its repetitive events and remarkably nonrising plot structure. One repeated narrative riff concerns white promises of employment or participation in unions; migration, or mobilization of blacks to grasp the promise; withdrawal of the promise by white capitalists *and* unions; and the consequent unemployment of blacks. In literary terms, this history is a "bad read." Fixed to the bottom, black workers' labor history has traditionally amounted to a *non*labor history, a story of struggle to gain the "privilege" of being exploited.[5]

Morrison's novel knows this nonrising plot structure well. *Sula's* plot bottoms out in the end the way it begins but with one exception: by the end of the novel (1965) even the richness of bottom values is being lost by a generation that (black nationalist pride aside) has moved toward whiter values without dramatic economic gain.[6] This generation has cut a path to whiteness but lost its contact with a Bottom that is "up": the only bottom they know is the valley, but by the time they have moved down, whites have moved up, and the Bottom is only, truly down. This story of how the Bottom was lost *requires* that Morrison play anal historian and write the sadistic fiction that bruises readers of *Sula*. Written in the early seventies and published in 1973, *Sula* bears the stamp of the Nixon fallout of the federal programs and promises initiated by LBJ. It is a story also tinged with the postwar unemployment blues for black men who returned from Vietnam.

If we should not be perplexed that Morrison already at the start concludes that the black Bottom collapsed, neither should we wonder why she commences with 1919 (all of her chapter titles are dates). For 1919 marks a crucial period toward the end of blacks' Great Migration from South to North during World War I, a migration that established a black industrial working class and an efflorescence of black hopes for livelihoods. The motif of promise and letdown figures here (and perhaps forms the structure of another "nigger joke"): lured from the South by "glowing reports of the high wages and better social conditions in the 'Negro Heaven' north of the Mason-Dixon line" (Foner 130), blacks found that labor opportunities disappeared with the end of the war, confirming their position at this Heaven's bottom.[7] With soldiers returning, employers replaced working blacks with white veterans, though black servicemen found no work.[8]

Morrison's autopsy on the Bottom begins in earnest, we shall see, with a black man who returns from World War I only to be "tucked up there in the Bottom" where black men discover the passivity of unemployment. How fitting for his place in this anal economy, where he finds himself stalled, that this black man discovers his "grave" black face in the toilet bowl's water.

Theoretical Coins: "The Gold Which the Devil Gives His Paramours Turns into Excrement"

As we explore this postmortem on the bottom, it is hard to ignore that other chronicler of anal erotism, Freud, whose theories on anality have migrated so successfully into popularized versions of anal-retentive personality types and a child's pleasure in producing its "presents." In *Sula's* world, black communal life is figuratively bound to a Freudian fascination: the obsessions, repressions, and expressions of anal economies in relation to the dominant order. Remarkably, given the dominant culture's stance against it, Morrison comes down on the side of the Bottom and on the side of those whom she represents as having *retained* anal erotism into adult life. Could Morrison be writing *Sula* so as to upend the negative cultural judgments grounding Freud on bottom values?

I have backed, once again, into my claims. Curiously, at this point, a Freudian theorist of gay male sex can help me dramatize why Morrison must value debasement and yet debase theorists such as Freud. In his fraught piece, "Is the Rectum a Grave?," Leo Bersani presses the nerve of debasement's value. I point particularly to Bersani's conclusion that sex can valuably shatter the self rather than "phallicize the ego":

> Phallocentrism is exactly that: not primarily the denial of power to women (although it has obviously also led to that, everywhere and at all times), but above all the denial of the *value* of powerlessness in both men and women. I don't mean the value of gentleness, or nonaggressiveness, or even of passivity, but rather of a more radical disintegration and humiliation of the self. For there is finally, beyond the fantasies of bodily power and subordination that I have just discussed, a transgressing of that very polarity which . . . may be the profound sense of both certain mystical experiences and of human sexuality. . . . Freud keeps returning to a line of speculation in which the opposition between pleasure and pain becomes irrelevant, in which the sexual emerges as the *jouissance* of exploded limits, as the ecstatic suffering into which the human organism momentarily plunges when it is "pressed" beyond a certain threshold of endurance. (217)

For a "general public," this troubling view of *sex as that which debases the self* is starkly symbolized by the sex act commonly associated with gay men: anal penetration. Even as far back as the Greeks, "to be penetrated is to abdicate power." "The only 'honorable' sexual behavior," Bersani writes, quoting Michel Foucault, " 'consists in being active, in dominating, in penetrating, and in thereby exercising one's authority' " (212). Domination and the will to exercise authority—presumed masculine (and white) pursuits—are demeaned in depictions of anal penetration. This is why these relations are feared and, according to Bersani, should be embraced. Bersani again:

> But what if we said, for example, not that it is wrong to think of so-called passive sex as "demeaning," but rather that *the value of sexuality itself is to demean the seriousness of efforts to redeem it?* "AIDS," [Simon] Watney writes, "offers a new sign for the symbolic machinery of repression, making the rectum a grave." . . . But if the rectum is the grave in which the masculine ideal (an ideal shared—differently—by men *and* women) of proud subjectivity is buried, then it should be celebrated for its very potential for death. Tragically, AIDS has literalized that potential as the certainty of biological death, and has therefore reinforced the heterosexual association of anal sex with a self-annihilation originally and primarily identified with the fantasmatic mystery of an insatiable, unstoppable female sexuality. It may, finally, be in the gay man's rectum that he demolishes his own perhaps otherwise uncontrollable identification with a murderous judgment against him. (222)

Clearly, Bersani's celebrations are dangerous. He only hints at the dangers for women involved in the "joys" of powerlessness and does not consider African Americans' representational fix as America's "bottom" class. My demurs not aside, I confess that Bersani holds me in sway because Morrison, elaborately, runs his risks. She *out*runs his risks. Morrison's black women become the anal penetrators of the novel's black men, not for love of domination but for reasons of empowering or releasing from suffering black male bodies on the bottom. By penetrating black men, Morrison's women reinforce why, being people of and for the bottom, blacks must demolish in rectal graves their "own perhaps otherwise uncontrollable identification with a murderous [white] judgment against [them]." *Sula's* black women, in their roles as anal penetrators, actively warn against the *loss* of bottom locations and stimulations, since these may be valued for their coinage in partially alternate economies. Thus, the novel implies—insists—that these women are brilliant at making waste count in the eyes of Heaven.

Can critical theories that in their origins are largely European, largely white, assist us with this riddle?[9] In her widely reprinted article, "The Race for Theory," Barbara Christian voices concern that critical theories are not supple enough to speak to an African American literature that seemingly has "the possibilities of rendering the world as large and as complicated as I experienced it, as sensual as I knew it was" (52). For Christian, "people of color have always theorized—but in forms quite different from the Western form of abstract logic"—"in narrative forms, in the stories we create, in riddles and proverbs, in the play with language, since dynamic rather than fixed ideas seem more to our liking" (52). "Theory," to her mind, even that forged by the Black Arts Movement of the 1960s, has been unrightfully "exalted" (Christian's term) over the fictions of black women and men. The words "devalue," "denigrate," and "discredit" pepper Christian's essay as she expresses anger over Western "philosophers'" power "to determine the ideas that we deemed valuable" (52). In this struggle over value, Christian wants to raise "black" fictions from a "low" designation ("denigrated" as political or just ignored) to a valued designation as a theorizing force, shattering the grip that a certain version of (white) theory holds.[10]

Taking to heart Christian's complaints, I propose that rather than exalting or avoiding "critical theories," we should, for a time, purposefully, explicitly, complexly *debase* them. By this I mean make their "high" theoretical moves lean "low" (I speak of their assigned positions not their actual values) *and so reveal their limits* by tucking their claims into contexts bound to trouble them. In this way, what Christian calls their "pallid" or "self-indulgent" qualities may stand apparent.

Yet there is a surprising twist to the "critical debasement" I propose: If Freud turns to shit in the face of black fiction, does his fall, his inadequacy to the anguish Morrison poses, devalue the importance of Freudian theory for reading black novels? The value, to the contrary, may reside *precisely in the debasement,* in what Morrison *makes visible* by folding Freud's claims into a bottom that she, unlike he, unambiguously champions. Clearly, debasement is no easy matter, especially if excrement proves part golden after all, as Freud entertains.[11] Indeed, as if in a cultural exchange, Morrison trades on the familiarity of Freudian notions, particularly feces as a kind of coin, in order to script an anal economy. More striking still, revealing the limits of Freudian thought for mapping black gender relations, Morrison reverses Freud's expectations.

Let me now schematize Freud on anality so that her reshiftings of Freud may emerge:

> Only by the help of psychoanalytic investigation of the neuroses has it become possible to penetrate so far back and to discover these still earlier phases of libido-development. . . . In this early period a loose sort of organization exists which we shall call *pre-genital;* for during this phase it is not the genital component-instincts, but the *sadistic* and *anal,* which are most prominent. The contrast between *masculine* and *feminine* plays no part as yet; instead of it there is the contrast between *active* and *passive,* which may be described as the forerunner of the sexual polarity with which it also links up later. That which in this period seems masculine to us, regarded from the stand-point of the genital phase, proves to be the expression of an impulse to mastery, which easily passes over into cruelty. ("Development" 336)

Freud sees the contrast masculine/feminine as not yet actuated but only foreshadowed in the pregenital phase, augured through the opposition active/passive. Although Freud states that "the contrast between masculine and feminine plays no part as yet," he nonetheless "links" masculinity to activity and, specifically, to mastery and cruelty. In effect, Morrison reverses Freud's relations so as to untie the Gordian relationship of black men and women to black and white economies. To loosen this knot, she must join black women to cruel-seeming mastery while binding black males to forms of passivity.

Morrison bends Freud's claims, furthermore, against the dominant order to which he reconciled patients. Back to Freud:

> The outer world first steps in as a hindrance at this point, a hostile force opposed to the child's desire for pleasure. . . . To induce him to give up these sources of pleasure he is told that everything connected with these functions is "improper," and must be kept concealed. In this way he is first required to exchange pleasure for value in the eyes of others. His

own attitude to the excretions is at the outset very different. . . . Even af-ter education has succeeded in alienating him from these tendencies, he continues to feel the same high regard for his "presents" and his "money." ("Sexual Life" 324)

"The outer world"—the dominant economy, one might say—invades the child's pleasure and demands not only that pleasure be exchanged for value but that anal pleasure be repressed as "improper." Even so, one's assimilation into dominant educations does not eliminate bottom pleasures, so that feces as an alternate coin (or medallion) may still count for something. One can see that if bottom values vitalize Morrison, then anality must receive its due in *Sula*. Morrison must valorize excretion as production and valorize, also, the mastery and cruelty that attend anality. Freud's own judgments concerning anality are caught in their ambivalence in a curious comment, made when he wrote a preface to John G. Bourke's *Scatologic Rites of All Nations:* "Men have chosen to evade the predicament by so far as possible denying the very existence of this inconvenient 'trace of the Earth.' . . . The wiser course would un-doubtedly have been to admit it and to make as much improvement in it as its nature would allow" ("Excretory Functions" 220). What would constitute this "improvement" Freud does not say.

Here is a final set of points from Freud: There are roughly three paths with regard to anal erotism, and these are spelled out in his essay "Char-acter and Anal Erotism" and in two of his introductory lectures on psy-choanalysis ("Aspects of Development and Regression: Aetiology" and "The Paths of Symptom-Formation"). For the sake of clarity, I call these paths regression, sublimation, and expression.

REGRESSION

Failure to "migrate" "successfully" past the anal phase leads to a fixation of the anal impulse that may predispose the libido to turn back "when the exercise of its function in a later and more developed form meets with powerful external obstacles, which thus prevent it from attaining the goal of satisfaction" ("Aspects" 350). Regression of the libido to the anal stage, along with repression, frequently forms an obsessional neu-rosis, in which symptoms substitute for the missing satisfaction but symptoms also convert satisfaction "into a sensation of suffering" ("Paths" 374).

Folding Freud into black American history, I find his opposition be-tween "success" at "migration" and "arrest" through "fixation" richly evocative of Morrison's lament. Freud's discussion of "powerful external obstacles" that impede "progress" toward "the goal," and that substitute "suffering" for "satisfaction," makes regression to an anal fixation sound like Morrison's Bottom history: migrations that have featured more arrests than success. Freud even offers two analogies to "inhibited development" that veer, strikingly, in Morrison's direction. First, he makes analogy to the vicissitudes of "migrating people," "small groups or bands" who "halted on the way, and settled down in . . . stopping-places, while the main body went further"; then, switching to physiology, he compares inhibited development to the *sometimes impeded migrations* of "the seminal glands" in higher mammals, "which are originally located deep in the abdominal cavity, [and which] begin a movement at a certain period of intra-uterine development which brings them almost under the skin of the pelvic extremity" ("Aspects" 349). When we meet Morrison's black male characters we must remember these analogies to psychic stalling—how Freud associates a people's stalled migration with the impeded migration of the seminal glands from their position "deep in the abdominal cavity."

Freud even brings regression into close proximity with debasement when he states emphatically: "In reality, wherever archaic modes of thought have predominated or persisted—in the ancient civilizations, in myths, fairy-tales and superstitions, in unconscious thinking, in dreams and in neuroses—money is brought into the most intimate relation with dirt" ("Character" 174). Rounding out the implications of regression as a journey back to more "primitive" stopping places or to "arrests" in intrauterine development, Freud later invokes "the word 'regression' in its general sense": that is, "reversion from a higher to a lower stage of development" ("Aspects" 351). His association of "excrement" with things "archaic" and "low" shows why Morrison's bottom values risk offense. His penchant for "improvement" shows why Morrison must debase him. In staking her claim with and for the bottom, Morrison seeks to invert entrenched cultural judgments about regression and, by implication, about debasement.

SUBLIMATION AND EXPRESSION

In contrast to regression, sublimation affirms the dominant values Morrison humiliates. Specifically, according to Freud, sublimation *redirects* a particular aim: *the aim to make money takes over for anal erotism.* As part of the development demanded by civilization, says Freud, shame, disgust, and morality are formed at the expense of anal excitations. Cleanliness, then, is a reaction-formation "against an interest in what is unclean and disturbing and should not be part of the body" ("Character" 172). The character traits of orderliness, miserliness, and obstinacy result from the sublimation of anal erotism. Conversely, those individuals who retain

anal erotism into adulthood and therefore express, rather than sublimate, anal interests do *not* show signs of anal character. By courtesy of
anal expressions, "no neurosis results; the libido succeeds in obtaining a
real, although not a normal satisfaction" ("Paths" 368). By "normal" society's standards, Freud continues, one who does not fall ill from expressing anal interests is, nonetheless, "perverse."[12] In Freud, this person is usually a homosexual; in *Sula,* it is Sula herself.

What interests me here is the way in which the character traits of sublimation (orderliness/miserliness/obstinacy) sound like a ticket to participation in the reigning white economy, whereas regression to and expression of anal interests sound like ties to the bottom values Morrison
affirms for black communities. We will see how these paths relate to
Morrison's development of characters. But first I will explain why Morrison, responsive to economic straits, must reverse Freud's expectation
that activity, at the anal stage, foreshadows masculinity, while passivity
adumbrates femininity.

The Bourgeoisie and the Hard Bottom Class: "We're a Typical White Family That Happens to Be Black"

Knowingly, Morrison sees this pair—masculine activity, feminine passivity—as the middle-class coupling of a white world anxious to flee its
bottom. Though she, as much as anyone, understands "the pain of being black" (the title of her interview with *Time* in 1989), Morrison refuses
to join the dominant order's plan to lure (but also shame) black families
into prescribed relations. Her refusal leads her to a lamentation different
from those who decry black men's "feminization" and the "devastating" outcome of the "female-headed home." For what Morrison mourns
is the reign of *white* gender: how it seduces blacks away from what she
depicts as the Bottom's communal bonds into the tight configuration of
the couple, how it courts; then jilts, the expectations of black men and
women.

Customarily, feminists have defined masculinity as access to the control of both capital and women (Delphy). But as numerous commenta-
tors have pointed out, problems emerge for extending this definition to
black men, for whom masculinity cannot so easily be defined along the
axis of economic power. Black masculinity cracks in early studies as diverse as the *Moynihan Report on the Negro Family* and Robert Staples's
Black Masculinity: The Black Male's Role in American Society. Staples's sociological study reveals the strain of fitting black men into (white) male supremacy. The dilemma for the "black man," according to Staples, involves his ability to "sire" children through "sexual adventures" (these

are Staples's terms) but his inability to provide for them once he "sires" them (136). This predicament fosters black men's self-destruction. In fact, Staples cites the 1970s as the period in which the "flowering of black manhood turned into a withering away of what little supremacy they had [over women]" (135). Unemployment is the culprit Staples has in mind—but also black men's "refus[al] to compromise their masculinity by indulging in 'feminine work'" (139). Here, for Staples, lies another trouble: He alludes to the *problem* of black women's employment that to his mind gives black women a competitive edge over black men and causes black men "to continue to fall behind black women in their education and economic progress" (19). Staples persistently voices his worry over gender reversal, even though at the start of his book he clearly states that, "despite having more education, black women consistently have a higher rate of unemployment and earn less income than black males" (17).

Black feminists, such as Angela Davis and Hortense J. Spillers, have argued that black women shatter white gender couplings that color femininity as passive. These scholars associate black women with work outside the home since neither leisure nor their own housework has formed the focus of black women's lives. Black women have not been privatized in their own domestic economies but have always been tied to production circuits in dominant economies (as sexual laborers, field laborers, factory laborers, or domestic laborers, under white management) (Davis).[13]

The fix for blacks in the face of white gender might go, then, like this: black women have been blocked from (the bourgeois ideal of) white feminine passivity, whereas black men have been blocked from (the bourgeois ideal of) white masculine activity. What counts as white masculine activity is the "privilege" of participating in the dominant (capitalist) economy as *either* exploiter *or* exploited (bourgeois or working class). Hence "activity" in this scheme should not be taken exclusively as "productive labor" in orthodox Marxist terms (according to which the proletariat, not the capitalist, performs productive labor). Rather, the bourgeois white man is culturally coded "active" though he doesn't, technically, "produce." In the same way, the enforced passivity of the bourgeois white woman may involve, in unorthodox Marxist terms, productive (domestic) labor, or even capitalist professional activity, but she is still culturally defined as more "passive."[14]

That is to say, as bodies climb up the economic ladder, tracing a trajectory from unemployed to working class to white collar to capitalist, they move increasingly into a whiter domain that, toward the top, has traditionally been governed (though now more precariously) by a masculine active/feminine passive binary couple. Threats to this governing opposition increasingly loom apparent. Yet, to a surprising extent, nineteenth- and early twentieth-century cultural codes (pre-civil rights and pre-women's movement) may still determine cultural associations of activity with white (bourgeois) masculinity and passivity with white (bourgeois) femininity, though the passive designation for bourgeois women is surely changing rapidly.

In suggesting that blacks can be bourgeois only by "going white," by conforming to a certain color of coupling, I am simply tracing Morrison's tracks through labor, sex, and love in *Sula*. Morrison makes no bed for a recognizable bourgeoisie among her black characters. After all, *Sula* centers on the 1940s—a period before blacks could even dream (á la Martin Luther King) of entering an era of corporate positions and suburban lifestyles; and though the novel ends in the civil rights era, the last chapter title, "1965," marks the year of the Moynihan report that spelled out the supposed "tangle of pathology" that makes the Negro family "fail" the "normal" genderings of the white middle class.

Popular national news magazines still tell us, quite pointedly, that *the bottom is defined by a certain configuration of gender:* the black man unemployed, the black woman heading the home. African Americans' sign of success—their bourgeois potential—is measured, therefore, by the extent to which they reverse bottom gender and mime white families. In a *Time* article by Richard Lacayo, "Between Two Worlds: The Black Middle Class Has Everything the White Middle Class Has except a Feeling that It Really Fits In," we learn in a punchline what "fitting in" means:

> For the black middle class, there are new preoccupations. Not just job-creation programs, but job promotions. Not just high school diplomas, but college tuition. Not just picket lines, but picket fences. An agenda, in short, for a full partnership in the American Dream.
>
> Superficially, middle-class blacks already seem to be living that dream. Leon and Cora Brooks have spent more than a decade at IBM, where he is a dealer account manager and she is a senior personnel specialist. They have a comfortable home in the affluent and mostly black Los Angeles neighborhood of Baldwin Hills; they have a Mercedes in the garage and a daughter at California State University at Northridge. Leon Brooks jokes, "We're a typical white family that happens to be black." (60)

But just how true is Brooks's joke? What *Time* and *Newsweek* anxiously index is the *incomplete* entry of African Americans into (white) bourgeois ranks. Bourgeois blacks are dogged by the bottom, according to *Newsweek,* only now the operative term is "underclass":

Devastating statistics: The isolation of the underclass was a hazard of the civil-rights movement. As it succeeded, more educated and entrepreneurial blacks moved to integrated neighborhoods, taking their gifts with them. It is an irony that distresses middle-class blacks: a deep class divide among blacks themselves. "We moved up the economic ladder and away from the old ghettoes," says Roger Wilkins, a senior fellow at the Institute for Policy Studies, a Washington-based think tank.

For those left behind the statistics are devastating. Around 55 percent of the families are headed by female parents. . . .

The steady economic growth that benefited many blacks gave way to economic stagnation in the mid-1970s. New plants and industries are taking root in suburban corridors, where poor blacks have little access to them. "You have to see the poverty of the urban underclass as likely to endure," says Michael Fix of the Urban Institute. "It raises the question of whether we're seeing the emergence of an American caste, a hard bottom class. . . . I do think that the urban underclass remains perhaps the signal issue of the next decade." ("Black and White" 20)

What remains specific to blacks, and recognizable as "black," according to these accounts, is their place on the bottom of an American caste system (spelled out for us, appropriately, by Mr. Fix). We notice that this bottom is truly down (what Morrison also hints in her chapter "1965"), depleted of its bottom values, says Mr. Fix, *by the accomplishments* of civil rights, successes that saw blacks part ways on the economic ladder, "buppies" taking with them "gifts" (easily cashed in for dollars), others left as a "hard bottom class."

This much Morrison would not deny and even foresees in the early 1970s when writing *Sula.* What she would not countenance is how this article warms up and re-serves the Moynihan report: The "devastating" specificity of the black bottom family is the female-headed home. This gender-configuration is *how we supposedly know* when blacks have failed to make it, when they are (on) the bottom (and pathological to boot!). Vestiges of the black matriarchy thesis—strong black women make black men weak: the black woman is elevated, the black man debased— remain in these discussions.

In her public commentary, Morrison cuts with a kinder knife a path to black gender and pain. In "The Pain of Being Black," she speaks to the issues of bottom gender and bottom values that do not duplicate white family relations:

> Q. *In one of your books you described young black men who say, "We have found the whole business of being black and men at the same time too difficult." You said that they then turned their interest to flashy clothing and to being hip and abandoned the responsibility of trying to be black and male.*

A. I said they took their testicles and put them on their chest. I don't know what their responsibility is anymore. They're not given the opportunity to choose what their responsibilities are. There's 60% unemployment for black teenagers in this city. What kind of choice is that?

Q. *This leads to the problem of the depressingly large number of single-parent households and the crisis in unwed teenage pregnancies. Do you see a way out of that set of worsening circumstances and statistics?*

A. Well, neither of those things seems to me a debility. I don't think a female running a house is a problem, a broken family. It's perceived as one because of the notion that a head is a man.

Two people can't raise a child any more than one. You need a whole community—everybody—to raise a child. The notion that the head is the one who brings in the most money is a patriarchal notion, that a woman—and I have raised two children, alone—is somehow lesser than a male head. Or that I am incomplete without the male. This is not true. And the little nuclear family is a paradigm that just doesn't work. It doesn't work for white people or for black people. Why we are hanging onto it, I don't know. It isolates people into little units—people need a larger unit. (122)

Morrison refutes the thesis that female headship constitutes a problem. What she offers is a warning that *coupledom* constitutes "a paradigm that just doesn't work." As for gender, Morrison locates black men as those bodies who wear (in the form of their genitals *as* their clothes) the failed promise of a dominant sign.

Taking this clue about failed promise, I would argue that Morrison carves out a specifically *black* masculinity in *Sula* (in a way that she does *not* designate a specifically black bourgeoisie) because she records black men's and women's *different expectations and letdowns* with regard to the promises made by dominant gender assignments. Defining themselves against "feminine work," black men may expect to participate in privileges that benefit white men. But black men, as opposed to their white male counterparts, are defined by their peculiar relation to unemployment and their peculiar uneven advance if employed. This is a form of masculinity, I would argue, *because it promises something not-feminine* (not-domestic, not-leisured); it *looks like femininity because of its letdown.* Black femininity bears a different relation to promise: it is promised nothing by a white culture's sign system. Yet, against all odds but for historical reasons (their lower cost to be capitalized and maintained; their possibilities for sexual and domestic labor in white economies; their active role in black domestic labor; and the lesser threat of their participation in capitalist productions), black women have discovered a promise for activity in capitalist circuits that seems incongruent with a double negative ("black woman").

In *Sula,* Morrison circumvents the stereotype of black males as "feminized" either by the dominant white order or by black women. The way she performs this—a stunning display—is to script the problem (no less harrowing) as black males stalled at an anal economic stage before the division into (white) masculinity and femininity that comes with employment. Morrison thus avoids examining black males' economic binds solely in relation to capitalist "success." Rather, she probes black gender in *Sula* as activity or passivity, mastery or nonmastery, with regard to capitalist *and* bottom productions. Posing these lessons in anal economics, Morrison concentrates readers on the pain of getting past an impasse, of migrating, of moving on—but without, one could say, leaving the pleasures of the bottom behind.

The Novel: Taking Freud Black to the Bottom

I want to begin this section by taking *Sula*'s first three chapters as a complex: the years 1919–21. Here Morrison not only roots her central issues but also hails her three main characters—Shadrack, Nel, and Sula—in succession. We can read these characters as figures for the three different paths that anal interests may take: regression (Shadrack), sublimation (Nel), and expression (Sula).

Shadrack's year is 1919. In him, we greet a character "blasted and permanently astonished by the events of 1917 . . . [who] returned to Medallion handsome but ravaged" (7). This is a black man "arrested" at the novel's start. It is important that he should be one of those veterans for whom no gainful work was waiting. Morrison even dramatizes this historical type and his economic halt in a peculiar way: she makes him shell-shocked as well as unemployable. Fitting for what would be his frustration in relation to a white capitalist economy if he were not undone by the war, Shadrack cannot control his "hands": "Slowly he directed one hand toward the cup and, just as he was about to spread his fingers, they began to grow in higgledy-piggledy fashion like Jack's beanstalk all over the tray and the bed" (9). Next, we are given more telling detail of the black man's privatized, sequestered relationship to an economy where he cannot find a place: Shadrack "wanted desperately to see his own face and connect it with the word 'private'—the word the nurse (and the others who helped bind him) had called him. 'Private' he thought was something secret, and he wondered why they looked at him and called him a secret. Still, if his hands behaved as they had done, what might he expect from his face?" (10). The word "private" binds together the black men in *Sula*—as if to chain-link them through common positioning (the deweys, we learn, "remained private and completely unhousebroken"; Plum "chuckled as if he had heard some private joke"; black men's genitals are several times referred to as their "privates"; even the honorary black Tar Baby wanted a place to die "privately"). But to return to Shadrack's privacy, we catch him in a particularly private moment that joins questions of face, identity, blackness, and hands together at the toilet.

Shadrack is in jail when it happens, newly released from the hospital, but literally arrested, "booked for vagrancy" (a denigrating name for unemployment):

> He lay in this agony for a long while and then realized he was staring at the painted-over letters of a command to fuck himself. . . . Like moonlight stealing under a window shade an idea insinuated itself: his earlier desire to see his own face. He looked for a mirror; there was none. Finally, keeping his hands carefully behind his back he made his way to the toilet bowl and peeped in. The water was unevenly lit by the sun so that he could make nothing out. Returning to his cot he took the blanket and covered his head, rendering the water dark enough to see his reflection. There in the toilet water he saw a grave black face. A black so definite, so unequivocal, it astonished him. He had been harboring a skittish apprehension that he was not real—that he didn't exist at all. But when the blackness greeted him with its indisputable presence, he wanted nothing more. In his joy he took the risk of letting one edge of the blanket drop and glanced at his hands. They were still. Courteously still. (13)

Regression to an anal economy is formative for identity and takes this character back to black as something to be celebrated. In reference to blackness (which is rendered as a greeting—a hailing or arresting of himself) his hands function—as if, courteously, an anal economy scripts a different scheme of productivity.[15] Momentously, in this anal version of the Lacanian imaginary, with the toilet bowl acting as mirror, Shadrack tucks, instead of fucks, himself: tucked up into his blanket, he renders the toilet water "dark enough to see his reflection," reversing the more familiar reliance upon lightness as a means of revelation.

Completing his context, Morrison makes Shadrack, "tucked up there in the Bottom," a kind of obsessional neurotic, fixed on bottom values. Not surprisingly, it is he who establishes National Suicide Day, one day, each year, devoted to the fear of death: a sadistic call, one might say, for neighbors "to kill themselves or each other" (14).

Freud, as it happens, pairs obsessive actions and religious practices in an essay by that name, written shortly before "Character and Anal

Erotism." He terms the neurotic's obsessive rituals a *"private* religion" (a nice phrase for Shadrack). More to the point for a reading of *Sula*'s religious themes, whether private or communal, Freud compares obsessive actions that express unconscious motives and ideas with religion, in which "something that is not yet absolutely forbidden is permitted" (124). I will argue that this religion in *Sula* functions to permit anal pleasures and values, even though it seems overtly to oppose the text's queen of anality, Sula Peace.

What does oppose anality in *Sula* is Nel's halting movement toward whiteness. Nel is a character traipsing the path of sublimation. Introduced in the chapter "1920," Nel, we learn, was raised by a proper, repressive mother: "Under Helene's hand the girl became obedient and polite. Any enthusiasms that little Nel showed were calmed by the mother until she drove her daughter's imagination underground" (18). Part of the novel's tension is strung with Nel's equivocal relation to this underground—that is, her relation to the Bottom, to blackness, and to Sula, who figures the sadistic pleasures that proper Nel has learned to guard against. But even here, early in *Sula,* we are being told that if one is black one cannot flee the bottom, only (incompletely) sublimate it. On a trip south by train, Helene and Nel are visually assaulted by the denigrating gaze of black soldiers suited in "shit-colored uniforms." They next must bear affront to their manners by using the "toilets" for "COL-ORED WOMEN" in the field beyond the stationhouse. Black women, the novel seems to say, have no equal access to white bourgeois manners if they are defined by having to void themselves in high grass. Helene gleans this point in a glimpse at Nel: "She gazed at her daughter's wet buttocks" (27). Perhaps Nel, too—like Shadrack who wraps himself into his blanket—tucks herself into the bottom darkness that renders identities dark enough to see, for we find her refusing her given name as Helene's proper daughter: " 'I'm me. I'm not their daughter. I'm not Nel. I'm me. . . . Me,' she murmured. And then, sinking deeper into the quilts, 'I want . . . I want to be . . . wonderful. Oh, Jesus, make me wonderful' " (28–29).

Morrison proceeds from Nel to Sula, Nel's girlhood friend who later, sadistically, brings Nel back to black and to the toilet by laying Nel's husband Jude on a whim. It is curious and important that this chapter ("1921"), which should be introducing us to Sula, largely offers a historical retrospective of Sula's grandmother Eva—a woman who masters anal economies on behalf of her son. I refer to the scene in which Eva's baby, Plum, cannot defecate and so must be saved by his mother's fortitude in the family outhouse (yet another toilet scene).

Retrospective to this moment, we are given a quick historical sketch of Eva's economic bind. Abandoned by her husband Boyboy, she is left with $1.65, along with five eggs and three beets. She is linked to white productions as a mother forced to seek employment outside of her home: "She would have to scrounge around and beg through the winter, until her baby was at least nine months old, then she could plant and maybe hire herself out to valley farms to weed or sow or feed stock until something steadier came along at harvest time" (33). As prelude to her economic solution, Eva must mobilize anal mastery when she discovers her baby has stopped having bowel movements:

> She wrapped him in blankets, ran her finger around the crevices and sides of the lard can and stumbled to the outhouse with him. Deep in its darkness and freezing stench she squatted down, turned the baby over on her knees, exposed his buttocks and shoved the last bit of food she had in the world (besides three beets) up his ass. Softening the insertion with the dab of lard, she probed with her middle finger to loosen his bowels. Her fingernail snagged what felt like a pebble; she pulled it out and others followed. Plum stopped crying as the black hard stools ricocheted onto the frozen ground. And now that it was over, Eva squatted there wondering why she had come all the way out there to free his stools. (34)

We encounter, again, a wrapping in blankets, a tucking linked to an anal feeding and a literal movement up the bottom—where tucking, by the way, can mean "to gather up in a fold," "to eat or drink heartily," or "to stick, pierce, or poke."[16] Here looms the clearest figuration of the black male's quandary in relation to the dominant white economy: *He can't produce*—either feces or coins. Eva's mastery of economies is signaled not only by her ability to free Plum's stools but also by the fact that there, in the outhouse, she envisions a solution to her family's hardship. What a cruel solution it is: Eva, we later learn, throws herself under a train, in order to lose her leg in order to collect insurance in order to raise the children her husband Boyboy sired. This astonishing twist on selling one's body proves, nonetheless, a masterful move within the white economy.

Eva's loss of her leg also proves a masterful move in castration economies, which Freud, of course, made famous as the means by which male and female bodies are gendered. Morrison's novel brilliantly cleaves to the anal stage, so that questions of castration are stalled and kept at bay. Even so, Morrison may imply that black women, perhaps *because* they are promised nothing and wear a double negative, are better able than black men to finesse castration economies. *Sula's* black males lack this mastery, stalled as they are at the threshold of production, saddled with the letdown of their phallic sign.

A reversal creeps into view again. In Jacques Lacan's return to Freud, he stresses the penis as that "pound of flesh which is mortgaged in [the male subject's] relationship to the signifier" (28), meaning that the penis-as-organic-reality must be relinquished as the male subject transits into the domain of signification that substitutes language, but also *privilege*, for organic reality. Morrison interrogates phallic privilege by limning black gender: In *Sula*, black males cannot convert the penis to the phallus (hence, the letdown of their phallic sign), whereas women can manipulate, and even mortgage, penile representatives. For it may be possible to read Eva's leg, along with the later depictions of Nel and Sula's phallic/fecal twigs and Sula's hand (by which she sifts Ajax's loam), as women's penile proxies. In Eva's case, she parts with her "penis" (the leg she loses) in order to tap white economic power.

In his essay "On Transformations of Instinct as Exemplified in Anal Erotism," Freud asserts that the feces are the first part of the body with which the child has to part; he claims, furthermore, that "in the products of the unconscious . . . the concepts faeces (money, gift), baby, and penis are ill-distinguished from one another and are easily interchangeable" (128). As if to beguile Freudian claims, Eva solves Plum's inability to part with his feces (a "concept" ill distinguished from penis) by, productively, parting with a "penis" of her own, as if she has not only castrated but also excreted her leg, turning this fecal appendage into coins. She even parts company with her "baby," Plum himself, as a way to secure him against his own loss.

This is why, at the end of this chapter ("1921"), we receive reminiscence of a scene of cruelty: Eva sets fire to Plum, now grown, while Plum sleeps in "snug delight":

> Now there seemed to be some kind of wet light [kerosene] traveling over his legs and stomach with a deeply attractive smell. It wound itself— this wet light—all about him, splashing and running into his skin. He opened his eyes and saw what he imagined was the great wing of an eagle pouring a wet lightness over him. Some kind of baptism, some kind of blessing, he thought. Everything is going to be all right, it said. Knowing that it was so he closed his eyes and sank back into the bright hole of sleep. (47)

As if we've sustained a narrative slap too smooth to sting, we encounter a liquid sadomasochism alive with this novel's aggressive truthtelling. The truth being told is that Plum grew up to be a veteran like Shadrack, who, ravaged by war and the unemployment for black men that followed, was exhausting himself in a backward spiral, seeking rebirth. Eva tells it this way: " 'There wasn't space for him in my womb. And he was crawlin' back. Being helpless and thinking baby thoughts and dreaming baby dreams and messing up his pants again and smiling all the time. . . . I birthed him once. I couldn't do it again. He was growed, a big old thing'" (71). In John 3, Nicodemus learns from Jesus that "a man cannot enter a second time into his mother's womb and be born." Rebirth takes some different form. Tucking Freud into this context, I imagine Morrison grazing his assertion that children are confused between the roles of the womb and the rectum for giving birth, so that "children are all united from the outset in the belief that the birth of a child takes place by the bowel; that is to say, that the baby is produced like a piece of feces" (Freud, "Sexual Life" 328). Morrison seems determined in *Sula* to conflate birthing with defecating, as if to say that rebirth can be thought only in close conjunction with the bottom—its values and pleasures.[17] In the case of Plum, however, the bottom truly is a grave, where Eva, helpless to heal, can only demolish the "murderous judgment against him" (Bersani 222). With a plash of penetration—the splashing kerosene "running into his skin"—Plum is gathered "back into the bright hole" of *death.*

Eva's moment of loving cruelty anticipates a later scene of like kind: Nel and Sula, twelve years old, "wishbone thin and easy-assed," accidentally kill a boy named Chicken Little. The scene occurs after Sula, on her way to the toilet, overhears her mother say that she loves but doesn't like her daughter. Nel and Sula escape to the woods where curious play with twigs takes place:

> Nel found a thick twig and, with her thumbnail, pulled away its bark until it was stripped to a smooth, creamy innocence. Sula looked about and found one too. When both twigs were undressed Nel moved easily to the next stage and began tearing up rooted grass to make a bare spot of earth. When a generous clearing was made, Sula traced intricate patterns in it with her twig. At first Nel was content to do the same. But soon she grew impatient and poked her twig rhythmically and intensely into the earth, making a small neat hole that grew deeper and wider with the least manipulation of her twig. Sula copied her. . . . Together they worked until the two holes were one and the same. (58)

By poking and piercing the ground with their twigs, these girls make a hole into which they stuff "all of the small defiling things they could find"—"paper, bits of glass, butts of cigarettes." This hole that they "tucked in," both in the sense of piercing and enfolding, the narrator calls "a grave" (59). One may be reminded by their phallic use of twigs, "poked rhythmically and intensely into the earth," along with their focus on "debris" and things "defiling," of Freud's discussion of the fecal "stick"—fecal mass—that Freud says stimulates the rectal lining just as a penis "excites" the vagina.[18] Here females wield the "penis," exciting another rectal grave.

Following upon this scene of construction as if, providentially, in "creamy innocence" they have built a bottom in which to tuck him, Chicken Little slips from Sula's hands, falls into the river, and drowns. This is yet another black male killed by a female who has cruelly or tenderly tucked him into death and taken him forever outside of oppressions. Important for the theological valence to this tucking, the narrator describes the women in church who mourn Chicken Little: "They acknowledged the innocent child hiding in the corner of their hearts, holding a sugar-and-butter sandwich. That one. The one who lodged deep in their fat, thin, old, young skin, and was the one the world had hurt. . . . [They] wondered if that was the way the slim, young Jew felt, he who for them was both son and lover and in whose downy face they could see the sugar-and-butter sandwiches" (65). These women tuck the black male into their hearts and into the folds of their various skins, by linking his hurts to the slim young Jew.

I leave this scene behind to press toward the book's middle ground, where a wedding, a betrayal, and an orgasm figure prominently. Nel has one of the few weddings in the Bottom (weddings being more of a valley affair). If this whitened ceremonial is not enough to put Nel back on the path of whiteness and sublimation, the representation of Nel's husband Jude surely does. Jude seeks the (white) masculinity that is yoked to active work and control over women. More specifically, he seeks to work on the construction of the new Medallion bridge. (Later, the bridge idea is dropped in favor of a tunnel.) We can grasp Jude's impetus to marriage only by unlocking his labor history and his own ambivalent realization that, ultimately, one cannot escape the bottom.

> More than anything he wanted the camaraderie of the road men: the lunch buckets, the hollering, the body movement that in the end produced something real, something he could point to. . . . It was after he stood in lines for six days running and saw the gang boss pick out thin-armed white boys . . . that he got the message. So it was rage, rage and a determination to take on a man's role anyhow that made him press Nel about settling down. He needed some of his appetites filled, some posture of adulthood recognized. . . . Whatever his fortune, whatever the cut of his garment, there would always be the hem—the tuck and fold that hid his raveling edges; a someone sweet, industrious and loyal to shore him up. And in return he would shelter her, love her, grow old with her. (82–83)

In spite of the white economy that forcefully stills Jude to forms of passivity, he is determined "to take on a man's role anyhow" by dominating Nel. Yet even his own determinations for sheltering are confused with a representation of tucking, where she is the tucker and he the tuckee. Can we be surprised that this wedding chapter, a chapter that can figure only a partial sublimation of the bottom, ends with a rear view? In the last paragraph, Nel watches Sula leave the wedding, and "even from the rear," the novel informs us, "Nel could tell that it was Sula and that she was smiling" (85).

The novel now skips from 1927 to 1937—a ten-year hiatus in which Sula has left Medallion for a college education while Nel has stayed at home in the Bottom with husband Jude. These events form another view—Eva's was the first—of a black woman's mastery of anal economics. For when Sula returns during the Bottom's plague of robins and their "pearly shit," she is college-educated *and* conversant with sadistic urges of bottom pleasures—so much so, in fact, that Morrison paints her as someone who is obviously unable to sublimate: "She was completely free of ambition, with no affection for money, property or things, no greed, no desire to command attention or compliments—no ego. For that reason she felt no compulsion to verify herself—be consistent with herself" (119); "Sula never competed; she simply helped others define themselves" (95). Sula's lack of sublimation makes her the bottom of the Bottom and lends her a peculiar theological agency within her community, demonstrated first in relation to Nel: she leads Nel back to the toilet and to God. She tenders Nel's passage by copulating with Nel's husband, for no stated reason. The effect is startling: the end of Nel's marriage and the beginning of a long journey back—*to Sula,* oddly enough.

To mark this shift in Nel's subjectivity, the narrative, for the first time, leaps to a short first-person narration of Nel's interiority. It is as if Nel's encounter with Sula's alternate economy—an anal economy that marks property in unaccustomed ways—creates a new space in which different forms of subjectivity can appear, a space, no less, in which even the narrator temporarily surrenders full possession. When Morrison returns to omniscient narration, we are at the toilet where Nel is newly contemplating God. This bathroom, in fact—"small and bright"— shows forth what Plum's "bright hole of sleep" could only shadow: rebirth needs some form of excretion, the back-end productions of grief over waste:

> The bathroom. It was both small and bright, and she wanted to be in a very small, very bright place. Small enough to contain her grief. Bright enough to throw into relief the dark things that cluttered her. Once inside, she sank to the tile floor next to the toilet. . . . There was stirring, a

movement of mud and dead leaves. She thought of the women at
Chicken Little's funeral. . . . What she had regarded since as unbecoming
behavior seemed fitting to her now; they were screaming at the neck of
God, his giant nape, the vast back-of-the-head that he had turned on
them in death. . . . They could not let that heart-smashing event pass un-
recorded, unidentified. It was poisonous, unnatural to let the dead go
with a mere whimpering, a slight murmur, a rose bouquet of good taste.
Good taste was out of place in the company of death, death itself was
the essence of bad taste. And there must be much rage and saliva in its
presence. (107) [19]

This is bottom theology—one of rage and saliva, of mud and dead leaves.
If Freud would read such ceremonials as obsessive acts, as a sort of communal regression to the toilet, Morrison would hold him to his point
about religion: "something that is not yet absolutely forbidden is [here]
permitted" ("Obsessive Actions" 124): a communal howl that breaks the
(white) canons of taste.

Yet Morrison's theology is not so simple. As Freud predicts, if religion
"reproduce[s] something of the pleasure which [it is] designed to prevent" ("Obsessive Actions" 125), it must, *on the surface of things,* still prevent this pleasure. Morrison portrays this complicated logic and *affirms*
the casuistry Freud would regard as religious hypocrisy: Morrison depicts how the Bottom makes Sula represent the devil, the bottom of the
Bottom, yet a devil around which the community is able, quite salvi-
fically, to define itself. The narrator reports: "Their conviction of Sula's
evil changed them in accountable yet mysterious ways. Once the source
of their personal misfortune was identified, they had leave to protect
and love one another. They began to cherish their husbands and wives,
protect their children, repair their homes and in general band together
against the devil in their midst. In their world, aberrations were as much
a part of nature as grace. It was not for them to expel or annihilate it"
(117-18). Sula stimulates the Bottom's theology, providing the hidden
outlet for her community's pleasure. If she undermines sublimation,
"the aim to make money that takes over for anal erotism" (as Freud
would say), is it any wonder that she should be figured as a devil in the
Bottom? Freud reminds us that the devil is directly aligned with anality;
in fact, in myth and fairy tales, "the gold which the devil gives his para-
mours turns into excrement" ("Character" 174).

Along this rich associative chain (gold/devil/paramours/excrement),
readers can discover, as if uncovering a reward for their pains, Morrison's
golden links to orgasm. Female orgasm (and, of course, it is Sula's) is rendered as a species of anal erotism, an orgasm seemingly in touch with excrement, or at least with soil. Prior to the moment, the narrator has told

us that sex is Sula's way of feeling deep sorrow. Her lovemaking hollows a space in which she "leap[s] from the edge into soundlessness and [goes] down howling, howling in a stinging awareness of the endings of things" (123). This descent into endings recalls not only bottom theology but also Bersani's meditations on debasement, especially his celebration of sex "as the *jouissance* of exploded limits, as the ecstatic suffering into which the human organism momentarily plunges when it is 'pressed' beyond a certain threshold of endurance" (217). This is clearly downward mobility in the sexual sense—but a movement down that effects Sula's rise. Now the narration shifts to Sula in first person, as it earlier did with Nel, suggesting a formation of Sula's subjectivity in the "high silence of orgasm":

> *If I take a chamois and rub real hard on the bone, right on the ledge of your cheek bone, some of the black will disappear. It will flake away into the chamois and underneath there will be gold leaf. . . .*
>
> How high she was over his wand-lean body, how slippery was his sliding sliding smile.
>
> *And if I take a nail file . . . and scrape away at the gold, it will fall away and there will be alabaster. . . .*
>
> The height and the swaying dizzied her, so she bent down and let her breasts graze his chest.
>
> *Then I can take a chisel and small tap hammer and tap away at the alabaster. It will crack then like ice under the pick, and through the breaks I will see the loam, fertile, free of pebbles and twigs. For it is the loam that is giving you that smell. . . . I will put my hand deep into your soil, lift it, sift it with my fingers, feel its warm surface and dewy chill below. . . .*
>
> He swallowed her mouth just as her thighs had swallowed his genitals, and the house was very, very quiet. (130–31)

As if her direct address might hem the reader, too, Sula rides the reader, on top of her lover, along a color spectrum of anality—from black to gold leaf to alabaster to loam—beginning at the cheek bone but ending where? Her rubbing and scraping and chiseling and swallowing surely color her active in intercourse. Joined by her seeming penetration of his "soil" by her hand, these piercing, abrasive invasions of Ajax's depths recall Eva's freeing Plum's stools with her finger and Nel and Sula's probings of their makeshift "grave" with their twigs (recall the fecal stick). This scene's siftings even transform Eva's earlier desperation, lending now suggestions of something languorous, sensual, and sumptuous to anal penetration.[20] Since the rich fertility of Ajax's loam contrasts sharply with Plum's hard stools, we might ask whether female orgasm moves black women to make black men productive and also *alive* to bottom values?

Now we have come full circle to a crux: What are the material limits of black folks embracing paradigms of downward mobility, whether Christian and/or sexual? Can there be alternative productions without possessions (white and capitalist) "up" in the bottom? As Morrison brings Nel and Sula's relation to a head, sharpening questions of traditional morality and possession, so too she draws to a point *Sula*'s economic and historical concerns. For this reason, Sula's parting question to Nel, asked before dying, "How do you know who was good?," extends to judgments about competing economies. This question is drawn to a point by a tunnel.

In the chapter entitled "1941," Bottom blacks attack the tunnel that they have been barred from helping to build. The date of the chapter places us during a wartime economy; jobs, once again, have been promised to black men and, once again, the promise reverts to a "nigger joke." By this time, as well, the Bottom's devil, Sula, has died—the black community's strongest link to its anal economics. The narrator laments: "A falling away, a dislocation was taking place. . . . [They] now had nothing to rub up against. The tension was gone and so was the reason for the effort they had made. Without her mockery, affection for others sank into flaccid disrepair" (153).

Already one senses the Bottom's collapse in the image of a "flaccid disrepair." Another sign of the Bottom's demise: Shadrack falls hopeless that National Suicide Day will do, or has ever done, any good for blacks. Even so, he leads a parade to the mouth of the tunnel, where again we encounter a womb/bowel image that swiftly and terribly converts to a grave. In a remarkable display of rage at their downward mobility, these people of the Bottom, who are losing bottom values, attack the tunnel that figures their relationship to white employment promises: "Their hooded eyes swept over the place where their hope had lain since 1927. There was the promise: leaf-dead. . . . They didn't mean to go in, to actually go down into the lip of the tunnel, but in their need to kill it all, all of it, to wipe from the face of the earth the work of the thin-armed Virginia boys, the bull-necked Greeks and the knife-faced men who waved the leaf-dead promise, they went too deep, too far. . . . A lot of them died there" (161–62). How should we read this angry penetration, motivated by the letdown of a promise made to black men? Does Morrison's affirmation of bottom values meet its death here? Must bottom values be put to death because the Bottom can never economically be "up"? Or is it precisely the attack that is wrongheaded? Is an alternate economy that nourishes the bottom possible, or even desirable?

Morrison does not solve this problem for us. Her narrative leaves off in 1965 with the certainty that the Bottom did collapse: Black people who made money during the war moved close to the valley, only to find that white people with money had moved up into the hills. The invocation of civil rights through the chapter title, "1965," plays sorrowfully, ironically. The era of civil rights was a time of symbolic reversal; civil rights, at least King's brand, was grounded in a bottom theology; and with its struggle over restrooms and buses, civil rights provided a veritable discourse on toilets and back passages. Does Morrison suggest that civil rights, because of its gains, led to blacks' assimilation of values that would then repress the bottom? Is this why the novel ends with ambivalent Nel calling out in sorrow *for Sula*—voicing a cry that has "no bottom and . . . no top, just circles and circles of sorrow" (174)?

I think Morrison worries in this direction. What a fix, indeed: if upward mobility proves theologically and sexually bankrupt but downward mobility spells economic suicide for racially marginalized people, what alternate economy will not in the end immobilize? Can people dispossess their way up the ladder? Can we search for the ceiling that will raise the bottom? Can there be a rising that refuses to leave one's bottom behind? Can we even pose this problem in terms of economies that we know?

In *Sula,* Morrison attempts an alternative—one that might be provisionally worth embracing. One could call its dynamic "tucking up the bottom," where "tucking" means simultaneously "to gather up in a fold," "to draw together," "to eat or drink heartily," and, by way of Old French and Middle Dutch, "to stick, pierce, or poke." The verb "tuck" itself seems to trouble distinctions between activity and passivity, between aggressor and receiver. It suggests a snug contact with the bottom that is restless nonetheless. And if "tucking" bears obvious maternal overtones, it avoids the softness that spells a white feminine passivity, being, after all, a folding that is also a piercing, a poking that is also a swallowing.

Has Morrison shown us how to write "fucking" as "tucking"—sexually, theologically, and economically—where to "tuck" each other in the bottom is to aggress against each other tenderly?

NOTES

This essay originated as a talk sponsored by the Humanities Center at the University of Utah, February 1989. It subsequently appeared in *Cultural Critique* 24 (Spring 1993): 81–118 and is reprinted here, with minor revisions, by permission of Oxford University Press. I gratefully acknowledge criticisms generously offered by Barry Weller, Stephanie Pace, Gillian Brown, Henry Staten, and, especially, this essay's most persistent troubleshooters, Peggy Pascoe and Melanee Cherry.

1. Despite the burgeoning critical attention focused on Toni Morrison, critics, as far as I know, have not addressed *Sula*'s anal focus. For major collections on Morrison, see Gates and Appiah, *Toni Morrison;* McKay, *Critical Essays on Toni Morrison* (with essays by Robert Grant and Deborah McDowell on *Sula*); and Bloom, *Toni Morrison* (esp. the essays by Cynthia Davis and Melvin Dixon). In addition, see Samuels and Hudson-Weems, *Toni Morrison;* Awkward, *Inspiriting Influences;* Butler-Evans, *Race, Gender, and Desire;* and Willis, *Specifying.*

2. In this essay, black (with or without quotation marks) carries the status not of an essence but of a cultural signifier—a label worn by people (sometimes willingly, sometimes not, sometimes habitually, sometimes shiftingly) and written on the surface of fictions, genders, economies, and locations often in ways that incalculably form them. In referring to black fiction, for example, I am reading according to the author's signature, not claiming a known character. Morrison, too, it seems to me, uses black and blackness in these ways.

3. In "Missionary Positions," Watney provides a trenchant analysis of how Western media have bastardized these complex links. He demonstrates how Western journalists' extreme focus on "promiscuity" in Africa has led to their "regarding black Africans and gay men as effectively interchangeable"; thus "Africa," he writes, "becomes a 'deviant' continent, just as Western gay men are effectively Africanized" (88). More specifically, since the symptoms of "African AIDS disease" correspond to familiar Western images of (African) famine ("lassitude, extreme weight loss, huge staring eyes"), AIDS becomes in these journalists' descriptions "a virus which eventually kills by transforming all its 'victims' into 'Africans,' and which threatens to 'Africanize' the entire world" (91–92).

4. In "The Motives of Jokes—Jokes as a Social Process," Freud claims that jokes may be used by a person who "finds criticism or aggressiveness difficult so long as they are direct, and possible only along circuitous paths" (*Jokes* 142). More interesting for my purposes, Freud further states that "aggressive tendentious jokes succeed best in people in whose sexuality a powerful sadistic component is demonstrable, which is more or less inhibited in real life" (143).

5. Morrison herself, in an interview with *Time* magazine, points to the unique economic placement of blacks in relation to European immigrants: "But in becoming an American from Europe, what one has in common with that other immigrant is contempt for me—it's nothing else but color. . . . Every immigrant knew he would not come as the very bottom. He had to come above at least one group—and that was us" ("Pain" 120).

6. By "whiteness" I mean the very things *Sula* implies are new (and formerly alien) to the black community in 1965: jobs in the dominant economy, homes in the valley, and the separateness of the nuclear family.

7. Foner quotes from a leaflet distributed throughout Alabama: "Are you happy with your pay envelope? Would you like to go North where the laboring man shares the profits with the Boss? . . . Let's Go Back North. Where no trouble or labor exists, no strikes, no lock outs, large coal, good wages, fair treatment, two weeks pay, good houses. If you haven't got all these things you had better see us. Will send you where you can have all these things. . . . Will advance you money if necessary. Go now. While you have the chance" (130).

8. "In April 1919, the Division of Negro Economics announced that 99% of Chicago's black veterans were still unemployed, with little prospect of work in the immediate future" (Foner 132).

9. We are now familiar with many black critics' deep hesitancy toward what we have come to call "critical theories" (see the debate in *New Literary History:* Joyce, "Black Canon" and " 'Who the Cap Fit' "; Gates, "What's Love"; and Baker, "In Dubious Battle"). Even those critics who use these theories (e.g., theories forged by Freud, Marx, Lacan, Althusser, Foucault, Derrida, Irigaray, Kristeva, and Wittig) caution against the specifically Western European limitations to their analytical presumptions and historical perspectives as applied to African American texts and contexts (e.g., Robinson, *Black Marxism* [2–5]; and Gates, *"Race," Writing, and Difference* [13–15]).

The whiteness of these theories is a vexed question, to be sure, for even the theorists are not all unquestionably white (Derrida, for instance, is a *pied noir* and a Jew; strictly speaking, his place of birth makes him an African). Moreover, the cultural relations they criticize are the dominant white order's formation of class and gender others. Because race is not a prominent category of investigation for most of these theorists, does it necessarily follow that these theories are "white," bound to an unacknowledged racial specificity? I leave this question unsettled. The problem that occupies me here can be sharpened to this: Can these critical theories (whether or not we deem them white) signify on the terrain of what we call, reading by the signature, black fiction?

10. Perhaps things have changed faster than Christian could have imagined when she published her article in 1987, or perhaps fictions do not possess quite the power to threaten institutions in the way we hope they would (more likely), for Morrison, I believe, is swiftly becoming canonical on English department syllabi and even on exam lists. My caveat, however, does not change the force of Christian's complaint, since now (perversely) it may be Morrison's status as the *one* black woman writer "we should read" that keeps other black writers from being read. With this assimilation, of course, the likelihood increases that academics will tame what is most subversive about Morrison's fiction—a situation that occasions my essay.

11. In theorizing the value of debasement, I am currently working on a theory of what I call "narrative slapping." I take as my paradigm the moment in Hurston's *Their Eyes Were Watching God* when Tea Cake slaps Janie:

> "Tea Cake, you sho is a lucky man," Sop-de-Bottom told him. "Uh person can see every place you hit her. Ah bet she never raised her hand tuh hit yuh back, neither. Take some uh dese ol' rusty black women and dey would fight yuh all night long and next day nobody couldn't tell you ever hit 'em. Dat's de reason Ah done quit beatin' mah woman. You can't make no mark on em at all. Lawd! wouldn't Ah love tuh whip uh tender woman lak Janie! Ah bet she don't even holler. She jus' cries, eh Tea Cake?"
>
> "Dat's right. . . . Mah Janie is uh high time woman and useter things. Ah didn't get her outa de middle uh de road. Ah got her outa uh big fine house. Right now she got money enough in de bank tuh buy up dese ziggaboos and give 'em away."
>
> "Hush yo' mouf! And she down heah on de muck lak anybody else!" (218–19)

This disturbing exchange suggests that debasement's value must be marked in reference to a prior elevation. So too, I would argue, the form of Hurston's novel—Janie's journey from poverty, to wealth, to the muck once more—can register the muck's richness only by administering a narrative slap that brings her down from a throne. Her drop into marriage with Tea Cake, her work on the land, and her autoerotic proximity to herself can be valued by readers only if we see her fall, slapped down, from a previous height.

In *Sula,* the value of the bottom, along with the value of Sula's deviltry, can best be measured after Sula has died and the Bottom is lost.

12. Freud notes: "The ego may countenance the fixation and will then be perverse to that extent"; for "regression of libido without repression would never give rise to a neurosis, but would result in a perversion" ("Aspects" 360, 353).

13. Though more directly focused on "the African female in captivity," Spillers also provides a crucial discussion of the black woman's differential relation to domesticity and gendering in "Mama's Baby, Papa's Maybe."

14. Clearly, it is the bourgeois, not the working-class, woman our culture still links most directly with passivity, since working-class women may not be privatized and may work outside the home in the dominant economy (even as domestic workers). This scheme, of course, may further raise the issue of white bourgeois women who themselves work in the dominant economy—as account executives, for example. More women are becoming petit bourgeois or bourgeois "in their own right" (not by marriage, that is). Since these women cannot be labeled passive or privatized, they bear a problematic relation to their gender sign as figured according to dominant codes. The copious advertisements and women's magazine articles devoted to helping "professional" women maintain their femininity surely highlight this problematic relation.

15. My mention of "hailing" makes obvious reference to Althusser's notion of subjectivity formation, which takes place, he argues, "by that very precise operation which I have called interpellation or hailing, and which can be imagined along the lines of the most commonplace everyday police (or other) hailing: 'Hey, you there!'" (174). That Althusser imagines here a hailing by police may lead us to connect hailing with "arresting" in the latter's double sense of stopping and being placed under law.

In the passage where "blackness greeted [Shadrack] with its indisputable presence," Morrison seems to imagine a moment of subjectivity formation that, while certainly not located outside of ideology, takes the character toward a positioning he can value more than whiteness.

16. These definitions are from *Webster's New World Dictionary.* The last sense of "tuck" as linked "to pierce" comes by way of Old French (*estoquier*) and Middle Dutch (*stocken*)—"to stick, pierce, poke"—giving rise to the archaic noun form of "tuck" that means "a thin sword."

17. In Freud's case study of Schreber, we discover Schreber's fascinating account of a question put to him by God, "'Why don't you sh—?'" and his subsequent experience: "When, upon the occasion of such a call, I actually succeed in evacuating—and as a rule, since I nearly always find the lavatory engaged, I use a pail for the purpose—the process is always accompanied by the generation of an exceedingly strong feeling of spiritual voluptuousness" (*Three Case Histories* 123).

18. Freud writes: "The relationship between the penis and the passage lined with mucous membrane which it fills and excites already has its prototype in the pregenital, anal-sadistic phase. The faecal mass, or as one patient called it, the faecal 'stick,' represents as it were the first penis, and the stimulated mucous membrane of the rectum represents that of the vagina" ("Transformations" 131).

19. The "vast back-of-the-head that [God] had turned on them in death" is not a simple image of a turning away. In fact, the revelation of God's back parts is invested with extraordinary richness—even tenderness—in the story of Moses, where, as a sign of his favor, God agrees to reveal his glory—backward (Exodus 33: 20–23). See also Freud's Wolf Man analysis for his discussion of a patient whose "first religious scruples" concerned "whether Christ had had a behind" ("Anal Eroticism" 79).

20. In his analysis of the Wolf Man, Freud refers to the belief "that sexual intercourse takes place at the anus" as "an older notion, and one which in any case completely contradicts the dread of castration" ("Anal Erotism" 78).

WORKS CITED

Althusser, Louis. *Lenin and Philosophy and Other Essays.* Trans. Ben Brewster. New York: Monthly Review Press, 1971.

Awkward, Michael. *Inspiriting Influences: Tradition, Revision, and Afro-American Women's Novels.* New York: Columbia University Press, 1989.

Baker, Houston A., Jr. "In Dubious Battle." *New Literary History* 18 (1987): 363–69.

Bersani, Leo. "Is the Rectum a Grave?" *October* 43 (Winter 1987): 197–222.

"Black and White in America." *Newsweek*, Mar. 7, 1988, pp. 18–23.

Bloom, Harold, ed. *Toni Morrison: Modern Critical Views.* New York: Chelsea House, 1990.

Butler-Evans, Elliott. *Race, Gender, and Desire: Narrative Strategies in the Fiction of Toni Cade Bambara, Toni Morrison, and Alice Walker.* Philadelphia: Temple University Press, 1989.

Christian, Barbara. "The Race for Theory." *Cultural Critique* 6 (Spring 1987): 51–63.

Davis, Angela. *Women, Race, and Class.* New York: Vintage, 1983.

Delphy, Christine. *Close to Home: A Materialist Analysis of Women's Oppression.* Trans. Diana Leonard. Amherst: University of Massachusetts Press, 1984.

Foner, Philip. *Organized Labor and the Black Worker, 1619–1981.* New York: International, 1981.

Franklin, John Hope. *From Slavery to Freedom: A History of Negro Americans.* New York: Alfred A. Knopf, 1988.

Freud, Sigmund. "Anal Erotism and the Castration Complex." *The Standard Edition of the Complete Psychological Works of Sigmund Freud.* Trans. and ed. James Strachey. 24 vols. London: Hogarth Press and the Institute of Psychoanalysis, 1959. 17:72–88.

——. "Aspects of Development and Regression: Aetiology." *General Introduction to Psychoanalysis.* Trans. Joan Riviere. New York: Pocket, 1953. 348–66.

——. "Character and Anal Erotism." *Standard Edition.* 9:167–75.

——. "Development of the Libido and Sexual Organizations." *General Introduction.* 329–47.

——. "The Excretory Functions in Psychoanalysis and Folklore." Rpt. in *Character and Culture.* Ed. Philip Rieff. New York: Collier, 1963. 219–22.

——. *Jokes and Their Relation to the Unconscious.* Trans. and ed. James Strachey. New York: Norton, 1963.

——. "Obsessive Actions and Religious Practices." *Standard Edition.* 9:117–27.

——. "On Transformations of Instinct as Exemplified in Anal Erotism." *Standard Edition.* 17:125–33.

———. "The Paths of Symptom-Formation." *General Introduction.* 367–85.

———. "The Sexual Life of Man." *General Introduction.* 312–28.

———. *Three Case Histories.* Ed. Philip Rieff. New York: Collier, 1963.

Gates, Henry Louis, Jr., ed. *"Race," Writing, and Difference.* Chicago: University of Chicago Press, 1986.

———. " 'What's Love Got to Do with It?': Critical Theory, Integrity, and the Black Idiom." *New Literary History* 18 (1987): 345–62.

Gates, Henry Louis, Jr., and K. A. Appiah, eds. *Toni Morrison: Critical Perspectives Past and Present.* New York: Amistad, 1993.

Hurston, Zora Neale. *Their Eyes Were Watching God.* 1937. Urbana: University of Illinois Press, 1978.

Joyce, Joyce A. "The Black Canon: Reconstructing Black American Literary Criticism." *New Literary History* 18 (1987): 335–44.

———. " 'Who the Cap Fit': Unconsciousness and Unconscionableness in the Criticism of Houston A. Baker, Jr. and Henry Louis Gates, Jr." *New Literary History* 18 (1987): 371–84.

Lacan, Jacques. "Desire and the Interpretation of Desire in *Hamlet.*" Trans. James Hulbert. *Yale French Studies* 55/56 (1977): 11–52.

Lacayo, Richard. "Between Two Worlds: The Black Middle Class Has Everything the White Middle Class Has except a Feeling that It Really Fits In." *Time,* Mar. 13, 1989, pp. 58–68.

McKay, Nellie Y., ed. *Critical Essays on Toni Morrison.* Boston: G. K. Hall, 1988.

Morrison, Toni. "The Pain of Being Black: An Interview with Toni Morrison." *Time,* May 22, 1989, pp. 120–22.

———. *Sula.* New York: New American Library, 1973.

Robinson, Cedric J. *Black Marxism: The Making of the Black Radical Tradition.* London: Zed, 1983.

Samuels, Wilfred D., and Clenora Hudson-Weems. *Toni Morrison.* Boston: Twayne, 1990.

Spillers, Hortense J. "Mama's Baby, Papa's Maybe: An American Grammar Book." *Diacritics* 17.2 (1987): 65–81.

Staples, Robert. *Black Masculinity: The Black Male's Role in American Society.* San Francisco: Black Scholar Press, 1982.

Watney, Simon. "Missionary Positions: AIDS, 'Africa,' and Race." *differences* 1 (Winter 1989): 83–100.

Willis, Susan. *Specifying: Black Women Writing the American Experience.* Madison: University of Wisconsin Press, 1987.

13 ◇ Reading the Figure of Dictation in Theresa Hak Kyung Cha's *Dictée*

In memoriam
Theresa Hak Kyung Cha (1951–82)

dictation: The pronouncing of words in order to their being written down. The school exercise of transcribing a dictated passage, especially one in a foreign language. Authoritative utterance or prescription. Arbitrary command; the exercise of dictatorship. Something dictated.

— *Oxford English Dictionary*

What is dictation—the speaking or the reading or the writing? When does it occur? Does dictation name that which is going to be read in order to be written, the reading of that which is to be written, that which has been read and is not yet written, the written that has been read, or the written that is going to be read? To whom does it belong—the reader or the writer or both or neither? Definitions of dictation assert distinctions in language that the process of dictation proceeds to dislocate: dictation thus draws the boundary between the oral and the written only to command the mutual transformation of one into the other. It articulates a reproductive principle in language that is also marvelously, formally transformatory, such that the audible turns visible and the visible becomes audible. It is both the pronouncement and the transcription: the pronouncement to be transcribed and the transcribed that has been pronounced.

What, then, would it mean to read a text as a written dictation? Theresa Hak Kyung Cha's *Dictée* both announces in its title its demand that it be read and introduces a complication into its mode of reception. For in naming her book a dictation, Cha begs the question of authorial voice (who is speaking in the text?), then defers it in favor of a gesture of submission to the reader, whose role is to correct, rewrite, and complete the text. The written dictation is primarily a transcription, a reproduction of speech not one's own. As the writing practiced by children in schools and secretaries in offices, dictation thus begins with a primary denial, a disowning of originality and of ownership; it is not an originary but a secondary, a sequential mode. Both a preliminary and a belated genre of writing, dictation awaits correction and approval by another—the other's authorizing signature. The gesture of postponement in the very naming of *Dictée* thus constructs a version of authorial anonymity and critically engages from the very start questions of priority and authority inherent in the processes of writing and reading. In blurring the distinction between writer and reader and reversing their roles, dictation indeed critiques the model of reading as mere reception as well as the notion of authorial originality.

"All along, you see her without actually seeing, actually having seen her" (*Dictée* 100). The irony of that gesture is that *Dictée* bears vividly nonetheless the name of its author, whose textual presence is highly commanding, precisely in the refusal to conform to standard dictates of literary production, in the rare demands on the reader who "do[es] not see her yet" (100). Cha, who described herself as "producer, director, performer, writer in video and film productions, installations, performances and published texts" (Roth 152), published *Dictée* shortly before her early and tragic death in 1982. Born in 1951 during the Korean War, Cha emigrated to the United States in 1962 at the age of eleven and was naturalized in 1977. Apart from *Apparatus,* the collection of theoretical essays on the cinematic apparatus that she edited and published in 1980, *Dictée* is her only book, both a departure from and the culmination of her prior engagement in video and performance art. Beginning with an apocryphal citation of Sappho and organized in nine sections around the names of the nine Greek muses, *Dictée* collects formally diverse texts in four languages (English, French, Korean, Chinese): Chinese calligraphy, French language exercises, handwritten drafts, cinematic scripts, letters, verse, prose, short narratives, and quotations from history books and religious texts, all ordered in a nonlinear, nonnarrative fashion. Interspersed within this assemblage, usually at the beginning and end of each section, are visual materials: anatomical diagrams, a geographical map of Korea, numerous unidentified photographs, a film still from Carl Theodor Dreyer's *Jeanne d'Arc,* grainy photocopies of a handprint, and a mural painting. In this way, *Dictée* mobilizes a staggering variety of materials in a conflictual manner, alluding to a personal yet vast and contrapuntal combination of traditions and cultures, both Eastern and Western.

Open paragraph   It was the first day   period
She had come from a far   period   tonight at dinner
comma   the families would ask   comma   open
quotation marks   How was the first day   interrogation mark   close quotation marks   at least to say
the least of it possible   comma   the answer would be
open quotation marks   there is but one thing   period
There is someone   period   From   a far   period
close quotation marks

— Cha, *Dictée*

If dictation provides one model for reading *Dictée,* it is also a mode that *Dictée* writes against and whose authority Cha parodies. As a schooling in a language, the written dictation reveals writing as learned convention, a formal system codified and fixed both by custom and "disciplinary artifice" (Lowe 41). As the apprenticeship primarily of linguistic form and knowledge, dictation is an exercise, a lesson. It performs in the context of compulsion or superior dictates; it installs in the sentence "a thing repugnant to spoken language and classified by grammar as subordination: the sentence becomes hierarchical," ordered, classified (Barthes, *Grain* 5). In dictation, the distance between speech and writing is amplified as the distance between speaker and transcriber and, often, as the distance between a mother tongue and a foreign one. At the same time, speech and writing achieve a contradictory conformity in dictation, for even as dictation transcribes speech into writing, speech in dictation is only textual citation, mere reading. In the child's dictation exercise, language is thus spoken but laboriously so, spoken as it is and should be written. An inversion thus takes place, so that punctuation marks—what Theodor W. Adorno calls "traffic signals," the silently visible "marks of oral delivery" (91)—become pronounced; the task then is to separate from the sounding of words those sounds to be spelled out, those to be merely obeyed in the placing of the hand on paper, and those to be translated into signs of vocal rest, pause, rise, and fall.

In the passage quoted above, yet another inversion is effected, and everything spoken as dictation is painstakingly written, with the result that, just as what is precisely usually silent in language is voiced, that which is usually least visible occupies the bulk of the text. In spelling out the punctuation marks, the passage thus effectively visualizes the contradiction inherent in dictation: its uneasy interpenetration of the vocality of speech and the materiality of writing even in their disjunction. Furthermore, in thematizing an unpronounced, though not unrecordable, inner writing of the subjunctive mood that anticipates rather than follows speech ("the families would ask," "the answer would be")—a writing that wills not the fullness and immediacy of speech but rather desires "to say the least of it possible"—this passage inscribes in speech itself distance, deliberation, and delay. Precisely in its failure to conform to the correct form of the dictée, the passage effectively visualizes its forms of coercion.

In assuming in such subversive form this predominantly feminized and infantile, foreign genre of writing as its title and topos, Cha thus draws attention to the directed and scripted, conscripting character of writing, as well as to its subjects who, in learning language, are simultaneously silenced. There are no self-representing subjects in dictation as it is practiced in schools: the reader only cites, and the writer only copies, all in the name of a correct collectivity of linguistic norms. In such a division of labor, what is at stake is not original expression but reproduction and transmission of the most exacting kind. In this way, *Dictée* names and critiques the ongoing processes of formalization and formation inherent in all linguistic interactions. Language is "that sedimented set of relations that stands ideally behind . . . [all] enunciations" (Benhabib 208),[1] "limits free plasticity[,] and rigidifies channels of development in the more autocratic way" (Whorf 156). As Edward Sapir pointedly put it:

> Human beings . . . are very much at the mercy of the particular language which has become the medium of expression for their society. It is quite an illusion to imagine that one adjusts to reality essentially without the use of language and that language is merely an incidental means of solving specific problems of communication or reflection. . . . We see and hear and otherwise experience very largely as we do because the language habits of our community predispose certain choices of interpretation. (qtd. in Whorf 134)

Language institutionalizes a basic conformity among its users, whose interactions are essentially mediated by it. Just as the successful dictation depends on the internalization of linguistic rules, every linguistic act already entails an interpretation of the world and shapes our experience of it. Dictation in this sense is a privileged site where language reveals its nature as law and where this law is actually voiced and articulated in the form of pedagogical commands. The implicit metaphor of the dictator in dictation asks readers of *Dictée* "to evaluate the hierarchic and imperative system of language as a transmission of orders, an exercise of power or of resistance to this exercise" (Deleuze and Guattari 65). Who are we serving when we read and write? And what is our source of critical authority involved in the reception of texts?

To come to a foreign language as an immigrant, as "someone From a far," particularly at a young age as Cha did, is to experience it vividly as a dictation, a coercive system of norms and rules, a primary means of correction and appraisal. The immigrant finds herself newly and repeatedly infantilized in the new language to which she comes belatedly as an outsider. She thus undergoes a sudden loss of the power of communication as well as the dramatic failure of the power of self-representation. Theresa Cha's profound achievement in *Dictée* is the inscription of such an autobiographical experience through the independent invention of a form and language that are capable of bearing the particulars of that experience as well as communicating its general significance. Cha's own work responds polemically to the problem of writing in a non-native language, "a second tongue a foreign tongue" (*Dictée* 80), by evincing resistance to a model of writing as either discursive mastery or the mere imitation and repetition of norms and by evoking a model of creative writing as the unlearning of language, the very antithesis of dictation. To read *Dictée* as a commentary on immigration, however, is not to simply trace and limit its meaning to a biographical one but to recognize in the mediated representation of the immigrant experience a commentary on the representation of identity.

Dispossessions: to be without voice and without authority, far "away from the land that is not your own," the homeland lost, mourned, "not your own any longer" (*Dictée* 45). The frontispiece to *Dictée* consists of a grainy reproduction of writing in Korean script originally etched in stone in a tunnel by a Korean migrant laborer in Japan during the period of Japan's colonization of Korea (1910–45). It is an incipient letter that obviously never reached its destination, petrified in its beginning movements by exile, hunger, the "terminal loss" of home (Said 357). Untranslated, unexplained, unsigned, the frontispiece represents, particularly for readers uneducated in Korean language and history, a visible but unreadable text, a cluster of hieroglyphs, mere pictorial signs. It thus interprets Walter Benjamin's statement: "Language is in every case not only communication of the communicable but also, at the same time, a symbol of the noncommunicable" ("Language" 331). It also performs as an anti-dictée: written during a time when the Japanese had forcibly outlawed the Korean language, it does not transcribe the spoken, foreign, and mandatory tongue but rather writes the unspeakable, forbidden mother tongue—in the enemy's land. It records not an official and public but a secret and familial language, born of enforced privation and reduction to childlike helplessness.

Beginning with the citation "Mother, I want to see you. I am hungry. I want to go home," Cha's text draws attention to the origin of language in a bodily expression of need, as well as the visceral relation of language to the kinships that bind us to what is given and dictated to us, what is originally not of our own choosing: family and home. Language, which "always appears as a heritage" (Saussure 71), is in general attached to such determinations, for they are at the root of our original and continuing being in the world that our language expresses; they are the site from which language first emerges. The Korean word translated as "home" here designates not so much a family house as a native place of birth, a province, town, country, community of belonging. The desire for home, expressed with terrible simplicity, is in this sense perhaps always present in our acts of language. Even the smallest linguistic act performed in solitude is thus an expression of solidarity; here it is precisely the boundaries of that solidarity that are crucially at stake.

Presenting such a text, Cha effectively enacts for the reader the secrecies and silences of language. In its requirement of translation, language thus confronts its own deep limitations and the intimation of its impotence and ultimate oblivion. Untranslatability is a kind of death, the erasure of being. The untranslated text dies with its secrets and becomes silence. If the task of translation identifies the essential solitude of languages, however, it also demands their community and communication: translation "ultimately serves the purpose of expressing the central reciprocal relationship between languages" (Benjamin, "Task" 72). Translation, our "somewhat provisional way of coming to terms with the foreignness of languages" (Benjamin, "Task" 75), thus aims not so much at the repetition or duplication of a language, whose copy it by definition cannot be, but at the redemption of that language by somehow relating to it and answering its call. The frontispiece is thus an emblem of *Dictée* itself, a work presented in terms of a task of translation. The frontispiece foreshadows the subject of *Dictée* as the inscription of loss and distance from places of origin and identifies it as a call and address. Cha introduces the frontispiece in such a manner, however, that it also becomes a hidden emblem whose possibility of recovery lies not so much in the learning of the Korean language as in the reading of *Dictée* itself. The implications of such a gesture are profound, for the work transforms the relation of languages to each other into an image of a language's self-relation: the task of translation in *Dictée* thus occurs within the English language become, as it were, foreign and strange. In this sense, the often halting, stuttering, unpropositional, and ungrammatical English of *Dictée* that appears to literalize, mimic, and parody the idea of a non-native tongue as an imperfect "Cracked tongue. Broken tongue" (75) serves not so much to vindicate the idea that it is impossible to write in a non-native tongue but rather to recuperate the experience of the foreignness of a language as itself an acknowledgment of that language's traditional ties to specific historical and sociocultural identities, as well as the possibility—the necessity—of reaching beyond them.

CLIO	HISTORY
CALLIOPE	EPIC POETRY
URANIA	ASTRONOMY
MELPOMENE	TRAGEDY
ERATO	LOVE POETRY
ELITERE	LYRIC POETRY
THALIA	COMEDY
TERPSICHORE	CHORAL DANCE
POLYMNIA	SACRED POETRY

—Cha, *Dictée*

The nine muses who organize *Dictée,* the nine daughters of Mnemosyne or memory, reveal in their genealogy a theory of creativity as essentially mediated by and derived from the past. Such a theory posits memory itself as a supernatural and incorporeal entity and the creative process as a dispossession or dictation where the poet, possessed by the muses, becomes a messenger of the supernatural and a medium of its intervention. The poet stands between the muse and the crowd, between past and present; she becomes an apparatus of annunciation. Like many mediating figures, the poet thus occupies a paradoxical place between absence and presence, revealing the incommensurability of the two even as they collapse and collide in her: her power depends on her power to surrender; she becomes visible to the degree that she is able to absent herself.

Dictée's recurring references to female martyrs both in colonial/national and religious contexts (e.g., the narrative of Yu Guan Soon's life, the still from Dreyer's *Jeanne d'Arc,* and quotations from Saint Theresa's autobiography) are related to this figure of the poet, for the martyr's power of recovery is linked directly to her power of self-erasure. In the case of the martyr, however, transcendence becomes not momentarily but permanently actual in the martyr's death. In death (that most discontinuous of forms, most unexchangeable of experiences, most terminal of losses), the martyr thus becomes a sign of transcendence paradoxically in the most immanent and historical form, a representative of a meaning whose power she cannot contain, in whose name she expires. The martyr's instrumentality is in this way more pure and more radical than that of the poet, and her forms of identification more violent:

whereas Greek poets preside over sacrifices, the martyr becomes the sacrifice, a human form that in its extinction has no consciousness but in its identity with the transcendent has an infinite one (to paraphrase Heinrich von Kleist's famous statement: "grace appears purest in that human form which has either no consciousness or an infinite one, that is, in a puppet or in a god" [244]).

What is always at stake in the poet's and martyr's performative acts of radical substitution is the nature of the uneasy and striking conjunction between self-representation and self-annihilation. The figures of both poet and martyr privilege models of selfhood that are strongly bound to the past and to the survival of the (in the case of the martyr, endangered) community; in both, the power of self-representation is always necessarily related to the power to represent that which is larger than oneself—a past beyond the bounds of individual memory, the identity of a community. In *Dictée,* Cha rewrites the traditional paradox of the poets and martyrs as a new historical and linguistic predicament, based not so much on the intolerable demands placed on these figures as on the rupture between the self and traditional communities, between the two aspects of language so skillfully united in the traditional figure of the poet—language as an instrument of communication and as the repository of a past cultural life of a people (Ngugi 439). *Dictée* thus describes a world in which the relationship between speaking and remembering is continually at risk, a world not governed by Mnemosyne but one from which Mnemosyne has withdrawn and absented herself, a world in which remembering is not so much a communal ritual as a private and solitary act, an impotent encounter: "Face to face with the memory, it misses. It's missing" (37). Mnemosyne in this sense is one of the unidentified "Dead gods. Forgotten. Obsolete" (130).

Early in *Dictée,* Cha describes the female speaker as a "diseuse" (French for female speaker), a word that Cha later elaborates in its specific meaning as a female fortune-teller and seer ("Diseuse de bonne aventure" [123]), and that plays on the English words "disease" and "disuse"; the diseuse is, however, a poor replica of the prophets. She does not speak with authority but is reduced to a tortured imitation of speech without originality, a mere "semblance of speech" (75): "She mimicks the speaking. That might resemble speech. (Anything at all.) Bared noise, groan, bits torn from words" (3). Weighed down by others' speech, "caught . . . in their thick motion in the weight of their utterance," she waits for their pauses, when "there might be an echo." "She might make the attempt then. The echo part. At the pause" (4).

In *Dictée* Cha speaks a language that does not bear her own cultural past, a language that for her has entailed the death of her own mother tongue and that is employed by a nation historically implicated in the political division of the original motherland: "I speak another tongue now, a second tongue" (80). How then is one to name the necessity of this unequal substitution, and in whose name does one speak after such loss? The instability and fracturing of voices in *Dictée,* the constant slippage between the first, second, and third persons, the unnaming of the "I," can thus be interpreted as transcribing an experience of the self as fragmentary with regard to both individual and collective pasts, as locating the instability of autobiography.

The fragmentary narrative of the colonial experience of Cha's mother as a teacher of Japanese to Korean children in Manchuria,[2] the narrative of Yu Guan Soon's life, and Cha's account of her return to a politically troubled Korea locate the historical distance traversed in the new construction of unspeakability in *Dictée* and serve as reminders of the historical sacrifices once made in the name of that language now newly lost. In the new configuration of unspeakability, the greatest threat is of forgetfulness and of the contingency and unavailability of shared communities. The repeated injunctions in *Dictée* to the mythical powers of the diseuse ("Let her call forth. Let her break open the spell cast upon time upon time again and again" [123]; "Let the one who is diseuse dust breathe away the distance of the well. Let the one who is diseuse again sit upon the stone nine days and nine nights. Thus. Making stand again, Eleusis" [130]; "Restore memory. Let the one who is diseuse, one who is daughter restore spring with her each appearance from beneath the earth" [133]) contain a reversal of the poetic trajectory outlined in the mythical construction of the muses: here writing does not record speech but precedes it as its invocation, and it is the task of the daughter to restore her mother's memory, to instigate her rebirth: "Dead words. Dead tongue. From disuse. Buried in Time's memory. Unemployed. Unspoken. History. Past. Let the one who is diseuse, one who is mother . . . be found" (133). There is no diseuse in *Dictée,* and the *written* calls for her to perform her function only serve as reminders that voice itself in the mythopoetic sense is a painfully absent phenomenon in the world. If what is at stake in *Dictée* is in mythical terms the sacrifice of the lost Korean mother tongue and its redemption, then what is lost is unrecoverable in the form in which it was lost, redeemable only through a process of almost unnatural translation.

> The extended journey, horizontal in form, in concept. From which a portion has been severed without the evidence of a mark even . . .
>
> — Cha, *Dictée*

In "Recalling Telling Retelling," an early essay on Cha, Susan Wolf noted that "Cha's sense of having a self formed in part by a past recalled only in fragments" (107) informed much of her work. The relevance of the fragmentation and disappearance of memory in *Dictée* is not limited to Cha's personal experience, however. *Dictée* describes the historical world in general as stricken with the disappearance of memory. In history, we do not serve Mnemosyne; rather, time dictates all: "What of time. Does not move. Remains there. Misses nothing. Time, that is. All else. All things else. All other, subject to time" (38). This "unaccountable, vacuous, amorphous" (140) "time that is oppression itself" (87), eternally fixed and eternally moving, precisely due to its unrelenting movement, its "onslaught" (140), threatens language with the "immobility of sediment" (159), with the fate of stone:

> Words cast each by each to weather
> avowed indisputably, to time.
> If it should impress, make fossil trace of word,
> residue of word, stand as a ruin stands,
> simply, as mark
> having relinquished itself to time to distance[.] (177)

The translation of experience into language is thus only made possible through "speech morsels" (56), brittle and "broken chips of stones" (56), the "fossil trace" and "residue" of language already bearing within itself the "weather" (177) of time. Because written language is only an imperfect preservation of the past, it becomes opaque and fragmentary, a visual "residue." As markers of a clearly human, yet ineffable intentionality, ruins are most like words and words most like ruins in their tendency toward the visual and in the incommunicability at the heart of their visibility. The task of writing, which can only work with fragments, is thus to "extract each fragment by each fragment from the word from the image another word another image the reply that will not repeat history in oblivion" (34).

Cha's photographs of ruins and of images receding into their background (e.g., the small hand or the figure with a mask) serve to reinforce the sense of visibility as itself subject to time. Her use of untitled photographic images is striking for, in severing the standard conjunctions of image and text where the image either simply illustrates the text or the text comments directly on the image, she reveals the opacity of the image—what is precisely silent and invisible in its immediacy—as its history, its own given context. Precisely in the unavailability of their contexts, these images are recognizable as citations, which puts them at a double removal from the viewer, for photography is, of course, the quintessential modern form of visual citation. One could indeed say that citation has found in photography its peerless ally, for its essential nature consists in its reproducibility, its supreme and uncanny citability. In its capacity to fix the essentially transitory, vanishing moment, photography makes of time an infinitely quotable though simultaneously absent text and becomes its radical kind of "still." What the photograph invokes and cites, then, is not only its absent referent but also the absence of that text whose readability depends crucially on the historical and cultural knowledge of its reader. In this way, though the photograph appears to be a "continuous messsage" "without a code," reality's "perfect analogon," it is also opaque in its very determinate detailedness—which is always historical, and the historical always recedes (Barthes, *Responsibility* 5). Thus, even as *Dictée*'s photographs represent ruins and murals, these ruins and murals themselves become images of photography.

Such a topography of citation in *Dictée* is not unrelated to the politics of immigration, for citation is a particularly homeless kind of text. Hans-Jost Frey's comments on citation are suggestive here. A citation is "a text that is displaced into another text," one that "belongs at the same time to two different contexts"—to the one from which it originates and to the one in which it finds new entry. Its ability to fit into different contexts does not diminish its uprootedness, however. The citation "is only incompletely integrated": it belongs in its new text "to the extent that it depends on the new context, but it does not belong in it to the extent that it is recognizable as a foreign text"—as part of the earlier text at once absent and alluded to. In this way, "the citation is a sort of intertext" connecting the two texts to which it both belongs and does not belong (287). The more the citation can adapt to different environments, the more errant it becomes and the more dislocated from its original home. Though citation usually carries with it for legal purposes all its identity papers—"documents, proof, evidence" (*Dictée* 56) written in the language of immigration officials (the language of authenticity, origin, identity)—it also confounds such a language by its essential mobility. Cha's use of citation, both visual and textual, preserves and heightens its intrusive and dislocated nature, its basic errancy. Her citations often turn out to be inexact (such as the names of the muses: "Elitere" for "Euterpe" and "Polymnia" for "Polyhymnia" [Kim 33]), as if they had undergone a kind of decay in their transposition. In this sense, citations describe, as it were, the fate of writing: its liability to fracture, its inevitable historical dislocation and disconnection from its original context, and its possibility of survival, however imperfect, precisely through its errancy, in a profoundly historical world. If the migrant citation and

the ruin as fateful images of Cha's own writings contain the acknowledgment of their fragility in history, the two images also complement
and temper each other to form in their conjunction an uncanny image
of hope.

> She could be seen sitting in the first few rows. . . . All dim,
> gently, slowly until in the dark, the absolute darkness the
> shadows fade. . . . The submission is complete. Relinquishes
> even the vision to immobility. Abandons all protests to that
> which will appear to the sight. About to appear. Forecast.
> Break. Break, by all means. The illusion that the act of view-
> ing is to make alteration of the visible. The expulsion is
> immediate. Not one second is lost to the replication of the
> totality. Total severance of the seen. Incision.
>
> — Cha, *Dictée*

"What has one seen / This view what has one viewed" (125). There are
several representations of female figures entering the cinema in *Dictée*
that are best understood in light of an immanent critique of cinema and
vision at work in the text, as well as the significantly filmic elements
in the literary strategy of the text. Cha disturbs the reader's desire for
passive spectatorship, figuring such desire as cinematic temptation. Her
striking experiment thus consists in the correction of such temptation
through a transformation of a filmic into a literary strategy. In her preface to *Apparatus,* Cha notes that the function of the "machinery" of
film, "inherent in its very medium, is to conceal from its spectator the
relationship of the viewer/subject to the work being viewed." Cinema
quite literally overshadows the audience. As Jean-Louis Baudry writes in
Apparatus, the cinema reproduces "in a striking way the mise-en-scene
of Plato's cave" (28) in its projection, in a darkened space, of a "halluci-
natory reality" made up of "virtual image[s]" before which the viewers
sit, wittingly or unwittingly, "chained, captured, or captivated" (32). In
Dictée, Cha similarly represents the viewer's experience of film as a self-
forgetting, an "expulsion" of the self. The visibility of the screen images
is a direct function of the "severance of the seen," a kind of cut or "inci-
sion" into the continuity of the visual world by means of the "simulated
night" (149), the artificially controlled darkness of the movie theater.

The contrast between the darkened, silenced immobility of the audience and the illuminated, virtuosic movement of the projected images
is not the only paradox of the cinema. For its successful projection and
imposition of illusion, the film must hide its central paradox: a film is
constructed out of visual fragments, discontinuous frames "that have

between them differences that are indispensable for the creation of an illusion of continuity, of a continuous passage (movement, time)" (Baudry 29) yet whose differences must at the same time be minimized as much as possible. For it is when the single frame differs least from the frames surrounding it that the illusion of continuous movement is heightened. Thus, "we could say that film—and perhaps in this respect it is exemplary—lives on the denial of difference: the difference is necessary for it to live, but it lives on its negation" (Baudry 29). Baudry argues that the "concealment of the technical base" in the visual form of the film has a specific ideological effect—namely, the elaboration of "a total vision which corresponds to the idealist conception of the fullness and homogeneity of 'being'" (28). That is, precisely in its unprecedented ability to depict movement, film becomes a transfixing rather than transformatory device of ideological identification. In the words of *Dictée,* through ideological operations the individual's "response is precoded to perform predictably however passively possible," "neutralized to achieve the no-response, to make absorb, to submit to the uni-directional correspondance [*sic*]" between viewer and image (33).

In *Dictée,* Cha employs a technique not unlike Sergei Eisenstein's "intellectual montage": each distinct and independent unit is juxtaposed with the next for "collision" rather than "linkage." Montage for Cha, as for Eisenstein, is polemically opposed to conventional uses of representational forms and continuity as a form of ordering. In *Dictée,* montage forestalls the sense of continuous movement or narrative, accentuates the differences of its individual components, and thereby counteracts the passivity of the audience. A salient use of montage is visible in the middle section of the book ("Erato") where Cha severs the spatial continuity between the left (verso) and right (recto) pages so that they become oppositional frames: the right page does not continue the text of the left but rather operates as a kind of inverse mirror of it, containing a different text in the spaces corresponding to the empty spaces of the left page (91–120).

In such a disparate collection and montage of materials, *Dictée* embodies a kind of scrapbook of an individual history—a history not as "total vision" but in fragments and citations, a history that in its very form depicts its profoundly mediated and material nature as fragmentary reconstruction from found and received materials. The performer of the text, the reader's hand, obviously a slow and unpredictable reel, is incomparable to the transfixing swiftness and regularity of the cinematic apparatus that disguises the fragment. Such a reader's hand better suits the double movement within the text itself that in turn resembles

the movement of memory: in memory, linkage does not obey the structure—the syntax—of logic but proceeds in jumps, starts, ellipses.

> They ask you identity. They comment upon your inability
> or ability to speak. Whether you are telling the truth or not
> about your nationality. They say you look other than you say.
> As if you didn't know who you were. You say who you are but
> you begin to doubt. They search you. They, the anonymous
> variety of uniforms, each division, strata, classification, any
> set of miscellaneous properly uni formed. They have the
> right, no matter what rank, however low their function they
> have the authority. Their authority sewn into the stitches of
> their costume. Every ten feet they demand to know who and
> what you are, who is represented. The eyes gather towards
> the appropriate proof. Towards the face then again to the
> papers . . .
> —Cha, *Dictée*

Theresa Cha returned to Korea for the first time in 1979 to work on a film
called *White Dust in Mongolia* (Kim 38). Cha's account of the Korean immigration officials' response to her upon her return poignantly reveals
the inadequacy of "papers" to the task of identification. The officials'
suspicion of Cha's papers recognizes such papers' inadequacy only in
terms of forgery and thus misidentifies the truth of that inadequacy—
the truth being that in fact "papers" cannot fully account for an identity. The origin of the "demand to know who and what you are" in uni-
formed and anonymous carriers of authority in this passage is in this
sense telling, for the impulse behind the demand can be read precisely as
the desire for uniformity and classifiability. If dictation as a theme in *Dictée* identifies through its very negativity the task of self-representation,
then such a task must be conceived in direct opposition to the supposed
representative work of identity papers and to the construction of identity as requiring adequate "proof"; rather, it must reach beyond the enforced, dictatory demand of such proof of authenticity that replicates
the very structures and categories according to which identities become
objectified. The originality of *Dictée* lies precisely in its ability to represent the denaturalizing, deterritorializing function of immigration in its
crossing of borders in our denaturalized world. Cha mobilizes that function through the declassifying, as it were, of literary form, for "to cut
across boundaries and borderlines is to resist the malaise of categories
and labels; it is to resist simplistic attempts at classifying, to resist the
comfort of belonging to a classification, and of producing classifiable
works" (Trinh 108).

NOTES

1. This quotation is taken from the context of Benhabib's exposition of Saussure.

2. Cha notes that this narrative is "based on the journals of Hyung Soon Huo" but suppresses the information that Huo is her mother. The narrative itself is structured as an address to "Mother."

WORKS CITED

Adorno, Theodor W. "Punctuation Marks." *Notes to Literature*. Vol. 1. Ed. Rolf Tiedemann. Trans. Shierry Weber Nicholsen. New York: Columbia University Press, 1991. 91–97

Barthes, Roland. *The Grain of the Voice: Interviews, 1962–1980*. Trans. Linda Coverdale. New York: Farrar, Straus, and Giroux, 1985.

———. *The Responsibility of Forms: Critical Essays on Music, Art, and Representation*. Trans. Richard Howard. New York: Farrar, Straus, and Giroux, 1985.

Baudry, Jean-Louis. "Ideological Effects of the Basic Cinematographic Apparatus." *Apparatus*. Ed. Cha. 25–37.

Benhabib, Seyla. *Situating the Self: Gender, Community and Postmodernism in Contemporary Ethics*. New York: Routledge, 1992.

Benjamin, Walter. "On Language as Such and on the Language of Man." *Reflections: Essays, Aphorisms, Autobiographical Writings*. Ed. Peter Demetz. Trans. Edmund Jephcott. New York: Schocken Books, 1986. 314–32.

———. "The Task of the Translator." *Illuminations*. Trans. Harry Zohn. New York: Schocken Books, 1968. 69–82.

Cha, Theresa Hak Kyung, ed. *Apparatus/Cinematic Apparatus: Selected Writings*. New York: Tanam Press, 1980.

———. *Dictée*. New York: Tanam Press, 1982.

Deleuze, Gilles, and Felix Guattari. "What Is a Minor Literature?" *Out There*. Ed. Ferguson, Gever, Trinh, and West. 59–69.

Ferguson, Russell, Martha Gever, Trinh T. Minh-ha, and Cornel West, eds. *Out There: Marginalization and Contemporary Cultures*. New York: New Museum of Contemporary Art, 1991.

Frey, Hans-Jost. "Intertextuality in Celan's Poetry: 'Zwolf Jahre' and 'Auf Reisen.'" *Word Traces: Readings of Paul Celan*. Ed. Aris Fioretos. Baltimore: Johns Hopkins University Press, 1994. 280–94.

Kim, Elaine H., and Norma Alarcón, eds. *Writing Self/Writing Nation: Essays on Theresa Hak Kyung Cha's Dictée*. Berkeley: Third Woman Press, 1994.

Kim, Young-Nan Nancy. "Memorable Losses: Writing in Exile and the Lessons of Writing in DICTEE." Senior thesis, Princeton University, 1991.

Kleist, Heinrich von. "On the Marionette Theater." *German Romantic Criticism*. Ed. A. Leslie Willson. New York: Continuum, 1982. 238–44.

Lowe, Lisa. "Unfaithful to the Original: The Subject of *Dictée*." *Writing Self/Writing Nation*. Ed. Kim and Alarcón. 35–69.

Ngugi wa Thiong'o. "The Language of African Literature." *Colonial Discourse and Post-Colonial Theory: A Reader*. Ed. Patrick Williams and Laura Chrisman. New York: Columbia University Press, 1994. 435–55.

Roth, Moira. "Theresa Hak Kyung Cha, 1951-1982: A Narrative Chronology." *Writing Self/Writing Nation.* Ed. Kim and Alarcón. 151-60.

Said, Edward W. "Reflections on Exile." *Out There.* Ed. Ferguson, Gever, Trinh, and West. 357-66.

Saussure, Ferdinand de. *Course in General Linguistics.* Ed. C. Bally and A. Sechehaye. Trans. Wade Baskin. New York: McGraw-Hill, 1959.

Trinh T. Minh-ha. *When the Moon Waxes Red: Representation, Gender and Cultural Politics.* New York: Routledge, 1991.

Whorf, Benjamin Lee. *Language, Thought and Reality: Selected Writings of Benjamin Lee Whorf.* Ed. John B. Carroll. Cambridge, Mass.: MIT Press.

Wolf, Susan. "Recalling Telling Retelling." *Fire over Water.* Ed. Reese Williams. New York: Tanam Press, 1986. 101-11.

14 ◇ A Journey toward Voice; or, Constructing One Latina's Poetics

> Narrative is radical, creating us at the very moment it is being created.
> — Toni Morrison, Nobel lecture

> Go on girl, do what come natural.
> — Victor Villanueva, personal communication

My journey has been marked by starts and stops, side trips, meanderings, and finding myself back where I began. The road winds on, always drawing me. To write this, I must write in reverse, weaving; hold on. Theorizing narratively, narratively theorizing, I do so with hesitancy. The road I travel through academia is one I make as I go, and I am never sure of the way. As a Latina, writer, teacher, scholar, mother, and feminist (to these markers, add working class to clarify how I came to the university—naive, grateful, uninitiated), the destination up ahead is one already charted for me—that of published writer/scholar, tenured, positioned securely in the ivory tower. Veering off track but keeping my voice and self intact, I just may get to that destination after all. Blending this voice with the one academia lauds—the one with the polemic, the theoretical, analytical one—has resulted in what I've come to call autobiographical cultural criticism. For me and others nurtured in oral traditions and communities, form is necessarily narrative dominant, although linguists, philosophers, and language theorists have argued that narrative is a fundamental way of making meaning in the world for all humans (e.g., Genette; Miner; Cazden and Hymes). How it began for me, this blending of voices, was with many beginnings. Though each one is as monumental as the next, life, like narrative, is not linear; even chronology misleads.

Crossing the border into academia, my first year as a junior faculty member, I applied for and was awarded a small grant to cover travel expenses to the Schomburg Center for Research on Black Culture: the Jersey girl going to the big city to work, a childhood fantasy; the junior faculty member going to Harlem to research the writer whose words haunt me, a grown-up fantasy. As I shift between the big city of my dreams and the little city of my birth, I keep a travel journal of sorts; the grant that allows me to be here is supposed to result in a bibliographic essay on Toni Morrison, but I've been yearning to write autobiographical literary criticism. I want to write about what this experience, this journey, is like: being childless and manless for a short time, being given the opportunity to write, read, think, sleep, study without being responsible to another, for another, being back in the small city I call my original home, the place where my self was made—biologically and psychologically. I walk the streets I walked as a youth when my youth was the first conscious thing I ever owned and ever hoped to have; I am near the people who have known me since before that moment when my self was made conscious. My best old girlfriend, Illy, and I are again together in the place where, yes, indeed, "we was girls together."

But the house I am staying at is not Illy's; this house belongs to a woman who is sister, confidante, and comfort of my soul, who watched me discover my youth and helped me shape and mold it but never controlled it. The woman whose gentle nature permits others to bare their trembling and bleeding insides to her, whose quivering insides gathered up my own last night. She lives here with her partner, a man whose youthful looks refuse to surrender to time. This man, this woman allow me into their home, allow me to make this house my home.

This place isn't the place where I learned what I do now—write. It isn't even where I discovered my love of language though it was where I learned to read it, speak it—two or three languages, actually. Urban talk and Spanish. And often a combination of the two. But I'm straying from my interest here, to record my research of Toni Morrison. My purpose is to go to the Schomburg library and research a writer whose words, characters, and presence haunt me and have haunted me for over ten years now. Should I go back that far? To the University of Miami and Rita Deutsch's Women Writers course and the reading of *Sula* in one sitting in that other library where I discovered Toni Morrison the enchantress? When I learned of other women writers of color who spoke directly to me? For the first time. For the first time, literature meant something to me. To me. Now, I write about this journey and hope that someone will discover something about this research that isn't in the proposal but far more interesting and meaningful.

I think I have been a feminist/womanist female for a very long time. I don't know if it was part of my genetic makeup though the line of women before me is strong indeed. Women who buried or divorced or bossed their men. Women whose fierce tongues can shatter an ego or buoy up a self. There are some incidents I remember that cause me to consider my feminism. Like the time in eighth grade catechism at Our Lady Star of the Sea—that church still figures in my dreams: gold leaf, dark wood, luminous marble and candles everywhere, shafts of colored light filtering through dust-racing incense-laden air. Church was religion. Sunday school was not. It was the first time, in seven or so years, that I had a nun for a catechism teacher. Those seven or so years that preceded this incident are pretty much the same in my mind—an endless campaign to sell candy, collect money, sell, sell, sell, so that we, presumably us public school kids who couldn't afford to go to Catholic school Monday through Friday, could reap the benefits—this money was for "our" classes, "our" church. I don't remember ever feeling I belonged there.

But this time, we were in a circle in a carpeted room with sofas and soft chairs—probably a teachers' lounge. It was a small group because after most of us made it through confirmation in the seventh grade, it was very difficult to get us to finish the last year. What for? We had gotten all we were supposed to get, I argued. But it didn't convince my mother and here I was with five or six other unpersuasive Catholic thirteen-year-olds talking about, for god's sake, abortion. It was 1973 and I didn't know what the procedure was but I sure didn't like the way this nun was talking about women being beholden to God and their bodies being God's temple and how women had no choice because of sin. We were all supposed to say what we felt about it and the right answer was yes, of course, abortion is a sin of murder, and, yes, God would punish these women in the hereafter who did this terrible, terrible thing. And they all conformed, said what she wanted to hear, her approval illustrated by emphatic nodding and hand-wringing. But I distinguished myself, my self. I said something like, I think women should be able to do whatever they want with their bodies.

When does one become a feminist? Womanish? Did it happen when those first few drops of rusty brown blood seeped down between my legs? Was it in my skin already, inextricably linked to that blood seeping down or sweat escaping my pores or hair falling out? Was womanism already ingrained in my brain through my female ancestors' legacy? Whenever it happened, its presence leaped up and out of my throat without any premonition on my part to the consequences of it. All I know and knew was that I was suddenly the cause for the nun's red, red face, shock, and then I was being escorted out, out of the class, out of the school. The stairs were quiet; our Sunday school principal wasn't notified—I was just put out. I gingerly walked through the waxed linoleum halls, slowly made my way back home. If my mother said anything to me, I can't conjure up the scene. In my mind there was no discussion of the incident. My mother and I never talked about abortion; she had no need to. Her nature and actions showed me the meaning of womanhood, a woman whose strength of character prohibited her from backing away from fighting back. Una fiera. Her example or her bloodline was already absorbed in me by then. At thirteen, I knew my body was mine. No need to discuss. It was over and I didn't go back.

Sula got into trouble, too. Nel and Sula reminded me of myself and Illy. Who was bad and who was good? Because she was dark, she was accused of being the bad one more often than me but what most mattered to us was that we should stick together. Like Sula and Nel. It was more important that she showed me her budding breasts when I was still wearing a sleeveless T-shirt and wanted more than life to wear a bra, a training, stretchy bra, anything, to show that I too was becoming grown up, womanish. Our intimacies, confidences, fears, and dreams effaced distracting judgments of us. After reading *Sula,* I decided right there and then that if I could write anything as perfect and profound and beautiful as this then I could die.

Perhaps womanism/feminism is linked to the condition of working-class women of color in America? Or maybe it is genetic, in the blood? My great-grandmother was one of those mulatas who was so beautiful, shapely, and alluring that even though she had two daughters from a previous union, my blue-eyed great-grandfather threw himself at her feet in awe, quit medical school, and preferred to be disowned by his light-skinned well-heeled family than to leave her. How much is true? Which part did I invent? The part about her flashing green eyes and sassiness? Or her succulent kisses and supple arms holding that ticket out of her caste so dearly? In Cuba, my grandmother didn't tell my mother much about her mother. Later, my mother's emigration and exile separated her, and in turn me, from our family on the island—and from the stories about my great-grandmother. It wasn't until much, much later that I began to understand the significance of this for me, of having una abuelita prieta; according to U.S. standards that makes me an octoroon who can pass, be accepted into Chestnutt's Blue Vein Society (Andrews). Not having known my nameless great-grandmother, she takes shape in my imagination: she who buried, killed, or left her man only to be worshipped, coveted, and married by another—a prime catch—someone with whom she could mejorar la raza, even if she already had two dark-skinned daughters. It's no use. What I need to know about her I know through writers in this country who never knew her, her historical moment. They can only give me the stories, U.S. versions of Cecilia Valdés, Maureen Peale, Jadine, or the oh-so-boring tragic mulata. Will I find her someday?

Dónde está tu Abuela?

The no name one, la prieta, the one who charmed El gallego
  (or el vasco?)
Dónde estás? Are you buried next to him? in that gorgeous,
  monstrous cemetery in Havana?
Who kept your keepsakes? What of your legacy?
Dónde estás? Did you leave me anything but the wild seed of
  imagination? The desire to recover you? The ability to
  recreate you?
Would you own me, abuela?

Another beginning is when the English department at SUNY–Albany, where I was earning my doctorate, hired Barbara McCaskill, whose specialization is African American women writers. I was blessed to be mentored by her for, at that time, no other professor specialized in this area; she was also the sole African American on the English faculty. It was shocking that this state school—not three hours from New York City—did not have more faculty members who were people of color. Of course, school officials proudly pointed to the fact that Toni Morrison was the Schweitzer Chair at Albany, but she wasn't really "part" of the English department. Her office was in a wing apart from the department, down by the elevator and bathroom; she could be in the stall next to me or share a ride up the elevator but I never saw her at readings, meetings, or any other department functions. But Morrison was the reason I had come to SUNY, so I diligently sought her out, through the double doors, down the narrow corridor, to the small office with two slits for windows, for advice on an exam list of contemporary African American women. Even though Morrison was an expert in that area, she had never taught such a class at Albany. Could it be that her special status, endowed chair, and big name kept Morrison an outsider? Or maybe she didn't want to be a part of the faculty network? But who really chooses? When I became the first and only Latina in my department I found myself in a similar situation—my own "special" status labeled me as an outsider. Institutional racism, sexism, and classism is so naturalized. See how irresistible, tempting it is to use the passive voice? No, it was deliberate; I was omitted/excluded from collegial networking and fellowship. I was left to my own devices.

At Albany, I never expected anyone to teach the work of Latino/as because I did not know such a canon existed (What!? Could I have been so sheltered? Latinos outnumbered all groups at the first undergraduate institution I attended, but I had no idea there was such a thing as a Latina writer, even while I was becoming one). It was in English departments that I had my formal training, but in women's studies and in Latin American and Caribbean studies departments my horizons were stretched far beyond the canon. Only after stopping at these places did I understand that, indeed, no English faculty member taught, discussed, or mentioned the literature of Latino/as. Ghettoization—only in the 'hood could I find myself in academia—or only in academia could I find myself in the 'hood. My attraction, love, and devotion to African American women writers stems mostly from a yearning to read about people who are more like my people and me than those hundreds of dead white men I had been coerced into studying as an undergraduate and master's student . . . and meanwhile, through the years, reading Morrison, thinking that's the way it was for me y mis amigas, feeling that's the way I want to write, wondering if I had it in me.

During my first year at community college, I explored an interest in journalism but my father dissuaded me from becoming a journalist because he was afraid I would go into war zones and get killed—we had watched the Vietnam war, mass civil rights demonstrations, and rebellions on television all through my childhood, so I knew he had a point. Trying to protect me from harm all of my life, my father was glad when I settled into the safe field of teaching, research, and writing; but he wasn't happy when I told him I would be doing some of that research at the Schomburg in Harlem.

Harlem, I must go to Harlem. What is it that causes such dread of the city, this city? I have internalized some of that myself. Is it that same darkness that besets American literature as Toni says in *Playing in the Dark?* The Africanist presence? People of color fear this city, too. But so many are "crazy about this city"—as the voice (the voice of tenderness, music, rememory?) says in *Jazz*.

In the last few pages of *Jazz* there is a "sweetheart" day in which light, clear, "steady and kind of kind," streams through that neighborhood. No chance of that today; it's overcast, cool. Good for walking though I've fallen back on my pace since the last time I was here. All that baggage weighing me down. Wanna fly, you gotta let go all that shit that weighs you down, Guitar tells Milkman Dead.

Light; that's what I saw when I climbed out of the subway hole. Light in a place that so many think of as dark, full of darkness, dark people, dark places. But I had been in the dark, in the tunnels, underground, anxious of the darkness above when there was only light, outside light and a wide, wide street that had very few tall buildings closing it in. No, there was light—overcast but light nonetheless.

I'm hearing the music in the book, the jazz in *Jazz*, and thinking that Morrison describes her Harlem in more detail, more lush detail, that is, than the city warrants. I was talking about it with my hosts. The city leaves little room for adornment. "It's tailored," my host said. Exactly, I said, the city is tailored; it either suits you, fits you, or it doesn't.

Violence seems so close here, a glance away. Just one look can kill you. My friend said to keep my head down and give dirty looks. Battle advice. Coming to this place is supposed to be like coming to battle. No one's bothered me yet. I know all the warnings; I've been here many times, love it here, miss it when I'm away from it too long. My father can't understand it; he escaped cities in the North for suburbs in the Southeast. I can't help just looking at the place, buildings rising up from years' worth of grime-grooved concrete. Coming up out of the subway, those mostly straight buildings reaching, trying to lift the closed-in sky. There is a sky but there's so much to see down here that not too many people bother looking for it. It just isn't as interesting.

Ay, but the people, they especially are. The voice in *Jazz* had almost forgotten the people, for it became so caught up in the city. The most diverse group of souls, speaking all tongues, betraying themselves with those tongues. Even the vagrants have style.

A beginning near the end of schooling: I had to own up to the label "writer" while completing my dissertation, a collection of short fiction. Even though I was resigned to being a teacher of writing, committed primarily to minority writers (most creative writing positions are for the entitled—folks with one or two books already under their belts), the dissertation proposal process required that I write a statement addressing my poetics in a theoretical, methodological way. Perhaps it is ironic that I was the first made to comply with this new regulation—the more traditional faculty members thought the creative writers were getting off too easily.

Groping, as best as I could, I wrote what I felt dealt with the dissertation proposal requirements. I wrote about my background and the literary influences on my writing; much of my piece detailed the politics of being a Latina feminist writer and what it meant to find others like me. I used to underline all the Spanish in my work, as one does with "foreign" languages. No matter how hard I tried, I could never reconcile the Spanish in my English and the English in my Spanish. After all, Spanish was my first language; the tongue spoken in my home. . . . I wrestled with this in my writing for a long time, and when I picked up *Cuentos* (and later *Getting Home Alive* by Aurora Levins Morales and Rosario Morales and after Nicholasa Mohr's work and then others), I was excited at how the stories were written in Spanish, English, and Spanglish. The *Cuentos* editors, Cherríe Moraga, Alma Gómez, Marian Romo-Carmona, and Myrtha Chabrán, helped me to see how important, indeed, legitimate, my usage is. They wrote that "*Cuentos* validates the use of spanglish and tex-mex. Mixing Spanish and English in our writing and talking is a legitimate and creative response to acculturation. It doesn't mean that we are illiterate or assimilated as we are sometimes labeled by the anglo or Latin American 'elite' " (xi).

When I read that introduction I felt liberated, as if a great weight had been removed from my tired shoulders. I had come home—home to language. And the voice of the proposal emerged from my Caribbean/urban/blue-collar/womanist dialects; its tone rang true. The proposal gave me a form—testimonio—but I didn't know it yet.

Another turn, two years later, during my first position in the academy: I was asked to write a piece on the legacy of Columbus for a women's journal, and once again I reconnected with the voice I had used in writing my dissertation proposal. How comforting it was to avoid the dry literary scholar's voice, the other "tongue" I imagined I had to use as an academic. That piece, not unlike this one, was conceived in my ear though written as text. It spoke of how languages (including Black English, Spanglish, and street talk) and storytelling framed my existence, stories about colonization, of exile and dispossession, of longing and lying. Of how I was sick of those stories, sick of diaspora and the familylessness I had in my cells. My father has seven siblings, my mother five; I am related to more than twenty cousins that never came to my birthday parties—most are nameless and faceless, their absence meant more than their presence would have. No abuela, no primos, no tías—what could I do but invent them? All the gaps in my life I filled with stories, lies. Storytelling and lying to fill in for the stories I didn't hear, wasn't privy to—all leading to writing. I called it "No Accents Allowed" but that wasn't enough. I was driven (by intuition?) to consult *Breaking Boundaries: Latina Writings and Critical Readings* and there it was, the testimonio—Sandra María Esteves's "Open Letter to Eliana," Bessy Reyna's "Cuban-Panamanian-American-Lawyer-Writer Now in Connecticut," Denise Chávez's "Heat and Rain." Then I remembered the ones in Cherríe Moraga and Gloria Anzaldúa's *This Bridge Called My Back*—Moraga's "La Güera," and especially Mirtha Quintanales's "I Paid Very Hard for My Immigrant Ignorance." Looking at these and other Latinas' testimonios led me to see that I wasn't playing in the dark, writing in a void; that there was a connection to other Latina writers, even very diverse writers. And I didn't need to study testimonio, shaping at the point of utterance;[1] the leap from utterance to testimonio is, then, what comes naturally.

So in "No Accents Allowed: un testimonio," I had come home to a form. Suddenly I saw a way to combat my dread of scholarly writing—those testimonios were theory with flesh, analysis with feeling. I joined others who were disaffected with dry academic discourse but how I met these requires another side trip. After sending my piece off, I began preparing to teach my first summer graduate seminar. While clearing off my desk, I found a call for papers—seeking examples of cross-genre academic writing—initiated by Diane P. Freedman, author of *An Alchemy of Genres: Cross-Genre Writing by American Feminist Poet Critics* and coeditor of *The Intimate Critique: Autobiographical Literary Criticism.* Intrigued by the descriptions and titles, I called this woman immediately. But since neither book was in print yet, I relied on provocative and encouraging conversations with Diane, my students, and friends to map out the possibilities ahead. I learned of Patricia Williams's *An Alchemy of Race and Rights,* which blended the language of law (with ethics) and autobiography, Ruth Behar's *Translated Woman: Crossing the Border with Esperanza's Story,* which combined ethnography with the ethnographer's story, Nicole Ward Jouve's *White Woman Speaks with Forked Tongue: Autobiography as Criticism,* which teases out the variations and responsibilities of the critic's "I," and many other books, old and new, combining the personal with the academic, expertise with experience.[2] Cross-genre writing, also known as hybridization, syncretism, or border crossing, became, in my mind and others', the only way to keep one's voice, in all its tonalities, inflections, and accents, intact. Slowly, not all at once, I returned to Alice Walker's essays, to Anzaldúa's *Borderlands*, to the prose—new and old—of Adrienne Rich, Virginia Woolf's *A Room of One's Own*, Audre Lorde's *Sister Outsider*, and everything by bell hooks. Gradually, over a year, I began collecting the books Diane listed; reading them is another story . . . writing like that, well, it's what I desire.

But then, a week before the summer session began, I got the editor's comments on "No Accents Allowed." The faxed copy of my testimonio was riddled with notes, comments, corrections—every single line was edited. In the telephone conversation that followed the facsimile, the editor said she liked my narrative but that she had extensively edited it in order to "reshape" my words into what she considered to be the appropriate form. I was stunned. What could I do? One week before my first graduate seminar—unpublished, the youngest female faculty member, thinking about my contract renewal, the sole income earner for my small family, remembering the unemployment checks and Medicaid cards. Heartsick, thinking of the ends rather than the means, I obliged. Agreeing to most of her suggestions with two or three exceptions about content, I squelched my anger; her editing was not detrimental to my project. There was relief, the reward of being in print would come soon. But like a bad taste in my mouth, resentment lingered. It wasn't until I was in the middle of teaching the course in U.S. minority literature that I realized that my voice in the narrative had been appropriated by the editor. During the week I was talking to students about the function of editors in minority writers' texts (authenticating and verifying voices in slave narratives, for example, such as Lydia Maria Child's editing of Harriet Jacobs's *Incidents in the Life of a Slave Girl* and John Neihardt's manipulation of Black Elk's story), I decided to distribute to them my original piece and the published one.

Their responses, some outraged when they saw the editorial markings on every sentence of the piece, helped me not only to confirm my own outrage but to affirm my commitment to the testimonio and cross-genre writing in academia. I knew I had a right to be angry, but I wasn't planning to leave academia. No, I was staying right here—to speak in my own voice, conceived in my own ear. After all, the trick is to remain in the system, while infiltrating it. The trailblazing works of Anzaldúa, Kingston, Freedman, and others facilitate my journey. My vehicle is language, and, with Morrison, I believe that language is agency, an act with consequences. I too aim to subvert the system of arrogant, seductive, mutant, pseudo-intellectual language of the academy that Morrison, in her Nobel Prize lecture, warns us is designed to throttle women. The danger is dogma, insistence on only one voice, one way. I sense the growing anger against the one forsaking multiplicity; maybe it isn't so risky for me after all.

All along the testimonio form has been close to the heart of my voice. For women of color, for the oppressed, telling their lives is testimony, witness. It's not so strange then that when I review my tenurable writing on composition, what do I see but autoethnographic narrative—"Rewards, Risks and Resistance: One Teacher's Story" and "Racism and the Marvelous Real"—both are driven by storytelling. It seems that I couldn't avoid it even if I wanted to.

There is a tense relationship about space here in the city. Inside space and outside space are so far apart, so disparately conceived of that I could not help but be alarmed by it, once again. People carefully look out of windows, blinds are drawn tightly or curtains blow in the closed breeze but the window itself is impenetrable. The higher up, the safer. Windows low to the ground are almost never open: locked tight, barred, alarm-ribboned, or just plain boarded up. Door etiquette does not stray far from that of windows. One must enter or exit quickly, for exposure to the outside must be kept at a minimum—someone might see what you have and want it. Someone may want to come in—someone you don't know, someone who could hurt you or your inside people.

Safety inside is contrasted with outside risk. Outside, the energy is sometimes frenetic but when you're in it, you can't lose. If you walk in that current, nothing can touch you because your own energy links with that of the city and allows you an insider's vision of the outside. "Just keep on walking; don't stop for anyone; don't hang around like a tourist, well, you don't look like a tourist." Warnings about the outside. "All you have to do is heed the design—the way it's laid out for you, considerate, mindful of where you want to go and what you might need tomorrow" (9). *Jazz* warnings about Harlem.

Even the trains have inside/outside dynamics. If you're waiting for a train, stay where others are, where you are seen, but don't look at anyone. Wait for the train and then rush into safety, into the rocking lines of lighted and electrified metal.

My host likes to hear about polite New Yorkers. She was pleased when I told her that while I was waiting at an empty information booth in the World Trade Center a man walking by stopped to ask me "Where do you need to go?" and then instructed me on the most efficient way to get there. And about the other man in the train who asked not five seconds after I pulled out a subway map, "Do you know where you're going?" and then made sure I got off where I needed to. "That's nice," she said.

My commuting back and forth between New Jersey and Harlem alarmed some light-skinned friends. One asked me if there were a lot of black people in the library. Another was worried I might be in danger because I hadn't called her to pick me up at the train station at the designated time. She said she was ready to call the police and tell them to look for me, telling them about my research—it would be some sort of measure of my character. That because I am a light-skinned Latina doing work on a dark-skinned writer that I should be left alone. I am not the enemy, in other words.

Here I am reading, writing, concerning myself with other people of color in the hopes of discovering more about my self, though none of my family sees it that way. They think I'm strange, that it's queer about me. That maybe my lifelong friendship con mi amiga somehow draws me to color. Delving deeper inside myself, I come up with all sorts of explanations and arguments for my scholarly interests—others seem to need to hear them articulated as such—perfectly logical reasons. There is the philosophical and aesthetic commitment to the work of black women. The mindfulness I express when acknowledging my debt, their influence, on my own work as a writer/scholar, as a Cuban American, as a Latina womanist. Concerns such as my other/outsider status within the dominant culture, the struggle for identity and survival and also the accessibility to ancestors' wisdom and how we, women in particular, use that information. From the horizon, the presence and absence of that abuelita summons me.

It was an uneventful commute back to Jersey. For the moment, the last one, since the research was done and my child and partner were coming to meet me. Uninteresting, really, except for the ladybug that lighted on me at the bus stop. I brushed it from my ear and saw she was black all over with only one red spot. She crawled over my palm then flew away as I confirmed the darkness.

NOTES

1. For his discussion of the value of spontaneous inventiveness, see Britton's essay by that title in *Prospect and Retrospect*. See also works by other composition and writing theorists, such as Berthoff, *The Making of Meaning,* and Knoblauch and Brannon, *Rhetorical Traditions,* that further develop Britton's theory.

2. The first handwritten bibliography Diane sent me included Mairs, *Remembering the Bone House;* Steedman, *Landscape for a Good Woman;* Miller, *Getting Personal;* and Heller, "Experience and Expertise," which Diane said helped to legitimate cross-genre writing.

WORKS CONSULTED

Andrews, William, ed. *The Collected Stories of Charles W. Chestnutt.* New York: Penguin, 1992.

Anzaldúa, Gloria. *Borderlands/La Frontera: The New Mestiza.* San Francisco: Aunt Lute, 1987.

Behar, Ruth. *Translated Woman: Crossing the Border with Esperanza's Story.* Boston: Beacon, 1992.

Berthoff, Ann E. *The Making of Meaning: Metaphors, Models and Maxims for Writing Teachers.* Montclair: BoyntonCook, 1981.

Britton, James. *Prospect and Retrospect: Selected Essays of James Britton.* Ed. Gordon Pradl. Montclair, N.J.: BoyntonCook, 1982.

Cazden, Courtney, and Dell Hymes. "Narrative Thinking and Story-telling Rights: A Folkorist's Clue to a Critique of Education." *Keystone Folklore* 22 (1978): 22–35.

Freedman, Diane P. *An Alchemy of Genres: Cross-Genre Writing by American Feminist Poet-Critics.* Charlottesville: University Press of Virginia, 1992.

Freedman, Diane P., Olivia Frey, and Frances M. Zauhar, eds. *The Intimate Critique: Autobiographical Literary Criticism.* Durham, N.C.: Duke University Press, 1993.

Genette, Gérard. *Narrative Discourse: An Essay in Method.* Ithaca, N.Y.: Cornell University Press, 1980.

Heller, Scott. "Experience and Expertise Meet in New Brand of Scholarship." *Chronicle of Higher Education,* May 6, 1992, p. A7-A9.

hooks, bell. *Black Looks: Race and Representation.* Boston: South End Press, 1992.

———. *Talking Back: Thinking Feminist, Thinking Black.* Boston: South End Press, 1989.

———. *Yearning: Race, Gender, and Cultural Politics.* Boston: South End Press, 1990.

Horno-Delgado, Asunción, Eliana Ortega, Nina M. Scott, and Nancy Saporta Sternbach, eds. *Breaking Boundaries: Latina Writings and Critical Readings.* Amherst: University of Massachusetts Press, 1989.

Jouve, Nicole Ward. *White Woman Speaks with Forked Tongue: Autobiography as Criticism.* London: Routledge, 1991.

Kingston, Maxine Hong. *The Woman Warrior: Memoirs of a Girlhood among Ghosts.* New York: Vintage, 1976.

Knoblauch, C. H., and Lil Brannon. *Rhetorical Traditions and the Teaching of Writing.* Montclair, N.J.: BoyntonCook, 1984.

Lorde, Audre. *Sister Outsider: Essays and Speeches.* Freedom, Calif.: Crossing Press, 1984.

Mairs, Nancy. *Remembering the Bone House: An Erotics of Place and Space.* New York: Harper, 1989.

Miller, Nancy K. *Getting Personal: Feminist Occasions and Other Autobiographical Acts.* New York: Routledge, 1991.

Miner, Earl. *Comparative Poetics: An Intercultural Essay on Theories of Literature.* Princeton, N.J.: Princeton University Press, 1990.

Mohr, Nicholasa. *Rituals of Survival.* Houston, Texas: Arte Publico Press, 1985.

Moraga, Cherríe, and Gloria Anzaldúa, eds. *This Bridge Called My Back: Writings by Radical Women of Color.* New York: Kitchen Table/Women of Color Press, 1981.

Moraga, Cherríe, Alma Gómez, Marian Romo-Carmona, and Myrtha Chabrán, eds. *Cuentos: Stories by Latinas.* Latham, N.Y.: Kitchen Table Press, 1983.

Morales, Aurora Levins, and Rosario Morales. *Getting Home Alive.* Ithaca, N.Y.: Firebrand Books, 1986.

Morrison, Toni. *Jazz.* New York: Alfred A. Knopf, 1992.

——. Nobel prize lecture. Random House audiotape. Dec. 1993.

——. *Playing in the Dark: Whiteness and the Literary Imagination.* Cambridge, Mass.: Harvard University Press, 1992.

——. *Sula.* New York: New American Library, 1973.

Rich, Adrienne. *On Lies, Secrets and Silence: Selected Prose, 1966–1978.* New York: W. W. Norton, 1979.

——. *What Is Found There: Notebooks on Poetry and Politics.* New York: W. W. Norton, 1993.

Steedman, Carolyn Kay. *Landscape for a Good Woman: A Story of Two Lives.* New Brunswick, N.J.: Rutgers University Press, 1987.

Walker, Alice. *In Search of Our Mother's Gardens: Womanist Prose.* New York: Harcourt Brace Jovanovich, 1979.

Williams, Patricia. *An Alchemy of Race and Rights.* Cambridge, Mass.: Harvard University Press. 1991.

◇ Contributors

KIMBERLY M. BLAESER is an associate professor at the University of Wisconsin, Milwaukee, where she teaches Native American literature and creative writing. An enrolled member of the Minnesota Chippewa Tribe from White Earth Reservation, Blaeser is the author of a book of poems, *Trailing You* (1994), which won the First Book Award from the Native Writers' Circle of the Americas, and a critical study, *Gerald Vizenor: Writing in the Oral Tradition* (1996). Her essays, short fiction, and poetry have also been anthologized in numerous collections, including *The Colour of Resistance; Earth Song, Sky Spirit; Narrative Chance; Women on Hunting; Returning the Gift; Blue Dawn, Red Earth; Unsettling America;* and *New Voices in Native American Literary Criticism.*

RENAE MOORE BREDIN is an assistant professor of women's studies at the College of New Jersey (a.k.a. Trenton State College). She has published articles on Native American literature and ethnography and is currently working on *Guerrilla Ethnography,* which deals with the construction of race and gender in an interdisciplinary framework.

JENNIFER BROWDY DE HERNANDEZ teaches English, women's studies, and Latin American literature courses at Simon's Rock College of Bard. Her essays on Native American women's autobiographies and Latin American women's testimonials have appeared in such works as *Memory and Cultural Politics: New Approaches to American Ethnic Literatures* (1996) and *Interventions: Feminist Dialogues on Third World Women's Literature and Film* (1997). She is currently exploring issues of reciprocal cultural translations in the works of Gayatri Chakravorty Spivak, Paula Gunn Allen, and Greg Sarris.

KIMBERLY N. BROWN is a Ph.D. candidate in English at the University of Maryland, College Park, where she teaches courses in African American literature. She is currently working on a dissertation tentatively titled "Revolutionary Black Woman: Their Images and Ideologies" and contributes reviews to *Tulsa Studies* and *Women's Literature*.

KING-KOK CHEUNG is an associate professor of English and Asian American studies at the University of California, Los Angeles. She is the author of *Articulate Silences: Hisaye Yamamoto, Maxine Hong Kingston, Joy Kogawa* (1993); the editor of *An Interethnic Companion to Asian American Literature* (1997), *"Seventeen Syllables"* (1994), and *Asian American Literatures: An Annotated Bibliography* (1988).

MARILYN EDELSTEIN is an associate professor of English at Santa Clara University, where she also teaches in the Women's Studies Program. She has published essays in the areas of feminist theory, postmodernism, literature and ethics, and contemporary American fiction. She is working on a project on postmodernist and feminist ethics.

DIONNE ESPINOZA holds the Chancellor's Postdoctoral Fellowship in the Department of Communication at the University of California, San Diego. She is currently working on a manuscript dealing with gender, youth culture, and militancy in the Chicana/o movement organization the Brown Berets.

ROBIN RILEY FAST teaches American literature and poetry at Emerson College. Coeditor, with Christine Mack Gordon, of *Approaches to Teaching Dickinson's Poetry* (1989), she has published articles in *American Quarterly, Melus, Contemporary Literature, Twentieth-Century Literature, Legacy, Kentucky Review,* and *ESQ.* She is currently completing a book on contemporary Native American poetry.

TOMO HATTORI, an assistant professor of English and ethnic studies at the University of Utah, teaches courses in postcolonial literature and theory and Asian American literature. He is currently working on a book on Asian American culture and postmodernism.

ANALOUISE KEATING, an associate professor of English at Eastern New Mexico University, is the author of *Women Reading Women Writing: Self-Invention in Paula Gunn Allen, Gloria Anzaldúa, and Audre Lorde* (1996) and essays on Chicana literature, queer theory, multiethnic, and canonical U.S. literature. She is currently working on a transformational theory and praxis of multicultural U.S. literature.

TIMOTHY LIBRETTI is an assistant professor of English at Northeastern Illinois University in Chicago. He has published essays on U.S. proletarian and third world literatures, Asian American, Chicana/o, and African American literature, and Marxism and cultural studies. He is currently working on *U.S. Literary History and Class Consciousness: Rethinking U.S. Proletarian and Third World Literatures,* which focuses on reconceptualizing Marxism and Marxist literary history through exploring radical writers of color working within the U.S. Left literary tradition.

CECILIA RODRÍGUEZ MILANÉS, an assistant professor at Indiana University of Pennsylvania, teaches courses on writing and U.S. writers of color. She has published fiction, poetry, and autobiographical cultural criticism in periodicals such as *Thirteenth Moon, Americas Review,* and the *Women's Review of Books.* She is currently working on several projects, including a novel, essays on color, class, and teaching, and a study of U.S. Caribbean Latina writers, using a womanist theoretical approach.

EUN KYUNG MIN is a Ph.D. candidate in comparative literature at Princeton University. She has taught Korean literature in translation and interdisciplinary classes in philosophy and literature. She is completing a dissertation on philosophical and literary discussions of identity and sensibility in Locke, Hume, Diderot, and Sterne.

SANDRA KUMAMOTO STANLEY, an associate professor of English at the California State University, Northridge, is the author of *Louis Zukofsky and the Transformation of a Modern American Poetics* (1994). She has published essays on modernist, contemporary, and multiethnic literature. She is currently working on a manuscript entitled *Miscegenated Spaces.*

KATHRYN BOND STOCKTON, an associate professor of English at the University of Utah, is the author of *God Between Their Lips: Desire Between Women in Irigaray, Bronte, and Eliot* (1994). Her articles have appeared in, among other places, *Boundary 2, Novel,* and *Cultural Critique.* She is currently writing a book on debasement, engaging switchpoints between black and queer connections to anal economics, miscegenation, stone butch wounds, and the brain's prophylactic relations with the dead.

◇ Index